Sexual Harassment
in America

SEXUAL HARASSMENT IN AMERICA

A Documentary History

LAURA W. STEIN

Primary Documents in American History and Contemporary Issues

GREENWOOD PRESS
Westport, Connecticut • London

Library of Congress Cataloging-in-Publication Data

Stein, Laura W., 1963–
    Sexual harassment in America : a documentary history / Laura W.
Stein.
        p.   cm.—(Primary documents in American history and
    contemporary issues, ISSN 1069-5605)
    Includes bibliographical references and index.
    ISBN 0-313-30184-0 (alk. paper)
        1. Sexual harassment—Law and legislation—United States—History—
    Sources.   2. Sex discrimination in employment—Law and legislation—
    United States—History—Sources.   I. Title.   II. Series: Primary
    documents in American history and contemporary issues series.
    KF3467.S74   1999
    344.7301'4133—dc21   98–23548

British Library Cataloguing in Publication Data is available.

Library of Congress Catalog Card Number: 98–23548
ISBN: 0-313-30184-0
ISSN: 1069-5605

First published in 1999

Greenwood Press, 88 Post Road West, Westport, CT 06881
An imprint of Greenwood Publishing Group, Inc.

Printed in the United States of America

The paper used in this book complies with the
Permanent Paper Standard issued by the National
Information Standards Organization (Z39.48–1984).

10 9 8 7 6 5 4 3 2 1

Copyright Acknowledgments

The author and publisher gratefully acknowledge permission to reprint materials from the following sources:

DOCUMENT 1: Susan Brownmiller and Dolores Alexander, "How We Got Here: From Carmita Wood to Anita Hill," *Ms.* (January–February 1992), © Susan Brownmiller and Dolores Alexander, reprinted by permission of the authors.

DOCUMENT 7: Ellen Frankel Paul, "Sexual Harassment as Sex Discrimination: A Defective Paradigm," *Yale Law and Policy Review* 8 (1990), reprinted courtesy of *Yale Law and Policy Review*.

DOCUMENT 8: Katherine M. Franke, "What's Wrong with Sexual Harassment?" *Stanford Law Review* 49 (1997) © 1997 by the board of Trustees of the Leland Stanford Junior University.

DOCUMENT 12: Reprinted by permission of *Harvard Business Review*. Excerpt from "Sexual Harassment . . . Some See It . . . Some Won't" by Eliza G. C. Collins and Timothy B. Blodgett, March/April 1981. Copyright © 1981 by the President and Fellows of Harvard College; all rights reserved.

DOCUMENT 33: Harriet Chiang, "Judge Halves $7.1 Million Award in Harassment Case But Bay Area Woman Will Still Get Record Sum," *San Francisco Chronicle*, November 29, 1994, © The San Francisco Chronicle. Reprinted with Permission.

DOCUMENT 34: Ellen E. Schultz and Junda Woo, "The Bedroom Ploy: Plaintiffs' Sex Lives Are Being Laid Bare in Harassment Cases," *Wall Street Journal*, September 19, 1994. Reprinted by permission of the Wall Street Journal, © 1994 Dow Jones & Company, Inc. All Rights Reserved Worldwide.

DOCUMENT 43: David Benjamin Oppenheimer, "Workplace Harassment and the First Amendment: A Reply to Professor Volokh," © 1996 by *Berkeley Journal of Employment and Labor Law*. Reprinted from *Berkeley Journal of Employment and Labor Law* 17, no. 2 (1996): 321–22, 325–26, by permission. Reprinted courtesy of David Benjamin Oppenheimer.

DOCUMENT 47: Reprinted by permission of Rosemary L. Bray, "Taking Sides Against Ourselves," *New York Times Magazine*, November 17, 1991. Copyright 1991. All rights reserved.

DOCUMENT 52: Grace M. Kang, "Laws Covering Sex Harassment and Wrongful Dismissal Collide," *Wall Street Journal*, September 24, 1992. Reprinted by permission of the Wall Street Journal, © 1992 Dow Jones & Company, Inc. All Rights Reserved Worldwide.

DOCUMENT 61: LCDR J. Richard Chema, "Arresting 'Tailhook': The Prosecution of Sexual Harassment in the Military," *Military Law Review* 140 (Spring 1993). Excerpts from this article are reprinted from the *Military Law Review*, Department of the Army Pamphlet 27–100–140, at 62–64 (Spring 1993). The opinions and conclusions expressed herein are those of the individual author, and do not necessarily represent the views of The Judge Advocate General's School, United States Army, or any other governmental agency.

DOCUMENT 64: Dana Priest and Jackie Spinner, "Issue of Race Emerges in Aberdeen Courtroom; Defense Says Army Targets Black Instructors," *The Washington Post*, May 6, 1997. © 1997, The Washington Post. Reprinted with permission.

DOCUMENT 65: Eric Schmitt, "Top Enlisted Man in the Army Stands Accused of Sex Assault," *New York Times*, February 4, 1997. Copyright © 1997 by The New York Times Co. Reprinted by Permission.

DOCUMENT 66: Richard Cohen, "Presumed Innocent; But Not for Long," *The Washington Post*, February 13, 1997. © 1997, The Washington Post. Reprinted with permission.

DOCUMENT 72: Nan Stein, Nancy L. Marshall, and Linda R. Tropp, *Secrets in Public: Sexual*

To my husband, Jeffrey Winkler, thanks for everything.

Contents

Series Foreword

This series is designed to meet the research needs of high school and college students by making available in one volume the key primary documents on a given historical event or contemporary issue. Documents include speeches and letters, congressional testimony, Supreme Court and lower court decisions, government reports, biographical accounts, position papers, statutes, and news stories.

The purpose of the series is twofold: (1) to provide substantive and background material on an event or issue through the texts of pivotal primary documents that shaped policy or law, raised controversy, or influenced the course of events, and (2) to trace the controversial aspects of the event or issue through documents that represent a variety of viewpoints. Documents for each volume have been selected by a recognized specialist in that subject with the advice of a board of other subject specialists, school librarians, and teachers.

To place the subject in historical perspective, the volume editor has prepared an introductory overview and a chronology of events. Documents are organized either chronologically or topically. The documents are full text or, if unusually long, have been excerpted by the volume editor. To facilitate understanding, each document is accompanied by an explanatory introduction. Suggestions for further reading follow the document or the chapter.

It is the hope of Greenwood Press that this series will enable students and other readers to use primary documents more easily in their research, to exercise critical thinking skills by examining the key documents in American history and public policy, and to critique the variety of viewpoints represented by this selection of documents.

Introduction

DEFINING SEXUAL HARASSMENT

Although sexual harassment has been around for a long time, it was only in 1986 that the U.S. Supreme Court held that sexual harassment could be an illegal form of sex discrimination. It was not until 1991, when law professor Anita Hill accused Supreme Court nominee Clarence Thomas of sexual harassment, that the issue became front-page news. The recognition that sexual harassment is a wrong that the law should remedy is thus very recent.

Given the recent attention the issue has received, it is not surprising that there are many open questions about sexual harassment. The most basic question is what exactly constitutes sexual harassment.

At its broadest, people sometimes use the term "sexual harassment" to describe any incident in which one person directs unwanted sexual attention at another person. The legal definition of sexual harassment, however, is narrower. Several federal, state, and local laws prohibit discrimination on the basis of sex in particular contexts, such as in employment or education. These laws, for example, prohibit employers from refusing to hire women. Sexual harassment is prohibited by these laws because it is considered to be a form of sex discrimination. Consequently, sexual harassment in the legal sense of the term occurs only in contexts in which the law prohibits sex discrimination. If a construction worker makes suggestive comments to a woman passing by, that does not violate current law, since there is no law that prohibits construction workers from discriminating against those walking by the construction site. On the other hand, if those same suggestive comments are made by a supervisor to an employee or by a teacher to a student, it is unlawful sexual harassment.

What types of behavior constitute sexual harassment? The law recognizes two types of illegal sexual harassment. The first, called "quid pro quo" harassment, involves situations in which a person in a position of power (like a supervisor or a teacher) demands sexual favors in exchange for a benefit or threatens the victim with some type of retaliation if the victim does not comply. For example, if a supervisor demands sexual favors in exchange for a promotion, that is quid pro quo sexual harassment. Similarly, if he threatens a worker by telling her that he will fire her if she does not comply with his sexual demands, that is also illegal quid pro quo harassment.

The second type of sexual harassment, called hostile environment harassment, involves situations in which a person is subjected to sexualized comments or behavior that is so severe or pervasive that it creates an abusive environment. Most of the cases of sexual harassment that have been reported in the news fit this model. These cases may involve making sexually charged remarks to the victim, displaying pornography to the victim, groping or inappropriate touching, and sometimes even rape.

There is some disagreement, however, among courts and commentators about how to decide whether a given environment is bad enough to be considered illegal. Some courts and commentators argue that the question should be whether the environment is hostile when viewed from the perspective of a reasonable person. Others argue that, because women and men often view sexualized conduct differently, the issue should be whether a reasonable woman would judge the environment to be hostile or abusive.

SEXUAL HARASSMENT AS A FORM OF SEX DISCRIMINATION

The idea that sexual harassment constitutes an illegal form of sexual discrimination was put forth by feminist commentators like Lin Farley and Catharine MacKinnon. They have argued that sexual harassment is foremost an abuse of power. It is one way in which powerful men keep less powerful women in subordinate roles in the workplace. Harassment, furthermore, contributes to cases in which women quit their jobs and thus never gain seniority and the increases in salary and benefits that go with it. In addition, it makes women feel like second-class citizens. Thus, they have argued that sexual harassment in employment should be prohibited under a federal law called Title VII of the Civil Rights Act of 1964, which bans sex discrimination in employment.

In 1986 the U.S. Supreme Court, in a case called *Meritor Savings Bank, FSB v. Vinson*, agreed that sexual harassment is sex discrimination and, thus, violates Title VII. The Court did not, however, endorse the idea that sexual harassment is illegal because it contributes to the subordination of women. Instead, although its reasoning is somewhat murky, it seems to have concluded that sexual harassment is a form of sex discrimination because it is a way in which people of one gender are treated differently from people of another gender. Thus, in the most common factual scenario, a woman or group of women are targeted for harassment; men are not similarly harassed. Consequently, the Court reasoned, the female victims are being treated unfavorably because of their gender and are thus the victims of sex discrimination.

Which theory one adopts does not make a difference when dealing with the standard situation in which a man harasses a woman; both theories consider such behavior to be unlawful sex discrimination. The choice of a theory can, however, make a difference in cases in which it is alleged that a woman has harassed a man or in the increasingly common cases in which a worker alleges that he or she has been harassed by someone of the same sex. If sexual harassment is illegal because it contributes to the subordination of women, some argue, men cannot be victims. On the other hand, if sexual harassment is wrong because it involves treating people of one sex differently than those of another, then either men or women could be victims, so long as the harasser targets only members of one gender.

Not surprisingly, given this theoretical confusion, there has been a great deal of controversy over the issue of whether and when same-sex sexual harassment is illegal. Courts were badly split over the issue. In 1998, however, the Supreme Court decided that same-sex harassment can be illegal, so long as the person bringing suit can establish that the harasser treated men and women differently.

SEXUAL HARASSMENT AS A CIVIL WRONG

For the most part, sexual harassment is considered to be a civil, rather than a criminal, wrong. That means that victims of sexual harassment are entitled to bring lawsuits and receive money damages and court orders to compensate them for the harm they have suffered; the perpetrators of sexual harassment, however, do not go to jail because they engaged in harassment. The behavior that constitutes sexual harassment may also be a crime for which the perpetrator can be punished; for example, if a supervisor rapes a subordinate at the workplace, this constitutes both the civil wrong of sexual harassment and the crime of rape. On the other hand, if a supervisor constantly makes sexual advances or sexually derogatory comments to a subordinate, that is sexual harassment, but it is not a crime.

Furthermore, when a victim succeeds in a sexual harassment lawsuit, it is generally the employer or school that pays the damages, rather than the individual perpetrator. The federal statutes that prohibit sex discrimination in employment and education make the employer or the school financially responsible for the actions of their agents.

The military, however, provides an exception to the rule that sexual harassment is a civil, not a criminal, wrong. Uniformed military personnel are not permitted to bring civil lawsuits and collect money damages for sexual harassment, but committing sexual harassment is a crime under military regulations. Under these regulations, a person committing sexual harassment can be dishonorably discharged and even jailed.

CONFLICTS BETWEEN SEXUAL HARASSMENT LAW AND FREE SPEECH

Recently, conservatives and civil libertarians have criticized the laws against hostile environment sexual harassment, arguing that they stifle free speech. They point out that forms of speech, such as making offensive comments or posting nude pictures, can contribute to a finding of a hostile environment. They argue that people will be afraid to engage in robust dialogue about issues relating to gender and sex for fear of being charged with harassment. They fear that those who are "politically incorrect" or, in other words, are not feminists, will be particularly deterred from speaking. They further argue that if the prohibition on sexual harassment is construed broadly, it may be unconstitutional, because it interferes with the right to freedom of speech guaranteed by the First Amendment of the United States Constitution.

Other commentators, however, defend the law against sexual harassment. They argue that since the law prohibits only hostile environment harassment that is severe or pervasive, it does not stifle much speech. Furthermore, they argue, it only bars speech that is truly harmful to the victims and thus can and should be restricted.

ABOUT THIS VOLUME

This volume reproduces important documents relating to sexual harassment. For the most part, it includes primary documents such as court opinions, regulations and reports put forth by federal agencies, statutes, and portions of congressional debate. It also includes some newspaper articles and commentary by experts in the field.

Because the law against sexual harassment has been developed primarily by the federal courts, this volume contains a number of court decisions. It is thus important that the reader have a rudimentary knowledge of the structure of the federal court system.

The federal courts are divided into three tiers. At the bottom are the trial courts, also called District Courts. Above them are the Courts of

Appeals. If any party is unhappy with a decision rendered by the District Court, that party may bring the case to a Court of Appeals. The federal Courts of Appeals are divided geographically into twelve divisions, which are called circuits. The circuits are not required to agree with each other. In the area of sexual harassment, the circuits have divided over a number of issues.

Above the Courts of Appeals is the United States Supreme Court. The Supreme Court decides which cases it wants to hear. Its decisions about the meaning of the law are binding on all of the Courts of Appeals and District Courts.

This book is divided into six sections. The first section explores the issue of what sexual harassment is and why it is considered to be an illegal form of sex discrimination. The next three sections explore sexual harassment as it has arisen in three contexts—the workplace, the military, and educational institutions. The fifth section deals with the ways in which the law is expanding beyond these specific areas, such as in the context of housing. The final section contains four Supreme Court decisions dealing with sexual harassment issues, which were released in 1998.

Within these sections, this volume explores the history of legal prohibitions on sexual harassment, setting forth the important cases that led to the development of the idea that sexual harassment is a legal wrong. It also focuses on current areas of controversy—such as whether same-sex sexual harassment should be illegal and whether sexual harassment law impermissibly interferes with free speech. Each section also contains bibliographical suggestions for further reading.

ACKNOWLEDGMENTS

For assistance with this book, thanks to my student research assistants Nicole Itkin and Stacey Matthews-Maurice.

Part I

Defining Sexual Harassment

HOW SEXUAL HARASSMENT BECAME ILLEGAL

Sexual harassment, a term coined in the 1970s, has existed a long time. It was in the 1970s that a consensus began to grow that such behavior was both morally and legally wrong. The following excerpt from *Ms.* magazine explains how a loose-knit group of women changed the way in which society viewed this type of behavior.

DOCUMENT 1: "How We Got Here: From Carmita Wood to Anita Hill" (Susan Brownmiller and Dolores Alexander, 1992)

The women's movement was full blown by the time Lin Farley, a 29-year-old activist, was teaching an experimental course on women and work at Cornell University in 1974. During a consciousness-raising session with her class, students talked about disturbing behavior they had been subjected to on summer jobs; in all cases, the women had been forced off the job by these unwanted advances.

Coincidentally, Carmita Wood, a 44-year-old administrative assistant, walked out of the office of a Cornell physicist after becoming physically ill from the stress of fending off his advances. When Ms. Wood filed for unemployment compensation in Ithaca, New York, claiming it wasn't her fault she had quit her job, the nascent movement acquired its first heroine, as well as a clear delineation of a problem as endemic as the abuse itself. The credibility of an office worker, a mother of four, was pitted against the reputation of an eminent scientist whose status was—

and remains—so lofty that to this day his name has not appeared in accounts of her case.

Farley and two Cornell colleagues, Susan Meyer and Karen Sauvigné, found a lawyer for Wood and brainstormed to invent a name for their newly identified issue: "sexual harassment." The young feminists and their complainant proceeded to hold a movement-style speak out (a technique that had been used effectively to articulate the issues of abortion and rape) in a community center in Ithaca in May 1975. A questionnaire collected after the meeting showed that an astonishing number of women had firsthand experience to contribute.

Eleanor Holmes Norton, then chair of the New York City Commission on Human Rights, was conducting hearings on women and work that year. Farley came to testify, half expecting to be laughed out of the room. "The titillation value of sexual harassment was always obvious," Farley recalls. "But Norton treated the issue with dignity and great seriousness." . . .

Reporter Enid Nemy covered the Human Rights Commission hearings for the *New York Times*. Her story, "Women Begin to Speak Out Against Sexual Harassment at Work," appeared in the *Times* on August 19, 1975, and was syndicated nationally, to a tidal wave of response from women across the country.

Sauvigné and Meyer set up the Working Women's Institute in New York City as a clearinghouse for inquiries, and to develop a data bank with an eye toward public policy. Wood lost her case; the unemployment insurance appeals board ruled her reasons for quitting were personal. Lin Farley's breakthrough book, *Sexual Shakedown: The Sexual Harassment of Women on the Job*, was published by McGraw-Hill in 1978—after 27 rejections. "I thought my book would change the workplace," Farley says. "It is now out of print."

Things had begun to percolate on the legal front. Working with a large map and color-coded pushpins, Sauvigné and Meyer matched up complainants with volunteer lawyers and crisis counselors. Initially, aggrieved women sought redress by filing claims for unemployment insurance after they'd quit their jobs under duress, or by bringing their complaints to local human rights commissions. Ultimately, the most important means of redress became the EEOC, the federal agency charged with investigating and mediating discrimination cases under Title VII of the 1964 Civil Rights Act. . . .

By 1977, three cases argued at the appellate level (*Barnes v. Costle; Miller v. Bank of America; Tomkins v. Public Service Electric & Gas*) had established a harassed woman's right, under Title VII, to sue the corporate entity that employed her. "A few individual women stuck their necks out," says Nadine Taub, the court-appointed attorney for Adrienne Tomkins against the New Jersey utilities company.

The Tomkins case, in particular, made it clear that the courts would no longer view sexual harassment as a personal frolic, but as sex discrimination for which the employer might be held responsible. A young woman named Catharine MacKinnon had followed these cases with avid interest while a law student at Yale; later she published an impassioned, if somewhat obfuscating, treatise, *Sexual Harassment of Working Women*, in 1979.

Job-threatening though it was, sexual harassment remained on a back burner of the public conscience, as life-threatening issues—rape, battery, child abuse, and the ongoing pro-choice battle—continued to dominate feminist activity and media attention. . . .

Slowly and quietly, case law broadened the definition of unlawful harassment. As women entered the work force in greater numbers, committing themselves not only to jobs but to careers, new cases went beyond those situations in which a boss suggested sex to a subordinate as a quid pro quo for keeping her job or getting a promotion. A court decision in Minnesota established that coworker harassment was as inimical to working conditions as harassment by a boss. A New York decision held that a receptionist could not be required to wear revealing clothes that brought her unwanted attention.

Meanwhile, a clerk-typist named Karen Nussbaum was pursuing her own mission to organize women office workers through a national network she called 9 to 5. An old friend from the antiwar movement, Jane Fonda, visited her headquarters in Cleveland with the idea of making a movie about underpaid and unappreciated secretaries in a large U.S. corporation.

9 to 5, produced by Fonda's IPC Films, and starring Fonda, Lily Tomlin, and Dolly Parton, was released in 1980. . . .

In the waning days of the Carter administration, when Eleanor Holmes Norton was chair of the EEOC, she seized the initiative by issuing a set of federal guidelines on sexual harassment. The guidelines, a single-page memorandum issued on November 10, 1980, as Norton's tenure was running out, stated with admirable brevity that sexual activity as a condition of employment or promotion was a violation of Title VII. The creation of an intimidating, hostile, or offensive working environment was also a violation. Verbal abuse alone was deemed sufficient to create a hostile workplace. The guidelines encouraged corporations to write their own memoranda and inform employees of appropriate means of redress.

Guidelines are interpretations of existing statutes and do not have the full authority of law. But in 1981 (while Anita Hill was working for Clarence Thomas at the Department of Education), the EEOC was required to defend itself in *Bundy v. Jackson*, said the former EEOC general counsel Leroy D. Clark. The District of Columbia circuit court ruled in favor of Sandra Bundy, a corrections department employee, and accepted the EEOC's guidelines as law, holding that Title VII could be violated even if a woman remained on the job.

Employers who were caught off guard were in for another surprise. During that same first year of the Reagan administration, the Merit Systems Protection Board, a regulatory agency that seldom makes news, released the results of a random survey of 20,100 federal employees. The findings revealed that a staggering 42 percent of the government's female workers had experienced an incident of sexual harassment on the job in the previous two years. "It was the first decent methodological study," says Freada Klein, who served as an adviser. "They did it again in 1988 and came up with the same figures."

It took the Supreme Court until 1986 to affirm unanimously, in *Meritor Savings Bank v. Vinson*, that sexual harassment even without economic harm was unlawful discrimination, although the court drew back in some measure from employer liability in hostile-environment cases.

Five years later, Anita Hill's testimony to 14 white male senators, and the merciless attacks on her credibility, echoed the agonies of her predecessors from Carmita Wood to Mechelle Vinson, who came forward at the risk of ridicule to tell about an abuse of power by a favored, institutionally protected, high-status male.

Detractors of the feminist role in social change have sought to create the impression that sexual harassment is yet another nefarious plot cooked up by an elite white movement to serve middle-class professionals. As it happens, veterans of the battle have been struck time and again by the fact that the plaintiffs in most of the landmark cases, brave women every one, have been workingclass and African American: Paulette Barnes, payroll clerk; Margaret Miller, proofing machine operator; Diane Williams, Justice Department employee; Rebekah Barnett, shop clerk; Mechelle Vinson, bank teller trainee.

We collected many speculations as to why black women have led this fight, but the last word goes to Eleanor Holmes Norton, who said succinctly, "With black women's historic understanding of slavery and rape, it's not surprising to me."

Source: Susan Brownmiller and Dolores Alexander, "How We Got Here: From Carmita Wood to Anita Hill," *Ms.*, January/February 1992, pp. 70–71.

DEFINITIONS OF SEXUAL HARASSMENT

Definitions by the Government

A federal statute called Title VII of the Civil Rights Act of 1964, reprinted below as Document 13, prohibits sex discrimination in employment. Since the late 1970s, courts have interpreted this statute to prohibit sexual harassment in the workplace.

The Equal Employment Opportunity Commission (EEOC) is the federal administrative agency in charge of investigating claims that employers have violated Title VII. In 1980 the EEOC adopted official guidelines that defined sexual harassment in employment and made it clear that such behavior is illegal. These guidelines, which are reprinted as Document 14, have served as the basis for defining sexual harassment in various contexts. In 1992 the EEOC published a document, called *Questions and Answers about Sexual Harassment* (Document 2), which explains in simpler terms what sexual harassment is and what can be done to prevent it.

As the document explains, the EEOC recognizes two types of sexual harassment as illegal: "quid pro quo" harassment and "hostile environment" harassment. As is explained in a different document put forth by the EEOC, the "EEOC Policy Guidance on Current Issues of Sexual Harassment" (Document 3), these two distinct theories of harassment sometimes blend together in particular cases. Consequently, victims may raise both theories in a single case, if the facts support such a position.

DOCUMENT 2: *Questions and Answers about Sexual Harassment* (Equal Employment Opportunity Commission, 1992)

Identifying Sexual Harassment

What Is Sexual Harassment?

Sexual harassment is a form of sex discrimination which is a violation of Title VII of the Civil Rights Act of 1964. The EEOC's guidelines define two types of sexual harassment: "quid pro quo" and "hostile environment."

What Is "Quid Pro Quo" Sexual Harassment?

Unwelcome sexual advances, requests for sexual favors, and other verbal or physical conduct of a sexual nature constitute "quid pro quo" sexual harassment when (1) submission to such conduct is made either explicitly or implicitly a term or condition of an individual's employment, or (2) submission to or rejection of such conduct by an individual is used as the basis for employment decisions affecting such individual.

What Is "Hostile Environment" Sexual Harassment?

Unwelcome sexual advances, requests for sexual favors, and other verbal or physical conduct of a sexual nature constitute "hostile environment" sexual harassment when such conduct has the purpose or effect
of unreasonably interfering with an individual's work performance or
creating an intimidating, hostile, or offensive working environment.

What Factors Determine Whether an Environment Is "Hostile?"

The central inquiry is whether the conduct "unreasonably interfered
with an individual's work performance" or created "an intimidating,
hostile, or offensive working environment." The EEOC will look at the
following factors to determine whether an environment is hostile: (1)
whether the conduct was verbal or physical or both; (2) how frequently
it was repeated; (3) whether the conduct was hostile or patently offensive; (4) whether the alleged harasser was a co-worker or supervisor; (5)
whether others joined in perpetrating the harassment; and (6) whether
the harassment was directed at more than one individual. No one factor
controls. An assessment is made based upon the totality of the circumstances.

What Is Unwelcome Sexual Conduct?

Sexual conduct becomes unlawful only when it is unwelcome. The
challenged conduct must be unwelcome in the sense that the employee
did not solicit or incite it, and in the sense that the employee regarded
the conduct as undesirable or offensive.

How Will the EEOC Determine Whether Conduct Is Unwelcome?

When confronted with conflicting evidence as to whether conduct was
welcome, the EEOC will look at the record as a whole and at the totality
of the circumstances, evaluating each situation on a case-by-case basis.
The investigation should determine whether the victim's conduct was
consistent, or inconsistent, with his/her assertion that the sexual conduct
was unwelcome.

Who Can Be a Victim of Sexual Harassment?

The victim may be a woman or a man. The victim does not have to
be of the opposite sex. The victim does not have to be the person harassed but could be anyone affected by the offensive conduct.

Who Can Be a Sexual Harasser?

The harasser may be a woman or a man. He or she can be the victim's
supervisor, an agent of the employer, a supervisor in another area, a co-
worker, or a non-employee.

Can One Incident Constitute Sexual Harassment?

It depends. In "quid pro quo" cases, a single sexual advance may
constitute harassment if it is linked to the granting or denial of employ-

ment or employment benefits. In contrast, unless the conduct is quite severe, a single incident or isolated incidents of offensive sexual conduct or remarks generally do not create a "hostile environment." A hostile environment claim usually requires a showing of a pattern of offensive conduct. However, a single, unusually severe incident of harassment may be sufficient to constitute a Title VII violation; the more severe the harassment, the less need to show a repetitive series of incidents. This is particularly true when the harassment is physical. For example, the EEOC will presume that the unwelcome, intentional touching of a charging party's intimate body areas is sufficiently offensive to alter the condition of his/her working environment and constitute a violation of Title VII.

Can Verbal Remarks Constitute Sexual Harassment?

Yes. The EEOC will evaluate the totality of the circumstances to ascertain the nature, frequency, context, and intended target of the remarks. Relevant factors may include: (1) whether the remarks were hostile and derogatory; and (2) whether the alleged harasser singled out the charging party; (3) whether the charging party participated in the exchange; and (4) the relationship between the charging party and the alleged harasser.

What Should a Sexual Harassment Victim Do?

The victim should directly inform the harasser that the conduct is unwelcome and must stop. It is important for the victim to communicate that the conduct is unwelcome, particularly when the alleged harasser may have some reason to believe that the advance may be welcomed. However, a victim of harassment need not always confront his/her harasser directly, so long as his/her conduct demonstrates that the harasser's behavior is unwelcome. The victim should also use any employer complaint mechanism or grievance system available. If these methods are ineffective, the victim should contact the EEOC as soon as possible. . . .

Preventing Sexual Harassment

What Specific Steps Can an Employer Take to Prevent Sexual Harassment?

Prevention is the best tool to eliminate sexual harassment in the workplace. Employers are encouraged to take all steps necessary to prevent sexual harassment from occurring. An effective preventive program should include an explicit policy against sexual harassment that is clearly and regularly communicated to employees and effectively implemented. The employer should affirmatively raise the subject with all supervisory and nonsupervisory employees, express strong disapproval, and explain the sanctions for harassment.

Should an Employer Have a Grievance Procedure?

The employer should have a procedure for resolving sexual harassment complaints. The procedure should be designed to encourage victims of harassment to come forward and should not require a victim to complain first to the offending supervisor. They can do so by establishing an effective complaint or grievance process and taking immediate and appropriate action when an employee complains. It should ensure confidentiality as much as possible and provide effective remedies, including protection of victims and witnesses against retaliation.

What If an Employer Asserts That It Has Eliminated the Harassment?

When an employer asserts it has taken remedial action, the EEOC will investigate to determine whether the action was prompt, appropriate and effective. If the EEOC determines that the harassment has been eliminated, the victims made whole, and preventive measures instituted, the Commission normally will administratively close the charge because of the employers' prompt remedial action. . . .

The above information is intended as a general overview of sexual harassment and does not carry the force of legal opinion.

Source: United States Equal Employment Opportunity Commission, *Questions and Answers about Sexual Harassment*, December 1992.

DOCUMENT 3: *EEOC Policy Guidance on Current Issues of Sexual Harassment* (Equal Employment Opportunity Commission, 1990)

Although "quid pro quo" and "hostile environment" harassment are theoretically distinct claims, the line between the two is not always clear and the two forms of harassment often occur together. For example, an employee's tangible job conditions are affected when a sexually hostile work environment results in her constructive discharge. Similarly, a supervisor who makes sexual advances toward a subordinate employee may communicate an implicit threat to adversely affect her job status if she does not comply. "Hostile environment" harassment may acquire characteristics of "quid pro quo" harassment if the offending supervisor abuses his authority over employment decisions to force the victim to endure or participate in the sexual conduct. Sexual harassment may culminate in a retaliatory discharge if a victim tells the harasser or her employer she will no longer submit to the harassment, and is then fired in retaliation for this protest. Under these circumstances it would be appropriate to conclude that both harassment and retaliation . . . have occurred.

Distinguishing between the two types of harassment is necessary when determining the employer's liability. . . . But while categorizing sexual harassment as "quid pro quo," "hostile environment," or both is useful analytically these distinctions should not limit the Commission's investigations, which generally should consider all available evidence and testimony under all possibly applicable theories.

Source: Equal Employment Opportunity Commission, *EEOC Policy Guidance on Current Issues of Sexual Harassment*, March 19, 1990 (footnotes omitted).

In 1981 the federal government released a study of sexual harassment in the federal workplace. The authors concluded that sexual harassment should be considered an abuse of power in the workplace rather than a simple matter of personal attraction.

DOCUMENT 4: *Sexual Harassment in the Federal Workplace: Is It a Problem?* (Merit Systems Protection Board, 1981)

Major Views of Sexual Harassment

Three major views of sexual harassment have emerged from most of th[e] literature: one concerning the underlying social-political basis for the behavior, the second concerning the vulnerability of particular groups to sexual harassment, and the third, concerning the motivation behind the behavior.

The three views are:

1. That sexual harassment is an abuse of power that is exercised by those with power, usually male supervisors, over low-status employees, usually women.
2. That individuals with certain low-status, low-power characteristics, such as youth and low salaries and who are tied economically to their jobs, are more vulnerable to sexual harassment than others.
3. That sexual harassment is an expression of personal attraction between men and women that cannot and should not be stopped.

The first two views are closely related. They grow out of a belief that sexual harassment is a form of sex discrimination and abuse of power used to keep women in their place at the low end of the economic scale. The view is based on the fact that on average women earn only 59 cents for every dollar that a man earns and that sexual harassment is one example of the sex discrimination that maintains this disparity. . . .

The third view reflects a fundamentally different view of the sex roles of men and women and the impact that these roles have on their relationships to each other on the job. This theory grows out of a belief that rather than being a source of power of men over women, the vagueness and broad nature of the definitions of sexual harassment . . . will undoubtedly lead to a barrage of trivial and unfounded complaints against men. Followers of this view also might be inclined to believe that the sexual relationships between men and women are expressions of personal attraction, and that although some of the consequences of these relationships may involve harassment, it is not appropriate for an employer to become involved. . . .

Based upon the findings in the study, we concluded that the first two explanations appear valid under some circumstances and we rejected the last. . . .

The following briefly discusses these views in light of the findings from the study.

Sexual Harassment Is an Abuse of Power

. . . [T]he findings show that most victims, both men and women, are harassed by coworkers rather than supervisors who presumably have more power. On its face this finding would tend to disprove the power theory, however, one must look closer at the data. The findings also show that victims, regardless of severity of harassment, were more likely to perceive and experience adverse consequences if their harasser was a supervisor rather than a coworker. This seems to indicate that, although not all harassment is an outgrowth of organizational power, those cases where consequences are greater are more likely to be examples of abuse of organizational power. The sexual harassment by coworkers probably has more to do with personal power and sex roles than with organizationally derived power. In any event, further research would be helpful in exploring this issue.

Individuals with Certain Characteristics Are More Vulnerable to Sexual Harassment

The view that those with low status and power characteristics are more vulnerable to sexual harassment has been proved in some respects and disproved in others. Some with low power and status, such as younger men and women and trainees, did report receiving sexual harassment disproportionately, but others such as those in low salary levels, low education levels, and women office and clerical workers, did not.

Sexual Harassment Is Not an Expression of Personal Sexual Attraction

The theory that sexual harassment is an expression of personal sexual attraction grows out of a view that sexual harassment is part of standard behavior between the sexes and that employers have no business interfering with these matters of love or personal attraction. This theory has been disproved on several counts.

That many harassers were reported to have harassed more than one victim casts doubt on the idea that sexual harassment is simply a matter of unique personal attraction. The finding that the rate of sexual harassment is not constant among all Federal agencies also somewhat negates the idea that sexual harassment is appropriate sexual behavior that occurs everywhere; that many victims report severe consequences also tends to negate that this behavior is and should be standard practice. In addition, the vast majority of respondents stated that sexual harassment is not something that "people should have to put up with." All of this indicates that sexual harassment should not be considered standard behavior at the workplace and is very much a matter of concern for employers such as the Federal Government.

Source: Merit Systems Protection Board, *Sexual Harassment in the Federal Workplace: Is It a Problem?* Report of the Merit Systems Protection Board Office of Merit Systems Review and Studies, March 1981, pp. 21–22, 101.

Definitions by Commentators

Commentators writing about sexual harassment have also explained what sexual harassment is and why it should be considered to be legally wrongful. In the first major book published on the topic of sexual harassment, *Sexual Shakedown: The Sexual Harassment of Women on the Job* (Document 5), Lin Farley identified sexual harassment in the workplace as a major factor contributing to women's second-class status at work. She sees sexual harassment as both a symptom of and a reinforcement of "patriarchy" or, in other words, a social system characterized by male dominance.

Catharine MacKinnon adopted a similar position to Farley's. In her book, *Sexual Harassment of Working Women* (Document 6), she became the first commentator to distinguish two types of sexual harassment: quid pro quo and hostile environment. She argued that both types were manifestations of women's oppression in a male-dominated society and thus were forms of discrimination against women.

DOCUMENT 5: *Sexual Shakedown: The Sexual Harassment of Women on the Job* (Lin Farley, 1978)

[O]ur society is first, last, and foremost a patriarchy. Essentially, this means that it is a social system organized according to a principle of male rule.... Throughout successive epochs the patriarchy has maintained itself by generating ideas that legitimize, i.e. make acceptable, the very conditions which make this rule possible....

Sexual harassment is best described as unsolicited nonreciprocal male behavior that asserts a woman's sex role over her function as worker. It can be any or all of the following: staring at, commenting upon, or touching a woman's body; requests for acquiescence in sexual behavior; repeated nonreciprocated propositions for dates; demands for sexual intercourse; and rape. These forms of male behavior frequently rely on superior male status in the culture, sheer numbers, or the threat of higher rank at work to exact compliance or levy penalties for refusal. The variety of penalties include verbal denigration of a woman sexually; noncooperation from male co-workers; negative job evaluations or poor personnel recommendations; refusal of overtime; demotions; injurious transfers and reassignments of shifts, hours, or locations of work, loss of job training; impossible performance standards and outright termination of employment. Sexual harassment also frequently influences many hiring situations, as when companies employ across-the-board policies of hiring only those women who are attractive sex objects regardless of skills, or where there will be an outright demand for some form of sexual behavior which will result in the reward of the job while refusal will result in a nonhire.

... Sexual harassment is ... an act of aggression at any stage of its expression, and in all its forms it contributes to the ultimate goal of keeping women subordinate at work.

Source: Lin Farley, *Sexual Shakedown: The Sexual Harassment of Women on the Job* (New York: McGraw-Hill, 1978), pp. xv–xvi, 14–15.

DOCUMENT 6: *Sexual Harassment of Working Women* (Catharine A. MacKinnon, 1979)

Sexual harassment, most broadly defined, refers to the unwanted imposition of sexual requirements in the context of a relationship of unequal power. Central to the concept is the use of power derived from one social sphere to lever benefits or impose deprivations in another. . . . American society legitimizes male sexual dominance of women and employer's control of workers, although both forms of dominance have limits and exceptions. Sexual harassment of women in employment is particularly clear when male superiors on the job coercively initiate unwanted sexual advances to women employees; sexual pressures by male coworkers and customers, when condoned or encouraged by employers, might also be included. Lack of reciprocal feeling on the woman's part may be expressed by rejection or show of disinclination. After this, the advances may be repeated or intensified; often employment retaliation ensues. . . .

Sexual harassment may occur in a single encounter or as a series of incidents at work. It may place a sexual condition upon employment opportunities at a clearly defined threshold, such as hiring, retention, or advancement; or it may occur as a pervasive or continuing condition of the work environment. Extending along a continuum of severity and unwantedness, and depending upon the employment circumstances, examples include

verbal sexual suggestions or jokes, constant leering or ogling, brushing against your body "accidentally," a friendly pat, squeeze or pinch or arm against you, catching you alone for a quick kiss, the indecent proposition backed by the threat of losing your job, and forced sexual relations.

Complex forms include the persistent innuendo and the continuing threat which is never consummated either sexually or economically. The most straightforward example is "put out or get out."

Source: Catharine A. MacKinnon, *Sexual Harassment of Working Women* (New Haven: Yale University Press, 1979), pp. 1–2. Quoting "Sexual Harassment on the Job: Questions and Answers" (Ithaca, NY: Working Women United Institute, 1975 [mimeograph]).

Other commentators disagree that sexual harassment is best viewed as a form of discrimination against women. They see it as a type of wrong that can visit members of either gender. Thus, they argue for a definition of sexual harassment that is gender neutral. One proponent of this position is Ellen Frankel Paul. She argues that sexual harassment is better defined as unequal treatment of people of one gender, rather than the oppression of women by men.

DOCUMENT 7: "Sexual Harassment as Sex Discrimination: A Defective Paradigm" (Ellen Frankel Paul, 1990)

Most commentators assume that sexual harassment involves men doing something objectionable to women—although they usually concede that the genders of harasser and victim could be reversed, or that a member of one sex could harass another of that same sex. Other more zealous partisans, however, inject male abuse of power and economic privilege into the very definition of sexual harassment. Catharine A. MacKinnon is perhaps the best known proponent of this view. . . .

Incorporating abuse of power into the definition, however, seems unduly limiting. While it mirrors accurately what transpires in the classic quid pro quo situation, it reflects only uneasily hostile environment sexual harassment by co-workers—unless one accepts the added, debatable, and more global assumption that males occupying any position in the workplace enjoy more power than women. If one favored such a claim, arguing for it directly, rather than importing it into the very definition of sexual harassment (thus begging the question and, perhaps, alienating those who might be sympathetic to the complaint but not the assumption), seems desirable.

I prefer a neutral definition of sexual harassment to MacKinnon's, which injects an ideological bias against men and the capitalist marketplace. This definition would eschew, as too confining, an implication of abuse of power. . . .

Source: Ellen Frankel Paul, "Sexual Harassment as Sex Discrimination: A Defective Paradigm," *Yale Law and Policy Review* 8 (1990): 333–35.

In an article published in 1997, Professor Katherine Franke thoroughly discussed the issue of why sexual harassment should be considered to be a form of sex discrimination (see Document 8). She summarizes three explanations given by other commentators as to why sexual harassment is a form of sex discrimination. The first theory finds sexual harassment to be sex discrimination because it constitutes a way in which men and women are sometimes treated differently in the workplace. Often women, but not men, are targeted for sexually abusive behavior, although in particular instances it can happen the other way around. So long as members of one gender are being singled out for abusive treatment, those espousing this argument contend, sex discrimination is occurring. This is the position adopted by Ellen Frankel Paul.

The second theory argues that sexual harassment is sex discrimination because it is sexual. These theorists argue that sexual behavior in the workplace has a particularly adverse effect on women and thus constitutes discrimination against women.

The third theory, the one espoused by Lin Farley and Catharine MacKinnon, argues that sexual harassment is sex discrimination because it is one way in which women are systematically subordinated by men. Men use sex in the workplace in order to preserve women's status as second-class citizens.

Professor Franke criticizes all these theories as incomplete; she argues that they do not fully explain what is discriminatory about sexual harassment. She argues that sexual harassment should be considered to be sex discrimination because it reinforces sexual stereotypes about the proper roles of men and women, under which men are required to be macho and women are required to be feminine. Thus, she argues, it should be just as illegal for men to harass effeminate men as it is for men to harass women—a point about which courts have differed.

DOCUMENT 8: "What's Wrong with Sexual Harassment?" (Katherine M. Franke, 1997)

V. Conclusion

Sexual harassment is something men do to women. This statement, while quite familiar and seemingly uncontroversial, is both descriptively underinclusive and theoretically short-sighted. The link between sexual harassment and sex discrimination is an important one, and it is one that is fair to assume is present in typical different-sex cases. But why? It is the why, not the what, of sexual harassment that I feel deserves closer theoretical attention. To date, the Supreme Court has been disinclined to do more than summarily conclude that sexual harassment is a form of sex discrimination. If courts are to continue to draw summary inferences and conclusions of sex discrimination in sexual harassment cases, and I believe that they should in most cases, it is imperative that a careful theory expounding the wrong of sexual harassment provide the context within which these evidentiary short cuts take place.

The wrong of sexual harassment must consist of something more than that the conduct would not have occurred "but for" the sex of the target, that the conduct was sexual in nature, or that it was something men do to women. The "something more" I suggest is that we regard sexual harassment as a tool or instrument of gender regulation. It is a practice, grounded and undertaken in the service of hetero-patriarchal norms. These norms, regulatory, constitutive, and punitive in nature, produce gendered subjects: feminine women as sex objects and masculine men as sex subjects. On this account, sexual harassment is sex discrimination precisely because its use and effect police hetero-patriarchal gender norms in the workplace.

I do not suggest that we reject existing doctrine, but rather that we work to develop a theoretical justification for inferring sex discrimination in traditional different-sex claims. This theoretical work will also provide the tools to consider whether same-sex sexual harassment raises the same kind of concerns as those present in the more central cases. All that I urge is renewed attention to the "based upon sex" element of the plaintiff's case, such that we view the wrong of sexual harassment in systemic terms, rather than in terms that elevate a method of proof ("but for") over the nature of the harm itself, or that conflate sex with sexism. To understand sexual harassment as a regulatory practice that constitutes gendered subjects by inscribing, enforcing, and policing hetero-patriarchal gender norms is to provide a better account of what sexual harassment is and what it does—in both different-sex and same-sex cases. Most importantly, this approach better explains why sexual harassment is a kind of sex discrimination.

Source: Katherine M. Franke, "What's Wrong with Sexual Harassment?" *Stanford Law Review* 49 (April 1997): 771–72 (footnotes omitted).

PART I: FOR FURTHER READING

Crenshaw, Kimberle. "Race, Gender, and Sexual Harassment." *Southern California Law Review* 65:3 (March 1992), 1467–76.

Hartel, Lynda Jones, and Helena M. Vonville. *Sexual Harassment: A Selected Annotated Bibliography*. Westport, CT: Greenwood Press, 1995.

Hill, Anita Faye, and Emma Coleman Jordan. *Race, Gender and Power in America: The Legacy of the Hill–Thomas Hearings*. New York: Oxford University Press, 1995.

Kreps, Gary L., ed. *Sexual Harassment: Communication Implications*. Cresskill, NJ: Hampton Press, 1993.

LeMoncheck, Linda, and Mane Hajdin. *Sexual Harassment—A Debate*. Lanham, MD: Rowman and Littlefield Publishers, 1997.

McCaghy, M. Dawn. *Sexual Harassment: A Guide to Resources*. Boston: G. K. Hall, 1985.

O'Donohue, William T., ed. *Sexual Harassment: Theory, Research and Treatment*. Boston: Allyn and Bacon, 1996.

Paludi, Michele A., and Richard B. Barickman. *Academic and Workplace Sexual Harassment: A Resource Manual*. Albany: State University of New York Press, 1991.

Skaine, Rosemarie. *Power and Gender: Issues in Sexual Dominance and Harassment*. Jefferson, NC: McFarland, 1996.

Stan, Adele M., ed. *Debating Sexual Correctness*. New York: Dell Publishing, 1995.

Wall, Edmund, ed. *Sexual Harassment: Confrontation and Decisions.* Buffalo, NY: Prometheus Books, 1992.

Wekesser, Carol, Karin L. Swisher, and Christina Pierce, eds. *Sexual Harassment.* San Diego, CA: Greenhaven Press, 1992.

Part II

Sexual Harassment in Employment

Sexual harassment was first declared to be illegal in the context of employment. In the 1970s, courts began interpreting preexisting laws that prohibited sex discrimination in employment to bar sexual harassment of workers.

THE PREVALENCE OF SEXUAL HARASSMENT IN EMPLOYMENT

In 1979 a subcommittee of the United States House of Representatives asked the Merit Systems Protection Board (MSPB), the agency that oversees federal workers, to conduct a study of sexual harassment in the federal workplace. The MSPB sent surveys to over 23,000 federal employees inquiring about their experiences with sexual harassment. The results of the MSPB's survey were published in 1981 (Document 9).

In 1988 and again in 1995, the MSPB updated its study (Documents 10, 11). These later studies found increased awareness of the problem of sexual harassment in the workplace; however, there was no decrease in the percentage of people who reported being sexually harassed.

DOCUMENT 9: *Sexual Harassment in the Federal Workplace: Is It a Problem?* **(Merit Systems Protection Board, 1981)**

Summary

The following major findings emerged from the study:

- Both men and women Federal workers generally agree that uninvited behaviors of a sexual nature constitute sexual harassment.
- The incidence rate of sexual harassment in the Federal workforce is widespread—42% of all female employees and 15% of all male employees reported being sexually harassed.
- Many sexual harassment incidents occur repeatedly and are of relatively long duration.
- The majority of Federal employees who had worked elsewhere feel sexual harassment is no worse in the Federal workplace than in state and local governments or in the private sector.
- Sexual harassment is widely distributed among women and men of various backgrounds, positions and locations; however, individuals with certain personal and organizational characteristics are more likely to be sexually harassed than others.
- The characteristics of harassers differ for women and men victims—for example, women report almost always being harassed by a man, whereas men report usually being harassed by a woman.
- Many harassers are reported to have bothered more than one victim at work.
- Few employees report having been accused of sexually harassing others.
- Those who are sexually harassed by supervisors and those who experience the more severe forms of sexual harassment are more likely than other victims to foresee penalties or possible benefits from the sexual harassment.
- Most victims neither anticipated nor received adverse consequences as a result of their sexual harassment, although a sizeable minority did, particularly women.
- A number of informal actions were found by victims to be effective in stopping sexual harassment, particularly the most direct and assertive responses.
- Few victims pursue formal remedies, but many who do find them helpful.
- The impact and cost of sexual harassment in dollars to the Federal Government is sizeable—an estimated minimum of $189 million over the 2-year period covered by the study.
- Although their experiences do not change the careers and work situations of most victims, a sizeable number of women and men do leave their jobs or suffer adverse consequences.
- Victims are more likely to think the sexual harassment negatively affected their personal well-being or morale than their work performance or that of their immediate work group.
- Victims and supervisors are generally unaware of available formal remedies and are skeptical about their effectiveness.
- Assertive informal actions are thought to be the most effective way employees can make others stop bothering them sexually.
- Most victims and supervisors think there is much management can do to reduce sexual harassment.

• In conclusion, the data show that sexual harassment is widespread, is costly, deeply felt by many of the victims, and that the 1979 Congressional investigation was indicative of a significant problem; however, the data also indicated that there is much that can be done to reduce that problem. . . .

Victims of Sexual Harassment

To determine who is sexually harassed and whether certain personal and organizational factors contributed to the likelihood of harassment, we looked at a number of demographic variables. . . . Based on these factors, we found that the typical men and women who are likely to be harassed are:

• young,
• not married,
• higher educated,
• members of a minority, racial or ethnic group (if male),
• hold trainee positions (or office/clerical positions, if male),
• hold non-traditional positions, for their sex (e.g., female law enforcement officers, male secretaries),
• have an immediate supervisor of the opposite sex,
• have an immediate work group composed predominately of the opposite sex. . . .

Perpetrators of Sexual Harassment

We found that most women reported that their harassers were male and that most men indicated that their harassers were female. However, men were far more likely than women to report being harassed by someone of their same sex.

Most harassers of women and men reportedly acted alone rather than in concert with another person. However, most women identified their harasser as being older than they, whereas men usually indicated that their harasser was usually younger than they. Although both women and men reported that their harasser was usually married, men were more likely to indicate that their harasser was divorced or single. Most victims in general reported being harassed by someone of their same race or ethnic background, although minority women were more likely to report that their harasser was of a different race or ethnicity.

One surprising finding was that women and men reported being harassed by fellow employees more often than by supervisors. This finding was surprising in that, before the study, most sexual harassment was thought to be perpetrated by the more powerful supervisors against their more vulnerable employees. However, a sizeable number of women also reported being harassed by supervisors. Thus, supervisors were found to be responsible for a number of sexual harassment incidents, although not the principle cause of the problem. . . .

Another major finding was that many women and men reported that their harasser had also bothered others at work. This somewhat negates the view that sexual harassment is principally a matter of isolated instances of personal sexual attraction. Thus it appears that some individuals are more likely to harass others and that sexual harassment is not necessarily normal interaction among men and women in the job, or that all men and women engage in it as has been intimated by some. . . .

. . . [One] in every 3 women employed by the Federal Government reported having been subjected to unwanted sexual remarks, 1 in 4 had been deliberately touched or cornered, 1 in 10 had been pressured for sexual favors, and 1 in 100 had faced actual or attempted rape or sexual assault. Since respondents were allowed to report more than one kind of behavior, many are counted more than once in these figures.

Source: Merit Systems Protection Board, *Sexual Harassment in the Federal Workplace: Is It a Problem?* Report of the Merit Systems Protection Board Office of Merit Systems Review and Studies, March 1981, pp. 3–4, 6, 9–10, 37.

DOCUMENT 10: *Sexual Harassment in the Federal Government: An Update* **(Merit Systems Protection Board, 1988)**

Summary of Findings

Compared to 7 years ago Federal workers are now more inclined to define certain types of behavior as sexual harassment. For example, in 1980 approximately 77 percent of all employees considered uninvited pressure for dates by a supervisor to be sexual harassment. In 1987 that percentage had increased to almost 84 percent. Likewise, in 1980, 84 percent of male employees and 91 percent of female employees considered unwanted supervisory pressure for sexual favors to be sexual harassment. In 1987 those percentages had increased to 95 percent and 99 percent, respectively. Similar changes were seen in employee attitudes about most other types of behavior.

In 1987, 42 percent of all women and 14 percent of all men reported they experienced some form of uninvited and unwanted sexual attention. Despite an apparent increase in the level of sensitivity about what behavior may be considered sexual harassment, there has been no significant change since the Board's last survey in 1980 in the percentage of Federal employees who say they have received such uninvited and unwanted attention. . . .

The most frequently experienced types of uninvited sexual attention is "unwanted sexual teasing, jokes, remarks, or questions." The least frequently experienced type of harassment—"actual or attempted rape or assault"—is also arguably the most severe. Sexual harassment takes many forms and an employee may experience more than one form. In answering the Board's 1987 survey, 35 percent of all female respondents and 12 percent of all male respondents said they experienced some type of "unwanted sexual teasing, jokes, remarks, or questions." Also in 1987, approximately .8 percent of all female respondents and .3 percent of male respondents said they experienced "actual or attempted rape or assault." . . .

Coworkers are much more likely than supervisors to be the source of sexual harassment. In 1987, 69 percent of female victims and 77 percent of male victims said they were harassed by a coworker or another employee without supervisory authority over them. Only 29 percent of the female victims and 19 percent of the male victims cited someone in their supervisory chain as the source of their harassment. This pattern is consistent with the Board's 1980 findings.

Some individuals are more likely than others to be victims of sexual harassment. For example, based on the data obtained in 1987, women who: are single or divorced; are between the ages of 20 and 44; have some college education; have a nontraditional job; or work in a predominantly male environment or for a male supervisor have the greatest chance of being sexually harassed. However, as the Board found in 1980, despite this generalization, sexual harassment is still widely distributed among women and men of all ages, backgrounds, and job categories.

Many victims tried more than one response to unwanted sexual attention. Although later judged ineffective by most of them, almost half of all victims tried to ignore the behavior or otherwise did nothing in response. In 1987, only 5 percent of both female and male victims said they took some type of formal action. Although most employees were aware of the availability of formal action—e.g., filing a grievance or a discrimination complaint—very few chose to use those potential remedies.

When victims of sexual harassment did take positive action in response to unwanted sexual attention, it was largely informal action and, in many cases, was judged to be effective. The most effective and frequently taken informal action was simply telling the harasser to stop. Forty-four percent of the female victims and 25 percent of the male victims said they took this action and, in over 60 percent of the cases, both groups said it "made things better." . . .

During the 2-year period from May 1985 through May 1987, sexual harassment cost the Federal Government an estimated $267 million.

This cost is in addition to the personal cost and anguish many of the victims had to bear. This conservative estimate is derived by calculating the cost of replacing employees who leave their jobs as a result of sexual harassment, of paying sick leave to employees who miss work as a consequence, and of reduced individual and work group productivity.

Source: Merit Systems Protection Board, *Sexual Harassment in the Federal Government: An Update*, Report of the Merit Systems Protection Board, June 1988, pp. 3–4.

DOCUMENT 11: *Sexual Harassment in the Federal Workplace: Trends, Progress, and Continuing Challenges* **(Merit Systems Protection Board, 1995)**

Findings

In 1994, 44 percent of women and 19 percent of men responding to our survey reported that they had experienced some form of unwanted sexual attention during the preceding 2 years—rates similar to 1987's 42 percent and 14 percent. The fact that the incidence of unwanted sexual attention has not decreased since the last Governmentwide survey is naturally a cause for concern. Despite very widespread training and information efforts that have successfully raised workforce sensitivity to the issues surrounding sexual harassment, the persistence of this amount of unwanted sexual attention in the Federal workplace suggests that the Government's programs to eradicate the problem need some serious re-examination.

At the same time, it is possible that at least some of this unwanted sexual attention was reported by survey respondents not *in spite* of efforts to increase awareness, but *because* of them. Individuals who formerly might have dismissed an uninvited look or remark, or persistent unwanted social invitations as mere rudeness or insensitivity, may now be more inclined to place those behaviors in one of the categories the Board's survey identifies as uninvited and unwanted sexual attention. (In fact, suggestive looks, sexual remarks, and employees pressuring co-workers for dates were the most frequently reported forms of sexual harassment, despite there being a number of respondents who said they would not characterize this conduct as sexual harassment.)

Formal responses, such as filing grievances or discrimination complaints are rare. Only about 6 percent of the 1994 survey respondents who had experienced sexually harassing behaviors indicated that they took formal action in response to the harassment. Of the self-identified victims who did *not* take formal action, the most common reason (given by half these victims) was that they did not think the situation was serious enough to warrant such action.

Federal agencies have been successful in educating the workforce and raising awareness about sexual harassment. Over 87 percent of Federal supervisors and 77 percent of nonsupervisory employees have received training in the area of sexual harassment. Some 78 percent of employees said that they know the channels to follow if they have been harassed and want to report it. All Federal agencies have policies prohibiting sexual harassment, and 92 percent of Federal employees are aware of those policies.

Sexual harassment cost the Federal Government an estimated $327 million during the 2-year period April 1992 to April 1994, but the overall ill effects of sexual harassment have decreased significantly. This amount includes the cost of sick leave, job turnover, and productivity losses, and represents an increase since the Board's last sexual harassment study, when Government costs were estimated at $267 million for the period May 1985 to May 1987. However, the increase reflects inflation and the rise in salaries to a greater degree than it reflects an increase in the ill effects of harassment. Since the 1987 study, there has been a significant drop in turnover and sick leave used in response to sexual harassment, as well as a decline in the severity and duration of productivity losses resulting from the disruptive effects of sexual harassment.

The definition of sexual harassment is expanding, as more Federal employees are defining more kinds of behavior as sexual harassment. Survey respondents were asked whether they would classify as sexual harassment six kinds of behavior, ranging from sexual comments to pressure for sexual favors. In virtually every case, whether the behavior was engaged in by a supervisor or by a coworker, the proportion of respondents—both men and women—who classified the six behaviors as sexual harassment rose between 1980 and 1987 and had increased again by 1994. Some of the increases are striking. For example, since the Board's first sexual harassment survey the proportion of men who categorize uninvited sexual teasing, jokes, remarks, or questions by coworkers as sexual harassment rose from 42 percent in 1980 to 64 percent in 1994.

As in previous surveys, 1994 survey results show that the less severe forms of sexually harassing behaviors are the most prevalent, while the most severe behaviors occur the least often. In 1994, 37 percent of women and 14 percent of men said they had experienced unwanted sexual teasing, jokes, remarks, or questions, generally considered less severe forms of sexual harassment. Actual or attempted rape or assault was reported by 4 percent of female respondents and 2 percent of males.

Coworkers and other employees, rather than individuals in the supervisory chain, continue to be the primary source of sexual harassment in the Federal workplace. In 1994, some 79 percent of male and 77 percent of female respondents who reported experiencing sexual harassment said that they had been harassed by coworkers or other employees. This contrasts with the 14 percent of men and 28 percent of women reporting sexual harassment who said that an immediate or higher level supervisor had been responsible for the harassment.

Some employees are at greater risk than others of being targets of unwanted sexual attention. Employees who have experienced unwanted sexual attention are more likely than those who have not experienced such attention to work exclusively or mostly with people of the opposite sex and to be supervised by members of the opposite sex. Employees of both sexes who reported having experienced unwanted sexual attention are more likely to be college-educated than those who have not experienced such attention. Also, employees under the age of 35 have a greater chance of experiencing unwanted sexual attention than those who are older. At the same time, the majority of employees who reported these experiences are 35 and older, since the population of employees in that age group is so large (83 percent of respondents).

The most effective responses to sexual harassment are informal, assertive ones such as confronting harassers and telling them to stop. Although the most common response to unwanted sexual attention is to ignore the behavior or do nothing (44 percent of respondents who had experienced harassment reacted that way), asking or telling a person to stop was identified by 88 percent of all survey respondents as the action they believed would be most effective in dealing with harassment. Of the respondents who had actually experienced sexual harassment and taken this action, 60 percent said it made things better.

A sizable number of employees, particularly men, are concerned about how they will be perceived by others in the workplace, in view of today's emphasis on sexual harassment. Some 63 percent of the male and half of the female respondents indicated that they believe that some people are too quick to take offense when someone expresses a personal interest in them through looks or remarks. One in three employees believes that normal attraction between people in the workplace is, to a moderate or great extent, misinterpreted as sexual harassment. Nearly half the men indicated they don't feel comfortable giving compliments because their remarks might be misinterpreted.

Most employees do not think that the emphasis on sexual harassment has made their workplaces uncomfortable. Employees' concern about how others perceive their words and actions may be causing people to think more critically about the effects of their conduct and to exercise more self restraint, but it apparently has not led to a chilling effect in the workplace. Only 18 percent of men and 6 percent of women indicated that fear of being accused of sexual harassment had made their organizations uncomfortable places in which to work.

Comments provided by survey respondents indicate that some perceive the penalties for harassment to be inappropriate or inconsistent. While it may be the case that most supervisors and managers want to stop harassment in their organizations, some may prefer to do it in a way that avoids harming the career of the harasser, who otherwise may be very valuable to the organization. Some survey respondents provided comments indicating that they see this as resulting in penalties that are too light or that demonstrate a double standard, with higher-level or managerial and executive personnel being treated less harshly than lower-level employees.

Source: Merit Systems Protection Board, *Sexual Harassment in the Federal Workplace: Trends, Progress, and Continuing Challenges*, Report of the Merit Systems Protection Board, October 1995, pp. viii–x.

Men's and Women's Perceptions of Sexual Harassment

In 1981 the *Harvard Business Review* published the results of a survey it conducted with *Redbook* magazine that was designed to elicit perceptions of sexual harassment in the workplace (Document 12). The study found that men and women generally agreed about what constitutes sexual harassment in egregious cases. In close cases, however, women were more likely than men to call the behavior sexual harassment. Furthermore, there was a significant disagreement between the sexes about the prevalence of sexual harassment and about whether complaints of sexual harassment are taken seriously by the employer. Women, more than men, believed that sexual harassment was common and believed it to be less likely that management would do anything about it.

DOCUMENT 12: "Sexual Harassment . . . Some See It . . . Some Won't" (Eliza G. C. Collins and Timothy B. Blodgett, 1981)

What is it & how much?

* * *

Not surprisingly, respondents to our survey agree about which extreme situations constitute sexual harassment but differ over the more ambiguous cases. For instance, 87% think that the following statement definitely indicates abuse: "I have been having an affair with the head of my division. Now I've told him I want to break it off, but he says I will lose out on the promotion I've been expecting." . . .

Opinions on these extreme cases differ little between men and women and between top and lower level management. For example, 89% of the men and 92% of the women think the first statement in Exhibit I is harassment ("I can't seem to go in and out of my boss's office without being patted or pinched"). Nearly 87% of top management and 91% of lower-level management also think it is.

In other, less extreme situations, however, people are less certain about the interpretation but still consider the behavior quite offensive. . . . An average of 40% say the situation where a man starts each day with a sexual remark and insists it's an innocent social comment is harassment; an average of 48% say it is possibly; 8% say it is not; and 4% don't know. According to many readers, a situation where a man often puts his hand on a woman's arm when making a point is even more innocent. . . .

The perceived seriousness of the harassment seems to depend on who is making the advance, the degree of interpreted intent, and the victim's perception of the consequences. The amount the victim appears to suffer, however, does not necessarily vary with the perceived seriousness. In many comments, for instance, the writers seemed more vexed by persistent low-level misbehavior, which, although covered by EEOC guidelines, is impractical to do something about and is often harder to prove than more extreme forms. . . .

Many people commented on how power influences perceptions of harassment. As one reader put it, "The indebtedness increases the harassment's potency." Some of our male readers were very aware of the implications of power differences: "There is a male code of silence regarding harassment of females that has to be broken, particularly in the area of male 'power' figures and females without power," said the 38-year-old male vice president of marketing in a large insurance company. "Either too many men never recover from being high school jocks or they understand that corporate power can be a new way to be attractive. Having suffered through both lessons, I feel free to comment."

The power phenomenon is not necessarily restricted to men, either. "The more power people have, the more able they are to let go of their inhibitions and act on their desires," testified a 36-year-old government administrator. "As a woman manager, I must admit to temptation! It is when the overtures are unwanted, persistent, and power based that they are unhealthy organizationally." . . .

Throughout the survey we found answers that could be explained only by a "that's the way men are" assessment on the part of both men and women—resignation or acceptance bred of recurring experience. Perhaps the more one sees behavior like that we described, the less one is stirred to call it misconduct.

How much?

* * *

The most striking finding on the question of how much abuse actually takes place is the difference in perception between men and women and between high-level and lower-level management. (Because most high-level managers in our survey were men and more lower-level managers were women, the two sets of responses often parallel each other.) The answers to the statement, "The amount of sexual harassment at work is greatly exaggerated," are:

	Agree or partly agree	Disagree or partly disagree
Top management	63%	22%
Middle management	62	30
Lower-level management	44	40
Women	32%	52%
Men	66	17

In most instances substantial differences appear in men's and women's perceptions of how frequently sexual harassment occurs. For example, one-third of the men, but a full half of the women, have witnessed or heard of a case where the man starts each day with a sexual remark that he insists is an innocent social comment. . . .

How can we explain the differences in viewpoint? Sexual harassment may not take place when male managers are around to observe it; and even if it does, they may not "see" it as women do. . . .

Even though men generally agree in the abstract with women about what harassment is, the gap in perception of what actually happens is real and significant. . . .

One factor that may help explain the difference in perception is social conditioning. For example, 44% of the women view the statement about the man who starts each day with a sexual remark . . . as only "possibly" misconduct. . . . Perhaps some women, accustomed to accept such incidents as a price of survival in the business world, have lost sensitivity. . . .

In extreme cases, higher-level executives report that they are generally unaware of what's going on. Perhaps one of the worst examples of abuse in our survey is epitomized by [the situation] . . . where the man gives the woman a poor evaluation because she refuses to have sex with him.

Ten percent of all respondents have heard of or observed this situation. The response by management level breaks down this way: top management, 5%; middle management, 9%; lower-level management, 13%; persons other than managers (a small number), 19%.

As in other situations, more women than men testify to knowledge of th[is] situation . . . 16% against 5%. Whether conditioning, denial, or lack of awareness explains these disparities, the gap in perception between different levels of management and between men and women poses a serious problem for policymakers.

What would you do?

* * *

The problem of disparities in perception appears throughout the survey. To probe differing attitudes, we sent two different versions of four vignettes in our split-sample questionnaire. In one we asked readers to say what they would do as managers in these situations; in the other, what typical managers would do. . . . One can draw many conclusions from the answers, but three disparities in perception stand out: (1) the differential treatment men and women employees receive after an unwanted advance, (2) how women should handle themselves, and (3) how responsible managers ought to act in the workplace.

Perceived differential treatment

The responses to the vignettes show that men and women hold very different opinions on how top managers will act in an ambiguous situation. Their opinions also differ depending on whether the victim is a female or male executive, a female executive or secretary, and on who is making the advance.

For example, in the first vignette a company president walks into his sales manager's office and finds him standing near his secretary, who looks upset and flustered. . . . On the colored questionnaire we asked what the typical president would do, and on the white form we asked what "you" would do. Nearly two-thirds of the women who filled out the colored form believed that the typical president would do nothing— being unaware of what happened or unwilling to confront the sales manager on a personal matter—while fewer than half the men voted this way.

In thinking that the typical president would do nothing, most of the women chose avoidance of confrontation as the motivation, while most men selected ignorance as the reason for inactivity. Women, it seems, tend to think that male executives take an uninvolved stance even when they know what is happening (and even when it is addressed in the guidelines). . . .

This assumption by women of how male executives will behave reveals itself in [other] vignette[s]. . . .

. . . [When asked how a male executive would react if another male executive made a remark to him about a female's body], "share the joke" received more votes from women than any other choice. . . .

The responses to [another] vignette also reveal perceived differential treatment of executive women and secretaries. Women disapprove of [a boss's unwanted sexual advances] slightly more when the victim is a secretary (40%) than when she is an executive (36%). One-quarter of all our respondents would express their disapproval to the secretary's boss, while one-fifth would do so on behalf of the executive. If secretaries are unprotected, executive women are even more so, although more respondents say they would give advice on how to deal with the behavior to executives than to secretaries (11% to 6%). . . .

If we look at the order of options that our female respondents think a typical division manager would choose in the case of [sexual harassment of] a woman executive [by a client], we see a discouraging picture of how much support women think management will give them in the face of sexual harassment. Rather than buttress them with a team (their next-to-last choice), back them regardless of the consequences, or encourage them to parry the advance, women assume that the division managers would want to transfer them. Whether women fear this most as the outcome or base their opinions on personal experience, their perceptions of how management would act should ring alarms for top officers.

What can a woman handle?

Do men and women hold different views on how women should or can deal with sexual advances? Women disagree among themselves here. Some think that women, to survive in the business world, have to handle whatever comes their way. . . .

Other women think that harassment within organizations is too much for any person to handle alone. . . .

We asked our readers whether "a smart woman employee ought to have no trouble handling an unwanted sexual approach." Fifty-nine percent of the women disagree or partly disagree and the same proportion of men agree or partly agree. Men seem to think that women can overcome sexual overtures through tact. . . .

Most women are less sure that they can deal with an unwanted sexual approach and, in fact, they wonder whether anything they do would make them safe from such behavior in the workplace. A full 78% of them disagree with the statement, "If a women dresses and behaves properly, she will not be the target of unwanted sexual approaches at work."

The same proportion of women, however, agree or partly agree with the statement, "Women can and often do use their sexual attractiveness to their own advantage" (compared with 86% of the men). . . .

Although we cannot assume that the opposite of the statement—"If a women dresses and behaves properly, she will not be the target of unwanted sexual approaches at work"—is true, the strong female disagreement with it indicates that women feel vulnerable on the issue.

Source: Reprinted by permission of *Harvard Business Review*. Excerpt from "Sexual Harassment . . . Some See It . . . Some Won't" by Eliza G. C. Collins and Timothy B. Blodgett, March/April 1981. Copyright © 1981 by the President and Fellows of Harvard College; all rights reserved.

LAWS PROHIBITING SEXUAL HARASSMENT IN EMPLOYMENT

Federal Law

In 1964 the U.S. Congress passed sweeping civil rights legislation. Title VII of the Civil Rights Act of 1964 prohibited discrimination in employment on the basis of certain enumerated characteristics, such as race and sex, by employers who employ at least fifteen workers, unions, and employment agencies. The main impetus behind this legislation was to combat discrimination against African Americans. While the legislation was being debated, however, congressmen who sought to defeat the bill added an amendment that also prohibited employment discrimination based on sex. To their surprise, the bill passed with the amendment.

Given this strange legislative history, there is very little detail in the statute about how to interpret the prohibition against sex discrimination in employment. As the excerpt below indicates, Title VII does not mention sexual harassment or say anything about what it is or whether it is prohibited.

DOCUMENT 13: Title VII of the Civil Rights Act of 1964, § 703(a) (1964)

(a) Employer practices

It shall be an unlawful employment practice for an employer—

(1) to fail or refuse to hire or to discharge any individual, or otherwise to discriminate against any individual with respect to his compensation, terms, conditions, or privileges of employment, because of such individual's race, color, religion, sex, or national origin; or

(2) to limit, segregate, or classify his employees or applicants for em-

ployment in any way which would deprive or tend to deprive any individual of employment opportunities or otherwise adversely affect his status as an employee, because of such individual's race, color, religion, sex or national origin.

Source: United States Code, Title 42, § 2000e-2(a) (1988).

As mentioned earlier, The Equal Employment Opportunity Commission (EEOC) is the federal administrative agency in charge of enforcing Title VII. It has the authority to investigate, mediate, and prosecute claims of discrimination in employment. In 1980 the EEOC adopted a regulation interpreting Title VII that defined and prohibited sexual harassment in employment (see Document 14).

The EEOC's definition has been widely accepted by the courts. Furthermore, similar definitions of sexual harassment are used in cases involving harassment in the military and in educational institutions.

In 1982 and 1987, the EEOC published more detailed directions about what it considers to be illegal sexual harassment as part of its Compliance Manual, a publication designed to give its employees guidance about how to enforce the law. It took a very broad perspective on what types of activities are illegal under Title VII, concluding that both men and women can be victims of sexual harassment, that co-employees as well as supervisors can commit illegal sexual harassment, and that the harasser and the victim can be of the same gender (see Document 15).

DOCUMENT 14: *Equal Employment Opportunity Commission's Guidelines on Discrimination Because of Sex* **(Equal Employment Opportunity Commission, 1980)**

---

§ 1604.11 Sexual harassment.

(a) Harassment on the basis of sex is a violation of section 703 of title VII.... Unwelcome sexual advances, requests for sexual favors, and other verbal or physical conduct of a sexual nature constitute sexual harassment when (1) submission to such conduct is made either explicitly or implicitly a term or condition of an individual's employment, (2) submission to or rejection of such conduct by an individual is used as the basis for employment decisions affecting such individual, or (3) such conduct has the purpose or effect of unreasonably interfering with an individual's work performance or creating an intimidating, hostile, or offensive working environment. . . .

(f) Prevention is the best tool for the elimination of sexual harassment.

An employer should take all steps necessary to prevent sexual harassment from occurring, such as affirmatively raising the subject, expressing strong disapproval, developing appropriate sanctions, informing employees of their right to raise and how to raise the issue of harassment under title VII, and developing methods to sensitize all concerned.

(g) Other related practices: Where employment opportunities or benefits are granted because of an individual's submission to the employer's sexual advances or requests for sexual favors, the employer may be held liable for unlawful sex discrimination against other persons who were qualified for but denied that employment opportunity or benefit.

Source: 29 *Code of Federal Regulations* § 1604.11 (1995).

DOCUMENT 15: *Equal Employment Opportunity Commission Compliance Manual* (Bureau of National Affairs, 1982, 1987)

(b) *Recognizing Sexual Harassment*—A finding of sexual harassment does not depend on the existence of any one given set of facts. Sexual harassment can occur in a wide variety of circumstances and encompass many variables. Although the most widely recognized fact pattern is that in which a male supervisor sexually harasses a female employee, this form of harassment is not the only one recognized by the EEOC. The Commission's view of sexual harassment includes, but is not limited to, the following considerations:

(1) A man as well as a woman may be the victim of sexual harassment, and a woman as well as a man may be the harasser.

(2) The harasser does not have to be the victim's supervisor. (S)he may also be an agent of the employer, a supervisory employee who does not supervise the victim, a non-supervisory employee (co-worker), or, in some circumstances, even a non-employee.

(3) The victim does not have to be of the opposite sex from the harasser. Since sexual harassment is a form of sex discrimination, the crucial inquiry is whether the harasser treats a member or members of one sex differently from members of the other sex. The victim and the harasser may be of the same sex where, for instance, the sexual harassment is based on the victim's sex (*not* on the victim's sexual preference) and the harasser does not treat employees of the opposite sex the same way. . . .

Example 1—If a male supervisor of male and female employees makes unwelcome sexual advances toward a male employee because the employee is male but does not make similar advances toward female employees, then the male supervisor's conduct may constitute sexual harassment since the disparate treatment is based on the male employee's sex.

Example 2—If a male supervisor harasses a male employee because of the employee's homosexuality, the the supervisor's conduct would *not* be sexual harassment since it is based on the employee's sexual preference, not on his gender. Title VII covers charges based on gender but not those based on sexual preference. . . .

(4) the victim does not have to be the person at whom the unwelcome sexual conduct is directed. (S)he may also be someone who is affected by such conduct when it is directed toward another person. For example, the sexual harassment of one female employee may create an intimidating, hostile, or offensive working environment for another female (or male) co-worker. . . .

615.3 *Sexual Harassment Guidelines*—For purposes of the following discussion, the term "Guidelines" refers specifically to § 1604.11 of the Commission's amended Guidelines on Discrimination Because of Sex. . . .

(1) *Section 1604.11(a)*—The first section of the Guidelines states that harassment on the basis of sex is a violation of § 703 of Title VII. Sexual harassment is sex discrimination not because of the sexual nature of the conduct to which the victim is subjected but because the harasser treats a member or members of one sex differently from members of the opposite sex. However, it is the sexual nature of the prohibited conduct which makes this form of sex discrimination sexual harassment. . . .

This section further states that unwelcome sexual advances, requests for sexual favors, and other verbal or physical conduct of a sexual nature constitute sexual harassment when any one of three criteria is met:

(1) Submission to such conduct is made either explicitly or implicitly a term or condition of an individual's employment.

Example—If a female laborer complains to her foreman that the male workers on the job direct sexually suggestive remarks and gestures at her and the foreman tells her that such conduct is to be expected as part of the job, then her submission to the sexually harassing conduct is made an explicit term or condition of her employment.

No such overt statement is necessary to show that submission to sexual harassment is a term or condition of employment where a connection between employment and submission can be inferred. Such an inference could be made where, for example, other women workers had complained to the employer, either directly or through an agent or supervisor, and had been told that if they did not like the conduct they could find other jobs. Because submission to such sexual conduct is an *additional* term or condition of employment, one not imposed on employees of the opposite sex, it is sex discrimination and, specifically, sexual harassment.

(2) Submission to or rejection of such conduct by an individual is used as the basis for employment decisions affecting such individual.

Example—If an employee's promotion depends on his or her granting certain sexual favors and the promotion is denied because the employee refuses to do so, then the employee is the victim of sexual harassment. The same result is reached if the employee does submit and consequently receives the promotion.

Basing any employment decision on whether the affected individual submits to or rejects unwelcome sexual conduct is sexual harassment where a similar decision affecting a member of the opposite sex is not so based. The decision need not have a concrete economic effect on the victim, although it often does, because the nature of the specific employment decision is irrelevant. Whether it involves promotion, discharge, transfer, training, work assignment, salary, overtime, or getting an office with a window—the decision cannot have a sexual string attached.

(3) Such conduct has the purpose or effect of unreasonably interfering with an individual's work performance or creating an intimidating, hostile, or offensive work environment.

Example 1—If a male co-worker of a female employee makes unwelcome sexual advances toward her, his conduct may depending on the total circumstances, unreasonably interfere with her ability to do her work. Likewise, his conduct may unreasonably interfere with the work performance of other employees, male or female.

Example 2—If certain male employees make sexual remarks, jokes, or gestures in the presence of or directed toward female employees, that conduct may make the work atmosphere intimidating or threatening for the female employees. The harassment of the female employees may also create an offensive work environment for other male employees.

In the example, the objectionable conduct may not be such that submission to it constitutes a term or condition of employment, and submission to or rejection of the conduct may not be the basis of an employment decision. Nonetheless, the conduct is sexual harassment if it unreasonably interferes with an employee's work performance or creates a negative work environment, even if the conduct is not specifically directed at the person who is affected by it. This section is intentionally broad enough to encompass types of sexual harassment which might not be covered in other ways.

Source: Equal Employment Opportunity Commission Compliance Manual, Bureau of National Affairs, 1982, 1987, pp. 615:0004–615:0006.

State Law

Most states also have laws that prohibit sex discrimination in employment. Like Title VII, most of these laws do not explicitly address sexual harassment, although state courts have found that these laws do prohibit such conduct. A handful of states, however, have statutes that explicitly prohibit sexual harassment in employment. For example, a Vermont statute both prohibits sexual harassment and requires employers to adopt and publicize internal mechanisms through which employees can complain about sexual harassment.

DOCUMENT 16: Vermont Fair Employment Practices Act (1993)

§ 495h. Sexual harassment

(a) All employers, employment agencies and labor organizations have an obligation to ensure a workplace free of sexual harassment.

(b) Every employer shall:

(1) Adopt a policy against sexual harassment which shall include:

(A) a statement that sexual harassment in the workplace is unlawful;

(B) a statement that it is unlawful to retaliate against an employee for filing a complaint of sexual harassment or for cooperating in an investigation of sexual harassment;

(C) a description and examples of sexual harassment;

(D) a statement of the range of consequences for employees who commit sexual harassment;

(E) if the employer has more than five employees, a description of the process for filing internal complaints about sexual harassment and the names, addresses, and telephone numbers of the person or persons to whom complaints should be made; and

(F) the complaint process of the appropriate state and federal employment discrimination enforcement agencies, and directions as to how to contact such agencies.

(2) Post in a prominent and accessible location in the workplace, a poster providing, at a minimum, the elements of the employer's sexual harassment policy required by subdivision (1) of this subsection.

(3) Provide to all employees an individual written copy of the employer's policy against sexual harassment.

(c) Employers shall provide individual copies of their written policies to current employees no later than November 1, 1993, and to new employees upon their being hired. Employers who have provided individual written notice to all employees within the 12 months prior to October 1, 1993, shall be exempt from having to provide an additional notice during the 1993 calendar year.

(d) The commissioner of labor and industry shall prepare and provide to employers subject to this section a model policy and a model poster, which may be used by employers for the purposes of this section.

(e) A claim that an individual did not receive the information required to be provided by this section shall not, in and of itself, result in the automatic liability of any employer to any current or former employee or applicant in any action alleging sexual harassment. An employer's compliance with the notice requirements of this section does not insulate the employer from liability for sexual harassment of any current or former employee or applicant.

(f) Employers and labor organizations are encouraged to conduct an education and training program within one year after September 30, 1993 for all current employees and members, and for all new employees and members thereafter within one year of commencement of employment, that includes at a minimum all the information outlined in this section. Employers are encouraged to conduct additional training for current supervisory and managerial employees and members within one year of September 30, 1993, and for new supervisory and managerial employees and members within one year of commencement of employment or membership, which should include at a minimum the information outlined in subsection (b) of this section and the specific responsibilities of supervisory and managerial employees and the methods that these employees must take to ensure immediate and appropriate corrective action in addressing sexual harassment complaints. Employers, labor organizations and appropriate state agencies are encouraged to cooperate in making this training available.

Source: Vermont Statutes Annotated, Ch. 21, § 495h (1995).

EARLY SEXUAL HARASSMENT CASES

Sexual harassment is a relatively new area of law. The first lawsuits arguing that sexual harassment in employment was illegal were brought in the mid-1970s.

Cases Holding That Harassment Is Not Sex Discrimination

The earliest sexual harassment cases involved claims of quid pro quo harassment (see Documents 17–21). The lawyers who brought these suits argued that such sexual harassment was a form of illegal sex discrimination in employment and thus violated Title VII.

The courts who heard the earliest cases, however, disagreed with the lawyers' arguments. They reasoned that sexual harassment was a personal matter between the employees involved, rather than a form of sex discrimination for which the employing company was responsible. Furthermore, they were concerned that finding for the plaintiffs would unleash a flood of lawsuits every time one employee made sexual advances to another. Finally, the courts were also troubled by the hypothetical bisexual harasser. How could it be sex discrimination, the courts wondered, if a harasser made sexual advances to both men and women, thus treating them equally? On the other hand, how could it make sense for heterosexual harassment to be illegal, while bisexual harassment would be permitted? These concerns prompted courts, including those that decided *Corne v. Bausch & Lomb, Inc.* (Document 17) and *Tomkins v. Public Service Electric & Gas Co.* (Document 18), to hold that sexual harassment was not illegal. The *Tomkins* case, however, was later reversed on appeal (see Document 21).

DOCUMENT 17: *Corne v. Bausch & Lomb, Inc.*, U.S. District Court (1975)

Plaintiffs Jane Corne and Geneva DeVane filed the present complaint alleging a violation of civil rights based on sex discrimination. The suit was instituted pursuant to . . . Title VII of the Civil Rights Act of 1964. . . . It is alleged that at the time the discriminatory acts occurred, plaintiffs were employed by defendant Bausch and Lomb and defendant Leon Price was in a supervisory capacity over plaintiffs.

. . . The complaint . . . alleges the following: plaintiffs worked in a clerical capacity for defendants in the period before the filing of the E.E.O.C. complaints; plaintiffs' employment conditions became increasingly onerous in that they were repeatedly subjected to verbal and physical sexual advances from defendant Price; defendant Price's illegal activities were directed not only to plaintiffs but also to other female employees and thus constituted a condition of employment that discriminates by sex in violation of Title VII; cooperation with defendant Price's illegal activities resulted in favored employment that discriminates by sex in violation of Title VII; immediately before the filing of the complaint with the E.E.O.C., defendant Price's activities directed to plaintiffs became so onerous that plaintiffs were forced to resign. . . .

Assuming that all allegations in the complaint are true, plaintiffs have failed to state a claim for relief under Title VII of the Civil Rights Act. . . .

. . . Plaintiffs allege that putting a male in a supervisory position over female employees, where the male supervisor persistently takes unsolicited and unwelcome sexual liberties with the female employees is the creation of a sex discriminatory condition, and a limitation that tends to deprive the women of equal employment opportunities; the plaintiffs seek to hold the employer liable because its administrative personnel knew or should have known of defendant Price's conduct toward female employees. . . .

In all of the . . . cases [in which courts have found illegal sex discrimination] the discriminatory conduct complained of arose out of company policies. There was apparently some advantage to, or gain by, the employer from such discriminatory practices. Always such discriminatory practices were employer designed and oriented. In the present case, Mr. Price's conduct appears to be nothing more than a personal proclivity, peculiarity or mannerism. By his alleged sexual advances, Mr. Price was satisfying a personal urge. Certainly no employer policy is here involved; rather than the company being benefited in any way by the conduct of Price, it is obvious it can only be damaged by the very nature of the acts complained of.

. . . [T]here is nothing in the Act which could reasonably be construed to have it apply to "verbal and physical sexual advances" by another employee, even though he be in a supervisory capacity where such complained of acts or conduct had no relationship to the nature of the employment.

It would be ludicrous to hold that the sort of activity involved here was contemplated by the Act because to do so would mean that if the conduct complained of was directed equally to males there would be no basis for suit. Also, an outgrowth of holding such activity to be actionable under Title VII would be a potential federal lawsuit every time any employee made amorous or sexually oriented advances toward another. The only sure way an employer could avoid such charges would be to have employees who were asexual.

Source: 390 *Federal Supplement* 161–164 (D. Arizona 1975) (footnotes omitted).

DOCUMENT 18: *Tomkins v. Public Service Electric & Gas Co.,* U.S. District Court (1976)

Plaintiff Adrienne Tomkins was formerly employed by defendant Public Service Electric and Gas Company (hereinafter PSE&G). She was fired by PSE&G under circumstances which are presently in dispute. After her termination plaintiff filed this lawsuit. . . . The gravamen of plaintiff's complaint is that she was subjected to sexual harassment by her male supervisor. She further alleges that the company retaliated against her when she protested the supervisor's actions. Plaintiff seeks to proceed under the authority of Title VII of the Civil Rights Act of 1964. . . .

Plaintiff was hired as an office worker at the company's Newark offices in 1971. Her progress through the lower grades of office employment was normal until she was assigned to the defendant supervisor. Plaintiff at this time was approaching eligibility for a promotion to a secretarial position. The complaint alleges that the supervisor requested that plaintiff take lunch with him outside the office premises, purportedly to discuss her prospects with the firm. Plaintiff contends that the supervisor used the opportunity to make sexual advances to her. She charges that she was detained by the supervisor against her will through economic threats and physical force.

... In sum, plaintiff claims that her superior's sexual advances coupled with his threats of reprisals, and the company's subsequent retaliation and ultimate termination of her services because of her complaints, constitute violations of Title VII. . . .

In company with three of the four district courts that have considered the issue, this Court holds that sexual harassment and sexually motivated assault do not constitute sex discrimination under Title VII. . . .

Title VII was enacted in order to remove those artificial barriers to full employment which are based upon unjust and long-encrusted prejudice. Its aim is to make careers open to talents irrespective of race or sex. It is not intended to provide a federal tort remedy for what amounts to physical attack motivated by sexual desire on the part of a supervisor and which happened to occur in a corporate corridor rather than a back alley. In this instance the supervisor was male and the employee was female. But no immutable principle of psychology compels this alignment of parties. The gender lines might as easily have been reversed, or even not crossed at all. While sexual desire animated the parties, or at least one of them, the gender of each is incidental to the claim of abuse. Similarly, the pleadings in this case aver that the supervisor's advances were spurned. Had they been accepted, however, and plaintiff thereby preferred, could co-workers be heard to complain in federal court as well? It is clear that such a claim is simply without the scope of the Act. The abuse of authority by supervisors of either sex for personal purposes is an unhappy and recurrent feature of our social experience. Such conduct is frequently illegal under the penal statutes of the relevant jurisdiction. Such conduct might well give rise to a civil action in tort. It is not, however, sex discrimination within the meaning of Title VII even when the purpose is sexual. E.E.O.C. urges that a contrary decision would not open the floodgates to litigation. The Commission argues that only sexual advances from a superior to a subordinate under the cloak of the superior's authority would be actionable under Title VII, and then only if such a practice contributed to an employment-related decision. But plaintiff's theory rests on the proposition, with which this Court concurs, that the power inherent in a position of authority is necessarily coercive. And, as the representative of the EEOC candidly conceded in oral argument, every sexual advance made by a supervisor would be made under the apparent cloak of that authority. Any subordinate knows that the boss is the boss whether a file folder or a dinner is at issue. Finally, the Court recalls [an earlier judge's statement that]: "The attraction of males to females and females to males is a natural sex phenomenon and it is probable that this attraction plays at least a subtle part in most personnel decisions." This natural sexual attraction can be subtle. If the plaintiff's view were to prevail, no superior could, prudently, attempt to open a social dialogue with any subordinate of either sex. An invitation to dinner could become an invitation to a federal lawsuit if a once harmonious relationship turned sour at some later time. And if an inebriated approach by a supervisor to a subordinate at the office Christmas party could form the basis of a federal lawsuit for sex discrimination if a promotion or a raise is later denied to the subordinate, we would need 4,000 federal trial judges instead of some 400.

Source: 422 *Federal Supplement* 553, 555–57 (D.N.J. 1976) (footnotes omitted).

Cases Holding That Harassment Is Sex Discrimination

In 1976 a trial court in the District of Columbia became the first court to hold that sexual harassment is a form of sex discrimination that is illegal under Title VII. That court, in a case called *Williams v. Saxbe* (Document 19), reasoned that, according to the plaintiff's claims, similarly situated men and women were being treated differently; women were forced to contend with harassment while men were not. That type of differential treatment, according to the court, is the very essence of sex discrimination. A number of appellate courts soon followed suit, agreeing that sexual harassment is illegal under Title VII. The cases of *Barnes v. Costle* (Document 20) and the appellate decision in *Tompkins v. Public Service Electric & Gas Co.* (Document 21) provide examples.

DOCUMENT 19: *Williams v. Saxbe*, U.S. District Court (1976)

Plaintiff, Diane R. Williams, brings this action to recover damages and for other relief as a result of defendants' alleged violations of the provisions of Title VII of the Civil Rights Act of 1964 . . . specifically, plaintiff alleges that she has been denied equal employment opportunities in the Department of Justice because of her sex. Plaintiff was a female employee of the Community Relations Service ("CRS") of the Department of Justice from approximately January 4, 1972 to September 22, 1972, at which time her employment with the CRS was terminated. Defendants are the Attorney General of the United States and the Director of the CRS of the Department of Justice. . . .

II. RETALIATORY ACTIONS OF A MALE SUPERVISOR, TAKEN BECAUSE A FEMALE EMPLOYEE DECLINED HIS SEXUAL ADVANCES, CONSTITUTES SEX DISCRIMINATION WITHIN THE DEFINITIONAL PARAMETERS OF TITLE VII OF THE CIVIL RIGHTS ACT OF 1964.

[T]he motion to dismiss presents the issue of whether the retaliatory actions of a male supervisor, taken because a female employee declined his sexual advances, constitutes sex discrimination within the definitional parameters of Title VII of the Civil Rights Act of 1964, as amended. This Court finds that it does. Defendants, however, make a cogent and almost persuasive argument to the contrary.

. . . . [Defendants argue that:]

"Plaintiff was allegedly denied employment enhancement not because she was a woman, but rather because she decided not to furnish the sexual consideration claimed to have been demanded. Therefore, plaintiff is in no different class from other employees, regardless of their gender or sexual orientation, who are made subject to such carnal demands." . . .

While defendants' argument is appealing, it obfuscates the fact that, taking the facts of the plaintiff's complaint as true, the conduct of the plaintiff's supervisor created an artificial barrier to employment which was placed before one gender and not the other, despite the fact that both genders were similarly situated. It is the opinion of this Court that plaintiff has therefore made out a cause of action under [Title VII]. . . . [6]

Finally, defendants argue that plaintiff has not made out a case of sex discrimination under the Act because the instant case was not the result of a policy or a regulation of the office, but rather, was an isolated personal incident which should not be the concern of the courts and was not the concern of Congress in enacting Title VII. But this argument is merely based upon defendants' view of the facts, coupled with a fear that the courts will become embroiled in sorting out the social life of the employees of the numerous federal agencies. . . . [T]he decision of the Court that plaintiff has stated a cause of action under Title VII will not have the feared result defendants urge. What the statute is concerned with is not interpersonal disputes between employees. Rather, the instant case reveals the statutory prohibition on the alleged discriminatory imposition of a condition of employment by the supervisor of an office of an agency. . . .

⁶This court also rejects any argument that this cannot be sex discrimination because the application of the rule would depend upon the sexual preference of the supervisor, as opposed to some other reason. But the reason for the discrimination under Title VII is not necessary to a finding of discrimination. *Cf. Griggs v. Duke Power Co.* . . . ("But Congress directed the thrust of the Act to the consequences of employment practices, not simply the motivation.") . . .

It is also notable that since the statute prohibits discrimination against men as well as women, a finding of discrimination could be made where a female supervisor imposed the criteria of the instant case upon only the male employees in her office. So could a finding of discrimination be made if the supervisor were a homosexual. And, the fact that a finding of discrimination could not be made if the supervisor were a bisexual and applied this criteria to both genders should not lead to a conclusion that sex discrimination could not occur in other situations outlined above.

Source: 413 *Federal Supplement* 654, 655–661 (D.D.C. 1976) (some footnotes omitted).

DOCUMENT 20: *Barnes v. Costle*, U.S. Court of Appeals for the District of Columbia (1977)

I

Appellant, a black woman, was hired by the director of the [Environmental Protection] Agency's equal employment opportunity division, who also is black, as his administrative assistant. . . . During a pre-employment interview, she asserts, he promised a promotion . . . within ninety days. Shortly after commencement of the employment, she claims, the director initiated a quest for sexual favors by "(a) repeatedly soliciting [her] to join him for social activities after office hours, notwithstanding [her] repeated refusal to do so; (b) by making repeated remarks to [her] which were sexual in nature; (c) by repeatedly suggesting to [her] that if she cooperated with him in a sexual affair, her employment status would be enhanced." Appellant states that she "continually resisted [his] overtures . . . and finally advised him that notwithstanding his stated belief that many executives 'have affairs with their personnel', she preferred that their relationship remain a strictly professional one." Thereafter, she charges, the director "alone and in concert with other agents of [appellee], began a conscious campaign to belittle [her], to harass her and to strip her of her job duties, all culminating in the decision of [appellee's] agent . . . to abolish [her] job in retaliation for [her] refusal to grant him sexual favors." These activities, appellant declares, "would not have occurred but for [her] sex." . . .

III

... The question debated, and the issue pivotal on this appeal, is whether the discrimination, in the circumstances described by appellant, was as a matter of law "based on ... sex ...."

We start with the statute as written, and, so measured, we think the discrimination as portrayed was plainly based on appellant's gender. Her thesis, in substance, is that her supervisor retaliated by abolishing her job when she resisted his sexual advances. More particularly, she states that he repeatedly told her that indulgence in a sexual affair would enhance her employment status; that he endeavored affirmatively but futilely to consummate his proposition; and that, upon her refusal to accede, he campaigned against her continued employment in his department and succeeded eventually in liquidating her position. So it was, by her version, that retention of her job was conditioned upon submission to sexual relations—an exaction which the supervisor would not have sought from any male. It is much too late in the day to contend that Title VII does not outlaw terms of employment for women which differ appreciably from those set for men, and which are not genuinely and reasonably related to performance on the job.

The District Court felt, however, that appellant's suit amounted to no more than a claim "that she was discriminated against, not because she was a woman, but because she refused to engage in a sexual affair with her supervisor." ... We cannot accept this analysis of the situation. ... But for her womanhood, from aught that appears, her participation in sexual activity would never have been solicited. To say, then, that she was victimized in her employment simply because she declined the invitation is to ignore the asserted fact that she was invited only because she was a woman subordinate to the inviter in the hierarchy of agency personnel.[55] Put another way, she became the target of her superior's sexual desires because she was a woman, and was asked to bow to his demands as the price for holding her job. The circumstance imparting high visibility to the role of gender in the affair is that no male employee was susceptible to such an approach by appellant's supervisor. Thus gender cannot be eliminated from the formulation which appellant advocates, and that formulation advances a prima facie case of sex discrimination within the purview of Title VII. ...

[55] It is no answer to say that a similar condition could be imposed on a male subordinate by a heterosexual female superior, or upon a subordinate of either gender by a homosexual superior of the same gender. In each instance, the legal problem would be identical to that confronting us now—the exaction of a condition which, but for his or her sex, the employee would not have faced. These situations, like that at bar, are to be distinguished from a bisexual superior who

conditions the employment opportunities of a subordinate of either gender upon participation in a sexual affair. In the case of the bisexual superior, the insistence upon sexual favors would not constitute gender discrimination because it would apply to male and female employees alike.

Source: 561 *Federal Reporter 2d* 983, 984–95 (D.C. Cir. 1977) (some footnotes omitted).

DOCUMENT 21: *Tomkins v. Public Service Electric & Gas Co.,* U.S. Court of Appeals for the Third Circuit (1977)

The question presented is whether appellant Adrienne Tomkins, in alleging that her continued employment with appellee Public Service Electric and Gas Co. [PSE&G] was conditioned upon her submitting to the sexual advances of a male supervisor, stated a cause of action under Title VII of the Civil Rights Act of 1964. . . . The district court determined that appellant did not state a claim under Title VII, and dismissed her complaint. . . . Taking the allegations of Tomkins' complaint as true . . . we find that a cognizable claim of sex discrimination was made and, accordingly, we reverse the dismissal of the complaint and remand the case to the district court for further proceedings. . . .

A.

Tomkins claims that the sexual demands of her supervisor imposed a sex-based "term or condition" on her employment. She alleges that her promotion and favorable job evaluation were made conditional upon her granting sexual favors, and that she suffered adverse job consequences as a result of this incident. In granting appellees' motion to dismiss, however, the district court characterized the supervisor's acts as "abuse of authority . . . for personal purposes." . . . The court thus overlooked the major thrust of Tomkins' complaint, *i.e.*, that her employer, either knowingly or constructively, made acquiescence in her supervisor's sexual demands a necessary prerequisite to the continuation of, or advancement in, her job.

The facts as alleged by appellant clearly demonstrate an incident with employment ramifications, one within the intended coverage of Title VII. The context within which the sexual advances occurred is itself strong evidence of a job-related condition: Tomkins was asked to lunch by her supervisor for the express purpose of discussing his upcoming evaluation of her work and possible recommendation of her for a promotion. But one need not infer the added condition from the setting alone. It is expressly alleged that the supervisor stated to Tomkins that her continued success and advancement at PSE&G were dependent upon her agreeing to his sexual demands. The demand thus amounted to a condition of employment, an additional duty or burden Tomkins was required by her supervisor to meet as a prerequisite to her continued employment. . . .

III.

. . . [W]e conclude that Title VII is violated when a supervisor, with the actual or constructive knowledge of the employer, makes sexual advances or demands toward a subordinate employee and conditions that employee's job status—evaluation, continued employment, promotion, or other aspects of career development—on a favorable response to those advances or demands, and the employer does not take prompt and appropriate remedial action after acquiring such knowledge.

IV.

We do not agree with the district court that finding a Title VII violation on these facts will result in an unmanageable number of suits and a difficulty in differentiating between spurious and meritorious claims. The congressional mandate that the federal courts provide relief is strong; it must not be thwarted by concern for judicial economy. More significant, however, this decision in no way relieves the plaintiff of the burden of proving the facts alleged to establish the required elements of a Title VII violation. Although any theory of liability may be used in vexatious or bad faith suits, we are confident that traditional judicial mechanisms will separate the valid from the invalid complaints.

Source: 568 *Federal Reporter 2d* 1044, 1045–49 (3d Cir. 1977) (footnotes omitted).

Hostile Environment Harassment Cases

The earliest sexual harassment lawsuits involved claims of quid pro quo harassment. It was not until 1981 that the first court recognized that hostile environment harassment, in which the employee may suffer no tangible harm, also constitutes illegal sex discrimination. In recognizing the illegality of hostile environment harassment, the United States Court of Appeals for the District of Columbia relied on earlier cases that held that racial harassment in employment that creates a hostile environment for minority workers is illegal.

DOCUMENT 22: *Bundy v. Jackson*, U.S. Court of Appeals for the District of Columbia (1981)

In *Barnes v. Costle* . . . we held that an employer who abolished a female employee's job to retaliate against the employee's resistance of his sexual advances violated Title VII of the Civil Rights Act of 1964. . . . The appellant in this case . . . asks us to extend *Barnes* by holding that an employer violates Title VII merely by subjecting female employees to sexual harassment, even if the employee's resistance to that harassment does not cause the employer to deprive her of any tangible job benefits. . . .

I. BACKGROUND

Appellant Sandra Bundy is now, and was at the time she filed her lawsuit, a Vocational Rehabilitation Specialist. . . .

The District Court's finding that sexual intimidation was a "normal condition of employment" in Bundy's agency finds ample support in the District Court's own chronology of Bundy's experiences there. Those experiences began in 1972 when Bundy . . . received and rejected sexual propositions from Delbert Jackson, then a fellow employee at the agency but now its Director. . . . It was two years later, however, that the sexual intimidation Bundy suffered began to intertwine directly with her employment, when she received propositions from two of her supervisors, Arthur Burton and James Gainey. . . .

We add that, although the District Court made no explicit findings as to harassment of other female employees, its finding that harassment was "standard operating procedure" finds ample support in record evidence that Bundy was not the only woman subjected to sexual intimidation by male supervisors.

In denying Bundy any relief, the District Court found that Bundy's supervisors did not take the "game" of sexually propositioning female employees "seriously," and that Bundy's rejection of their advances did not evoke in them any motive to take any action against her. . . . The record, however, contains nothing to support this view, and indeed some evidence directly belies it. For example, after Bundy complained . . . Burton began to derogate her for alleged malingering and poor work performance, though she had not previously received any such criticism. . . . Burton also arranged a meeting with Bundy and Gainey to discuss Bundy's alleged abuse of leave, though he did not pursue his charges at this meeting. . . .

Beyond these actions, Bundy's supervisors at least created the impression that they were impeding her promotion because she had offended them, and they certainly did nothing to help her pursue her harassment claims through established channels. . . .

We . . . made clear in *Barnes* that sex discrimination within the meaning of Title VII is not limited to disparate treatment founded solely or categorically on gender. Rather, discrimination is sex discrimination whenever sex is for no legitimate reason a substantial factor in the discrimination. . . .

We thus readily conclude that Bundy's employer discriminated against her on the basis of sex. What remains is the novel question whether the sexual harassment of the sort Bundy suffered amounted by itself to sex discrimination with respect to the "terms, conditions, or privileges of employment." . . .

Bundy's claim on this score is essentially that "conditions of employment" include the psychological and emotional work environment that the sexually stereotyped insults and demeaning propositions to which she was indisputably subjected and which caused her anxiety and debilitation . . . illegally poisoned that environment. This claim invokes the Title VII principle enunciated by Judge Goldberg in *Rogers v. Equal Employment Opportunity Com'n*. . . . The plaintiff in *Rogers*, a Hispanic, did not claim that her employer, a firm of opticians, had deprived her of any tangible job benefit. Rather, she claimed that by giving discriminatory service to its Hispanic *clients* the firm created a discriminatory and offensive work environment for its Hispanic *employees*. Granting that the express language of Title VII did not mention this situation, Judge Goldberg stated:

Time was when employment discrimination tended to be viewed as a series of isolated and distinguishable events, manifesting itself, for example, in an employer's practices of hiring, firing, and promoting. But today employment discrimination is a far more complex and pervasive phenomenon, as the nuances and subtleties of discriminatory employment practices are no longer confined to bread and butter issues. As wages and hours of employment take subordinate roles in management-labor relationships, the modern employee makes ever-increasing demands in the nature of intangible fringe benefits. Recognizing the importance of these benefits, we should neither ignore their need for protection, nor blind ourselves to their potential misuse.

. . . [That court] then concluded that the employer had indeed violated Title VII, Judge Goldberg explaining that "terms, conditions, or privileges of employment"

is an expansive concept which sweeps within its protective ambit the practice of creating a work environment heavily charged with ethnic or racial discrimination. . . .

The relevance of these "discriminatory environment" cases to sexual harassment is beyond serious dispute. Racial or ethnic discrimination against a company's minority clients may reflect no intent to discriminate directly against the company's minority employees, but in poisoning the atmosphere of employment it violates Title VII. . . . Racial slurs, though intentional and directed at individuals, may still be just verbal insults, yet they too may create Title VII liability. How then can sexual harassment, which injects the most demeaning sexual stereotypes into the general work environment and which always represents an intentional assault on an individual's innermost privacy, not be illegal? . . .

Indeed, so long as women remain inferiors in the employment hierarchy, they may have little recourse against harassment beyond the legal recourse Bundy seeks in this case. The law may allow a woman to prove that her resistance to the harassment cost her her job or some economic benefit, but this will do her no good if the employer never takes such tangible actions against her.

And this, in turn, means that so long as the sexual situation is constructed with enough coerciveness, subtlety, suddenness, or one-sidedness to negate the effectiveness of the woman's refusal, or so long as her refusals are simply ignored while her job is formally undisturbed, she is not considered to have been sexually harassed. C. MACKINNON, SEXUAL HARASSMENT OF WORKING WOMEN 46–47 (1979). It may even be pointless to require the employee to prove that she "resisted" the harassment at all. So long as the employer never literally forces sexual relations on the employee, "resistance" may be a meaningless alternative for her. If the employer demands no response to his verbal or physical gestures other than good-natured tolerance, the woman has no means of communicating her rejection. She neither accepts nor rejects the advances; she simply endures them. She might be able to contrive proof of rejection by objecting to the employer's advances in some very visible and dramatic way, but she would do so only at the risk of making her life on the job even more miserable. . . .

Bundy proved that she was the victim of a practice of sexual harassment and a discriminatory work environment permitted by her employer. Her rights under Title VII were therefore violated.

Source: 641 *Federal Reporter 2d* 934, 938–47 (D.C. Cir. 1981).

> *Henson v. City of Dundee* (Document 23), decided by a Court of Appeals in 1982, remains one of the leading cases on hostile environment harassment. It was the first case to lay out a clear five-part test for assessing whether a plaintiff has established a claim of hostile environment sexual harassment.

DOCUMENT 23: *Henson v. City of Dundee*, U.S. Court of Appeals for the Eleventh Circuit (1982)

In deciding this appeal, we must determine the proper application of Title VII principles to claims of sexual harassment at the workplace. Appellant, Barbara Henson, filed a Title VII action against the City of Dundee, Florida alleging sexual harassment on her job with the police department. . . .

Henson was hired as a dispatcher in the five-officer Dundee police department on January 14, 1975. Her position was funded by the federal government under the Comprehensive Employment Training Act (CETA). There were five other CETA employees who worked as dispatchers for the department, one female employee who generally worked with Henson during her shift, Carolyn Dicks, and four male employees.

Henson claims that during the two years she worked for the Dundee police department, she and her female coworker were subjected to sexual harassment by the chief of the Dundee police department, John Sellgren. She alleges that this harassment ultimately led her to resign under duress on January 28, 1977. In May 1977 Henson filed a complaint against the City of Dundee with the Equal Employment Opportunity Commission (E.E.O.C.) alleging sexual harassment. . . .

At trial, Henson attempted to prove three types of sexual harassment. First, she claimed that Sellgren created a hostile and offensive working environment for women in the police station. She and her former coworker, Dicks, testified that Sellgren subjected them to numerous harangues of demeaning sexual inquiries and vulgarities throughout the course of the two years during which Henson worked for the police department. Henson stated that in addition to these periodic harangues, Sellgren repeatedly requested that she have sexual relations with him. The district court, however, did not permit Henson's attorney to present evidence that Sellgren had also made sexual advances to Dicks. Henson testified further that she complained of Sellgren's conduct in 1976 to the city manager, Jane Eden, but that Eden took no action to restrain Sellgren. . . .

I. Sexual harassment and work environment

* * *

Title VII prohibits employment discrimination on the basis of gender, and seeks to remove arbitrary barriers to sexual equality at the workplace with respect to "compensation, terms, conditions, or privileges of employment." . . . "[T]erms, conditions, or privileges of employment" include the state of psychological well being at the workplace. . . . Therefore, courts have held that an employer violates Title VII simply by creating or condoning an environment at the workplace which significantly and adversely affects an employee because of his race or ethnicity, regardless of any other tangible job detriment to the protected employee. . . .

Sexual harassment which creates a hostile or offensive environment for members of one sex is every bit the arbitrary barrier to sexual equality at the workplace that racial harassment is to racial equality. Surely, a requirement that a man or woman run a gauntlet of sexual abuse in return for the privilege of being allowed to work and make a living can be as demeaning and disconcerting as the harshest of racial epithets. A pattern of sexual harassment inflicted upon an employee because of her sex is a pattern of behavior that inflicts disparate treatment upon a member of one sex with respect to terms, conditions, or privileges of employment. There is no requirement that an employee subjected to such disparate treatment prove in addition that she has suffered tangible job detriment. . . .

Of course, neither the courts nor the E.E.O.C. have suggested that every instance of sexual harassment gives rise to a Title VII claim against an employer for a hostile work environment. Rather, the plaintiff must allege and prove a number of elements in order to establish her claim. These elements include the following:

(1) *The employee belongs to a protected group.* As in other cases of sexual discrimination, this requires a simple stipulation that the employee is a man or a woman.

(2) *The employee was subject to unwelcome sexual harassment.* The E.E.O.C. regulations helpfully define the type of conduct that may constitute sexual harassment: "sexual advances, requests for sexual favors, and other verbal or physical conduct of a sexual nature." . . . In order to constitute harassment, this conduct must be unwelcome in the sense that the employee did not solicit or incite it, and in the sense that the employee regarded the conduct as undesirable or offensive. . . .

(3) *The harassment complained of was based upon sex.* The essence of a disparate treatment claim under Title VII is that an employee or applicant is intentionally singled out for adverse treatment on the basis of a prohibited criterion. . . . In proving a claim for a hostile work environment due to sexual harassment, therefore, the plaintiff must show that but for the fact of her sex, she would not have been the object of harassment. . . .

In the typical case in which a male supervisor makes sexual overtures to a female worker, it is obvious that the supervisor did not treat male employees in a similar fashion. It will therefore be a simple matter for the plaintiff to prove that but for her sex, she would not have been subjected to sexual harassment. . . . However, there may be cases in which a supervisor makes sexual overtures to workers of both sexes or where the conduct complained of is equally offensive to male and female workers. . . . In such cases, the sexual harassment would not be based upon sex because men and women are accorded like treatment. Although the plaintiff might have a remedy under state law in such a situation, the plaintiff would have no remedy under Title VII. . . .

(4) *The harassment complained of affected a "term, condition, or privilege" of employment*. [T]he state of psychological well being is a term, condition, or privilege of employment within the meaning of Title VII.... [H]owever ... the "mere utterance of an ethnic or racial epithet which engenders offensive feelings in an employee" does not affect the terms, conditions, or privileges of employment to a sufficiently significant degree to violate Title VII." ... For sexual harassment to state a claim under Title VII, it must be sufficiently pervasive so as to alter the conditions of employment and create an abusive working environment....

(5) *Respondeat superior*. Where, as here, the plaintiff seeks to hold the employer responsible for the hostile environment created by the plaintiff's supervisor or coworker, she must show that the employer knew or should have known of the harassment in question and failed to take prompt remedial action.... The employee can demonstrate that the employer knew of the harassment by showing that she complained to higher management of the harassment ... or by showing the pervasiveness of the harassment, which gives rise to the inference of knowledge or constructive knowledge....

In this case, Henson has made a prima facie showing of all elements necessary to establish a violation of Title VII. Dismissal of her claim was therefore erroneous. She is entitled to prove her claim on remand to the district court for a new trial.

Source: 682 *Federal Reporter 2d* 897, 899–905 (11th Cir. 1982).

THE SUPREME COURT SPEAKS

In 1986, a little more than ten years after the first court decided that sexual harassment in employment was illegal, the U.S. Supreme Court took up the issue. The case involved a lawsuit brought by a woman, Mechelle Vinson, who had lost her job at a bank. Ms. Vinson alleged that her supervisor, Sidney Taylor, had insisted that she have sex with him and that she complied out of fear that she would otherwise lose her job. Furthermore, she alleged that he had fondled her in front of other employees and had raped her. Mr. Taylor denied ever having sex with Ms. Vinson.

The trial court treated the case as a quid pro quo harassment case. It found for the bank that no harassment had occurred. The court reasoned that if any sexual relations had taken place, they had been "voluntary" and did not affect any tangible aspects of Ms. Vinson's employment.

An appellate court, however, reversed. That court saw the case as one involving hostile environment harassment and ordered that it be sent back for trial to consider that theory. It further held that it was irrelevant if the alleged sexual relationship between the parties was voluntary, in the sense that Ms. Vinson had not been actually forced to have sex, so long as she could establish that the advances were "unwelcome." Finally, that court objected to the trial court's permitting the defendants to introduce evidence at trial about the way in which Ms. Vinson dressed and about personal sexual fantasies that she had discussed at work.

Finally, the Supreme Court took the case. The Court unanimously held that both forms of sexual harassment are illegal under Title VII. Furthermore, it held that in order to make out a claim of hostile environment harassment, the plaintiff must show that the conduct directed at her was "unwelcome" and that it was "sufficiently severe or pervasive" to alter the conditions of her employment. The Supreme Court agreed with the appellate court that it was irrelevant if some of the sexual contact was voluntary. It concluded, however, that evidence about the way in which the plaintiff dressed at work and about her publicly expressed sexual fantasies could be admitted into court at the trial court judge's discretion.

The Justices of the Supreme Court, however, split on the issue of how to determine when an employing company should be held legally responsible and forced to pay damages for the acts of one of its supervisors. That issue is taken up later in Documents 27, 28, and 95.

DOCUMENT 24: *Meritor Savings Bank v. Vinson*, U.S. Supreme Court (1986)

II

Title VII of the Civil Rights Act of 1964 makes it "an unlawful employment practice for an employer . . . to discriminate against any individual with respect to his compensation, terms, conditions, or privileges of employment, because of such individual's race, color, religion, sex, or national origin." . . .

Respondent argues, and the Court of Appeals held, that unwelcome sexual advances that create an offensive or hostile working environment violate Title VII. Without question, when a supervisor sexually harasses a subordinate because of the subordinate's sex, that supervisor "discriminate[s]" on the basis of sex. Petitioner apparently does not challenge this proposition. It contends instead that in prohibiting discrimination with respect to "compensation, terms, conditions, or privileges" of employment, Congress was concerned with what petitioner describes as "tangible loss" of "an economic character," not "purely psychological aspects of the workplace environment." . . .

We reject petitioner's view. First, the language of Title VII is not limited to "economic" or "tangible" discrimination. The phrase "terms, conditions, or privileges of employment" evinces a congressional intent " 'to strike at the entire spectrum of disparate treatment of men and women' " in employment. . . . Petitioner has pointed to nothing in the Act to suggest that Congress contemplated the limitation urged here.

Second, in 1980 the EEOC issued Guidelines specifying that "sexual harassment," as there defined, is a form of sex discrimination prohibited by Title VII. As an "administrative interpretation of the Act by the enforcing agency," . . . these Guidelines, " 'while not controlling upon the courts by reason of their authority, do constitute a body of experience and informed judgment to which courts and litigants may properly resort for guidance.' " . . . The EEOC Guidelines fully support the view that harassment leading to noneconomic injury can violate Title VII.

In defining "sexual harassment," the Guidelines first describe the kinds of workplace conduct that may be actionable under Title VII. These include "[unwelcome] sexual advances, requests for sexual favors, and other verbal or physical conduct of a sexual nature." . . . Relevant to the charges at issue in this case, the Guidelines provide that such sexual misconduct constitutes prohibited "sexual harassment," whether or not it is directly linked to the grant or denial of an economic *quid pro quo*, where "such conduct has the purpose or effect of unreasonably interfering with an individual's work performance or creating an intimidating, hostile, or offensive working environment." . . .

Of course . . . not all workplace conduct that may be described as "harassment" affects a "term, condition, or privilege" of employment within the meaning of Title VII. . . . For sexual harassment to be actionable, it must be sufficiently severe or pervasive "to alter the conditions of [the victim's] employment and create an abusive working environment." . . . Respondent's allegations in this case—which include not only pervasive harassment but also criminal conduct of the most serious nature—are plainly sufficient to state a claim for "hostile environment" sexual harassment.

The question remains, however, whether the District Court's ultimate finding that respondent "was not the victim of sexual harassment" . . . effectively disposed of respondent's claim. The Court of Appeals recognized, we think correctly, that this ultimate finding was likely based on one or both of two erroneous views of the law. First, the District Court apparently believed that a claim for sexual harassment will not lie absent an *economic* effect on the complainant's employment. . . . Since it appears that the District Court made its findings without ever considering the "hostile environment" theory of sexual harassment, the Court of Appeals' decision to remand was correct.

Second, the District Court's conclusion that no actionable harassment occurred might have rested on its earlier "finding" that "[i]f [respondent] and Taylor did engage in an intimate or sexual relationship . . . that relationship was a voluntary one." . . . But the fact that sex-related conduct was "voluntary," in the sense that the complainant was not forced to participate against her will, is not a defense to a sexual harassment suit brought under Title VII. The gravamen of any sexual harassment claim is that the alleged sexual advances were "unwelcome." . . . While the question whether particular conduct was indeed unwelcome presents difficult problems of proof and turns largely on credibility determinations committed to the trier of fact, the District Court in this case erroneously focused on the "voluntariness" of respondent's participation in the claimed sexual episodes. The correct inquiry is whether respondent by her conduct indicated that the alleged sexual advances were unwelcome, not whether her actual participation in sexual intercourse was voluntary.

Petitioner contends that even if this case must be remanded to the District Court, the Court of Appeals erred in one of the terms of its remand. Specifically, the Court of Appeals stated that testimony about respondent's "dress and personal fantasies," . . . which the District Court apparently admitted into evidence, "had no place in this litigation." The apparent ground for this conclusion was that respondent's voluntariness *vel non* in submitting to Taylor's advances was immaterial to her sexual harassment claim. While "voluntariness" in the sense of consent is not a defense to such a claim, it does not follow that a complainant's sexually provocative speech or dress is irrelevant as a matter of law in determining whether he or she found particular sexual advances unwelcome. To the contrary, such evidence is obviously relevant. The EEOC Guidelines emphasize that the trier of fact must determine the existence of sexual harassment in light of "the record as a whole" and "the totality of circumstances, such as the nature of the sexual advances and the context in which the alleged incidents occurred." . . . Respondent's claim that any marginal relevance of the evidence in question was outweighed by the potential for unfair prejudice is the sort of argument properly addressed to the District Court. In this case the District Court concluded that the evidence should be admitted, and the Court of Appeals' contrary conclusion was based upon the erroneous, categorical view that testimony about provocative dress and publicly expressed sexual fantasies "had no place in this litigation." . . . While the District Court must carefully weigh the applicable considerations in deciding whether to admit evidence of this kind, there is no *per se* rule against its admissibility.

Source: 477 U.S. Reports 57, 57–69 (1986).

Prior to 1998, the Supreme Court decided only one other case involving sexual harassment in employment. In 1993, in a case called *Harris v. Forklift Systems, Inc.,* the Court considered the issue of whether a hostile environment sexual harassment plaintiff must show that she suffered severe psychological injury in order to win her lawsuit. The unanimous Supreme Court held for the plaintiff that she was not required to make such a showing. Instead, she need only show that the conduct complained of is sufficiently severe or prevalent to create an atmosphere that she viewed and that a reasonable person would view as hostile or abusive.

Justice Antonin Scalia filed a concurring opinion in the case. He was concerned that the words "hostile" and "abusive" were too vague to give juries deciding future cases much guidance.

DOCUMENT 25: *Harris v. Forklift Systems, Inc.,* U.S. Supreme Court (1993)

In this case we consider the definition of a discriminatorily "abusive work environment" (also known as a "hostile work environment") under Title VII of the Civil Rights Act of 1964. . . .

II

Title VII of the Civil Rights Act of 1964 makes it "an unlawful employment practice for an employer . . . to discriminate against any individual with respect to his compensation, terms, conditions, or privileges of employment, because of such individual's race, color, religion, sex, or national origin." . . . As we made clear in *Meritor Savings Bank, FSB v. Vinson* . . . this language "is not limited to 'economic' or 'tangible' discrimination. The phrase 'terms, conditions, or privileges of employment' evinces a congressional intent 'to strike at the entire spectrum of disparate treatment of men and women' in employment," which includes requiring people to work in a discriminatorily hostile or abusive environment. . . . When the workplace is permeated with "discriminatory intimidation, ridicule, and insult," . . . that is "sufficiently severe or pervasive to alter the conditions of the victim's employment and create an abusive working environment," . . . Title VII is violated.

This standard, which we reaffirm today, takes a middle path between making actionable any conduct that is merely offensive and requiring the conduct to cause a tangible psychological injury. As we pointed out in *Meritor*, "mere utterance of an . . . epithet which engenders offensive feelings in a [*sic*] employee" . . . does not sufficiently affect the conditions of employment to implicate Title VII. Conduct that is not severe or pervasive enough to create an objectively hostile or abusive work environment—an environment that a reasonable person would find hostile or abusive—is beyond Title VII's purview. Likewise, if the victim does not subjectively perceive the environment to be abusive, the conduct has not actually altered the conditions of the victim's employment, and there is no Title VII violation.

But Title VII comes into play before the harassing conduct leads to a nervous breakdown. A discriminatorily abusive work environment, even one that does not seriously affect employees' psychological well-being, can and often will detract from employees' job performance, discourage employees from remaining on the job, or keep them from advancing in their careers. Moreover, even without regard to these tangible effects, the very fact that the discriminatory conduct was so severe or pervasive that it created a work environment abusive to employees because of their race, gender, religion, or national origin offends Title VII's broad rule of workplace equality. The appalling conduct alleged in *Meritor*, and the reference in that case to environments " 'so heavily polluted with discrimination as to destroy completely the emotional and psychological stability of minority group workers,' " . . . merely present some especially egregious examples of harassment. They do not mark the boundary of what is actionable.

We therefore believe the District Court erred in relying on whether the conduct "seriously affected plaintiff's psychological well-being" or led her to "suffer injury." Such an inquiry may needlessly focus the factfinder's attention on concrete psychological harm, an element Title VII does not require. Certainly Title VII bars conduct that would seriously affect a reasonable person's psychological well-being, but the statute is not limited to such conduct. So long as the environment would reasonably be perceived, and is perceived, as hostile or abusive, . . . there is no need for it also to be psychologically injurious.

This is not, and by its nature cannot be, a mathematically precise test. We need not answer today all the potential questions it raises. . . . But we can say that whether an environment is "hostile" or "abusive" can be determined only by looking at all the circumstances. These may include the frequency of the discriminatory conduct; its severity; whether it is physically threatening or humiliating, or a mere offensive utterance; and whether it unreasonably interferes with an employee's work performance. The effect on the employee's psychological well-being is, of course, relevant to determining whether the plaintiff actually found the environment abusive. But while psychological harm, like any other relevant factor, may be taken into account, no single factor is required. . . .

JUSTICE SCALIA, concurring.

Meritor Savings Bank, FSB v. Vinson . . . held that Title VII prohibits sexual harassment that takes the form of a hostile work environment. The Court stated that sexual harassment is actionable if it is "sufficiently severe or pervasive 'to alter the conditions of [the victim's] employment and create an abusive work environment.' " . . . Today's opinion elaborates that the challenged conduct must be severe or pervasive enough "to create an objectively hostile or abusive work environment—an environment that a reasonable person would find hostile or abusive." . . .

"Abusive" (or "hostile," which in this context I take to mean the same thing) does not seem to me a very clear standard—and I do not think clarity is at all increased by adding the adverb "objectively" or by appealing to a "reasonable person['s]" notion of what the vague word means. Today's opinion does list a number of factors that contribute to abusiveness . . . but since it neither says how much of each is necessary (an impossible task) nor identifies any single factor as determinative, it thereby adds little certitude. As a practical matter, today's holding lets virtually unguided juries decide whether sex-related conduct engaged in (or permitted by) an employer is egregious enough to warrant an award of damages. One might say that what constitutes "negligence" (a traditional jury question) is not much more clear and certain than what constitutes "abusiveness." Perhaps so. But the class of plaintiffs seeking to recover for negligence is limited to those who have suffered harm, whereas under this statute abusiveness is to be the test of whether legal harm has been suffered, opening more expansive vistas of litigation.

Be that as it may, I know of no alternative to the course the Court today has taken. One of the factors mentioned in the Court's nonexhaustive list—whether the conduct unreasonably interferes with an employee's work performance—would, if it were made an absolute test, provide greater guidance to juries and employers. But I see no basis for such a limitation in the language of the statute. Accepting *Meritor's* interpretation of the term "conditions of employment" as the law, the test is not whether work has been impaired, but whether working conditions have been discriminatorily altered. I know of no test more faithful to the inherently vague statutory language than the one the Court today adopts. For these reasons, I join the opinion of the Court.

Source: 510 *United States Reports* 17, 18–25 (1993).

In 1998 the Supreme Court decided four more cases involving alle-

gations of sexual harassment in employment. Excerpts from those decisions are set forth in Part VI of this book (Documents 93–96).

PROVING "UNWELCOMENESS"

The Supreme Court in *Meritor Savings Bank v. Vinson* (Document 24)
held that, in order to win on a sexual harassment claim, the plaintiff
must establish that the sexual words or conduct to which she was subjected were "unwelcome." The issue whether the plaintiff welcomed
the conduct is critical in many sexual harassment trials. In 1990, EEOC
issued "Policy Guidance" (Document 26) stating its position on what
constitutes unwelcome behavior. The agency explained that the conduct must be offensive to the victim and must not have been solicited
or incited by him or her. It is helpful to the plaintiff's case if he or she
protested when the harassment occurred, although such protests are
not absolutely required.

DOCUMENT 26: *EEOC Policy Guidance on Current Issues of Sexual Harassment* (Equal Employment Opportunity Commission, 1990)

A. Determining Whether Sexual Conduct Is Unwelcome

Sexual harassment is "unwelcome . . . verbal or physical conduct of a
sexual nature. . . ." Because sexual attraction may often play a role in the
day-to-day social exchange between employees, "the distinction between
invited, uninvited-but-welcome, offensive-but-tolerated, and flatly rejected" sexual advances may well be difficult to discern. . . . But this distinction is essential because sexual conduct becomes unlawful only when
it is unwelcome. The Eleventh Circuit provided a general definition of
"unwelcome conduct" in *Henson v. City of Dundee* . . . : the challenged
conduct must be unwelcome "in the sense that the employee did not
solicit or incite it, and in the sense that the employee regarded the conduct as undesirable or offensive."

When confronted with conflicting evidence as to welcomeness, the
Commission looks "at the record as a whole and at the totality of circumstances" . . . evaluating each situation on a case-by-case basis. When
there is some indication of welcomeness or when the credibility of the
parties is at issue, the charging party's claim will be considerably
strengthened if she made a contemporaneous complaint or protest. Particularly when the alleged harasser may have some reason (e.g., a prior
consensual relationship) to believe that the advances will be welcomed,

it is important for the victim to communicate that the conduct is unwelcome. Generally, victims are well-advised to assert their right to a workplace free from sexual harassment. This may stop the harassment before it becomes more serious. A contemporaneous complaint or protest may also provide persuasive evidence that the sexual harassment in fact occurred as alleged. . . . Thus, in investigating sexual harassment charges, it is important to develop detailed evidence of the circumstances and nature of any such complaints or protests, whether to the alleged harasser, higher management, co-workers or others.

While a complaint or protest is helpful to charging party's case, it is not a necessary element of the claim. Indeed, the Commission recognizes that victims may fear repercussions from complaining about the harassment and that such fear may explain a delay in opposing the conduct. If the victim failed to complain or delayed in complaining, the investigation must ascertain why. The relevance of whether the victim has complained varies depending upon "the nature of the sexual advances and the context in which the alleged incidents occurred." . . .

Example—Charging Party (CP) alleges that her supervisor subjected her to unwelcome sexual advances that created a hostile work environment. The investigation into her charge discloses that her supervisor began making intermittent sexual advances to her in June, 1987, but she did not complain to management about the harassment. After the harassment continued and worsened, she filed a charge with EEOC in June, 1988. There is no evidence CP welcomed the advances. CP states that she feared that complaining about the harassment would cause her to lose her job. She also states that she initially believed she could resolve the situation herself, but as the harassment became more frequent and severe, she said she realized that intervention by EEOC was necessary. The investigator determines CP is credible and concludes that the delay in complaining does not undercut CP's claim.

When welcomeness is at issue, the investigation should determine whether the victim's conduct is consistent, or inconsistent, with her assertion that the sexual conduct is unwelcome. . . .

In some cases the courts and the Commission have considered whether the complainant welcomed the sexual conduct by acting in a sexually aggressive manner, using sexually-oriented language, or soliciting the sexual conduct. Thus, in *Gan v. Kepro Circuit Systems* . . . the plaintiff regularly used vulgar language, initiated sexually-oriented conversations with her co-workers, asked male employees about their marital sex lives and whether they engaged in extramarital affairs, and discussed her own sexual encounters. In rejecting the plaintiff's claim of "hostile environment" harassment, the court found that any propositions or sexual remarks by co-workers were "prompted by her own sexual aggressiveness and her own sexually-explicit conversations." . . .

Conversely, occasional use of sexually explicit language does not necessarily negate a claim that sexual conduct was unwelcome. Although a
charging party's use of sexual terms or off-color jokes may suggest that
sexual comments by others in that situation were not unwelcome, more
extreme and abusive or persistent comments or a physical assault will
not be excused, nor would "quid pro quo" harassment be allowed.

Any past conduct of the charging party that is offered to show "welcomeness" must relate to the alleged harasser. . . . [E]vidence concerning
a charging party's general character and past behavior toward others has
limited, if any, probative value and does not substitute for a careful
examination of her behavior toward the alleged harasser.

A more difficult situation occurs when an employee first willingly participates in conduct of a sexual nature but then ceases to participate and
claims that any continued sexual conduct has created a hostile work
environment. Here the employee has the burden of showing that any
further sexual conduct is unwelcome, work-related harassment. The employee must clearly notify the alleged harasser that his conduct is no
longer welcome. If the conduct still continues, her failure to bring the
matter to the attention of higher management or the EEOC is evidence,
though not dispositive, that any continued conduct is, in fact, welcome
or unrelated to work. In any case, however, her refusal to submit to the
sexual conduct cannot be the basis for denying her an employment benefit or opportunity; that would constitute a "quid pro quo" violation.

Source: Equal Employment Opportunity Commission, *EEOC Policy Guidance on
Current Issues of Sexual Harassment*, March 19, 1990 (footnotes omitted).

LEGAL RESPONSIBILITY FOR SEXUAL HARASSMENT

When the Employer Must Pay

Sexual harassment lawsuits are typically brought as sex discrimination
claims pursuant to Title VII of the Civil Rights Act of 1964 or pursuant
to state antidiscrimination law. These laws provide that it is illegal for
employers to discriminate on the basis of sex. They further provide that
the employer is responsible for the acts of its "agents." For example,
if an individual supervisor whom the employer has delegated the
power to hire employees refuses to hire women, it is the company that
is legally responsible. The principle that employers must pay for wrongful acts by their agents committed within the scope of their employment
is referred to by the Latin term *respondeat superior*, which translates
as "let the master answer."

It is common, therefore, for sexual harassment suits to be brought
against the employing company instead of (or, sometimes, in addition

to) the person who engaged in the harassing behavior. But courts have been puzzled by the issue of when an employer should have to pay for an employee's harassing behavior. They have applied the law of agency, an area of law that seeks to provide a general answer to the question of when a company is legally responsible for the behavior of its workers. Agency law makes employers responsible for wrongs committed by their employees within the scope of their employment.

They have disagreed, however, about what the result of applying agency principles to the area of sexual harassment should be. In 1980 the EEOC analyzed the problem. It adopted guidelines (Document 27) providing that employers should always be responsible for harassment perpetrated by supervisors. On the other hand, the employer should not be held responsible for harassment perpetrated by a coworker or a nonemployee unless it knew, or should have known of the behavior but failed to correct the problem.

DOCUMENT 27: *Equal Employment Opportunity Commission's Guidelines on Discrimination Because of Sex* (Equal Employment Opportunity Commission, 1980)

§ 1604.11 Sexual harassment.

* * *

(c) Applying general title VII principles, an employer, employment agency, joint apprenticeship committee or labor organization (hereinafter collectively referred to as "employer") is responsible for its acts and those of its agents and supervisory employees with respect to sexual harassment regardless of whether the specific acts complained of were authorized or even forbidden by the employer and regardless of whether the employer knew or should have known of their occurrence. The Commission will examine the circumstances of the particular employment relationship and the job functions performed by the individual in determining whether an individual acts in either a supervisory or agency capacity.

(d) With respect to conduct between fellow employees, an employer is responsible for acts of sexual harassment in the workplace where the employer (or its agents or supervisory employees) knows or should have known of the conduct, unless it can show that it took immediate and appropriate corrective action.

(e) An employer may also be responsible for the acts of non-employees, with respect to sexual harassment of employees in the work-place, where the employer (or its agents or supervisory employees) knows or should have known of the conduct and fails to take immediate and appropriate corrective action. In reviewing these cases the Commission will consider the extent of the employer's control and any other legal responsibility which the employer may have with respect to the conduct of such non-employees.

Source: 29 *Code of Federal Regulations* § 1604.11.

In 1986, in *Meritor Savings Bank v. Vinson* (Document 28), the U.S. Supreme Court confronted the issue. The majority of the Supreme Court declined to give a firm answer to the question of when employers should be held legally responsible for harassment that occurs within their companies. Nonetheless, it suggested that it agreed with a revised position recently adopted by EEOC: employers should always be liable for quid pro quo harassment, but they should only be liable for hostile environment harassment if the employer knew about the harassment but failed to correct the problem or if they did not provide a reasonable way for employees to notify management of sexual harassment claims.

In contrast, Justice Thurgood Marshall, who was joined by three other Justices, filed a separate opinion, arguing that the EEOC's original test was the appropriate one.

In 1998 the Supreme Court revisited the issue of when the employer could be held responsible for both hostile environment and quid pro quo harassment. Those cases, *Burlington Industries, Inc. v. Ellerth* (Document 94) and *Faragher v. City of Boca Raton* (Document 95), are discussed in Part VI.

DOCUMENT 28: *Meritor Savings Bank v. Vinson*, U.S. Supreme Court (1986)

[In this case, Mechelle Vinson, a former bank employee, sued the bank for damages, based on allegations that her supervisor, Sidney Taylor, had demanded that she have sex with him, had fondled her at work, and had raped her. The Supreme Court treated this case as a hostile environment case]. . . .

III

[The trial court] went on to consider the question of the bank's liability. Finding that "the bank was without notice" of Taylor's alleged conduct, and that notice to Taylor was not the equivalent of notice to the bank, the court concluded that the bank therefore could not be held liable for

Taylor's alleged actions. The Court of Appeals took the opposite view, holding that an employer is strictly liable for a hostile environment created by a supervisor's sexual advances, even though the employer neither knew nor reasonably could have known of the alleged misconduct. The court held that a supervisor, whether or not he possesses the authority to hire, fire, or promote, is necessarily an "agent" of his employer for all Title VII purposes, since "even the appearance" of such authority may enable him to impose himself on his subordinates.

The parties . . . suggest several different standards for employer liability. Respondent [Vinson], not surprisingly, defends the position of the Court of Appeals. Noting that Title VII's definition of "employer" includes any "agent" of the employer, she also argues that "so long as the circumstance is work-related, the supervisor is the employer and the employer is the supervisor." . . . Notice to Taylor that the advances were unwelcome, therefore, was notice to the bank.

Petitioner [the Bank] argues that respondent's failure to use its established grievance procedure, or to otherwise put it on notice of the alleged misconduct, insulates petitioner from liability for Taylor's wrongdoing. A contrary rule would be unfair, petitioner argues, since in a hostile environment harassment case the employer often will have no reason to know about, or opportunity to cure, the alleged wrongdoing.

The EEOC, in its brief . . . contends that courts formulating employer liability rules should draw from traditional agency principles. Examination of those principles has led the EEOC to the view that where a supervisor exercises the authority actually delegated to him by his employer, by making or threatening to make decisions affecting the employment status of his subordinates, such actions are properly imputed to the employer whose delegation of authority empowered the supervisor to undertake them. . . . Thus, the courts have consistently held employers liable for the discriminatory discharges of employees by supervisory personnel, whether or not the employer knew, should have known, or approved of the supervisor's actions. . . .

The EEOC suggests that when a sexual harassment claim rests exclusively on a "hostile environment" theory, however, the usual basis for a finding of agency will often disappear. In that case, the EEOC believes, agency principles lead to

"a rule that asks whether a victim of sexual harassment had reasonably available an avenue of complaint regarding such harassment, and, if available and utilized, whether that procedure was reasonably responsive to the employee's complaint. If the employer has an expressed policy against sexual harassment and has implemented a procedure specifically designed to resolve sexual harassment claims, and if the victim does not take advantage of that procedure, the employer should be shielded from liability absent actual knowledge of the sexually hostile environment (obtained, e.g., by the filing of a charge with the EEOC or a comparable state agency). In all other cases, the employer will be liable if it has actual knowledge of the harassment or if, considering all the facts of the case, the victim in question had no reasonably available avenue for making his or her complaint known to appropriate management officials." ...

This debate over the appropriate standard for employer liability has a rather abstract quality about it given the state of the record in this case. We do not know at this stage whether Taylor made any sexual advances toward respondent at all, let alone whether those advances were unwelcome, whether they were sufficiently pervasive to constitute a condition of employment, or whether they were "so pervasive and so long continuing ... that the employer must have become conscious of [them]. ..."

We therefore decline the parties' invitation to issue a definitive rule on employer liability, but we do agree with the EEOC that Congress wanted courts to look to agency principles for guidance in this area. While such common-law principles may not be transferable in all their particulars to Title VII, Congress' decision to define "employer" to include any "agent" of an employer ... surely evinces an intent to place some limits on the acts of employees for which employers under Title VII are to be held responsible. For this reason, we hold that the Court of Appeals erred in concluding that employers are always automatically liable for sexual harassment by their supervisors. ... For the same reason, absence of notice to an employer does not necessarily insulate that employer from liability. ...

Finally, we reject petitioner's view that the mere existence of a grievance procedure and a policy against discrimination, coupled with respondent's failure to invoke that procedure, must insulate petitioner from liability. While those facts are plainly relevant, the situation before us demonstrates why they are not necessarily dispositive. Petitioner's general nondiscrimination policy did not address sexual harassment in particular, and thus did not alert employees to their employer's interest in correcting that form of discrimination. ... Moreover, the bank's grievance procedure apparently required an employee to complain first to her supervisor, in this case Taylor. Since Taylor was the alleged perpetrator, it is not altogether surprising that respondent failed to invoke the procedure and report her grievance to him. Petitioner's contention that respondent's failure should insulate it from liability might be substantially stronger if its procedures were better calculated to encourage victims of harassment to come forward. ...

Justice Marshall, with whom Justice Brennan, Justice Blackmun, and Justice Stevens join, concurring in the judgment.

I fully agree with the Court's conclusion that workplace sexual harassment is illegal, and violates Title VII. Part III of the Court's opinion, however, leaves open the circumstances in which an employer is responsible under Title VII for such conduct. Because I believe that question to be properly before us, I write separately.

The issue the Court declines to resolve is addressed in the EEOC Guidelines on Discrimination Because of Sex, which are entitled to great deference. . . .

The Commission, in issuing the Guidelines, explained that its rule was "in keeping with the general standard of employer liability with respect to agents and supervisory employees. . . . [T]he Commission and the courts have held for years that an employer is liable if a supervisor or an agent violates the Title VII, regardless of knowledge or any other mitigating factor." . . . I would adopt the standard set out by the Commission.

An employer can act only through individual supervisors and employees; discrimination is rarely carried out pursuant to a formal vote of a corporation's board of directors. Although an employer may sometimes adopt companywide discriminatory policies violative of Title VII, acts that may constitute Title VII violations are generally effected through the actions of individuals, and often an individual may take such a step even in defiance of company policy. Nonetheless, Title VII remedies, such as reinstatement and backpay, generally run against the employer as an entity. The question thus arises as to the circumstances under which an employer will be held liable under Title VII for the acts of its employees.

The answer supplied by general Title VII law . . . is that the act of a supervisory employee or agent is imputed to the employer. Thus, for example, when a supervisor discriminatorily fires or refuses to promote a black employee, that act is, without more, considered the act of the employer. The courts do not stop to consider whether the employer otherwise had "notice" of the action, or even whether the supervisor had actual authority to act as he did. . . . Following that approach, every Court of Appeals that has considered the issue has held that sexual harassment by supervisory personnel is automatically imputed to the employer when the harassment results in tangible job detriment to the subordinate employee. . . .

The brief filed by the . . . EEOC in this case suggests that a different rule should apply when a supervisor's harassment "merely" results in a discriminatory work environment. The Solicitor General concedes that sexual harassment that affects tangible job benefits is an exercise of authority delegated to the supervisor by the employer, and thus gives rise to employer liability. But, departing from the EEOC Guidelines, he argues that the case of a supervisor merely creating a discriminatory work environment is different because the supervisor "is not exercising, or threatening to exercise, actual or apparent authority to make personnel decisions affecting the victim." . . . In the latter situation, he concludes, some further notice requirement should therefore be necessary.

[This] position is untenable. A supervisor's responsibilities do not begin and end with the power to hire, fire, and discipline employees, or with the power to recommend such actions. Rather, a supervisor is charged with the day-to-day supervision of the work environment and with ensuring a safe, productive workplace. There is no reason why abuse of the latter authority should have different consequences than abuse of the former. In both cases it is the authority vested in the supervisor by the employer that enables him to commit the wrong: it is precisely because the supervisor is understood to be clothed with the employer's authority that he is able to impose unwelcome sexual conduct on subordinates. There is therefore no justification for a special rule, to be applied *only* in "hostile environment" cases, that sexual harassment does not create employer liability until the employee suffering the discrimination notifies other supervisors. No such requirement appears in the statute, and no such requirement can coherently be drawn from the law of agency.

Source: 477 *United States Reports* 57, 69–73, 74–78 (1986).

When the Individual Harasser Must Pay

Sometimes victims of sexual harassment try to sue the individual who harassed them in addition to or instead of the employing company. This strategy is somewhat unusual because, in many cases, the individual does not have enough money to pay the plaintiff any significant damages.

In lawsuits brought under Title VII, the majority of courts hold that individuals cannot be held legally responsible. Either the company must pay or nobody must. The case of *Tomka v. Seiler Corp.* (Document 29) is representative of the courts that take this view.

This result may seem strange to non-lawyers, since it lets the party most responsible for the harassment off the hook, but courts reach this conclusion by looking closely at the language of the statute. Title VII prohibits *employers*, not individual people, from discriminating.

A few courts, however, have reached the opposite conclusion—that individual supervisors can be held liable for sexual harassment under Title VII. These courts reason that Title VII's purpose of eliminating sex discrimination in employment would be better served if individuals were aware that they could be punished if they engaged in sexual harassment. Judge Parker's dissent in *Tomka v. Seiler Corp.* explains this view.

If a victim wants to collect damages from the individual harasser, there is a path that can be used. Instead of, or in addition to, suing under Title VII, the victim can also sue under state tort law. A tort is a civil wrong. Tort law prohibits such things as assault and battery, the intentional infliction of emotional distress, and invasion of privacy. Under these laws, the person who causes the harm—the individual harasser—is legally responsible and must pay money damages.

DOCUMENT 29: *Tomka v. Seiler Corp.*, U.S. Court of Appeals for the Second Circuit (1995)

D. Individual Liability

... We ... hold that individual defendants with supervisory control over a plaintiff may not be held personally liable under Title VII.

1. Title VII

The starting point in any statutory construction case, of course, is the language of the statute. . . . Title VII defines "employer" in relevant part as "a person engaged in an industry affecting commerce who has fifteen or more employees . . . and any *agent* of such a person." . . . The meaning of "agent" as used in this section has engendered a significant split among federal courts. Some courts have held that the literal language means supervisory personnel and other agents of the employer are statutory "employers" who may be held individually liable for discriminatory acts. . . . By contrast, at least three circuits and a number of district courts have interpreted this section not as creating individual liability but as a simple expression of respondeat superior: discriminatory personnel actions taken by an employer's agent only create liability for the employer-entity. . . .

a. The Statutory Scheme

The agent clause is part of a sentence that limits liability to employers with fifteen or more employees. . . . [T]he Ninth Circuit reasoned that Congress decided to protect small employers "in part because Congress did not want to burden small entities with the costs associated with litigating discrimination claims." . . . Thus, the court held that it was "inconceivable" that a Congress concerned with protecting small employers would simultaneously allow civil liability to run against individual employees. . . . We agree with this analysis. . . .

b. Title VII's Remedial Provisions

Title VII's remedial provisions also lead us to conclude that Congress never intended to hold agents individually liable for violations of the Act. Before Congress enacted the Civil Rights Act of 1991 . . . ("CRA of 1991"), a successful Title VII plaintiff was typically limited to reinstatement and backpay as potential remedies. . . . Clearly, backpay and reinstatement are equitable remedies which are most appropriately provided by employers, defined in the traditional sense of the word. . . .

The CRA of 1991 adds compensatory and punitive damages to the remedies available to a victim of intentional discrimination. Although money damages are of the type that an individual can normally be expected to pay, Congress calibrated the maximum allowable damage award to the size of the employer and failed to repeal the exemption for defendants with less than fifteen employees. In addition, the CRA of 1991 does not contain similar limits on damage awards against agents of an employer, or even address the subject of individual liability. Thus, it appears that Congress contemplated that only employer-entities could be held liable for compensatory and punitive damages, because "if Congress had envisioned individual liability . . . it would have included individuals in this litany of limitations and discontinued the exemption for small employers" . . .

. . . Accordingly, we hold that an employer's agent may not be held individually liable under Title VII. . . .

Parker, Circuit Judge, dissenting:
I write separately in dissent only as to the narrow issue of whether an employer's agent may be held individually liable for discriminatory acts under Title VII. I believe that the express language of the statute permits individual liability under Title VII and that sound jurisprudence counsels giving that statutory language its full effect. . . .

. . . Title VII specifically defines the term "employer" as "a person engaged in an industry affecting commerce who has fifteen or more employees . . . and any agent of such a person." . . .

Based on a literal reading of the statutory language, I would hold that Title VII permits a successful plaintiff to receive all relief provided for under the statute . . . against an employer "and any agent of such a person," jointly and severally, as outlined below. For this reason I disagree with, and respectfully dissent from, the majority opinion holding that an employer's agent cannot be individually liable under Title VII.

Source: 66 Federal Reporter 3d 1295, 1313–17, 1318–24 (2d Cir. 1995).

REMEDIES AVAILABLE IN CASES OF HARASSMENT

Originally, Title VII provided a limited range of remedies that a plaintiff could collect. Section 706(g) of Title VII provided that a plaintiff in a discrimination suit could get back pay, which is an award of money to make up for any wages lost because of discrimination, and get court orders reinstating her in her job, awarding her a promotion that she should have gotten, or ordering the employer to cease discriminating. Furthermore, the defendant could be forced to pay the plaintiff's attorney's fees.

However, the plaintiff was not entitled to so-called compensatory damages, which is money awarded to compensate for things like the emotional injury caused by the harassment or medical bills for counseling. Nor could a plaintiff get punitive damages, which are designed to punish the defendant for engaging in particularly bad behavior.

DOCUMENT 30: Title VII of the Civil Rights Act of 1964, § 706(g) (1964)

(g) **Injunctions; appropriate affirmative action; equitable relief; accrual of back pay; reduction of back pay; limitations on judicial orders**

(1) If the court finds that the respondent has intentionally engaged in or is intentionally engaging in an unlawful employment practice charged in the complaint, the court may enjoin the respondent from engaging in such unlawful employment practice, and order such affirmative action as may be appropriate, which may include, but is not limited to, reinstatement or hiring of employees, with or without back pay (payable by the employer, employment agency, or labor organization, as the case may be, responsible for the unlawful employment practice), or any other equitable relief as the court deems appropriate. Back pay liability shall not accrue from a date more than two years prior to the filing of a charge with the Commission. Interim earnings or amounts earnable with reasonable diligence by the person or persons discriminated against shall operate to reduce the back pay otherwise allowable.

(2)(A) No order of the court shall require the admission or reinstatement of an individual as a member of a union, or the hiring, reinstatement, or promotion of an individual as an employee, or the payment to him of any back pay, if such individual was refused admission, suspended, or expelled, or was refused employment or advancement or was suspended or discharged for any reason other than discrimination on

account of race, color, religion, sex, or national origin or in violation [of
the section of the Act that prohibits retaliation against those who exercise
their rights under the Act].

Source: 42 *United States Code* § 2000e–5(g) (1964).

The Civil Rights Act of 1991 (Document 31), another federal statute,
changed this by authorizing plaintiffs to collect both compensatory and
punitive damages in employment discrimination cases brought under
Title VII. It also gave parties the right to a jury trial on discrimination
claims; earlier Title VII cases had been heard by judges.

As a political compromise, however, the amount of money that the
plaintiff can get has been capped at varying amounts depending on the
size of the employer. Employers with more than 500 employees can
be forced to pay up to $300,000. In contrast, employers with one hun-
dred employees or fewer cannot be forced to pay more than $50,000
in compensatory and punitive damages. These caps have been criticized by women's groups. Although a group of senators and congressmen introduced a bill to abolish these caps, called the Equal Remedies
Act (Document 32), it has not been enacted and, at the present time,
its prospects do not look promising.

DOCUMENT 31: Civil Rights Act of 1991, § 102 (1991)

§ 1977A Damages in cases of intentional discrimination in employment

(a) Right of Recovery

(1) **Civil Rights**. In an action brought by a complaining party under . . .
the Civil Rights Act of 1964 . . . against a respondent who engaged in
unlawful intentional discrimination (not an employment practice that is
unlawful because of its disparate impact) prohibited under . . . the Act
. . . the complaining party may recover compensatory and punitive damages as allowed in subsection (b) of this section in addition to any relief
authorized by section 706(g) of the Civil Rights Act of 1964, from the
respondent. . . .

(b) Compensatory and punitive damages

(1) **Determination of punitive damages**. A complaining party may
recover punitive damages under this section against a respondent (other
than a government, government agency, or political subdivision) if the
complaining party demonstrates that the respondent engaged in a discriminatory practice or discriminatory practices with malice or with reck-

less indifference to the federally protected rights of an aggrieved individual.

(2) **Exclusions from compensatory damages**. Compensatory damages awarded under this section shall not include backpay, interest on backpay, or any other type of relief authorized under section 706(g) of the Civil Rights Act of 1964. . . .

(3) **Limitations**. The sum of the amount of compensatory damages awarded under this section for future pecuniary losses, emotional pain, suffering, inconvenience, mental anguish, loss of enjoyment of life, and other nonpecuniary losses, and the amount of punitive damages awarded under this section, shall not exceed for each complaining party—

(A) in the case of a respondent who has more than 14 and fewer than 101 employees in each of 20 or more calendar weeks in the current or preceding calendar year, $50,000;

(B) in the case of a respondent who has more than 100 and fewer than 201 employees in each of 20 or more calendar weeks in the current or preceding calendar year, $100,000; and

(C) in the case of a respondent who has more than 200 and fewer than 501 employees in each of 20 or more calendar weeks in the current or preceding calendar year, $200,000; and

(D) in the case of a respondent who has more than 500 employees in each of 20 or more calendar weeks in the current or preceding calendar year, $300,000. . . .

(c) **Jury trial**. If a complaining party seeks compensatory or punitive damages under this section—

(1) any party may demand a trial by jury; and

(2) the court shall not inform the jury of the limitations described in subsection (b)(3).

Source: 42 *United States Code* § 1981A (1991).

DOCUMENT 32: U.S. Senate, Statements on Introduced Bills and Joint Resolutions—The Equal Remedies Act (1995)

EQUAL REMEDIES ACT

Mr. KENNEDY. Mr. President, on behalf of myself and 20 other Senators, it is an honor to reintroduce the Equal Remedies Act to repeal the caps on the amount of damages available in employment discrimination cases brought under the Civil Rights Act of 1991.

The Civil Rights Act of 1991 for the first time gave women, religious minorities, and the disabled the right to recover compensatory and punitive damages when they suffer intentional discrimination on the job—but only up to specified limits. Victims of discrimination on the basis of race or national origin, by contrast, can recover such damages without such limits. No similar caps on damages exist in other civil rights laws, and they are not appropriate in this instance.

The Equal Remedies Act will end this double standard by removing the caps on damages for victims of intentional discrimination on the basis of sex, religion, or disability.

The caps on damages deny an adequate remedy to the most severely injured victims of discrimination. For example, if a woman proves that as a result of discrimination or sexual harassment she needs extensive medical treatment exceeding the caps, she will be limited to receiving only partial compensation for her injury.

In addition, the caps on punitive damages limit the extent to which employers who intentionally discriminate—particularly the worst violators—are punished for their discriminatory acts and deterred from engaging in such conduct in the future. The more offensive the conduct and the greater the damages inflicted, the more the employer benefits from the caps.

The caps on damages in the Civil Rights Act of 1991 were a compromise necessitated by concern about passing a bill that President Bush would sign. The issue was only one of the important issues covered in that piece of legislation, which also reversed a series of Supreme Court decisions that had made it far more difficult for working Americans to challenge discrimination.

The bill as a whole represented a significant advance in the ongoing battle to overcome discrimination in the workplace. In order to guarantee that the bill would become law, the unfortunate compromise on damages was included. However, many of us made clear that we intended to work for enactment of separate legislation to remove the caps. By reintroducing the Equal Remedies Act today, we reaffirm our commitment. We must end the double standard that relegates women, religious minorities, and the disabled to second-class remedies under the civil rights laws.

Source: 141 *Congressional Record S* 1758–88, January 30, 1995.

Because of the caps on damages, plaintiffs often turn to state law in addition to raising claims under Title VII. State laws often provide for unlimited damages. Huge damage awards, like the one described in the excerpt from the *San Francisco Chronicle* (Document 33), are the result of lawsuits brought under state law. The case described in the

Chronicle article, *Weeks v. Baker & McKenzie*, was recently upheld on appeal.

DOCUMENT 33: "Judge Halves $7.1 Million Award in Harassment Case But Bay Area Woman Will Still Get Record Sum" (Harriet Chiang, 1994)

A San Francisco judge yesterday cut in half a $7.1 million sexual harassment verdict awarded to a former legal secretary, ruling that the jury "overreached" in issuing the record-setting penalty against the megafirm where she worked.

Even with the reduction, the $3.5 million verdict in favor of Rena Weeks remains the nation's largest verdict awarded to an individual in a sexual harassment case.

While halving the award, Superior Court Judge John Munter upheld the jury's basic finding that Weeks was sexually harassed by Martin Greenstein, a high-powered trademark lawyer in the Palo Alto offices of Baker & McKenzie, the world's biggest law firm.

The judge also agreed that Baker & McKenzie knew that Greenstein had harassed Weeks and other women at the law firm over the course of several years but that it continued to employ him.

"Greenstein's harassment was severe and pervasive," Munter wrote in his 15-page decision. The law firm clearly knew that Greenstein was harassing women, the judge said, but kept him on "with a conscious disregard of the rights of the plaintiffs and other women in the workplace."

Weeks was hired by the firm in 1991 and was employed for less than three months, including 25 days as a secretary for Greenstein, a big moneymaker with a stable of high-paying Silicon Valley clients. But in that short span, she testified, he repeatedly subjected her to unwelcome sexual advances and groping.

In his decision, the judge left intact the jury's $50,000 award to Weeks for the emotional trauma she had suffered, a sum legal experts say is appropriate given her short term of employment.

Munter also upheld the $225,000 in punitive damages against Greenstein. But, he said, the $6.9 million punitive-damages award against Baker & McKenzie was excessive.

Noting that Weeks' own attorneys had asked the jury for $3.5 million, Munter wrote: "The sum of $3.5 million is a fair and reasonable sum. ... An award of $6.9 million is not." He added that $3.5 million is 5 percent of the firm's net worth. . . .

Weeks, who worked at Baker & McKenzie's Palo Alto offices until September 1991, sued Greenstein and the firm in May 1992. She claimed that Greenstein sexually harassed her by groping her breast while pouring M&Ms down her front shirt pocket, lunging at her in the office with his arms outstretched, and grabbing her while she was loading file cabinets and pressing himself against her.

The former secretary charged that Baker & McKenzie put up with Greenstein's misconduct because he was a powerful lawyer with influential and affluent clients.

Weeks alleged that Greenstein harassed at least eight other women beginning in 1987, when he was in the firm's Chicago office.

The firm fired Greenstein a year ago after learning that he had backdated some documents. Greenstein is now a partner at a small law firm in San Jose.

In slicing in half the jury award, Munter noted that the $6.9 million was 138 times the $50,000 awarded to Weeks for her emotional suffering. Under the law, punitive damages must be "reasonably related" to the compensatory damages. The judge also found that the $3.5 million is a sufficient deterrent to further harassment at the law firm.

"Baker's conduct was not the product of a deliberate and purposeful policy aimed at violating the rights of anyone," said Munter. The judge noted that the firm will be required to pay Weeks' attorney fees—her lawyers have requested a little over $2.7 million. And, he added, the firm has taken steps to improve its handling of sexual harassment cases.

Source: Harriet Chiang, "Judge Halves $7.1 Million Award in Harassment Case But Bay Area Woman Will Still Get Record Sum," *San Francisco Chronicle*, November 29, 1994, p. A-15.

EVIDENCE ABOUT THE PLAINTIFF'S SEXUAL HISTORY

In sexual harassment cases, defendants sometimes try to introduce evidence about the plaintiff's sexual behavior. Often, the defendant tries to use this evidence to prove that the plaintiff welcomed the sexual advances; therefore, the advances were not illegal. Indeed, the Supreme Court in *Meritor Savings Bank, FSB v. Vinson* (Document 24) held that evidence of a plaintiff's "sexually provocative speech or dress" and "publicly expressed sexual fantasies" might in some cases be relevant and might properly be admitted into evidence.

Sometimes, however, as the excerpt from the *Wall Street Journal* (Document 34) explains, lawyers seek to discover and introduce such evidence in order to intimidate the plaintiff into dropping the lawsuit. In response to this concern, in 1994, Congress amended the Federal Rules of Evidence—the rules that govern what evidence can be admitted in trials in federal courts—to give plaintiffs some protection from having this type of evidence introduced against them. Specifically, Congress extended a modified version of the "rape shield" law, which makes it difficult to introduce evidence of a victim's sexual past in criminal rape cases, to apply in civil cases involving "sexual misconduct."

The new rule (Document 35) makes evidence of a plaintiff's "other sexual behavior" or "sexual predisposition" presumptively inadmissible in sexual harassment lawsuits. Such evidence can be admitted only if its importance to a fair judgment in the case (in legal terms, its "probative value") substantially outweighs the danger that it will harm the victim or will unfairly prejudice the litigation. The rule also requires that a party seeking to introduce such evidence follow specified procedures designed to protect the victim's privacy, such as filing papers relating to the matter under seal, so that the public cannot get access to them.

DOCUMENT 34: "The Bedroom Ploy: Plaintiffs' Sex Lives Are Being Laid Bare in Harassment Cases" (Ellen E. Schultz and Junda Woo, 1994)

Weeping on the witness stand in federal court in Norfolk, Va., Rosemary J. Martin tackled a lawyer's tough question: Did she ever watch X-rated films with her husband? Later a witness was asked: Didn't Ms. Martin sleep with her husband before marriage? Before dating him, did she date other men?

Ms. Martin could hardly believe her ears. But this wasn't a rape trial, where such questions probably would have been barred. Ms. Martin had filed a civil suit alleging sexual harassment, and lawyers don't face a rape-shield barrier in civil court. "I felt dirty and cheap," she says.

What she faced was the unexpected fallout from the Civil Rights Act of 1991.

That federal law was intended to support sexual-harassment and discrimination suits, by allowing punitive damages, emotional-distress awards and the right to a jury trial. But the law raised the stakes so sharply that defense lawyers are increasingly resorting to harsh tactics, asking about sex lives, childhood molestation, abortions and venereal disease.

Some lawyers for companies that are sued bemoan the unseemly questions they feel compelled to ask. "I may be uncomfortable doing it—it's certainly something I'd prefer not to do—but I don't allow myself the luxury of regret," says Ronald M. Green, a partner at Epstein Becker & Green, a New York firm that represents many companies.

Defense attorneys blame plaintiffs' lawyers who, they say, charge into court with often meritless but potentially costly allegations. With juries awarding big verdicts, these defense attorneys say, cases can't easily be settled for nuisance amounts, and companies are fighting back with every legal weapon at hand. "It's the fear of giant verdicts and the fear of juries," Mr. Green says.

So, defense lawyers, contending they are only doing their duty to clients, are going straight into the bedroom. In sexual-harassment cases, they are challenging the way women talk, dress and behave in an effort to prove that the plaintiff "welcomed" a boss's behavior and thus wasn't protected by federal law.

"If the plaintiff talked about sex on the job, it makes inquiries into her sexual background relevant," says Denise Hummell, a Denver lawyer currently defending a manager accused by eight women of harassment. "If she claims the harassment interfered with her sex life, her extramarital affairs become relevant."

And suits claiming emotional distress—a claim first authorized in federal sex-bias cases by the 1991 law—make an alleged victim's mental state relevant. So, defendants may have a legitimate interest in discovering whether something other than the alleged discrimination or harassment caused the distress.

"They want to show that the plaintiff is a nut or a slut," contends Philip Kay, a San Francisco lawyer who recently won a $7.1 million California state-court jury verdict in a sexual-harassment case against Chicago law firm Baker & McKenzie.

Although most of the plaintiffs are women, men are affected, too. In a federal civil case in New York, a female office worker hastily settled a race-bias case before trial. Her lawyer says she backed off when she learned that her husband would be questioned about his impotence— something the defense learned from her gynecology records.

Complaints about the tough legal tactics have reached Congress. An amendment seeking to curb such maneuvers is included in the crime bill just enacted. The amendment bars evidence about a plaintiff's sexual history unless that evidence is so crucial to the defendant's case that any harm to the accuser would be "substantially outweighed."

That wording is an attempt to straddle a delicate problem, says federal Judge Ralph K. Winter, head of the drafting panel. He says courts should exclude irrelevant evidence that merely embarrasses the accuser but should allow evidence that shows the accuser wasn't upset by the behavior or even invited it. "There will be a lot of intermediate cases,"

Judge Winter says. "And the courts will just have to work it out case by case."

That indicates, defense lawyers say, that they still will have a lot of maneuvering room. First, the pretrial stage allows broad inquiries. "As long as you can argue that a question could lead to evidence, you can ask it," says Tracy Higgins, associate professor of civil procedure at Fordham University School of Law in New York.

Then, at trial, judges have some discretion over what evidence is admitted. Consequently, their decisions run along a broad spectrum, and lawyers, both for the defense and for the plaintiff, have few grounds for objection. Even if an appeals court reviews a judge's decision, rulings on what evidence is reasonable and relevant are highly subjective. . . .

In the Virginia case, Ms. Martin alleged that her then-supervisor, Daniel P. Batchelor, raped her several times at Virginia Beach's Cavalier Hotel, where both worked. Mr. Batchelor's lawyer, James A. Thurman, says that his client didn't rape the 95-pound woman, adding that she is "sexually unappealing."

Mr. Thurman says his team asked about X-rated videos to suggest that the 43-year-old Ms. Martin had concocted her allegations from movies she might have seen. The questions about premarriage dating, he adds, were intended to show that her husband wasn't a jealous man and that she, if raped, could have confided in him. "We by no stretch of the imagination were trying to show that Rosemary Martin was promiscuous," he says.

A jury found that Mr. Batchelor had engaged in assault and battery but not sexual harassment. It awarded Ms. Martin $102,000 from him and the hotel, which denied that rape occurred. Ms. Martin lost on her claims of emotional distress and wrongful termination. While the case is on appeal, Mr. Batchelor continues to work as the hotel's general manager. . . .

Plaintiffs' lawyers say many women drop cases or settle for unfairly low amounts after realizing the interrogations they are likely to face. Ellen Sacks, former head of the employment-law section of the Association of Trial Lawyers of America, can rattle off instances where she dropped emotional-distress claims to prevent knowledge of a client's mastectomy, adoption or childhood sexual abuse. "Unless you've had a perfect life—and most people's lives are not like that—it's a real problem," she says.

Source: Ellen E. Schultz and Junda Woo, "The Bedroom Ploy: Plaintiffs' Sex Lives Are Being Laid Bare in Harassment Cases," *Wall Street Journal*, September 19, 1994, p. A-1.

DOCUMENT 35: Federal Rule of Evidence 412 (1994)

Rule 412. Sex Offense Cases; Relevance of Alleged Victim's Past Sexual Behavior or Alleged Sexual Predisposition

(a) Evidence generally inadmissible.—The following evidence is not admissible in any civil or criminal proceeding involving alleged sexual misconduct except as provided in subdivisions (b) and (c):

(1) Evidence offered to prove that any alleged victim engaged in other sexual behavior.

(2) Evidence offered to prove any alleged victim's sexual predisposition.

(b) Exceptions.— . . .

(2) In a civil case, evidence offered to prove the sexual behavior or sexual predisposition of any alleged victim is admissible if it is otherwise admissible under these rules and its probative value substantially outweighs the danger of harm to any victim and of unfair prejudice to any party.

Evidence of an alleged victim's reputation is admissible only if it has been placed in controversy by the alleged victim.

(c) Procedure to determine admissibility.

(1) A party intending to offer evidence under subdivision (b) must—

(A) file a written motion at least 14 days before trial specifically describing the evidence and stating the purpose for which it is offered unless the court, for good cause requires a different time for filing or permits filing during trial; and

(B) serve the motion on all parties and notify the alleged victim or, when appropriate, the alleged victim's guardian or representative.

(2) Before admitting evidence under this rule the court must conduct a hearing *in camera* and afford the victim and parties a right to attend and be heard. The motion, related papers, and the record of the hearing must be sealed and remain under seal unless the court orders otherwise.

Source: Federal Rule of Evidence 412 (1994).

SAME-SEX HARASSMENT

The earliest theorists who argued that sexual harassment was sex discrimination contended that harassment represented one way in which men oppressed women. Indeed, the overwhelming majority of sexual harassment cases involve allegations that a man has harassed a woman.

There are, however, a small number of cases in which the gender tables are turned—a man alleges he has been harassed by a woman.

The courts considering these cases have universally held that it is also sex discrimination for women to harass men. They reason that the statutes prohibiting sex discrimination are written in gender-neutral terms; they protect men and women equally.

More confusion has been caused, however, by cases in which the harasser and the victim are of the same gender. Back in the earliest sexual harassment decisions, courts puzzled about this situation. It was not long before these same-sex harassment cases actually began to arise, and courts have disagreed about how to resolve them.

Some courts, like the court in *Goluszek v. H. P. Smith* (Document 36), have rejected same-sex harassment claims entirely, finding that such behavior cannot be sex discrimination under Title VII. Many other courts, however, have tried to draw distinctions, finding some types of same-sex harassment to be illegal, while others are not.

Same-sex harassment cases have been brought under both quid pro quo and hostile environment theories. In the quid pro quo cases, the plaintiff, often (although not always) a heterosexual, argues that a homosexual supervisor demanded sexual favors in exchange for job benefits or in order to avoid being punished on the job. The majority of courts have found that such harassment is illegal under Title VII.

The hostile environment cases, in contrast, largely fall into three categories. In some cases, the victims, homosexual or perceived to be homosexual, have experienced hostile acts at the hands of their supervisors or coworkers because of their sexual orientation. In other cases, a heterosexual worker claims that a homosexual supervisor or coworker subjected him to a hostile environment by propositioning or groping him. In still other cases, both the victim and alleged harasser are heterosexual, and the victim is objecting to prevalent sexualized horseplay in the workplace that has been directed at him or her.

There has been much disagreement among the courts about whether any of these behaviors constitute illegal sex discrimination under Title VII. In general, however, people complaining of mistreatment by homosexuals have fared better in the courts than those who complain of mistreatment by heterosexuals.

Some courts, however, have disagreed with distinctions based on the sexual orientation of the parties and have found that same-sex hostile environment harassment can be illegal regardless of the orientation of either the harasser or the victim. These courts, like the court in *Quick v. Donaldson* (Document 37), reason that so long as the harasser is making people of one sex and not the other the targets of offensive behavior, that is illegal sex discrimination.

In March 1998, the U.S. Supreme Court weighed in on this issue. In *Oncale v. Sundowner Offshore Services* (Document 93), the Court held that same-sex harassment can be illegal, but only if the victim can establish that he or she was targeted because of his or her gender. That decision is discussed further in Part VI.

DOCUMENT 36: *Goluszek v. H. P. Smith*, U.S. District Court (1988)

In this Title VII case, the plaintiff Anthony Goluszek claims that he was the victim of sexual harassment by other males who worked for the defendant H. P. Smith. . . .

Facts

Anthony Goluszek has never been married nor has he lived anywhere but at his mother's home. According to Goluszek's psychiatrist, Goluszek comes from an "unsophisticated background" and has led an "isolated existence" with "little or no sexual experience." Goluszek "blushes easily" and is abnormally sensitive to comments pertaining to sex. . . .

Shortly after Goluszek started at H. P. Smith in December of 1976, a number of machine operators questioned him as to why he had no wife or girlfriend and joked that one had to be married to work there. . . . In 1978, [another employee, named] Adair on one occasion told Goluszek that if Goluszek could not fix a machine he would be sent to a sausage factory. Adair also said Goluszek needed to "get married and get some of that soft pink smelly stuff that's between the legs of a woman." Goluszek responded that Adair should not comment on Goluszek's personal life. . . .

Sometime subsequently in 1979, H. P. Smith transferred Goluszek to the day shift. On a number of occasions on this shift, employees driving jeeps threatened to knock Goluszek off of his ladder. Goluszek complained about this practice to his supervisors. They assured him the matter would be investigated. . . .

H. P. Smith transferred Goluszek back to the night shift sometime in 1981. On that shift, the operators periodically asked Goluszek if he had gotten any "pussy" or had oral sex, showed him pictures of nude women, told him they would get him "fucked," accused him of being gay or bisexual, and made other sex-related comments. The operators also poked him in the buttocks with a stick. Goluszek complained to General Foreman Bill Clemente about the remarks, but Clemente did nothing. Goluszek has admitted that the employees on both shifts talked about sex with one another and used words such as "fuck" in those conversations. He also admits that comments about sex were made that were not directed at him. . . .

I
Sexual Harassment

* * *

H. P. Smith claims that Goluszek cannot prove that he was harassed because of his sex by his co-workers. Goluszek easily rebuts that argument, however, by citing the 1972 letter warning a male employee to lay off a female employee. . . . Although the letter is dated, the court considers it significant probative evidence of H. P. Smith's reacting differently to female complaints of sexual harassment than to male complaints. Reading the record as a whole, the court finds that a fact-finder could reasonably conclude that if Goluszek were a woman H. P. Smith would have taken action to stop the harassment, that such action would have stopped the harassment and that the harassment was pervasive and continuous from the time Goluszek began until he was fired.

The more convincing argument for dismissal is one H. P. Smith failed to make. Simply stated, the defendant's conduct was not the type of conduct Congress intended to sanction when it enacted Title VII. The goal of Title VII is equal employment opportunity. . . . That goal is accomplished in part by imposing an affirmative duty on employers to maintain a working environment free of discriminatory intimidation. . . . The discrimination Congress was concerned about when it enacted Title VII is one stemming from an imbalance of power and an abuse of that imbalance by the powerful which results in discrimination against a discrete and vulnerable group. . . . Title VII does not make all forms of harassment actionable, nor does it even make all forms of verbal harassment with sexual overtones actionable. The "sexual harassment" that is actionable under Title VII "is the exploitation of a powerful position to impose sexual demands or pressures on an unwilling but less powerful person." . . . Actionable sexual-harassment fosters a sense of degradation in the victim by attacking their sexuality. . . . In effect, the offender is saying by words or actions that the victim is inferior because of the victim's sex. . . .

During the times relevant to his claim, Goluszek was a male in a male-dominated environment. . . . The argument that Goluszek worked in an environment that treated males as inferior consequently is not supported by the record. In fact, Goluszek may have been harassed "because" he is a male, but that harassment was not of a kind which created an anti-male environment in the workplace. . . . A wooden application of the verbal formulations created by the courts would salvage Goluszek's sexual-harassment claim. The court, however, chooses instead to adopt a reading of Title VII consistent with the underlying concerns of Congress and grants H. P. Smith summary judgment on that claim.

Source: 697 Federal Supplement 1452, 1453–56 (N.D. Ill. 1988).

DOCUMENT 37: *Quick v. Donaldson*, U.S. Court of Appeals for the Eighth Circuit (1996)

This case raises hostile environment sexual harassment claims based on allegations that male co-workers physically and verbally harassed Phil Quick for two years and that his employer, Donaldson Company, Inc. (Donaldson), knew of the harassment but failed to respond with proper remedial action. . . .

I.

Phil Quick joined Donaldson in January 1991 as a welder and press operator in its muffler production plant in Grinell, Iowa. About eighty-five percent of the 279 employees at the plant are male. Quick claims he was the workplace victim of "bagging," physical assault, and verbal harassment, including taunting about being homosexual.[1] He asserts that he has an action . . . for sex discrimination based on sexual harassment in a hostile work environment.

Quick alleges that at least twelve different male co-workers bagged him on some 100 occasions from January 1991 through December 1992. "Bagging" is defined in the record in various ways, but typically involved an action aimed at a man's groin area. . . .

The majority of the 100 bagging incidents involving Quick occurred between January and September of 1991. During this time, Quick also saw at least one other male employee being bagged every day. In August 1991, Quick complained to supervisor Daniels about being bagged. No remedial action was taken by Daniels or Donaldson. After Daniels observed employees bag Quick on several occasions, Quick says Daniels told him that the next time somebody bagged him "to turn around and bag the shit out of them." The bagging incidents decreased after Quick was transferred to another department on September 3, 1991. Between that time and December 1992, Quick was bagged by a male co-worker on some six occasions.

Sometime during the fall of 1992, Schoen, the plant manager, instructed the supervisors to stop the bagging actions and reviewed with them the company's written sexual harassment policy. According to supervisor Musgrove, each supervisor then reviewed that policy with department employees and explained why the practice could not continue. One employee, David Ashburn, also stated that Donaldson circulated a memo around that time saying that bagging was harassment. After this, the bagging apparently ended.

Quick also claims that male co-workers assaulted him on two occasions. . . .

Quick alleges in addition that he was verbally harassed and falsely labeled a homosexual. . . .

As a result of these actions, Quick obtained medical and psychological treatment, which he asserts will continue in the future. He currently experiences a bobbing sensation in his left testicle due to the alleged assault and battery in August 1991. . . .

II.

* * *

A.

. . . In order to state a claim for sex discrimination based on a hostile environment, a plaintiff must show that: (1) [he] belongs to a protected group; (2) [he] was subject to unwelcome sexual harassment; (3) the harassment was based on sex; (4) the harassment affected a term, condition, or privilege of employment; and (5) [the employer] knew or should have known of the harassment and failed to take proper remedial action. . . .

The first factor, membership in a protected group, is satisfied by showing that the plaintiff employee is a man or a woman. . . . Congress did not limit Title VII protection to only women or members of a minority group. Rather, the broad rule of workplace equality under Title VII strikes "at the entire spectrum of disparate treatment of men and women in employment" in order to provide a workplace free of "discriminatory intimidation, ridicule and insult." *Harris v. Forklift Systems, Inc.* . . . Neither a man nor a woman is required to run a "gauntlet of sexual abuse in return for the privilege of being allowed to work and make a living." *Meritor.* . . . The term "sex" as used in Title VII has accordingly been interpreted to mean either "man" or "woman," and to bar workplace sexual harassment against women because they are women and against men because they are men. . . .

The third required element is that the harassment complained of was based upon sex. Although there is little legislative history as to what discrimination "based on sex" means, the key inquiry is whether "members of one sex are exposed to disadvantageous terms or conditions of employment to which members of the other sex are not exposed." . . . Evidence that members of one sex were the primary targets of the harassment is sufficient to show that the conduct was gender based. . . . The motive behind the discrimination is not at issue because "[a]n employer could never have a legitimate reason" for creating or permitting a hostile work environment. . . .

B.

. . . Protection under Title VII is not limited to only disadvantaged or vulnerable groups. It extends to all employees and prohibits disparate treatment of an individual, man or woman, based on that person's sex. . . . The district court therefore erred in requiring Quick to show evidence of an anti-male or predominantly female work environment.

The district court also erred in determining that the challenged conduct was not of a genuine sexual nature and therefore not sexual harassment. The court concluded that neither bagging nor the physical attacks expressed sexual interest nor involved sexual favors or comments. A worker "need not be propositioned, touched offensively, or harassed by sexual innuendo" in order to have been sexually harassed, however. . . . Intimidation and hostility may occur without explicit sexual advances or acts of an explicitly sexual nature. . . . Moreover, physical aggression, violence, or verbal abuse may amount to sexual harassment. . . . The bagging [and some of the assaults were] aimed at Quick's sexual organs . . . [and he was taunted with sexually suggestive names]. Whether or not these actions, when viewed in the totality of the circumstances, constituted prohibited sexual harassment remains a genuine issue of material fact for trial. . . .

The district court also incorrectly concluded that the alleged harassment was not gender based because it found the underlying motive was personal enmity or hooliganism. A hostile work environment is not so easily excused, however. . . . The fact that Quick might have been unpopular could not justify conduct that otherwise violated Title VII. . . .

The proper inquiry for determining whether discrimination was based on sex is whether "members of one sex are exposed to disadvantageous terms or conditions of employment to which members of the other sex are not exposed." *Harris* . . . (Ginsburg, J., concurring). Although Donaldson claims that female employees could theoretically be bagged, our review is limited to the record developed below. . . . That record contains only incidents of bagging male employees. A female employee was apparently once asked to bag a male supervisor, but she refused. On this record, with all facts and inferences drawn in Quick's favor, a fact-finder could reasonably conclude that the treatment of men at Donaldson was worse than the treatment of women. Thus, Quick has raised a genuine issue of material fact as to whether the alleged harassment was gender based.

[1]There is no dispute that Quick is in fact heterosexual.

Source: 90 *Federal Reporter 3d* 1372, 1374–79 (8th Cir. 1996).

SPECIAL ISSUES IN HOSTILE ENVIRONMENT HARASSMENT

The "Reasonable Woman" Standard

In *Meritor Savings Bank v. Vinson* (Document 24), the Supreme Court held that, in order to be illegal under Title VII, hostile environment sexual harassment must be sufficiently "severe or pervasive" so that it alters the victim's working conditions. Stray sexist remarks are not enough to demonstrate illegal sexual harassment.

Lower courts have been faced with the question of how to determine whether particular behavior meets this legal standard. Some courts have held that a victim must demonstrate both that the behavior seemed severe or pervasive to her and that a "reasonable person" would agree with that assessment. Commentators, however, objected to the use of a reasonable person standard. They argue that men and women view sexualized speech and conduct differently and that the law should take into account this fact, rather than judge the conduct on a gender-neutral basis. These commentators argued that when the plaintiff is a woman, courts should employ a "reasonable woman" standard, under which it would ask the fact finder to determine if the conduct in question would seem severe or pervasive to a reasonable woman. Several courts have followed this approach.

Some courts, however, have rejected the reasonable woman standard, arguing that legal standards should be the same regardless of the gender of the plaintiff. The case of *Ellison v. Brady* (Document 38) illustrates both of these approaches. The majority in that case found that the reasonable woman standard was appropriate, but a dissenting judge disagreed.

DOCUMENT 38: *Ellison v. Brady*, U.S. Court of Appeals for the Ninth Circuit (1991)

II

* * *

. . . [A] hostile environment exists when an employee can show (1) that he or she was subjected to sexual advances, requests for sexual favors, or other verbal or physical conduct of a sexual nature, (2) that this conduct was unwelcome, and (3) that the conduct was sufficiently severe or pervasive to alter the conditions of the victim's employment and create an abusive working environment. . . .

III

* * *

. . . [W]e believe that in evaluating the severity and pervasiveness of sexual harassment, we should focus on the perspective of the victim. . . . If we only examined whether a reasonable person would engage in allegedly harassing conduct, we would run the risk of reinforcing the prevailing level of discrimination. Harassers could continue to harass merely because a particular discriminatory practice was common, and victims of harassment would have no remedy.

We therefore prefer to analyze harassment from the victim's perspective. A complete understanding of the victim's view requires, among other things, an analysis of the different perspectives of men and women. Conduct that many men consider unobjectionable may offend many women. . . .

We realize that there is a broad range of viewpoints among women as a group, but we believe that many women share common concerns which men do not necessarily share.[9] For example, because women are disproportionately victims of rape and sexual assault, women have a stronger incentive to be concerned with sexual behavior. Women who are victims of mild forms of sexual harassment may understandably worry whether a harasser's conduct is merely a prelude to violent sexual assault. Men, who are rarely victims of sexual assault, may view sexual conduct in a vacuum without a full appreciation of the social setting or the underlying threat of violence that a woman may perceive.

In order to shield employers from having to accommodate the idiosyncratic concerns of the rare hyper-sensitive employee, we hold that a female plaintiff states a prima facie case of hostile environment sexual harassment when she alleges conduct which a reasonable woman[11] would consider sufficiently severe or pervasive to alter the conditions of employment and create an abusive working environment.

We adopt the perspective of a reasonable woman primarily because we believe that a sex-blind reasonable person standard tends to be male-biased and tends to systematically ignore the experiences of women. The reasonable woman standard does not establish a higher level of protection for women than men. . . . Instead, a gender-conscious examination of sexual harassment enables women to participate in the workplace on an equal footing with men. By acknowledging and not trivializing the effects of sexual harassment on reasonable women, courts can work towards ensuring that neither men nor women will have to "run a gauntlet of sexual abuse in return for the privilege of being allowed to work and make a living." . . .

We note that the reasonable victim standard we adopt today classifies conduct as unlawful sexual harassment even when harassers do not realize that their conduct creates a hostile working environment. Well-intentioned compliments by co-workers or supervisors can form the basis of a sexual harassment cause of action if a reasonable victim of the same sex as the plaintiff would consider the comments sufficiently severe or pervasive to alter a condition of employment and create an abusive working environment. That is because Title VII is not a fault-based tort scheme. "Title VII is aimed at the consequences or effects of an employment practice and not at the . . . motivation" of co-workers or employers. . . . To avoid liability under Title VII, employers may have to educate and sensitize their workforce to eliminate conduct which a reasonable victim would consider unlawful sexual harassment. . . .

Sexual harassment is a major problem in the workplace. Adopting the victim's perspective ensures that courts will not "sustain ingrained notions of reasonable behavior fashioned by the offenders." . . . Congress did not enact Title VII to codify prevailing sexist prejudices. To the contrary, "Congress designed Title VII to prevent the perpetuation of stereotypes and a sense of degradation which serve to close or discourage employment opportunities for women." . . . We hope that over time both men and women will learn what conduct offends reasonable members of the other sex. When employers and employees internalize the standard of workplace conduct we establish today, the current gap in perception between the sexes will be bridged.

[9] One writer explains: "While many women hold positive attitudes about un-coerced sex, their greater physical and social vulnerability to sexual coercion can make women wary of sexual encounters. Moreover, American women have been raised in a society where rape and sex-related violence have reached unprecedented levels, and a vast pornography industry creates continuous images of sexual coercion, objectification and violence. Finally, women as a group tend to hold more restrictive views of both the situation and type of relationship in which sexual conduct is appropriate. Because of the inequality and coercion with which it is so frequently associated in the minds of women, the appearance of sexuality in an unexpected context or a setting of ostensible equality can be an anguishing experience." Abrams, *Gender Discrimination and the Transformation of Workplace Norms*, 42 VAND. L. REV. 1183, 1205 (1989). . . .

[11] Of course, where male employees allege that co-workers engage in conduct which creates a hostile environment, the appropriate victim's perspective would be that of a reasonable man.

Stephens, District Judge, dissenting:

* * *

Nowhere in section 2000e of Title VII, the section under which the plaintiff in this case brought suit, is there any indication that Congress intended to provide for any other than equal treatment in the area of civil rights. The legislation is designed to achieve a balanced and generally gender neutral and harmonious workplace which would improve production and the quality of the employees' lives. In fact, the Supreme Court has shown a preference against systems that are not gender or race neutral, such as hiring quotas. . . . While women may be the most frequent targets of this type of conduct that is at issue in this case, they are not the only targets. I believe that it is incumbent upon the court in this case to use terminology that will meet the needs of all who seek recourse under this section of Title VII. Possible alternatives that are more in line with a gender neutral approach include "victim," "target," or "person."

The term "reasonable man" as it is used in the law of torts, traditionally refers to the average adult person, regardless of gender, and the conduct that can reasonably be expected of him or her. For the purposes of the legal issues that are being addressed, such a term assumes that it is applicable to all persons. Section 2000e of Title VII presupposes the use of a legal term that can apply to all persons and the impossibility of a more individually tailored standard. It is clear that the authors of the majority opinion intend a difference between the "reasonable woman" and the "reasonable man" in Title VII cases on the assumption that men do not have the same sensibilities as women. This is not necessarily true. A man's response to circumstances faced by women and their effect upon women can be and in given circumstances may be expected to be understood by men.

It takes no stretch of the imagination to envision two complaints emanating from the same workplace regarding the same conditions, one brought by a woman and the other by a man. Application of the "new standard" presents a puzzlement which is born of the assumption that men's eyes do not see what a woman sees through her eyes. I find it surprising that the majority finds no need for evidence on any of these subjects. I am not sure whether the majority also concludes that the woman and the man in question are also reasonable without evidence on this subject. . . .

The focus on the victim of the sexually discriminatory conduct has its parallel in rape trials in the focus put by the defense on the victim's conduct rather than on the unlawful conduct of the person accused. Modern feminists have pointed out that concentration by the defense upon evidence concerning the background, appearance and conduct of women claiming to have been raped must be carefully controlled by the court to avoid effectively shifting the burden of proof to the victim. It is the accused, not the victim who is on trial, and it is therefore the conduct of the accused, not that of the victim, that should be subjected to scrutiny. . . .

. . . I believe that a gender neutral standard would greatly contribute to the clarity of this and future cases in the same area.

Source: 924 *Federal Reporter 2d* 872, 873–81, 884–85 (9th Cir. 1991) (some footnotes omitted).

In 1990 the EEOC announced its position on this controversy in its new *Policy Guidance on Current Issues of Sexual Harassment* (Document 39), which adopted the reasonable person test. The agency cautioned, however, that "the reasonable person standard should consider the victim's perspective and not stereotyped notions of acceptable behavior."

DOCUMENT 39: *Policy Guidance on Current Issues of Sexual Harassment* (Equal Employment Opportunity Commission, 1990)

In determining whether unwelcome sexual conduct rises to the level of a "hostile environment" in violation of Title VII, the central inquiry is whether the conduct "unreasonably interfer[es] with an individual's work performance" or creates "an intimidating, hostile, or offensive working environment." . . . Thus, sexual flirtation or innuendo, even vulgar language that is trivial or merely annoying, would probably not establish a hostile environment.

1) Standard for Evaluating Harassment—In determining whether harassment is sufficiently severe or pervasive to create a hostile environment, the harasser's conduct should be evaluated from the objective standpoint of a "reasonable person." Title VII does not serve "as a vehicle for vindicating the petty slights suffered by the hypersensitive." . . . Thus, if the challenged conduct would not substantially affect the work environment of a reasonable person, no violation should be found.

Example—Charging Party alleges that her co-worker made repeated unwelcome sexual advances toward her. An investigation discloses that the alleged "advances" consisted of invitations to join a group of employees who regularly socialized at dinner after work. The co-worker's invitations, viewed in that context and from the perspective of a reasonable person, would not have created a hostile environment and therefore did not constitute sexual harassment.

A "reasonable person" standard also should be applied to the more basic determination of whether challenged conduct is of a sexual nature.

Thus, in the above example, a reasonable person would not consider the co-worker's invitations sexual in nature, and on that basis as well no violation would be found.

This objective standard should not be applied in a vacuum, however. Consideration should be given to the context in which the alleged harassment took place. As the Sixth Circuit has stated, the trier of fact must "adopt the perspective of a reasonable person's reaction to a similar environment under similar or like circumstances." . . .

The reasonable person standard should consider the victim's perspective and not stereotyped notions of acceptable behavior. For example, the Commission believes that a workplace in which sexual slurs, displays of "girlie" pictures, and other offensive conduct abound can constitute a hostile work environment even if many people deem it to be harmless or insignificant. . . .

2) Isolated Instances of Harassment—Unless the conduct is quite severe, a single incident or isolated incidents of offensive sexual conduct or remarks generally do not create an abusive environment. As the Court noted in *Vinson*, "mere utterance of an ethnic or racial epithet which engenders offensive feelings in an employee would not affect the conditions of employment to a sufficiently significant degree to violate Title VII." . . . A "hostile environment" claim generally requires a showing of a pattern of offensive conduct. In contrast, in "quid pro quo" cases a single sexual advance may constitute harassment if it is linked to the granting or denial of employment benefits.

But a single, unusually severe incident of harassment may be sufficient to constitute a Title VII violation; the more severe the harassment, the less need to show a repetitive series of incidents. This is particularly true when the harassment is physical. . . .

The Commission will presume that the unwelcome, intentional touching of a charging party's intimate body areas in [sic] sufficiently offensive to alter the conditions of her working environment and constitute a violation of Title VII. More so than in the case of verbal advances or remarks, a single unwelcome physical advance can seriously poison the victim's working environment. If an employee's supervisor sexually touches that employee, the Commission normally would find a violation. In such situations, it is the employer's burden to demonstrate that the unwelcome conduct was not sufficiently severe to create a hostile work environment.

When the victim is the target of both verbal and non-intimate physical conduct, the hostility of the environment is exacerbated and a violation is more likely to be found. Similarly, incidents of sexual harassment directed at other employees in addition to the charging party are relevant to a showing of hostile work environment. . . .

3) Non-physical Harassment—When the alleged harassment consists

of verbal conduct, the investigation should ascertain the nature, frequency, context, and intended target of the remarks. Questions to be explored might include:

—Did the alleged harasser single out the charging party?
—Did the charging party participate?
—What was the relationship between the charging party and the alleged harasser(s)?
—Were the remarks hostile and derogatory?

No one factor alone determines whether particular conduct violates Title VII. As the Guidelines emphasize, the Commission will evaluate the totality of the circumstances. In general, a woman does not forfeit her right to be free from sexual harassment by choosing to work in an atmosphere that has traditionally included vulgar, anti-female language. . . .

. . . [A] woman does not assume the risk of harassment by voluntarily entering an abusive, anti-female environment. "Title VII's precise purpose is to prevent such behavior and attitudes from poisoning the work environment of classes protected under the Act." . . . Thus . . . a district court found that a hostile environment was established by the presence of pornographic magazines in the workplace and vulgar employee comments concerning them; offensive sexual comments made to and about plaintiff and other female employees by her supervisor; sexually oriented pictures in a company-sponsored movie and slide presentation; sexually oriented pictures and calendars in the workplace; and offensive touching of plaintiff by a co-worker. . . . The court held that the proliferation of pornography and demeaning comments, if sufficiently continuous and pervasive, "may be found to create an atmosphere in which women are viewed as men's sexual playthings rather than as their equal coworkers." . . . The Commission agrees that, depending on the totality of circumstances, such an atmosphere may violate Title VII.

Source: Equal Employment Opportunity Commission, *Policy Guidance on Current Issues of Sexual Harassment*, March 28, 1990.

Many lawyers believed that the Supreme Court would clear up the disagreement about the reasonable woman standard in 1993 when it decided *Harris v. Forklift Systems, Inc.* (Document 25). Several briefs filed with the Court specifically raised this issue. For example, the brief filed by the American Psychological Association (Document 40) argued that women are much more likely than men to view sexual behavior at work as harassment.

In contrast, the brief filed by the Women's Legal Defense Fund (Document 41) argued against both the reasonable person and the reasonable woman standards. The authors of this brief contended that all that a plaintiff should be required to show is that she was subjected to unwelcome sexualized conduct that made the environment abusive to her; there should be no consideration of how the harasser's behavior would have affected a reasonable person or a reasonable woman. They were concerned that using either a reasonable person or a reasonable woman test legitimates harassing behavior that is commonplace today; so long as harassment occurs frequently, a court might find that a reasonable person or woman would not be offended by the conduct. Furthermore, they were concerned that using the reasonable woman standard stereotyped women as unduly sensitive in matters relating to sex.

The Supreme Court's opinion in *Harris*, however, did not discuss the debate, although it did use the words "reasonable person" throughout. This has left lawyers confused about the state of the law. Some claim that, by using the words "reasonable person," the Supreme Court adopted that standard. Others claim that, because it did not discuss the debate over the issue, the Court simply left the issue unresolved.

DOCUMENT 40: Brief for Amicus Curiae American Psychological Association in Support of Neither Party, *Harris v. Forklift Systems, Inc.* (1993)

II. WOMEN AND MEN DIFFERENTLY PERCEIVE BEHAVIOR THAT CAN BE CHARACTERIZED AS SEXUAL HARASSMENT.

Many courts of appeals, in determining whether particular conduct is sufficiently severe or persistent to alter conditions of employment, have expressly applied an objective test to hostile work environment claims. . . . In deciding which test to adopt, the Court may wish to consider data suggesting that men and women tend to evaluate sexual behavior in the workplace dissimilarly.

Survey and laboratory research has generally shown that women are more likely than men to label sexually aggressive behavior at work as harassment. There is a gap between men's and women's perceptions with respect to every category of sexual harassment, but the gap is most pronounced with respect to gender-based insults and ridicule and less explicit forms of sexual advances. Studies also show that men are more likely to be tolerant of sexual harassment than women. One study, for example, concluded that men were four times more likely than women to predict they would be flattered by sexual overtures at work and four times less likely to predict they would be insulted.

Although there is considerable empirical data establishing the differential, there is less understanding of why such a differential exists.... [One study] suggested that women may view sexual overtures as threatening to their positions at work.... It also appears that sexual liaisons with co-workers raise a man's status in the work organization but lower a woman's status....

Related studies have shown that men are significantly more likely to attribute the causes of harassing behavior to characteristics of the victim, while women are more likely to attribute the causes to characteristics of the perpetrators. Men are also more likely than women to attribute harassment complaints to an external factor, such as career competition between the complainant and the alleged perpetrator. Several researchers have suggested that these results are consistent with notions of harm avoidance and blame avoidance. More women fear victimization and more men fear being accused of harassment.

The courts of appeals are split on the appropriate reasonableness standard for assessing whether given conduct is sufficiently severe and pervasive to violate Title VII. Evidence from social science research indicates that the choice of a reasonableness standard will measurably affect the results generated.

Source: Brief for Amicus Curiae American Psychological Association in Support of Neither Party, *Harris v. Forklift Systems, Inc.*, No. 92–1168 (April 30, 1993).

DOCUMENT 41: Brief of Amici Curiae Women's Legal Defense Fund, the National Women's Law Center, et al., in Support of Petitioner, *Harris v. Forklift Systems, Inc.* (1993)

II. IF THE COURT CHOOSES TO SPEAK MORE BROADLY ON THE ELEMENTS OF A HOSTILE ENVIRONMENT HARASSMENT CASE, IT SHOULD CORRECT TWO ADDITIONAL LEGAL ERRORS COMMITTED BY THE COURTS BELOW.

* * *

B. Application Of "Reasonableness" Standards For Determining The Severity Or Pervasiveness Of Harassing Conduct Has Legitimated Discriminatory Conduct And Reinforced Stereotypes.

* * *

Experience has shown that application of a "reasonableness" criterion has served as a barrier to full realization of the right to a workplace that is free from "discriminatory intimidation, ridicule, and insult." *Meritor*. . . . It has provided courts with a yardstick that is infected with discriminatory assumptions that serve to bar legitimate claims. In the sections below, we explain some of the more significant difficulties that have arisen in connection with these "reasonableness" standards, discussing both the "reasonable person" and the "reasonable woman" standards.

1. *Application of a "Reasonable Person" Standard Has Had the Effect of Perpetuating Discriminatory Conditions and Stereotypes.*

A number of lower courts have held that, for conduct to be "severe or pervasive enough 'to alter the conditions of [the victim's] employment and create an abusive working environment,' " *Meritor* . . . it must have had that effect not only on the plaintiff herself, but also on a "reasonable person." On its face, this formulation sounds harmless enough. In application, however, it has the potential to perpetuate the very discriminatory conditions that Title VII was intended to eliminate. In some cases, the "reasonable person" standard has served as a powerful engine of the status quo.

One of the most disturbing examples is the majority opinion [of the U.S. Court of Appeals for the Sixth Circuit] in *Rabidue [v. Osceola Refining Co.]*. The *Rabidue* majority held that a court must "adopt the perspective of a reasonable person's reaction to a similar environment under essentially like or similar circumstances." . . . The court refused to find Title VII liability despite evidence of highly offensive sexual conduct in the plaintiff's workplace. As grounds for condoning such conduct, the majority quoted with approval the district court's reference to the widespread existence of abusive conduct in society at large:

"Indeed, it cannot seriously be disputed that in some work environments, humor and language are rough hewn and vulgar. Sexual jokes, sexual conversations and girlie magazines may abound. Title VII was not meant to—or can—change this. It must never be forgotten that Title VII is the federal court mainstay in the struggle for equal employment opportunity for the female workers of America. But it is quite different to claim that Title VII was designed to bring about a magical transformation in the social mores of American workers."

. . . The majority concluded that the prevalence of "erotica" in society at large rendered the effect of the harassing conduct on the plaintiff's work environment "de minimis." . . .

The "reasonable person" through whose eyes the *Rabidue* majority viewed the conduct at issue must have been the men working at Osceola Refining prior to the time Ms. Rabidue arrived. . . . Application of this standard grandfathered any conduct that predated the plaintiff's arrival in the workplace, presenting a highly effective barrier for any person unwilling to accept that workplace "as is."

The implications of that ruling are stark. Under *Rabidue*'s application of the "reasonable person" standard, a woman must endure truly outrageous conduct as a condition of her employment. For example, a requirement of Ms. Rabidue's job was that she meet regularly with a fellow manager who "routinely referred to women as 'whores,' 'cunt,' 'pussy,' and 'tits.' " . . . The *Rabidue* court's application of the "reasonable person" standard also condones widespread display in the workplace of pictorial displays that demean women. . . .

A "reasonable person" standard almost inevitably condones offensive and demeaning conduct at some level because it incorporates the views of those doing the harassing—or those who are indifferent or blind to the barriers to equal access erected by others' harassment. . . . After all, the perpetrators of much conduct that courts have characterized as harassment presumably think their conduct is perfectly reasonable. But if the harasser's conduct erects a barrier to equal access to the workplace, his viewpoint—or that of others like him—about the reasonableness of the conduct or the environment it creates should be irrelevant.

Finally, courts may wrongly assume that it is appropriate to include within the universe of "reasonable persons" members of protected groups who appear to have been, like many of the female clerical employees at Forklift Systems, "conditioned to accept denigrating treatment." . . . Some of these employees may have endured denigrating treatment in silence because of fears of retribution. Such conditioning or silent endurance must not set the standard for what constitutes actionable harassment. Title VII cannot be limited by the acquiescence of some—or even of all but one—to barriers to equal access.

Even if the fact-finder believes that he or she is viewing the conduct at issue objectively, that view may well be a product of his or her own subjective biases, biases at odds with Title VII's goals. The Court should apply the *Meritor* standards as stated, without importing a reasonableness inquiry.

2. Application of a "Reasonable Woman" Standard Can Also Create Or Perpetuate Discriminatory Stereotypes.

In an effort to address some of the problems inherent in the "reasonable person" test described above, a number of courts have substituted a "reasonable woman" test for the "reasonable person" test of *Rabidue* and its progeny. Nevertheless, the "reasonable woman" test has the potential to undermine Title VII's goals as much as the "reasonable person" test.

First, the "reasonable woman" standard suffers some of the same infirmities as the "reasonable person" standard. A court may incorporate into the standard the reactions of women who have endured harassment in silence or who have been "conditioned to accept it." Indeed, the courts below did just that. . . . For example, a court may assume that if women employees other than the plaintiff did not complain about the harassment, it must not have altered *their* working conditions, and therefore should not have altered the plaintiff's. But that assumption would perpetuate discriminatory conditions that Congress wished to eliminate.

Second, fact-finders applying a "reasonable woman" test may imbue that standard with their own biases about the types of jobs that women ought to accept or about the "types" of women who take certain jobs. A fact-finder who believed that women should not work as, say, managers, or welders, or construction workers, might be inclined to find that any woman who would accept such a position "is asking for it." . . . Such a finding would directly contravene Title VII's promise of equal job opportunity to any person who can perform the work.

Finally, although any court reviewing a sex-based or sexual harassment claim must take account of the realities women face, the "reasonable woman" test presents the risk of limiting opportunities for women based on gender stereotypes. It would be inappropriate and contrary to Title VII's purposes to apply any standard that expressly or impliedly rested on, for example, an assumption that women are somehow more delicate than men, and are therefore less able than men to cope with ordinary workplace pressures. Gender-specific standards based on such stereotypes have historically been used to "protect" women in a manner that denied them opportunities in the workplace. . . . Such a "protective" approach would only perpetuate the notion that women are incapable of handling the work-related stresses and conflicts that accompany many jobs. Title VII does not and should not insulate women from work-related stresses and conflicts incident to a particular career or occupation.

Seven years ago, this Court held that unwelcome, sex-based conduct constitutes actionable sexual harassment if it is "sufficiently severe or pervasive 'to alter the conditions of [the victim's] employment and create an abusive working environment.' " *Meritor.* . . . The working environment of concern to this Court in *Meritor* was the victim's, not that of some hypothetical composite plaintiff. The Court should reaffirm the standards articulated in *Meritor.*

Source: Brief of Amici Curiae Women's Legal Defense Fund, the National Women's Law Center, et al., in Support of Petitioner, *Harris v. Forklift Systems, Inc.*, No. 92–1168 (April 30, 1993).

Sexual Harassment Law versus Free Speech

The First Amendment to the United States Constitution provides that "Congress shall make no law . . . abridging the freedom of speech."

Indeed, freedom of speech is one of the most dearly held American values.

Some critics charge that the law against sexual harassment can illegitimately interfere with the right of people to speak freely in their workplaces. They point out that courts have found that forms of speech like sexual jokes and banter or displaying nude pictures in the workplace can contribute to a finding of hostile environment sexual harassment. They fear that, in order to avoid having to pay damages in sexual harassment lawsuits, employers will severely restrict what employees can say to each other, as well as what they can look at or read while on the job.

Feminists for Free Expression (FFE), an advocacy group of feminist women concerned about both equality and free speech rights, has filed briefs arguing that the law against hostile environment harassment should be construed narrowly, to avoid infringing on freedom of speech. FFE argues that if sexual harassment law were construed broadly to prohibit all sexual expression at work, it would stigmatize women as prudes and would prohibit some types of expression that are clearly protected by the First Amendment. Consequently, FFE argues that a plaintiff should be able to win a sexual harassment lawsuit only if she can demonstrate that the speech or conduct at issue specifically targeted her, that a reasonable person would have experienced it as harassment, and that it has demonstrably hindered her job performance. To date, however, this test has not been adopted by any court.

DOCUMENT 42: Brief for Amicus Curiae Feminists for Free Expression in Support of Petitioner, *Harris v. Forklift Systems, Inc.* (1993)

INTEREST OF THE AMICUS

Feminists for Free Expression (FFE) is an organization of diverse feminist women who share a commitment both to gender equality and to preserving the individual's right and responsibility to read, view, and produce media materials of her or his choice, without the intervention of the government "for our own good." . . .

FFE's participation in these cases is motivated by a conviction that the rights of free expression are both indivisible and of crucial importance to feminists and to women generally. . . . Indeed, any written or visual work which deals frankly with women's lives and sexuality is at risk in a climate of pervasive censorship. Because the freedom to put forth controversial feminist ideas and to combat ignorance regarding sexuality is so essential to women's rights and well-being, FFE believes that it is particularly incumbent upon women to oppose censorship initiatives, including the disturbing trend toward overly-intrusive workplace regulations under the aegis of compliance with Title VII. . . .

. . . FFE submits this brief as amicus curiae in an attempt to assist this Court in formulating appropriate standards which will at once protect all workers from invidious harassment while also maintaining due regard for our society's fundamental values of pluralism and free expression.

ARGUMENT

I. THE PREVAILING CONCEPT OF A "HOSTILE WORK ENVIRONMENT" MUST BE RE-EXAMINED IN ORDER TO AVOID SUBSTANTIAL DETRIMENT TO IMPORTANT FIRST AMENDMENT INTERESTS, BY RESTORING AS THE PROPER FOCUS OF THAT THEORY THE NOTION OF DISCRIMINATORY HARASSMENT.

* * *

. . . For the most part, the courts have relied on inappropriately subjective standards for discerning actionable harassment, either facilely equating mere "offensiveness" with harassment, or, as in this case, requiring that the plaintiff demonstrate serious psychological harm before conduct becomes actionable. This focus on the plaintiff's subjective reactions to various types of workplace conduct or speech has distracted the courts from a proper emphasis on the objective inquiry as to whether the complained-of behavior is in fact reasonably regarded as harassment, blurring necessary distinctions between conduct or expression that targets an employee for abuse, and protected expression that does not. . . .

"Title VII is not a 'clean language act,' " as some courts and commentators have wisely noted. . . . Its purpose is to eradicate workplace discrimination, including invidious harassment on the basis of race or gender. Judicial attempts to expand its focus to sanitize the workplace of all "offensiveness" or sexuality yield unconstitutionally censorial results. Under the wide-ranging approach to Title VII liability which has emerged in the reported decisions, courts and employers are imposing restrictions designed to "reduce the adult population to reading only what is fit for children," an unconstitutional result this Court has condemned. . . .

Moreover, such efforts are in fact counter-productive in terms of the statutory goal of gender equality. The paternalistic project of sanitizing workplace speech in defense of women workers enshrines archaic stereotypes of women as delicate, asexual creatures who require special protection from mere words and images. It may very well create additional antagonisms toward women whose entry into male-dominated professions is perceived as occasioning unwarranted intrusions into the sphere of personal liberty. Also, such overbroad regulations of speech threaten not only to censor the speech of the swearing male dockworker, but to curtail the free speech of the woman who chooses to read *Playgirl* on her lunch break or to display a pro-choice poster which might offend co-workers on religious grounds. . . .

A. *Women deserve Title VII protection from gender-based harassment, but neither need nor ultimately benefit from misguided attempts to rid the workplace of all expression regarding sexuality.*

* * *

In *Meritor Savings Bank v. Vinson,* . . . the [Supreme] Court endorsed the EEOC guidelines which define "sexual harassment" to include "verbal or physical conduct of a sexual nature [that] has the purpose or effect of unreasonably interfering with an individual's job performance or creating an intimidating, hostile or offensive work environment." . . .

. . . [The] lack of clarity [provided by these guidelines] regarding the concept of harassment has created a wellspring of confusion to the detriment of any comprehensive hostile work environment theory. First, these guidelines are both under-inclusive and misleading in their one-sided definition of actionable harassment as involving behavior "of a sexual nature," instead of defining the offense as gender-based harassment regardless of whether the abuse is sexual in nature. Second, . . . the definition of sexual harassment to include any "verbal conduct" that creates an "offensive" work environment is egregiously overbroad and viewpoint discriminatory in its application to protected expression, and must be narrowed to comport with the First Amendment.

As the present case illustrates, a wide range of abusive behavior, such as habitually referring to women employees as "stupid" or "incompetent," may constitute gender-based harassment of the sort this Court considered actionable discrimination under Title VII where "sufficiently severe or pervasive 'to alter the conditions of . . . employment.' " . . . Although the EEOC's definition of "sexual harassment" is to some extent understandable because of the prevalence of claims involving actual sexual conduct, it also creates confusion due to the double meaning of "sexual" to denote both gender and sexuality. . . .

This approach focusing primarily on sexuality rather than gender-based discrimination fundamentally disserves women by perpetuating stereotypes that women are so delicate in their sensibilities that exposure to erotic materials, frank sexual discussion, or jokes will inherently intimidate and demoralize them. "The assumption that women as a group may be more offended by profanity than men as a group seems like just the sort of stereotype that Title VII was intended to erase." . . .

This paternalistic approach is also harmful to both men and women workers because it is increasingly spawning court orders and employer regulations censoring virtually any sexual expression, including possession of protected materials as innocuous as *Cosmopolitan* and calendars featuring swimsuit-clad models. . . .

Coupled with the courts' failure to narrow the concept of "harassment" appropriately, this undue and apparently growing emphasis on cleansing the workplace of all sexual expression adversely affects all workers by occasioning such gratuitous infringement of their First Amendment rights. Undoubtedly, this over-regulation also generates hostility on the part of male workers who conclude that women's entry into the workplace has occasioned this diminution of their personal freedoms. For these reasons, the anti-sexual assumptions increasingly embedded in hostile work environment cases are not only offensively paternalistic but also probably as counter-productive to the pursuit of equality as they are destructive of free speech rights.

It is therefore crucial that this Court clarify that the gravamen of the Title VII theory is not sexuality or offensiveness but rather gender-based discrimination, whatever form the complained-of harassment may take. By returning this theory to its proper basis of liability for discriminatory harassment, and by distinguishing harassment from protected speech, this Court would both effectuate the statutory purpose and avoid an unnecessary clash between that purpose and First Amendment rights.

B. *Under current law, the failure to distinguish harassment from protected speech renders Title VII overbroad and viewpoint discriminatory, violating the First Amendment rights of all workers including important free speech rights of women.*

The caselaw regarding hostile work environment liability reveals an alarming failure to limit the definition of "harassment" so as to exclude protected First Amendment activities. Because the courts have increasingly applied an extremely vague, subjective concept of harassment in many of these cases, sometimes resting liability on "offensive" expression such as Penthouse centerfolds and sexual or sexist jokes, employers are compelled to restrict such speech in order to avoid liability. . . .

Imposing liability for protected expression renders this Title VII theory unconstitutionally overbroad; yet numerous reported decisions involve various forms of protected speech found to constitute or contribute to a hostile work environment for women and minorities. This development is both unfortunate and unnecessary, because protected speech can easily be filtered out simply by defining "harassment" in objective terms, as that word is commonly understood, limiting the concept to a course of conduct or expression targeting the plaintiff for invidious abuse, and which a reasonable person would regard as harassment.

Such harassing insults and other verbal abuse targeting individuals do not constitute protected speech because they directly effectuate the unlawful end of employment discrimination and are thus properly regarded as discrimination or harassment rather than as any real part of the marketplace of ideas. . . .

. . . [T]here is a great need for this Court to distinguish harassment from "more generally directed communication," to avoid unconstitutional applications of the hostile work environment theory. . . . A prime example of the misuse of this cause of action is [the case of *Robinson v.*] *Jacksonville Shipyards [Inc.].* . . .

. . . [T]he court [in that case] fashioned an incredibly broad remedial order, requiring the employer . . . to prohibit its workers from engaging in a wide variety of protected expressive activities, including "reading . . . in the work environment materials that are in any way sexually revealing [or] sexually suggestive," and displaying pictures "of a person of either sex who is not fully clothed or in clothes that are not suited to or ordinarily accepted for the accomplishment of routine work in and around the shipyard and who is posed for the obvious purpose of displaying or drawing attention to private portions of his or her body." . . . The overbreadth of this remedy, and the prior restraint it imposes on protected expression, egregiously violate the First Amendment.

Often, such restrictions are viewpoint-discriminatory as well. For example, they may prohibit expressions of opinion that women do not belong in the workplace, while allowing the contrary view to be expressed freely. . . .

II. PETITIONER CORRECTLY ASSERTS THAT THE COURTS BELOW ERRED IN REQUIRING THAT TITLE VII PLAINTIFFS DEMONSTRATE SERIOUS PSYCHOLOGICAL HARM IN ORDER TO PREVAIL IN A HOSTILE WORK ENVIRONMENT ACTION.

* * *

B. *Title VII cannot constitutionally create liability for expression protected by the First Amendment, e.g. mere display or possession of "offensive" materials, at least absent an additional showing of discriminatory intent to harass women or minorities.*

* * *

For all the reasons noted above, non-targeted speech such as erotic posters, "Archie Bunker for President" buttons, or general expressions of biased opinion like, "Women don't belong in the legal profession," may not be censored merely on grounds that they are "offensive" to women or minorities. Although these modes of expression and the attitudes they represent may be (and hopefully are) noxious to a great many Americans, the First Amendment does not allow the government to suppress them either directly by court order or indirectly by imposing Title VII liability on employers.

Certainly, if what purported to be a generalized expression of opinion were shown to be intended as harassment, it might be deemed unprotected much like the stream of personalized racial invective. For example, display of a Ku Klux Klan poster or continual remarks that women workers are incompetent, shown in the circumstances to be intended as threats or demoralizing taunts implicitly directed at black or women employees, might become actionable in an appropriate case. Absent such a showing, however, the generalized opinion or the "offensive" poster remains protected by the First Amendment and may not form the basis for Title VII liability.

Any other approach trivializes the much more serious types of gender or racially-biased behavior which effectively discriminate against women and minorities. The standard suggested here protects against those forms of harassment, encouraging employers to regulate against targeted, harassing expressions of racial or gender animus while protecting employees' rights of free expression. It avoids spurious stereotypes that all women have delicate sensibilities and require protection from sexual imagery and off-color jokes. It entails an acknowledgement that the adult working public cannot, consistent with the First Amendment, be reduced to reading and viewing only that material which the most sensitive member of the work force would find inoffensive. Because the First Amendment requires no less, Amicus FFE respectfully urges this Court to adopt this objective standard and to exclude protected expression from the purview of Title VII liability.

Source: Brief for Amicus Curiae Feminists for Free Expression in Support of Petitioner, *Harris v. Forklift Systems, Inc.*, No. 92–1168 (April 30, 1993).

Not all commentators agree with the FFE's arguments. Professor David Benjamin Oppenheimer argues that the restrictions on speech provided by laws prohibiting sexual harassment are no worse than the restrictions posed by laws preventing other types of harmful speech—like defamation and intentional infliction of emotional distress. He emphasizes the fact that, under current law, employers cannot be held liable for "mere words," but can be held liable only when these words are severe or pervasive enough to harm the complaining party by altering her conditions of work.

DOCUMENT 43: "Workplace Harassment and the First Amendment: A Reply to Professor Volokh" (David Benjamin Oppenheimer, 1996)

When the government assesses damages against an employer based on the speech of the employer's employees, the employer is entitled to the protections of the First Amendment to the United States Constitution. . . .

Private employers are, of course, generally free to impose restrictions on employee speech without governmental interference. Thus, employers may insist that employees treat one another with courtesy and respect, and refrain from uttering unwanted slurs, suggestive comments, or rude statements; such rules imposed privately by employers are of no interest to the state. The problem arises when employers who have chosen to refrain from enacting or enforcing such rules are sued by employees who have been harmed by harassment suffered on the job. The state's involvement, and thus the concern of Constitutional law, is the enactment of legal standards and the operation of a legal system in which employers are ordered by the state to compensate employees injured by workplace harassment. Where the harassment is verbal, rather than physical, the state is in the position of restricting verbal conduct; the potential for interference with freedom of expression is obvious.

Despite the potential for Constitutional infirmity, in reality employers are well protected. To begin with, Title VII prohibits workplace harassment only under circumstances where the harassment has verifiable effects on employees. . . .

It is, of course, axiomatic that the right of free speech is not absolute. Some speech simply falls outside the purview of the First Amendment. Obscenity, for example, is not protected. Blackmail, extortion, and fraud are carried out through words alone, yet those words have no Constitutional shield. The same is true for "fighting words"—words used to provoke violence. Some commentators describe these as categories of "no-value" speech. Workplace harassment, like fighting words, is conduct, or language, which provokes actual injury, in the form of an injurious and verifiably altered work environment. The wrong is not simply in engaging in the harassment, but in causing foreseeable injury to another—injury not only subjectively experienced by the plaintiff, but objectively injurious to a reasonable person. Unwelcome conduct, whether words or deeds, which constitutes intimidation, ridicule or insult and is objectively sufficiently severe or pervasive to alter the conditions of its workplace, making it abusive to employees, may be properly regarded as outside the protection of the First Amendment.

Moreover, even if verbal workplace harassment is entitled to some Constitutional protection under the First Amendment, protected speech is subject to government regulation. Some speech is considered to be sufficiently low in value that it may be regulated, although not altogether banned. The key to determining whether speech is "low-value" is a balancing test, in which the Court asks both how harmful the speech is, and how important it may be in promoting core democratic values. Under this reasoning, speech deemed "indecent" may be banned from the airwaves at certain hours. During union election campaigns, the time, place and manner, and even the content of speech by employers may be regulated; certain speech during campaigns is simply prohibited. Persons deemed "captive audiences" such as public transit riders, school students, medical patients and persons enjoying the privacy of their own homes may be protected from unwanted speech, even when the speech is political, thus implicating the core values of the First Amendment.

Women and minority group members in the workplace are a captive audience in much the same way as school students, medical patients, or employees facing a union election. For example, unlike the targets of street harassment, they cannot simply walk away from on-the-job harassment. They look to their employer to protect them, just as they expect protection from other unsafe working conditions. Having forfeited a certain amount of autonomy in exchange for their employment, they take in exchange an increased expectation of protection. . . .

Nor should the government's regulation of workplace harassment appear extraordinary. That the state is entitled to regulate such conduct as tortious, even when it takes the form of speech, is well established. Many torts empower the government to assess liability for verbal conduct. The tort of assault, for example, can be carried out through words alone. A threat of violence, accompanied by the capacity to carry it out, is sufficient to impose liability even where no physical touching occurs. Nonetheless the state may award damages against the assault tortfeasor without violating his or her First Amendment rights. The same is true of the torts of intentional infliction of emotional distress, invasion of privacy, defamation, and misrepresentation. In each case the defendants' speech alone may properly be the basis of a finding of liability.

These traditional expressive torts are not entirely outside the protections of the First Amendment. Each is protected from abuse by the shield of Constitutional privilege. As a result, the tortfeasor accused of a verbal tort is entitled to a requirement that the plaintiff prove actual fault and actual damages; strict liability may not be imposed, nor may damages be presumed. . . . [T]he Supreme Court and Circuit Courts of Appeals have applied these requirements to limit the effect of hostile work environment law under Title VII, just as they have to defamation, invasion of privacy, and infliction of emotional distress.

It bears repeating that to prove a violation of Title VII the plaintiff must prove a good deal more than "mere words." She must prove that she suffered an actual injury, and that a reasonable person would have similarly experienced the wrongful conduct as injurious. . . .

In sum, . . . Title VII's prohibition on workplace harassment does not infringe on legitimate rights of free expression. And, given the high barriers imposed on Title VII plaintiffs, it should not have the effect of chilling permissible speech.

Source: David Benjamin Oppenheimer, "Workplace Harassment and the First Amendment: A Reply to Professor Volokh," *Berkeley Journal of Employment and Labor Law* 17, no. 2 (1996): 321–22, 325–26, 331 (footnotes omitted).

SEXUAL HARASSMENT BY GOVERNMENT OFFICIALS

Clarence Thomas and Anita Hill

In the last few years there have been several cases in which prominent government officials have been accused of sexual harassment. The most famous involves Professor Anita Hill's accusations against now Supreme Court Justice Clarence Thomas. The 1991 hearings in which Professor Hill accused Justice Thomas of harassment brought the issue of sexual harassment to the forefront of the American consciousness.

At the time of his confirmation hearings, Justice Thomas was a judge on the U.S. Court of Appeals. Prior to that, he had served as chairman of the Equal Employment Opportunity Commission (EEOC), the federal agency charged with investigating and redressing sexual harassment in employment.

During the hearings, documents were leaked to the media detailing accusations by Anita Hill, who had been a subordinate of Justice Thomas's at the EEOC, that Justice Thomas had sexually harassed her. In response to these leaks, the committee scheduled additional days of hearings to deal with the accusations. As the following excerpts from the hearing illustrate, Justice Thomas and Professor Hill told very different stories about what happened during their tenure at the EEOC. Shortly after the hearings, a poll conducted by the *New York Times* and CBS News found that Americans, by a margin of two to one, believed Justice Thomas, rather than Professor Hill. One year after the hearings, however, polls showed Americans more evenly split about whom to believe.

In the wake of the hearings, the number of complaints filed with the EEOC alleging sex discrimination in employment rose dramatically. In 1990, the year before the hearings, only 5,572 claims of sexual harassment were filed with the EEOC; by 1993, that number had more than doubled, to 11,908.

DOCUMENT 44: Testimony of Hon. Clarence Thomas, Nomination of Judge Clarence Thomas to Be Associate Justice of the Supreme Court of the United States, *Hearings before the Committee on the Judiciary of the United States Senate* (1991)

Mr. Chairman, Senator Thurmond, members of the committee: as excruciatingly difficult as the last 2 weeks have been, I welcome the opportunity to clear my name today. No one other than my wife and Senator Danforth, to whom I read this statement at 6:30 a.m., has seen or heard the statement, no handlers, no advisers.

The first I learned of the allegations by Prof. Anita Hill was on September 25, 1991, when the FBI came to my home to investigate her allegations. When informed by the FBI agent of the nature of the allegations and the person making them, I was shocked, surprised, hurt, and enormously saddened.

I have not been the same since that day. For almost a decade my responsibilities included enforcing the rights of victims of sexual harassment. As a boss, as a friend, and as a human being I was proud that I have never had such an allegation leveled at me, even as I sought to promote women, and minorities into nontraditional jobs. . . .

I have been wracking my brains, and eating my insides out trying to think of what I could have said or done to Anita Hill to lead her to allege that I was interested in her in more than a professional way, and that I talked with her about pornographic or x-rated films.

Contrary to some press reports, I categorically denied all of the allegations and denied that I ever attempted to date Anita Hill when first interviewed by the FBI. I strongly reaffirm that denial. . . .

Mr. Chairman, something has happened to me in the dark days that have followed since the FBI agents informed me about these allegations. And the days have grown darker, as this very serious, very explosive, and very sensitive allegation or these sensitive allegations were selectively leaked, in a distorted way to the media over the past weekend.

As if the confidential allegations, themselves, were not enough, this apparently calculated public discourse has caused me, my family, and my friends enormous pain and great harm. . . .

I am not going to allow myself to be further humiliated in order to be confirmed. I am here specifically to respond to allegations of sex harassment in the work place. I am not here to be further humiliated by this committee, or anyone else, or to put my private life on display for a prurient interest or other reasons. I will not allow this committee or anyone else to probe into my private life. This is not what America is all about.

I will not provide the rope for my own lynching or for further humiliation. I am not going to engage in discussions, nor will I submit to roving questions of what goes on in the most intimate parts of my private live [sic] or the sanctity of my bedroom. These are the most intimate parts of my privacy, and they will remain just that, private.

Source: U.S. Senate, *Hearings before the Committee on the Judiciary United States Senate*, 102d Cong., 1st sess., October 11–13, 1991. S. Hrg. 102–1084, Pt. 4, J-102–40, pp. 5–10.

DOCUMENT 45: Testimony of Anita F. Hill, Nomination of Judge Clarence Thomas to Be Associate Justice of the Supreme Court of the United States, *Hearings before the Committee on the Judiciary of the United States Senate* (1991)

In 1981, I was introduced to now Judge Thomas by a mutual friend.

. . . After approximately three months of working [with Clarence Thomas at the Department of Education], he asked me to go out socially with him. What happened next and telling the world about it are the two most difficult things, experiences of my life. It is only after a great deal of agonizing consideration and a number of sleepless nights that I am able to talk of these unpleasant matters to anyone but my close friends.

I declined the invitation to go out socially with him, and explained to him that I thought it would jeopardize what at the time I considered to be a very good working relationship. I had a normal social life with other men outside of the office. I believed then, as now, that having a social relationship with a person who was supervising my work would be ill advised. I was very uncomfortable with the idea and told him so.

I thought that by saying "no" and explaining my reasons, my employer would abandon his social suggestions. However, to my regret, in the following weeks he continued to ask me out on several occasions. He pressed me to justify my reasons for saying "no" to him. These incidents took place in his office or mine. They were in the form of private conversations which would not have been overheard by anyone else.

My working relationship became even more strained when Judge Thomas began to use work situations to discuss sex. On these occasions, he would call me into his office for reports on education issues and projects or he might suggest that because of the time pressures of his schedule, we go to lunch to a government cafeteria. After a brief discussion of work, he would turn the conversation to a discussion of sexual matters. His conversations were very vivid.

He spoke about acts that he had seen in pornographic films involving such matters as women having sex with animals, and films showing group sex or rape scenes. He talked about pornographic materials depicting individuals with large penises, or large breasts involved in various sex acts.

On several occasions, Thomas told me graphically of his own sexual prowess. Because I was extremely uncomfortable talking about sex with him at all, and particularly in such a graphic way, I told him that I did not want to talk about these subjects. I would also try to change the subject to education matters or to nonsexual personal matters, such as his background or his beliefs. My efforts to change the subject were rarely successful.

Throughout the period of these conversations, he also from time to time asked me for social engagements. My reaction to these conversations was to avoid them by limiting opportunities for us to engage in extended conversations. . . .

During the latter part of my time at the Department of Education, the social pressures and any conversation of his offensive behavior ended. I began to believe and hope that our working relationship could be a proper, cordial, and professional one.

When Judge Thomas was made chair of the EEOC, I needed to face the question of whether to go work for him. I was asked to do so and I did. The work, itself, was interesting, and at the time, it appeared that the sexual overtures, which had so troubled me, had ended. . . .

For my first months at the EEOC, where I continued to be an assistant to Judge Thomas, there were no sexual conversations or overtures. However, during the fall and winter of 1982, these began again. The comments were random and ranged from pressing me about why I didn't go out with him, to remarks about my personal appearance. I remember him saying that "some day I would have to tell him the real reason that I wouldn't go out with him."

He began to show displeasure in his tone and voice and his demeanor in his continued pressure for an explanation. He commented on what I was wearing in terms of whether it made me more or less sexually attractive. The incidents occurred in his inner office at the EEOC.

One of the oddest episodes I remember was an occasion in which Thomas was drinking a Coke in his office, he got up from the table at which we were working, went over to his desk to get the Coke, looked at the can and asked, "Who has put pubic hair on my Coke?"

On other occasions he referred to the size of his own penis as being larger than normal and he also spoke on some occasions of the pleasures he had given to women with oral sex. At this point, in late 1982, I began to feel severe stress on the job. I began to be concerned that Clarence Thomas might take out his anger with me by degrading me or not giving me important assignments. I also thought that he might find an excuse for dismissing me. . . .

On, as I recall, the last day of my employment at the EEOC in the summer of 1983, I did have dinner with Clarence Thomas. We went directly from work to a restaurant near the office. We talked about the work that I had done. . . . Finally he made a comment that I will vividly remember. He said, that if I ever told anyone of his behavior that it would ruin his career. This was not an apology, nor was it an explanation. That was his last remark about the possibility of our going out, or reference to his behavior.

Source: U.S. Senate, *Hearings before the Committee on the Judiciary United States Senate*, 102d Cong. 1st sess., October 11–12, 13, 1991. S. Hrg. 102–1084, Pt.4, J-102–40, pp. 36–38.

DOCUMENT 46: Further Testimony of Hon. Clarence Thomas, Nomination of Judge Clarence Thomas to Be Associate Justice of the Supreme Court of the United States, *Hearings before the Committee on the Judiciary of the United States Senate* (1991)

Senator, I would like to start by saying unequivocally, uncategorically that I deny each and every single allegation against me today that suggested in any way that I had conversations of a sexual nature or about pornographic material with Anita Hill, that I ever attempted to date her, that I ever had any personal sexual interest in her, or that I in any way ever harassed her.

Second, and I think a more important point, I think that this hearing should never occur in America. This is a case in which this sleaze, this dirt was searched for by staffers of members of this committee, was then leaked to the media, and this committee and this body validated it and displayed it in prime time over our entire Nation. . . .

. . . This is a circus. It is a national disgrace. And from my standpoint as a black American, as far as I am concerned, it is a high-tech lynching for uppity-blacks who in any way deign to think for themselves, to do for themselves, to have different ideas, and it is a message that, unless you kow-tow to an old order, this is what will happen to you, you will be lynched, destroyed, caricatured by a committee of the U.S. Senate, rather than hung from a tree.

Source: U.S. Senate, *Hearings before the Committee on the Judiciary of the United States Senate,* 102d Cong. 1st sess., October 11–12, 13, 1991. S. Hrg. 102–1084, Pt.4., J-102–40, pp. 156–58.

As the article by Rosemary Bray (Document 47) explains, Professor Hill's allegations against Justice Thomas raised issues of race as well as gender. Many African Americans were critical of Professor Hill, arguing that, regardless of what might have happened to her at EEOC, it was wrong for her to level accusations against a prominent African American. Justice Thomas also explicitly made race an issue when, in his testimony before the committee, he referred to the hearings as "a high-tech lynching for uppity-blacks who in any way deign to think for themselves." His invocation of the lynching metaphor was extremely powerful and is thought by many commentators to have shifted public opinion to his side.

The metaphor, however, was criticized by some as an improper invocation of historical tragedy for Justice Thomas's personal gain. These commentators point out that, as a historical matter, black men were lynched based on allegations of sexual contact with white women, not with African American women like Professor Hill.

DOCUMENT 47: "Taking Sides Against Ourselves" (Rosemary L. Bray, 1991)

The Anita Hill–Clarence Thomas hearings are over; Judge Thomas is Justice Thomas now. Yet the memories linger on and on. Like witnesses to a bad accident, many of us who watched the three days of Senate hearings continue to replay the especially horrible moments. We compare our memories of cool accusation and heated denial; we weigh again in our minds the hours of testimony, vacuous and vindictive by turn. In the end, even those of us who thought we were beyond surprise had underestimated the trauma. . . .

The near-mythic proportions that the event has already assumed in the minds of Americans are due, in part, to the twin wounds of race and gender that the hearings exposed. If gender is a troubling problem in

American life and race is still a national crisis, the synergy of the two embodied in the life and trials of Anita Hill left most of America dumbstruck. Even black people who did not support Clarence Thomas's politics felt that Hill's charges, made public at the 11th hour, smacked of treachery. Feminist leaders embraced with enthusiasm a woman whose conservative political consciousness might have given them chills only a month earlier. . . .

The heated debates about gender and race in America have occurred, for the most part, in separate spheres; the separation makes for neater infighting.

But black women can never skirt these questions; we are their living expression. The parallel pursuits of equality for African-Americans and for women have trapped black women between often conflicting agendas for more than a century. We are asked in a thousand ways, large and small, to take sides against ourselves, postponing a confrontation in one arena to address an equally urgent task in another. Black men and white women have often made claims to our loyalty and our solidarity in the service of their respective struggles for recognition and autonomy, understanding only dimly that what may seem like liberty to each is for us only a kind of parole. Despite the bind, more often than not we choose loyalty to the race rather than the uncertain allegiance of gender.

Ours is the complicity of guilty survivors. A black man's presence is often feared; a black woman's presence is at least tolerated. . . .

As difficult as the lives of black women often are, we know we are mobile in ways black men are not—and black men know that we know. They know that we are nearly as angered as they about their inability to protect us in the traditional and patriarchal way, even as many of us have moved beyond the need for such protection. And some black men know ways to use our anger, our sorrow, our guilt, against us.

In our efforts to make a place for ourselves and our families in America, we have created a paradigm of sacrifice. And in living out such lives, we have convinced even ourselves that no sacrifice is too great to insure what we view in a larger sense as the survival of the race.

That sacrifice has been an unspoken promise to our people; it has made us partners with black men in a way white women and men cannot know. Yet not all of us view this partnership with respect. There are those who would use black women's commitment to the race as a way to control black women. There are those who believe the price of solidarity is silence. It was that commitment that trapped Anita Hill. And it is a commitment we may come to rue.

As I watched Hill being questioned that Friday by white men, by turn either timid or incredulous, I grieved for her. The anguish in her eyes was recognizable to me. Not only did she dare to speak about events more than one woman would regard as unspeakable, she did so publicly.

Not only did she make public accusations best investigated in private, she made them against a man who was black and conservative, as she was—a man who in other ways had earned her respect.

"Here is a woman who went to Sunday school and took it seriously," says Cornel West, director of the African-American Studies department at Princeton University and a social critic who felt mesmerized by what he called "the travesty and tragedy" of the hearings. "She clearly is a product of the social conservatism of a rural black Baptist community." For black women historically, such probity, hard-won and tenaciously held, was social salvation. For white onlookers, it suggested an eerie primness out of sync with contemporary culture.

In the quiet and resolute spirit she might very well have learned from Sunday school, Hill confronted and ultimately breached a series of taboos in the black community that have survived both slavery and the post-segregation life she and Clarence Thomas share. Anita Hill put her private business in the street, and she downgraded a black man to a room filled with white men who might alter his fate—surely a large enough betrayal for her to be read out of the race.

By Sunday evening, Anita Hill's testimony lay buried under an avalanche of insinuation and innuendo. Before the eyes of a nation, a tenured law professor beloved by her students was transformed into an evil, opportunistic harpy; a deeply religious Baptist was turned into a sick and delusional woman possessed by Satan and in need of exorcism; this youngest of 13 children from a loving family became a frustrated spinster longing for the attentions of her fast-track superior, bent on exacting a cruel revenge for his rejection.

These skillful transformations of Anita Hill's character by some members of the Senate were effective because they were familiar, manageable images of African-American womanhood. What undergirds these images is the common terror of black women out of control. We are the grasping and materialistic Sapphire in an "Amos 'n' Andy" episode; the embodiment of a shadowy, insane sexuality; the raging, furious, rejected woman. In their extremity, these are images far more accessible and understandable than the polished and gracious dignity, the cool intelligence that Anita Hill displayed in the lion's den of the Senate chamber. However she found herself reconstituted, the result was the same. She was, on all levels, simply unbelievable.

Anita Hill fell on the double-edged sword of African-American womanhood. Her privacy, her reputation, her integrity—all were casualties of an ignorance that left her unseen by and unknown to most of those who meant either to champion or abuse her. As credible, as inspiring, as impressive as she was, most people who saw her had no context in which to judge her. The signs and symbols that might have helped to place Hill were long ago appropriated by officials of authentic (male) blackness, or by representatives of authentic (white) womanhood. Quite simply, a woman like Anita Hill couldn't possibly exist. . . .

. . . [H]er profound self-possession, particularly in the face of the behavior she ascribed to Thomas, seemed impossible to observers—in large part because her response was not the conditioned one for black women. Hill showed no signs of the Harriet Tubman Syndrome, the fierce insistence on freedom or death that made Tubman an abolitionist legend. Anita Hill grabbed no blunt objects with which to threaten her superior, she did not thunder into his office in righteous anger or invoke the power to bring suit. She was not funny, or feisty, or furious in response to the behavior she described. She was disgusted, embarrassed and ambivalent. Therefore, it must have been a dream. . . .

. . . That week in October, my phone rang nonstop. Friends called to talk about their stories of sexual harassment, their memories of vengeful, jealous women who lie, their theories of self-loathing black men who act out their hostility toward black women while lusting after white women. . . .

The buses and trains and elevators were filled with debates and theories of conspiracy. Hill set up Thomas to bring a black man down. Thomas was a man; what man didn't talk about his prowess? In a Harlem restaurant where I sat with a cup of tea and the papers that Saturday, the entire kitchen staff was in an uproar. The cook, an African woman, wanted to know why Hill waited 10 years to bring it up. The waitress, an African-American woman, said she couldn't tell what to think. . . .

Yet the issues of race and sex illuminated by the hearings remain. So, too, do the myriad ways in which race and gender combine to confuse us. But for the first time in decades, the country has been turned, for a time, into a mobile social laboratory. A level of discussion between previously unaligned groups may have begun with new vigor and candor.

Segments of the feminist movement have been under attack for their selective wooing of black women. Yet many of these same women rallied to Hill with impressive speed. Some black women who had never before considered sexism as an issue serious enough to merit collective concern have begun to organize, including a group of black female academics known as African American Women in Defense of Ourselves. And even in brusque New York, people on opposite sides of this issue, still traumatized by the televised spectacle, seem eager to listen, to be civil, to talk things over. . . .

What was most striking about the hearings, in the end, was the sense of destiny that surrounded them. There was something rewarding about seeing what began as a humiliating event become gradually transformed only in its aftermath. Two African-Americans took center stage in what became a national referendum on many of our most cherished values. In the midst of their shattering appearances, Anita Hill and Clarence

Thomas each made us ask questions that most of us had lost the heart to ask.

They are exactly the kinds of questions that could lead us out of the morass of cynicism and anger in which we've all been stuck. That is an immensely satisfying measurement of the Hill-Thomas hearings. It would not be the first time that African-Americans have used tragedy and contradiction as catalysts to make America remember its rightful legacy.

Source: Rosemary L. Bray, "Taking Sides Against Ourselves," *New York Times*, November 17, 1991, sec. 6, pp. 56, 94, 101 (Magazine Desk).

The debate in the Senate over whether to confirm Clarence Thomas became bitter at times. One of Justice Thomas's strongest critics, both before and after Professor Hill's allegations surfaced, was Senator Edward Kennedy of Massachusetts. He argued that, if there was any doubt about who was telling the truth, Judge Thomas should not be confirmed. The Senate, however, did confirm him by a vote of 52 to 48.

DOCUMENT 48: Remarks of Senator Edward Kennedy of Massachusetts, Debate on the Nomination of Clarence Thomas to Be Associate Justice of the United States Supreme Court (1991)

Mr. KENNEDY.

Mr. President, the question before the Senate today is not a referendum on the credibility of Judge Clarence Thomas—or of Prof. Anita Hill. The issue before us is the fate of the Supreme Court and the Constitution, now and for decades to come.

It is no secret that I oppose Judge Thomas' nomination.

The extreme views he expressed before his confirmation hearings demonstrate that he lacks a deep commitment to the fundamental constitutional values at the core of our democracy. . . .

But over the past 9 days, the debate on this nomination has been transformed—and the Nation has been transfixed—by the charges of sexual harassment made by Prof. Anita Hill, and by the Judiciary Committee's hearings into those charges over the past weekend.

With extraordinary courage and dignity, Professor Hill expressed the pain and anguish experienced by so many women who have been victims of sexual harassment on the job.

She described the suffering and the humiliation that a woman encounters when her career and her livelihood are threatened by a supervisor who fills every workday with anxiety about when the next offensive action and the next embarrassing incident will occur.

The hearings on Professor Hill's charges were exhaustive, and they were difficult and painful for all of the participants—witnesses and Senators alike. But the hearings educated the country on an issue of great and growing significance.

Overnight, as on perhaps no other issue in our history, the entire country made a giant leap of understanding about sexual harassment. That offensive conduct will never be treated lightly again. All women—and all men too—owe Professor Hill a tremendous debt of gratitude for her willingness to discuss her experience, and for the courage and dignity with which she did so.

The most distressing aspect of the hearings was the eagerness with which many of Judge Thomas' supporters resorted to innuendos and scurrilous attacks on Professor Hill for her testimony about her charges of deeply offensive and humiliating actions by Judge Thomas.

They have charged that Professor Hill's allegations were an effort to play on racial fears and racial stereotypes. But the issue here is sexual oppression, not racial oppression.

I have spent much of my public life fighting against discrimination in all its ugly forms, and I intend to keep on making that fight.

I reject the notion that racism is relevant to this controversy. It involves an African-American man and an African-American woman—and, ultimately, it involves the character of America itself. The struggle for racial justice, in its truest sense, was meant to wipe out all forms of oppression. No one, least of all Judge Thomas, is entitled to invoke one form of oppression to excuse another.

The deliberate, provocative use of a term like lynching is not only wrong in fact; it is a gross misuse of America's most historic tragedy and pain to buy a political advantage.

The Senate today is not passing judgment solely on Judge Thomas or Professor Hill. The Senate is making a fundamental statement about our values and our conscience. Make no mistake about it. We in the Senate are also passing judgment on ourselves.

Are we an old boys' club, insensitive at best, and perhaps something worse? Will we strain to concoct any excuse, to impose any burden, to tolerate any unsubstantiated attack on a woman, in order to rationalize a vote for this nomination?

Will we refuse to heed the rights and claims of the majority of Americans who are women but who are so much a minority in this Chamber? What kind of Senate are we?

Because if we cannot listen and respond to this woman, as credible as she is and with the significant corroboration she offers, then what message are we sending to women across America? What American woman in the future will dare to come forward?

There is no proof that Anita Hill has perjured herself—and shame on anyone who suggests that she has.

There is no proof that any advocacy groups made Anita Hill say what she said or made up a story for her to repeat—and shame on anyone who suggests that this is what happened.

There is no proof, no proof at all that Anita Hill is fantasizing these charges or is mentally unbalanced—and shame on anyone desperate enough to suggest that she is.

The treatment of Anita Hill is what every women fears who thinks of lifting the veil and revealing her sexual harassment. Here in the Senate, and in the Nation, we need to establish a different, better, higher standard.

When confronted with all of the evidence that corroborates Professor Hill's charges, Judge Thomas' supporters abandoned the craven charge that she had concocted the story in recent weeks. Instead, they resorted to the meanest, and most unfounded, cut of all—that this tenured law professor, who testified with such grace and dignity, is delusional, that she somehow fantasized the entire horrible experience. That baseless charge is an insult to Professor Hill, and to the millions of American women who have been the victims of sexual harassment.

For too long, persons accused of sexual harassment have responded by charging their victims with being "sick," with "making the whole thing up," with "living in a fantasy world," or that such allegations "amount to nothing more than women taking a passing word in the wrong way."

Calculated slurs of that kind scare other women into silence.

And the greatest irony of all is that the very same people who are now making that irresponsible charge are those who have criticized Professor Hill for not making her own charges sooner.

If we allow these kinds of vicious attacks on Professor Hill to stand, if we dismiss her charges as fantasy or delusion, the message to women throughout America will be a chilling one—suffer in silence or pay a terrible price. . . .

Judge Thomas and his supporters have pointed with outrage to the harm that these hearings have done to him. But what about the harm that was done to Professor Hill? And I am not talking only about the Senate proceedings that she was so reluctant to set in motion. I am talking about the 2 years of harm that she endured because of this harassment. I am talking about 8 more years of harm she endured because of the silence she was forced to accept in a society that has been hostile to such claims for so long.

It has never been easy for any woman to bring a charge of sexual harassment. Attitudes are changing in our society. Our national consciousness has been raised by the events of recent days. And the lesson of these changes should be part of the consciousness of the Supreme Court, too. . . .

I believe Professor Hill. I recognize that most of the country is left with doubts about what really happened, and so are many Senators.

There is no conclusive answer—yet. But the Senate has to vote today, and what is the Senate to do?

In my view, Senators who are unsure about who is telling the truth should vote against this nomination.

The Bush administration is urging the Senate to give the benefit of the doubt to the nominee. If this were a criminal proceeding, or even a civil lawsuit, that assertion would be correct.

But the issue before the Senate today is a proceeding of a very different kind. The question is whether Judge Clarence Thomas should be appointed to the highest court in the land, whether he should be entrusted with the solemn power to have the last word on the meaning of the Constitution and the fundamental rights of all Americans.

Throughout the two centuries of our history, many—if not all—of the most important issues of our democracy have been resolved by the Supreme Court. All Americans—men and women—must have faith in the fairness and the integrity of the members of that Court, in their ability to do justice for every citizen, and in their commitment to doing justice. . . .

If we make a mistake today, the Supreme Court will be living with it and the Nation will be living with it for the next 30 or 40 years. That is too high a price to pay, too great a risk to take. To give the benefit of the doubt to Judge Thomas is to say that Judge Thomas is more important than the Supreme Court. . . .

The Senate has a constitutional responsibility to the Supreme Court and to the American people. The risk of being wrong is too great. Judge Thomas will continue to be a judge, but he should not be confirmed as a member of the Nation's highest court.

Source: Congressional Record, 137th Cong., 1st Sess., 1991, S14626–02, pp. S14641–42.

Senator Robert Packwood

Sexual harassment allegations have hit the other branches of the federal government as well. In 1992 the Senate Select Committee on Ethics began investigating allegations that Senator Robert Packwood of Oregon, a moderate Republican who had served in the Senate since

1968, had sexually harassed eighteen women, many of whom had served as members of his staff. In 1995 the committee found the allegations to be credible and voted unanimously that he be expelled from the Senate.

Two documents from the Senate committee's investigation have been included. The first is the committee's Resolution for Investigation (Document 49), released in May 1995, in which the committee announced its preliminary conclusions in the matter. The second, the committee's Resolution for Disciplinary Action (Document 50), released in September 1995, represents the committee's final conclusions and its recommendation to the full Senate that Senator Packwood be expelled. In the end, Senator Packwood resigned from the Senate in order to avoid expulsion.

DOCUMENT 49: Resolution for Investigation of Senator Bob Packwood (United States Senate Select Committee on Ethics, 1995)

RESOLUTION FOR INVESTIGATION

Whereas, the Select Committee on Ethics on December 1, 1992, initiated a Preliminary Inquiry (hereafter "Inquiry") into allegations of sexual misconduct by Senator Bob Packwood, and subsequently, on February 4, 1993, expanded the scope of its Inquiry to include allegations of attempts to intimidate and discredit the alleged victims, and misuse of official staff in attempts to intimidate and discredit, and notified Senator Packwood of such actions; and. . . .

Whereas, on the basis of evidence received during the Inquiry, there are possible violations within the Committee's jurisdiction. . . .

It is therefore *Resolved*:

I. That the Committee makes the following determinations regarding the matters set forth above:

(a) With respect to sexual misconduct, the Committee has carefully considered evidence, including sworn testimony, witness interviews, and documentary evidence, relating to the following allegations:

(1) That in 1990, in his Senate Office in Washington, D.C., Senator Packwood grabbed a staff member by the shoulders and kissed her on the lips;

(2) That in 1985, at a function in Bend, Oregon, Senator Packwood fondled a campaign worker as they danced. Later that year, in Eugene, Oregon, in saying goodnight and thank you to her, Senator Packwood grabbed the cam-

paign worker's face with his hands, pulled her towards him, and kissed her on the mouth, forcing his tongue into her mouth;

(3) That in 1981 or 1982, in his Senate office in Washington, D.C., Senator Packwood squeezed the arms of a lobbyist, leaned over and kissed her on the mouth;

(4) That in 1981, in the basement of the Capitol, Senator Packwood walked a former staff assistant into a room, where he grabbed her with both hands in her hair and kissed her, forcing his tongue into her mouth;

(5) That in 1980, in a parking lot in Eugene, Oregon, Senator Packwood pulled a campaign worker toward him, put his arms around her, and kissed her, forcing his tongue in her mouth; he also invited her to his motel room;

(6) That in 1980 or early 1981, at a hotel in Portland Oregon, on two separate occasions, Senator Packwood kissed a desk clerk who worked for the hotel;

(7) That in 1980, in his Senate office in Washington, D.C., Senator Packwood grabbed a staff member by the shoulders, pushed her down on a couch, and kissed her on the lips; the staff member tried several times to get up, but Senator Packwood repeatedly pushed her back on the couch;

(8) That in 1979, Senator Packwood walked into the office of another Senator in Washington, D.C., started talking with a staff member, and suddenly leaned down and kissed the staff member on the lips;

(9) That in 1977, in an elevator in the Capitol, and on numerous occasions, Senator Packwood grabbed the elevator operator by the shoulders, pushed her to the wall of the elevator and kissed her on the lips. Senator Packwood also came to this person's home, kissed her, and asked her to make love with him;

(10) That in 1977, in a motel room while attending the Dorchester Conference in coastal Oregon, Senator Packwood grabbed a prospective employee by her shoulders, pulled her to him and kissed her;

(11) That in 1975, in his Senate office in Washington, D.C., Senator Packwood grabbed the staff assistant referred to in (4), pinned her against a wall or desk, held her hair with one hand, bending her head backwards, fondling her with his other hand, and kissed her, forcing his tongue into her mouth;

(12) That in 1975, in his Senate office in Washington, D.C., Senator Packwood grabbed a staff assistant around her shoulders, held her tightly while pressing his body into hers, and kissed her on the mouth;

(13) That in the early 1970's, in his Senate Office in Portland, Oregon, Senator Packwood chased a staff assistant around a desk;

(14) That in 1970, in a hotel restaurant in Portland, Oregon, Senator Packwood ran his hand up the leg of a dining room hostess and touched her crotch area;

(15) That in 1970, in his Senate office in Washington, D.C., Senator Packwood grabbed a staff member by the shoulders and kissed her on the mouth.

(16) That in 1969, in his Senate office in Washington, D.C., Senator Packwood made suggestive comments to a prospective employee.

(17) That in 1969, at his home, Senator Packwood grabbed an employee of another Senator who was babysitting for him, rubbed her shoulders and back, and kissed her on the mouth. He also put his arm around her and touched her leg as he drove her home;

(18) That in 1969, in his Senate office in Portland, Oregon, Senator Packwood grabbed a staff worker, stood on her feet, grabbed her hair, forcibly pulled her head back, and kissed her on the mouth, forcing his tongue into her mouth. Senator Packwood also reached under her skirt and grabbed at her undergarments.

Based upon the Committee's consideration of evidence related to each of these allegations, the Committee finds that there is substantial credible evidence that provides substantial cause for the Committee to conclude that violations within the Committee's jurisdiction ... may have occurred; to wit, that Senator Packwood may have abused his United States Senate Office by improper conduct which has brought discredit upon the United States Senate, by engaging in a pattern of sexual misconduct between 1969 and 1990.

Notwithstanding this conclusion, for purposes of making a determination at the end of its Investigation with regard to a possible pattern of conduct involving sexual misconduct, some Members of the Committee have serious concerns about the weight, if any, that should be accorded to evidence of conduct alleged to have occurred prior to 1976, the year in which the federal court recognized quid pro quo sexual harassment as discrimination under the Civil Rights Act, and the Senate passed a resolution prohibiting sex discrimination in the United States Senate, and taking into account the age of the allegations.

Source: U.S. Senate Select Committee on Ethics, Resolution for Investigation of Senator Bob Packwood, Appendix A to Senate Report 104–137, 104th Cong., 1st sess., pp. 9–11 (September 5, 1995).

DOCUMENT 50: Resolution for Disciplinary Action of Senator Bob Packwood (United States Senate Select Committee on Ethics, 1995)

MR. MCCONNELL, from the Select Committee on Ethics,
submitted the following
REPORT
IV. FINDINGS OF THE COMMITTEE

The Committee makes the following findings respecting the matters which are the subject of the Committee's Investigation.

The Committee finds that Senator Packwood engaged in improper conduct which reflects upon the Senate. . . .

. . . [T]he Committee further finds, on the basis of the evidence before it, that Senator Packwood committed violations of the law and rules within the Committee's jurisdiction. . . . Specifically, the Committee finds that:

Senator Packwood endeavored to obstruct and impede the Committee's Inquiry by withholding, altering and destroying relevant evidence, including his diary transcripts and audio taped diary material. . . . The Committee further finds that these illegal acts constitute a crime against the United States Senate, and are reprehensible and contemptuous of the Senate's constitutional self-disciplinary process. Further, Senator Packwood's illegal acts constitute a violation of his duty of trust to the Senate and an abuse of his position as a United States Senator, reflecting discredit upon the United States Senate.

Senator Packwood engaged in a pattern of abuse of his position of power and authority as a United States Senator by repeatedly committing sexual misconduct, making at least 18 separate unwanted and unwelcome sexual advances between 1969 and 1990. In most of these instances, the victims were members of Senator Packwood's staff or individuals whose livelihoods were dependent upon or connected to the power and authority held by Senator Packwood. These improper acts bring discredit and dishonor upon the Senate and constitute conduct unbecoming a United States Senator.

Senator Packwood abused his position of power and authority as a United States Senator by engaging in a deliberate and systematic plan to enhance his personal financial position by soliciting, encouraging and coordinating employment opportunities for his wife from persons who had a particular interest in legislation or issues that Senator Packwood could influence. These improper acts bring discredit and dishonor upon the Senate and constitute conduct unbecoming a United States Senator.

V. Recommendation and Referrals

A. Recommendation for Expulsion

Based on the findings specified above, the Committee hereby recommends that the Senate agree to the following Resolution:

Resolved: That pursuant to Article 1, Section 5, Clause 2 of the United States Constitution, Senator Packwood is expelled from the Senate for his illegal actions and improper conduct in attempting to obstruct and impede the Committee's Inquiry; engaging in a pattern of sexual misconduct in at least 18 instances between 1969 and 1990; and engaging in a plan to enhance his financial position by soliciting, encouraging and coordinating employment opportunities for his wife from individuals with interests in legislation or issues which he could influence.

President William Jefferson Clinton

In 1994 Paula Corbin Jones, a former employee of the Arkansas state government, accused President Bill Clinton of harassing her while he was the governor of Arkansas. She claimed that the president exposed himself to her and made sexual advances toward her after a state trooper summoned her to his hotel room during a state function. President Clinton denied the allegations. Ms. Jones filed a lawsuit against the president alleging both that he sexually harassed her and that he defamed her character by claiming that she had lied about the incident. Excerpts from the legal complaint, in which Ms. Jones details her allegations, are reprinted below (Document 51).

President Clinton asked the courts to delay the suit until his term as president expires, claiming that it would interfere with his duties as president if he had to defend against the suit while in office. In June 1997, however, the Supreme Court refused to allow the president to delay the suit. In the spring of 1998, the trial court dismissed Ms. Jones's lawsuit. The judge reasoned that, even if all of her allegations were true, she still could not win a sexual harassment case because she failed to show any connection between the alleged behavior and her employment. Ms. Jones has appealed that decision.

DOCUMENT 51: Complaint of Paula Corbin Jones, *Paula Corbin Jones v. William Jefferson Clinton and Danny Ferguson* (1994)

COMPLAINT

Plaintiff Paula Corbin Jones, by counsel, brings this action to obtain redress for the deprivation and conspiracy to deprive Plaintiff of her federally protected rights as hereafter alleged, and for intentional infliction of emotional distress, and for defamation. . . .

THE PARTIES

3. Plaintiff Paula Corbin Jones (hereafter "Jones") is a citizen of the State of California. Prior to her marriage on December 28, 1991, Plaintiff was known as Paula Rosalee Corbin.

4. Defendant William Jefferson Clinton (hereafter "Clinton") is a citizen of the State of Arkansas or alternatively of the District of Columbia.

5. Defendant Danny Ferguson (hereafter "Ferguson") is a citizen of the State of Arkansas.

FACTS

6. On or about March 11, 1991, Jones began work as an Arkansas State employee for the Arkansas Industrial Development Commission (hereafter "AIDC"), an agency within the executive branch of the State of Arkansas. The Governor of Arkansas is the chief executive officer of the executive branch of the State of Arkansas.

7. On May 8, 1991, the AIDC sponsored the Third Annual Governor's Quality Management Conference (hereafter "Conference"), which was held at the Excelsior Hotel in Little Rock, Arkansas. Clinton, then Governor of Arkansas, delivered a speech at the Conference on that day.

8. Also on that day, Jones worked at the registration desk at the Conference along with Pamela Blackard (hereafter "Blackard") another AIDC employee.

9. A man approached the registration desk and informed Jones and Blackard that he was Trooper Danny Ferguson, Bill Clinton's bodyguard. Defendant Ferguson was at that time a law enforcement officer within the ranks of the Arkansas State Police and assigned to the Governor's Security Detail. He was in street clothes and displayed a firearm on his person. He made small talk with Jones and Blackard and then left.

10. At approximately 2:30 p.m. on that day, Ferguson reappeared at the registration desk, delivered a piece of paper to Jones with a four digit number written on it and said: "The Governor would like to meet with you" in this suite number. Plaintiff had never met Defendant Clinton and saw him in person for the first time at the Conference.

11. A three-way conversation followed between Ferguson, Blackard and Jones about what the Governor could want. Jones, who was then a rank-and-file Arkansas state employee being paid approximately $6.35 an hour, thought it was an honor to be asked to meet the Governor. Ferguson stated during the conversation: "It's okay, we do this all the time for the Governor."

12. Jones agreed to meet with the Governor because she thought it might lead to an enhanced employment opportunity with the State. Blackard told Jones that she would assume Plaintiff's duties at the registration desk.

13. Trooper Ferguson then escorted Jones to the floor of the hotel suite whose number had been written on the slip of paper Trooper Ferguson had given to Jones. The door was slightly ajar when she arrived at the suite.

14. Jones knocked on the door frame and Clinton answered. Plaintiff entered. Ferguson remained outside.

15. The room was furnished as a business suite, not for an overnight hotel guest. It contained a couch and chairs, but no bed.

16. Clinton shook Jones' hand, invited her in, and closed the door.

17. A few minutes of small talk ensued, which included asking Jones about her job. Clinton told Jones that Dave Harrington is "my good friend." On May 8, 1991, David Harrington was Director of the AIDC, having been appointed to that post by Governor Clinton. Harrington was Jones' ultimate superior within the AIDC.

18. Clinton then took Jones' hand and pulled her toward him, so that their bodies were in close proximity.

19. Jones removed her hand from his and retreated several feet.

20. However, Clinton approached Jones again. He said: "I love the way your hair flows down your back" and "I love your curves." While saying these things, Clinton put his hand on Plaintiff's leg and started sliding it toward the hem of Plaintiff's culottes. Clinton also bent down to attempt to kiss Jones on the neck.

21. Jones exclaimed, "What are you doing?" and escaped from Clinton's physical proximity by walking away from him. Jones tried to distract Clinton by chatting with him about his wife. Jones later took a seat at the end of the sofa nearest the door. Clinton asked Jones: "Are you married?" She responded that she had a regular boyfriend. Clinton then approached the sofa and as he sat down he lowered his trousers and underwear [and continued with his sexual advance]. . . .

23. Jones became horrified, jumped up from the couch, stated that she was "not that kind of girl" and said: "Look, I've got to go." She attempted to explain that she would get in trouble for being away from the registration desk.

24. . . . As Jones left the room Clinton looked sternly at Jones and said: "You are smart. Let's keep this between ourselves."

25. Jones believed "Dave" to be the same David Harrington, of whom Clinton previously referred. Clinton, by his comments about Harrington to Jones, affirmed that he had control over Jones' employment, and that he was willing to use that power. Jones became fearful that her refusal to succumb to Clinton's advances could damage her in her job and even jeopardize her employment.

26. At no time, nor in any manner, did Jones encourage Clinton to turn the meeting toward a sexual liaison. To the contrary, the unwanted sexual advances made by Clinton were repugnant and abhorrent to Jones who took all reasonable steps she could think to do to terminate Clinton's perverse attention and actions toward her.

27. Jones left the hotel suite and came into the presence of Trooper Ferguson in the hallway. Ferguson did not escort Plaintiff back to the registration desk. Jones said nothing to Ferguson and he said nothing to her during her departure from the suite. . . .

40. Jones terminated her employment and separated from AIDC service on February 20, 1993. On May 4, 1993, Plaintiff, her husband and child moved to California.

41. In January, 1994, Plaintiff visited her family and friends in Arkansas. While Jones was in Arkansas, [a friend] telephoned Jones to arrange a meeting for lunch. During the telephone conversation, [the friend] read to Plaintiff a paragraph from an article published in the January, 1994 issue of The American Spectator magazine regarding Plaintiff's hotel suite encounter with Clinton. . . .

42. The American Spectator account asserts that a woman by the name of "Paula" told an unnamed trooper (obviously Defendant Ferguson), who had escorted "Paula" to Clinton's hotel room, that "she was available to be Clinton's regular girlfriend if he so desired," thus implying a consummated and satisfying sexual encounter with Clinton, as well as a willingness to continue a sexual relationship with him. These assertions are untrue. The article, using information apparently derived from Ferguson, also incorrectly asserts that the encounter took place in the evening.

43. The American Spectator account also asserted that the troopers' " 'official' duties included facilitating Clinton's cheating on his wife. This meant that, on the State payroll, and using State time, vehicles and resources, they were instructed by Clinton on a regular basis to approach women and to solicit their telephone numbers for the Governor, to drive him in State vehicles to rendezvous points and guard him during sexual encounters; to secure hotel rooms and other meeting places for sex; . . ." and various other things to facilitate Clinton's sex life including "to help Clinton cover-up his activities by keeping tabs on Hillary's whereabouts and lying to Hillary about her husband's whereabouts." Although this pattern of conduct by Clinton may be true, the magazine article concluded, evidently from interviews with troopers from Clinton's Security Detail, including Ferguson, that "all of the women appear to have been willing participants in the affairs and liaisons. . . ."

44. Since Jones ("Paula") was one of the women preyed upon by Clinton and his troopers, including by Defendant Ferguson, in the manner described above, those who read this magazine account could conclude falsely that Jones ("Paula") had a sexual relationship and affair with Clinton. Jones' reputation within her community was thus seriously damaged. . . .

47. Because the false statements appearing in The American Spectator article that Jones was willing to have sex with Clinton (and the innuendo that she had already done so when she left the hotel suite) threatened her marriage, her friendships, and her family relationships, Plaintiff spoke publicly on February 11, 1994, that she was the "Paula" mentioned in The American Spectator article, that she had rebuffed Clinton's sexual advances, and that she had not expressed a willingness to be his girlfriend. Jones and her lawyer asked that Clinton acknowledge the inci-

dent, state that Jones had rejected Clinton's advances, and apologize to Jones.

48. Clinton, who is now President of the United States of America[,] responded to Jones' request for an apology by having his press spokespersons deliver a statement on his behalf that the incident never happened, and that he never met Plaintiff. Thus, by innuendo and effect, Clinton publicly branded Plaintiff a liar. Moreover, as recently as the week this Complaint was filed, Clinton, through his White House aides, stated that Plaintiff's account of the hotel room incident was untrue and a "cheap political trick."

49. Clinton hired an attorney, who, as Clinton's agent, said that Jones' account "is really just another effort to rewrite the results of the election [i.e., for President of the United States] and . . . distract the President from his agenda." The attorney further asked the question: "Why are these claims being brought now, three years after the fact?" The attorney also asked how Jones' allegations could be taken "seriously." These comments by Clinton's counsel, on behalf of Clinton, imply that Jones is a liar.

50. Dee Dee Meyers, White House Spokeswoman, said of Jones' allegations: "It's just not true." Thus, the pattern of defaming Jones continues to this date.

51. Clinton knows that Jones' allegations are true and that his, and his attorney's, spokespersons', and agents' denials are false.

52. The outrageous nature of Clinton's branding of Jones as a liar is aggravated in that a greater stigma and reputation loss is suffered by Jones by the statements of the President of the United States in whom the general public reposes trust and confidence in the integrity of the holder of that office. . . .

57. Clinton's actions and omissions above stated caused Jones embarrassment, humiliation, fear, emotional distress, horror, grief, shame, marital discord and loss of reputation.

Source: Paula Corbin Jones v. William Jefferson Clinton and Danny Ferguson, Civil Action No. LR-C-94–290, U.S. District Court for the Eastern District of Arkansas, Western Division, 1994.

LAWSUITS BROUGHT BY THOSE ACCUSED OF HARASSMENT

Sexual harassment law can put employers in a difficult position. If an employee makes a credible claim that she has been harassed, and the employer does not remedy the situation, the employer may be forced to pay damages to the victim. If, however, the employer responds by punishing the person accused of harassment, that person might sue the employer and argue that he has been unfairly treated.

In recent years, several lawsuits have been brought by men who were disciplined or fired after being accused of sexual harassment. Often these suits allege that the employer has defamed the plaintiff by calling him a harasser.

Employers usually win these lawsuits. Courts usually hold that employers are entitled to inform their employees and sometimes even the community that they believe someone has committed sexual harassment. But these victories often come only after the employer has spent a substantial amount of money in defense costs, making them somewhat hollow. An article from the *Wall Street Journal* (Document 52) explains this dilemma well.

DOCUMENT 52: "Laws Covering Sex Harassment and Wrongful Dismissal Collide" (Grace M. Kang, 1992)

Companies that fire employees for sexual harassment increasingly are finding they've simply exchanged one set of problems for another. Accused employees are suing for reinstatement or damages—whether or not they deny the charges—and in some courts, they're winning.

Employers in this tight spot are confronted with conflicting laws governing sexual harassment and wrongful discharge. Federal law requires companies to maintain a workplace free of sexual harassment. But some states allow workers to sue if they're fired without sufficient reason. And an employer who hesitates in order to investigate accusations risks a suit by the victim of the harassment.

The predicament is becoming more common as the number of sexual harassment suits increase, triggered in part by the publicity surrounding the charges against Supreme Court Justice Clarence Thomas during his confirmation hearings last year. The tough economic climate has also prompted more suits by fired employees, who would rather fight for their jobs than face the bleak job market.

"It's a tightrope," says Barbara Brown, an employment law specialist at Paul, Hastings, Janofsky & Walker in Washington. Stephen Tallent, a lawyer in the Washington office of the Los Angeles firm Gibson, Dunn & Crutcher, says that in "about one in five cases you'll get at least the threat of a wrongful-termination lawsuit." Most cases are settled to avoid adverse publicity, Ms. Brown says.

When the disputes have gone to trial, judges have ruled both ways on whether fired workers should be reinstated or awarded damages. The legal question is whether federal law and the Equal Employment Opportunity Commission's guidelines requiring "immediate and appropriate corrective action" when an employee complains of sexual abuse take precedent over state law and employment agreements that say the employer must have cause before firing the target of the accusations.

Employers may be wiser to fire the alleged harasser and risk a wrongful-termination suit, suggests Richard T. Seymour, director of the employment discrimination project of the Lawyers Committee for Civil Rights Under Law in Washington. The alternative, he says, may be multiple suits by sexual harassment victims. Harassers may often affect more than one co-worker, and the employer would face "much larger liability for failing to take action," he notes.

No matter what a company decides to do, it can end up mired in lengthy and expensive litigation. And the outcome is uncertain even when the company strongly believes the harassment occurred. . . .

The adequacy of investigations comes up repeatedly in wrongful-discharge cases involving harassment. Mr. Seymour, of the Lawyers Committee for Civil Rights Under Law, recommends that employers faced with sexual harassment accusations interview co-workers and managers, weigh the circumstances, provide the accused with the information and give the accused an opportunity to respond.

Jay W. Waks, a management employment specialist at the New York law firm Kaye, Scholer, Fierman, Hays & Handler, advises that "in particularly sensitive cases, an employer may be well advised to bring in outside counsel to evaluate the facts, if not to actually perform the investigation."

But sometimes an investigation is not enough to keep a company safe from a wrongful-discharge case. When confronted with allegations that Curtis Ashway had harassed a co-worker, Ferrellgas Inc., a propane gas distributor based in Liberty, Mo., interviewed other workers and supervisors and weighed their credibility. The company also gave Mr. Ashway, a district manager, an opportunity to respond to a written statement of the charges.

But a federal appeals court in San Francisco last year ruled that the company's good-faith belief that Mr. Ashway was guilty wasn't enough to fire him under the relevant state law, which requires a higher standard of proof. The appeals court reversed a lower court ruling and ordered the case retried.

Marigene Dessaint, Mr. Ashway's lawyer, says the ruling was a "recognition that the accused person also has rights." Ferrellgas is asking the U.S. Supreme Court for a hearing before the case is retried.

Source: Grace M. Kang, "Laws Covering Sex Harassment and Wrongful Dismissal Collide," *Wall Street Journal*, September 24, 1992, p. B–1.

PART II: FOR FURTHER READING

Aaron, Titus, and Judith A. Isaksen. *Sexual Harassment in the Workplace: A Guide to the Law and Research Overview for Employers and Employees.* Jefferson, NC: McFarland, 1993.

Baxter, Ralph H., Jr., and Lynne C. Hermle. *Sexual Harassment in the Workplace: A Guide to the Law.* New York: Executive Enterprises, 1994.

Browne, Kingsley. "Title VII as Censorship: Hostile-Environment Harassment and the First Amendment." *Ohio State Law Journal* 52:2 (1991), 481–550.

Chan, Anja Angelica. *Women and Sexual Harassment: A Practical Guide to the Legal Protections of Title VII and the Hostile Environment Claim.* New York: Hawoth Press, 1994.

Ehrenreich, Nancy S. "Pluralist Myths and Powerless Men: The Ideology of Reasonableness in Sexual Harassment Law." *Yale Law Journal* 99:6 (April 1990), 1177–234.

Estrich, Susan. "Sex at Work." *Stanford Law Review* 43 (April 1991), 813–61.

Friedman, Joel, Marcia Mobilia Boumil, and Barbara Ewert Taylor. *Sexual Harassment.* Deerfield Beach, Fla.: Health Communications, 1992.

Gutek, Barbara A. *Sex and the Workplace: The Impact of Sexual Behavior and Harassment on Women, Men, and Organizations.* San Francisco: Jossey-Bass, 1985.

Mayer, Jane, and Jill Abramson. *Strange Justice: The Selling of Clarence Thomas.* New York: Penguin Books, 1995.

Morrison, Toni, ed. *Race-ing Justice, En-gendering Power: Essays on Anita Hill, Clarence Thomas, and the Construction of Social Reality.* New York: Pantheon Books, 1992.

Segrave, Kerry. *The Sexual Harassment of Women in the Workplace, 1600 to 1993.* Jefferson, NC: McFarland, 1994.

Smitherman, Geneva, ed. *African American Women Speak Out on Anita Hill-Clarence Thomas.* Detroit: Wayne State University Press, 1995.

Part III

Sexual Harassment in the Military

We rely on the men and women of the Armed Forces to defend our rights. It is therefore particularly troubling when members of the military engage in sexual harassment.

When a civilian who is employed by the military suffers sexual harassment in the workplace, he or she may bring a lawsuit under Title VII, just like any other federal employee. Courts have held, however, that uniformed members of the armed services have no right to bring such civil suits. Thus, such service members must turn to internal military regulations and to the Uniform Code of Military Justice for redress of sexual harassment.

As is discussed more fully below, in 1989, the Department of Defense issued regulations defining and prohibiting sexual harassment and calling upon each branch of the service to promulgate internal policies to redress the problem. Unlike Title VII, however, these internal policies do not permit victims of sexual harassment to receive money damages. Instead, they provide mechanisms by which victims can complain of sexual harassment, direct superior officers to take complaints of sexual harassment seriously, and provide for potential criminal penalties and dishonorable discharge, under the military system of justice, for those who violate the policies.

Unfortunately, despite these policies, sexual harassment has been widespread within the military. The incident that received the most attention from the public is the Tailhook scandal, in which a group of naval aviators assaulted and groped women during their annual convention in Las Vegas in 1991. Not only was the public shocked by the behavior of these servicemen, but there was a concern that, rather than immediately responding to the allegations of abuse, Naval officials seemed more intent on covering up the matter.

THE PREVALENCE OF SEXUAL HARASSMENT IN THE MILITARY

Even before the Tailhook scandal, there were reports that sexual harassment in the military was rampant. For example, in 1988, the Department of Defense commissioned a survey of active duty military personnel to determine how frequently sexual harassment occurred within the military, under what circumstances it occurred, and how effective the military's anti-harassment policies were. The survey (Document 53) found that an astonishing 64 percent of women, along with 17 percent of men, reported experiencing some form of sexual harassment during the year prior to the survey.

DOCUMENT 53: *Sexual Harassment in the Military: 1988* (Melanie Martindale, 1990)

EXECUTIVE SUMMARY

Background

Mandated in 1988 by then Secretary of Defense Frank Carlucci in response to a recommendation of the Task Force on Women in the Military, the *1988/89 DoD Surveys of Sex Roles in the Active-Duty Military* consists of two confidential mail surveys of scientifically selected samples of active-duty military personnel conducted in 1988 and 1989. Results from the much larger 1988 survey, which targeted about 38,000 personnel in the active DoD [Department of Defense] services and Coast Guard and experienced a corrected response rate of about 60 percent, are the focus of this report.

Definition of Sexual Harassment

Respondents were not asked directly and explicitly about "sexual harassment" experiences, but rather were asked about specific, behaviorally described "uninvited and unwanted sexual attention" received at work. The term "sexual harassment" was used in the survey questionnaire only when asking respondents about policies and official actions. Consistent with DoD policy, the language of this report calls reported experiences of uninvited and unwanted sexual talk and behavior, as perceived by respondents, sexual harassment.

Limitations of the Survey

Like all studies, this survey has several limitations. First, it is the first survey of sexual harassment to be conducted in the military environment, and there is little with which to compare it. Second, the data are self-report data, which are always subject to problems of memory decay and unintended reporting error. Third, the measurement of sexual harassment is problematic, generally lacking in standardized terms, and characterized by fluid definitions that vary both across and within individuals because the topic tends to be emotionally charged for many people.

Experiences of Sexual Harassment

The questionnaire asked all respondents about their experiences of sexual harassment. These data are weighted estimates which assume nonrespondents would have answered the same way as respondents. The estimates can be generalized to the active-duty military population. . . .

Level of Sexual Harassment

- The percentage of active-duty military personnel experiencing at least one form of sexual harassment at least once while at work in the year prior to the survey is estimated to be about 22 percent of respondents of all four DoD services and the Coast Guard.
  —Female personnel (64 percent) were almost four times as likely as male personnel (17 percent) to experience some form of sexual harassment.

Types of Sexual Harassment

- The two most severe forms of sexual harassment are pressure for sexual favors and actual or attempted rape or sexual assault. Fifteen percent of the female and 2 percent of the male respondents reported pressure for sexual favors. Five percent of the female and 1 percent of the male respondents reported actual or attempted rape or sexual assault.
- Although verbal types of sexual harassment occur more frequently than other forms of sexual harassment, just 4 percent of respondents (Female: 9 percent; Male: 3 percent) experienced *only* verbal forms.
- The types of sexual harassment reported in the year prior to the survey by the *majority* of all *victims* (who are 64 percent of female personnel and 17 percent of male personnel) were:
  —Sexual teasing jokes, remarks or questions (Female victims: 82 percent; Male victims: 74 percent)
  —Sexually suggestive looks, gestures or body language (Female victims: 69 percent; Male victims 58 percent)
  —Touching, leaning over, cornering, pinching or brushing against of a deliberately sexual nature (Female victims: 60 percent; Male victims: 51 percent)

- A majority of female victims (59 percent) also experienced whistles, calls, hoots or yells of a sexual nature; 27 percent of male victims experienced this.

- Female victims (88 percent) are more likely than male victims (73 percent) to report experiencing two or more of the ten forms of sexual harassment listed on the questionnaire.

- Female victims generally experienced sexual harassment more frequently than male victims, although frequency of occurrence varied by type of sexual harassment. . . .

Described Experiences of Sexual Harassment

The questionnaire asked respondents who had experienced sexual harassment while on duty during the year prior to the survey to select one experience of sexual harassment which occurred in that time period and answer questions about it. . . .

Perpetrators and Described Experiences

- Most of the described experiences involved perpetrators of the opposite gender acting alone, although almost a quarter of them involved multiple perpetrators. . . .

- Perpetrators were most likely (45 percent) to be other military co-workers.

- Other military persons were next most frequently mentioned (Female: 32 percent; Male 26 percent).

- Military superiors were more likely to be the perpetrators of women's than men's described experiences. . . .

Actions to Reduce Sexual Harassment and Attitudes of Leaders

The questionnaire asked all respondents their perceptions of and opinions about various actions taken to reduce sexual harassment and about the attitudes of military leaders toward sexual harassment. . . .

Effectiveness of Formal Complaints

- The majority of both female and male personnel believe that reporting sexual harassment to the perpetrators' chain of command or filing formal complaint are effective ways to stop sexual harassment.

- Some personnel think that formal complaints would make things worse or would not be effective (Female: 11 percent; Male: 5 percent).

Actions at Installations

- Seventy-two percent of female and 77 percent of male personnel report that policies have been established at their installations/ships to reduce sexual harassment.

- About a quarter of personnel either do not know or believe no policies have been established prohibiting sexual harassment at their duty stations.

- A majority of personnel either do not know or believe no penalties against sexual harassers have been enforced (Female: 61 percent; Male: 53 percent).

Attitudes of Leaders

- The majority of both female and male personnel believe that the senior leadership of their Services, the senior leadership of their installations/ships, and their immediate supervisors/commanding officers make reasonable, honest efforts to stop sexual harassment.

- Over 30 percent of personnel do not know about their leaders' efforts to stop sexual harassment or believe that their leaders are not making reasonable and honest efforts to stop sexual harassment.

Source: Melanie Martindale, *Sexual Harassment in the Military: 1988*, Defense Manpower Data Center, September 1990), xi–xix.

In 1995 the Department of Defense commissioned a new study on sexual harassment. This study (Document 54) concluded that incidents of sexual harassment had declined substantially, but the number of victims was still significant.

DOCUMENT 54: *Department of Defense 1995 Sexual Harassment Survey*, Executive Summary (Lisa D. Bastian, Anita R. Lancaster, and Heidi E. Reyst, 1996)

In March 1994, the Deputy Secretary of Defense asked the Secretary of the Air Force and the Under Secretary of Defense for Personnel and Readiness to develop a sexual harassment policy action plan. This plan was provided in April 1994, and included among its elements (1) the establishment of a Defense Equal Opportunity Council (DEOC) Task Force on Discrimination and Sexual Harassment to review the Military Services' discrimination complaints systems and recommend improvements, and (2) the conduct of a Department-wide sexual harassment survey. . . .

Major Findings

How do 1995 results compare to those obtained in 1988? (Form A)
Form A, the replication of the 1988 survey, was fielded for the sole purpose of comparing reports of unwanted sexual attention in 1995 and 1988. Senior DoD officials believed these indicator data would be ex-

tremely important in answering the overall question, "Have we improved?"

Based on responses to Form A, reports of sexual harassment declined significantly since 1988. In 1988, 22 percent of active-duty military personnel (64% of women and 17% of men) reported one or more incidents of unwanted, uninvited sexual attention while at work during the year prior to the survey. In 1995, 19 percent of personnel (55% of women and 14% of men) reported one or more incidents while at work in the year prior to the survey.

Were there differences, across the Services, in reporting unwanted, uninvited sexual attention?
Overall, rates declined significantly across all Services except the Coast Guard, where there was no significant change. Navy women exhibited the greatest decline in reporting, dropping 13 percentage points, from 66 percent in 1988 to 53 percent in 1995.

In 1988, a larger percentage of women in the Marine Corps than in the other Services reported one or more incidents of unwanted, uninvited sexual attention (75% of active-duty Marine women reported experiencing one or more incidents). Army and Navy women reported at about the same levels (68% and 66%, respectively), Coast Guard was 62 percent, and Air Force was lowest at 57 percent. In 1995, the percentage of women reporting one or more incidents of unwanted, uninvited sexual attention continued to be highest for the Marine Corps (64%, down 11 percentage points from 1988), but the Army rate, at 61 percent (down seven points), is now not statistically different than the Marines. The Navy's incidence rate, at 53 percent (down 13 points), is much lower and not statistically different than that of the Air Force (at 49%, down eight percentage points from 1988). In 1988, 62 percent of Coast Guard women reported experiencing one or more incidents, compared to 59 percent in 1995, not a statistically significant change.

Why was a second survey (Form B) used and what was learned from it?
Form A replicated the 1988 survey and permitted comparisons to that baseline, but the 1988 survey had limitations for use in a 1995 sexual harassment study. Form B contained new items of interest to Defense policy officials (e.g., how much training was being provided, how effective was the training, opinions of the complaint process). It also contained a considerably expanded list of behaviors that might be checked by a respondent in reporting unwanted sexual attention (e.g., sexist behavior items). To cover the spectrum of behaviors that might be construed as sexual harassment, an extensive, behaviorally-based incident

reporting list, consisting of 25 items (versus the 10 items used in 1988), was developed and used in Form B. After the data were collected, the 25 items were factor analyzed and reported in five broad categories: (1) Crude/Offensive Behavior (e.g., unwanted sexual jokes, stories, whistling, staring); (2) Sexist Behavior (e.g., insulting, offensive and condescending attitudes based on the gender of the person); (3) Unwanted Sexual Attention (e.g., unwanted touching, fondling; asking for dates even though rebuffed); (4) Sexual Coercion (e.g., classic quid pro quo instances of job benefits or losses conditioned on sexual cooperation); and (5) Sexual Assault (e.g., unsuccessful attempts at and having sex without the respondent's consent and against his or her will).

Form B more than doubled the possible categories of reporting and broadened the circumstances under which incidents that might be considered to be harassment could be reported to include off-duty hours, off-base, etc. Thus, we expected that the rates would be higher on Form B than on the Form A/1988 survey. Based on responses to the 25 items from Form B, 43 percent of active-duty military (78% of women and 38% of men) indicated they had experienced one or more of the behaviors listed in the survey during the previous 12 months.

Form B also contained many new items designed to help the Department of Defense broaden its understanding of sexual harassment and related behaviors. For example, items were included on where such behaviors were occurring and to whom. Results of new items on Form B are summarized below under "Other Findings."

Did service members consider the experiences they reported to be sexual harassment?
Many did not. Because numerous new items were included on the Form B survey, a question was added that asked respondents if they considered any of the behaviors they checked in the 25-item list "sexual harassment." Although 78 percent of women and 38 percent of men checked one or more items, only 52 percent of women and nine percent of men both checked one or more items and indicated they considered at least some of those experiences to be sexual harassment.

Did service members think sexual harassment in the military had declined?
Yes, nearly three-quarters of military members with six to 10 years of service indicated harassment was occurring less often than a few years ago. Fewer women than men expressed this opinion (60% vs. 76%). Women in the Navy and Coast Guard (71% and 70%) were more likely than women in the other Services to report sexual harassment had declined. . . .

Summary of Major Findings

Based on the data collected in this study, there is evidence that sexual harassment is declining significantly in the active-duty Military Services. Between 1988 and 1995, the percentage of women reporting incidents of sexual harassment declined nine percentage points, and the percentage of men reporting incidents declined three percentage points. On the other hand, sexual harassment remains a major challenge that all the Services must continue to combat.

Other Findings

Who reported they had experienced uninvited, unwanted sex/gender-related behaviors?

Clearly, as noted earlier, women reported at considerably higher rates than men. In addition, for active-duty military, junior enlisted personnel (E1-E4) were more likely to report they had experienced behaviors than were senior enlisted (E5-E9) or officers. Among junior enlisted, 49 percent reported experiencing one or more such instances compared to 40 percent of senior enlisted and 39 percent of officers. For women, 83 percent of junior enlisted reported experiencing uninvited and unwanted gender-related behaviors, compared to 74 percent for senior enlisted and 75 percent for officers.

The analysis of Form B indicated that black men reported incidents at slightly higher rates than white men (43% vs. 36%). The overall rates for black and white women were not significantly different (76% vs. 78%).

Who were the offenders?

The most frequently cited sources of unwanted sex/gender-related behaviors, by both women and men, were military co-workers (44% of women and 52% of men), other military personnel of higher rank/grade (43% of women and 21% of men), and other military persons (24% of women and 22% of men). Active-duty women and men were far less likely to mention civilians. For example, only six percent of women and seven percent of men reported civilian co-workers had bothered them.

Where and when did the uninvited, unwanted sex/gender-related behaviors occur?

These behaviors primarily occurred on military installations, at work, and during duty hours. For example, 88 percent of women and 76 percent of men reported that in the situation that had the greatest effect on them, all or most of the uninvited, unwanted sex/gender-related behaviors occurred on a military installation.

In terms of when the reported experiences occurred, 74 percent of women and 68 percent of men reported that all or most of the experiences occurred while at work. In addition, 77 percent of women and 68 percent of men reported that all or most of the experiences occurred during duty hours. Only five percent of women reported none occurred on an installation, 14 percent said none occurred at work, and nine percent said none occurred during duty hours.

Did service members report their experiences and, if so, to whom?
Approximately 24 percent of those who indicated experiencing an incident said they reported the incident (40% of women and 17% of men). Members experiencing these behaviors most often reported the incidents to their immediate supervisor (26% of women and 11% of men), someone else in the chain of command (21% of women and 8% of men), and the supervisor of the person bothering them (18% of women and 8% of men).

What actions did organizations take in response to members' reports?
Fifty percent of women and 22 percent of men reported that the person who bothered them was talked to about the behavior and 20 percent of women and 10 percent of men reported that the person who bothered them was counseled. Fourteen percent of women and four percent of men indicated their complaint was being investigated. However, 39 percent of men and 15 percent of women indicated no action was taken and 23 percent of women and 16 percent of men said their complaint was discounted or not taken seriously. About 10 percent of those who reported their experiences said they did not know what action was taken.

If service members did not report their experiences, why not?
Where members indicated they did not report an incident, women most commonly gave as a reason for not reporting that they took care of the problem themselves (54%). Men, more frequently than women, said that they did not think the matter was important (51% of men and 35% of women). Twenty percent of women and 10 percent of men said they did not think anything would be done. In terms of negative consequences, 25 percent of women and 13 percent of men indicated they did not report because it would make their work situations unpleasant. Seventeen percent of women and eight percent of men thought they would be labeled troublemakers. Thirteen percent of women and 10 percent of men did not want to hurt the person who bothered them.

Did service members experience reprisal?
Some did. In the section of the survey where members who had experienced unwanted behaviors were describing the one situation that had the greatest effect on them, they were asked if they had experienced "a performance rating that was unfairly lowered." Twenty percent of women and nine percent of men who had experienced such behaviors indicated this had occurred to a small, moderate, or large extent.

All respondents on the survey were asked if they felt "free to report sexual harassment without fear of bad things happening" to them. Eighty percent of women and 86 percent of men said that was true to a small, moderate, or large extent.

To what extent were members who said they reported the behaviors to someone satisfied with the complaint process?
Of those who said they reported their experiences, 35 percent of women and 33 percent of men were dissatisfied with the complaint process overall. About a third were neither satisfied nor dissatisfied and a third were satisfied.

Had service members received training and, if so, what was their opinion of the effectiveness of the training?
Seventy-nine percent of women and 85 percent of men reported receiving sexual harassment training. In terms of how much training had occurred in the last 12 months, 26 percent of women and 34 percent of men reported receiving more than 4 hours of training. Forty percent of women and 42 percent of men reported receiving one to four hours of training. In addition, 98 percent of women and men reported they knew what kinds of words or actions are considered sexual harassment. When asked how effective the training was in reducing or preventing sexual harassment, 54 percent of women and 65 percent of men said "moderately to very effective," 33 percent of women and 27 of men said "slightly," and 12 percent of women and eight percent of men said "not effective." . . .

What did active-duty service members think of their leadership's efforts to make honest and reasonable efforts to stop sexual harassment?
When asked their opinion about whether leadership at different levels made honest and reasonable efforts to stop sexual harassment, 53 percent of women and 67 percent of men answered "yes" for senior leadership of their Service, 52 percent of women and 67 percent of men answered "yes" for the senior leadership of their installation/ship, and 59 percent of women and 68 percent of men answered "yes" for their immediate supervisor. Ten percent of women and five percent of men said that senior leadership was not making honest and reasonable efforts to stop sexual harassment while about a third said they did not know.

Summary

These survey results are encouraging. They document a decline in harassment experiences and reflect DoD and the Services' increased emphasis on combating sexual harassment. At the same time the surveys were being developed and fielded, other significant DEOC-related initiatives were implemented. It should be noted the timing of this study precluded measuring the effects of those initiatives. No doubt, the additional initiatives of the DEOC Task Force on Discrimination and Sexual Harassment will advance the ability of the Department of Defense to combat sexual harassment.

Source: Lisa D. Bastian, Anita R. Lancaster, and Heidi E. Reyst, *Department of Defense 1995 Sexual Harassment Survey*, DMDC Report No. 96–014 Executive Summary, December 1996 (available on the Internet at www.dcticas.dtic.mil/prhome).

THE TAILHOOK SCANDAL

The Tailhook Association is a private organization composed of active and retired members of the U.S. Navy and U.S. Marine Corps. It received some financial support from the Navy. For many years, many of those who attended its annual convention drank excessively and engaged in destructive behavior.

Things came to a head during the 1991 convention, which was held in September in Las Vegas, Nevada. Reports began to trickle out of misconduct by some who attended the convention. The most serious allegations involved the existence of "the gauntlet," a group of male aviators who, stationed in a hallway in the Las Vegas Hilton, grabbed women who passed by on their breasts and buttocks and sometimes partially undressed them. Some of these women were service members; others were civilians who had no connection with the Navy. Although one of the victims, Lieutenant Paula Coughlin, complained to her superior officer, he did not authorize an investigation, and no disciplinary actions were taken against those involved.

Several weeks after the convention, the media found out and began to publicize the activities. In October 1991, Senator John McCain of Arizona, himself a former naval aviator, alerted his colleagues in Congress to the scandal in a speech on the floor of the U.S. Senate.

DOCUMENT 55: Remarks of Senator John McCain regarding the Tailhook Association, Senate Proceedings and Debates of the 102d Congress, 1st Session (1991)

THE TAILHOOK ASSOCIATION

Mr. MCCAIN. Mr. President, I take the floor at this moment very disturbed about an incident that has been reported now in the media to have taken place in Las Vegas sometime around September 15, at the so-called Tailhook reunion, a reunion which is led by naval aviators and their supporters. It is a tradition in the Navy. Although it is a private organization, attendance at this gathering is encouraged by the Department of Defense and by naval authorities, both civilian and military, to the point where, Mr. President, flights to this convention, which has now been held for some 35 years, are taken in military aircraft.

Mr. President, in the last couple of days—remember that this convention took place well over a month ago—information has surfaced of some very despicable behavior taking place as far as sexual harassment is concerned at this convention. I refer to a copy of a letter from the president of the Tailhook Association, who is an active duty naval aviator. . . .

He sent this letter, and in it he talks about events that took place at this convention. He says:

This year our total damage bill was to the tune of $23,000.00. Of that figure, $18,000 was to install new carpeting as a result of cigarette burns and drink stains. We narrowly avoided a disaster when a "pressed ham"[*] pushed out an eighth-floor window which subsequently fell on the crowd below. Finally, and definitely the most serious, was "the Gauntlet" on the third floor. I have five separate reports of young ladies, several of whom had nothing to do with Tailhook, who were verbally abused, had drinks thrown on them, were physically abused and were sexually molested. Most distressing was the fact an underage young lady was severely intoxicated and had her clothing removed by members of the Gauntlet.

Mr. President, I cannot tell you the distaste and displeasure that I have as a naval aviator taking the floor concerning this incident. Additionally, there is report of a Navy lieutenant aide who was at this gathering who was also physically abused.

I believe in attendance of this meeting—I am sure not at the exact location—were senior ranking naval officers and civilian personnel.

Mr. President, I have contacted the Secretary of the Navy demanding a full and immediate convening of a high-ranking panel of civilian and military members in order to investigate this incident. I hesitate to even use the word allegation because there are several reports corroborating this. I have also talked to the Secretary of Defense. We must address these incidents.

The Navy's official or unofficial participation in the so-called Tailhook reunion must be suspended until such time as this is thoroughly investigated and appropriate action taken for those who are responsible.

Mr. President, there is no time in the history of this country that something like this is more inappropriate, and we cannot allow it. It is unconscionable. And we in the military, who pride ourselves on the equal opportunity that is extended to everyone in the military, should be ashamed and embarrassed—ashamed and embarrassed that this kind of activity went on. And there is no excuse for it.

The first question that I have of the Secretary of the Navy is, if this has been known now for over a month, why has action not been initiated until such time as this became known in the media?

As I said at the beginning of my remarks, it is with great displeasure that I take the floor on this issue. But the American people, the taxpayers and, very important, the women of America who serve in the military, or who are contemplating service in the military, deserve a prompt investigation and a thorough one; and those who are responsible for these incidents be given the appropriate punishment.

*[According to the Navy Inspector General's report, a " 'pressed ham' is naked buttocks pressed against a window pane." Office of Inspector General, Department of Defense, *Tailhook 91*, Part 1: "Review of the Navy Investigations" (September 1992)].

Source: Congressional Record, 102d Cong., 1st sess., October 29, 1991, 137, S15334–01.

In June 1992 the Secretary of the Navy, H. Lawrence Garrett III, requested that the Inspector General of the Department of Defense investigate both the incidents at the convention and the way in which senior officers had responded to the reports of misconduct. The Inspector General's office issued a scathing two-part report documenting serious misconduct both by those attending the convention and by senior military personnel who sought to cover up the activities, rather than to punish those involved. The second report noted that the Inspector General had referred numerous participants to the Navy for possible discipline based on their misconduct at the convention. In the end, however, no one was ever court-martialed based on activity at Tailhook, although about fifty Navy and Marine officers did receive administrative discipline, a lesser form of punishment.

DOCUMENT 56: *Tailhook 91*, Part 2: "Events at the 35th Annual Tailhook Symposium" (Office of Inspector General, Department of Defense, 1993)

SECTION I
EXECUTIVE SUMMARY

This report covers Part 2 of our inquiry into events relating to the 35th Annual Symposium of the Tailhook Association (Tailhook 91) held at the

Las Vegas Hilton Hotel from Thursday, September 5 to Sunday, September 8, 1991. The inquiry was initiated in response to a request from the Secretary of the Navy on June 18, 1992.

This report is primarily focused on the events at Tailhook 91; Part 1, issued on September 21, 1992, detailed our review of the Navy investigations of Tailhook 91 and related matters. Part 1 of the report concluded that the scope of the Navy's earlier investigations should have been expanded beyond the indecent assaults to encompass other violations of law and regulation as they became apparent and should have addressed individual accountability for the leadership failure that created an atmosphere in which the assaults and other misconduct took place. In that regard, the first part of our report examined the actions and inactions of Navy leadership responsible for the Navy's investigations of Tailhook 91.

In conducting the second part of our inquiry, we interviewed over 2,900 people who attended Tailhook 91 and obtained documents and other evidence relating to crimes and misconduct by naval aviators at Tailhook 91. . . .

Many attendees viewed the annual conference as a type of "free fire zone" wherein they could act indiscriminately and without fear of censure or retribution in matters of sexual conduct and drunkenness. Some of the Navy's most senior officers were knowledgeable as to the excesses practiced at Tailhook 91 and, by their inaction, those officers served to condone and even encourage the type of behavior that occurred there.

Our investigation disclosed that 83 women and 7 men were assaulted during the three days of the convention. Virtually all the assaults took place in the third floor area (including the adjoining patio which continued to be open to the public during the convention) of the Las Vegas Hilton Hotel where the squadron hospitality suites were located.

Through the use of detailed interviews and other investigative techniques, 23 officers were determined to warrant referral to the Navy for having participated in indecent assaults, and an additional 23 in indecent exposure. In total, 117 officers were implicated in one or more incidents of indecent assault, indecent exposure, conduct unbecoming an officer or failure to act in a proper leadership capacity while at Tailhook 91. Further, 51 individuals were found to have made false statements to us during our investigation. Evidence concerning all such matters has been referred to the Navy and/or the Department of Justice for appropriate action. . . . It should also be noted that the number of individuals involved in all types of misconduct or other inappropriate behavior was more widespread than these figures would suggest. Furthermore, several hundred other officers were aware of the misconduct and chose to ignore it. . . .

SECTION IV
WITNESS AND NAVY COOPERATION

We found the Secretary of the Navy, the Chief of Naval Operations and the Commandant of the Marine Corps were fully supportive of our efforts and went to all necessary lengths to ensure that our logistical and scheduling needs were met. The Navy also assisted in identifying Tailhook attendees and adjusting flight and training schedules where necessary to make officers available for interview. . . .

In contrast to the organizational cooperation described above, we found a wide variance in the level of cooperation shown by aviation officers. Most of the officers interviewed responded in a serious and cooperative fashion. Other officers were far less cooperative and attempted to limit their responses so as to reveal only minimal information. Many officers refused to offer information pertinent to the investigation unless asked very specific questions. For example, a common tactic taken by many officers in response to general questioning was to answer that they simply had no knowledge of the subject. However, we experienced a number of situations in which facts disclosed later in the investigation suggested that many of the same individuals did indeed have pertinent knowledge or information. A typical response to questions posed in follow-up interviews was that the investigator had not asked the "right" question. It is our belief that several hundred of the 2,384 naval officers we interviewed responded in that fashion.

The evidence revealed that other officers deliberately provided false information to us. Some squadron members appeared to maintain unified responses that were often contradicted by the testimony of witnesses not assigned to those squadrons. Similarly, individual officers specifically lied to us about their activities unless directly confronted with conflicting evidence. In one instance, a Navy lieutenant repeatedly denied that he indecently exposed himself. After he was shown a photograph clearly depicting him publicly exposing himself at Tailhook 91, the officer told us he had lied because he did not know that we had a picture and his career was worth the risk of being caught in a lie. . . .

In many instances, we were able to overcome attempts to mislead our investigators. In many others, however, we were not. . . .

Our investigators encountered repeated and deliberate attempts to obstruct their efforts. For instance, some witnesses who had been identified as having taken photographs at Tailhook 91 told us that they had misplaced or destroyed all such photographs. However, when these individuals were presented with a DoD IG subpoena, in most cases these "lost" photographs were produced. One Marine Corps aviator's commanding officer (CO) informed us that, after the aviator was interviewed, he overheard the officer telephone other aviators and tell them what they should and should not say to investigators relating to improper activity engaged in at Tailhook 91. A few officers reported the existence of a "Lieutenants' Protective Association (LPA)" and a "Junior Officers' Protective Association (JOPA)." The LPA and JOPA were described as being an allegiance among officers. One officer told us that, according to LPA and JOPA "rules," a junior officer will not "give up" another junior officer just because he has done "something stupid." ...

SECTION VI
INDECENT ASSAULTS

A. Gauntlet

Our investigation disclosed that the word "gauntlet," as applied in the context of Tailhook 91, was variously interpreted by the many people we interviewed. Some officers strongly disputed or denied even the existence of a gauntlet. One Navy lieutenant, for example, told us he thought the gauntlet was a "figment of someone's imagination" and he could not believe that a hundred guys would just stand around and allow someone to be assaulted. Other officers said they believed the gauntlet and Tailhook-related problems were created by the media. One Navy lieutenant simply asserted that "there is no such thing as the gauntlet." Another officer, a longstanding member of the Tailhook Association who attended numerous Tailhook conventions, said the gauntlet, as described in media reports as an organized effort by naval officers to grope females, "unequivocally does not exist."

Others told us the gauntlet existed, but did not involve assaultive behavior. Those witnesses defined the gauntlet as a very crowded hallway where people were drinking and socializing and where it was difficult to move without having drinks spilled on oneself. Yet others reported that the gauntlet consisted of "drunk" and "obnoxious" junior officers who pushed and shoved each other and anyone else in the hallway. Some described the gauntlet as a bunch of drunken male aviators who yelled catcalls, insults and suggestive remarks to women as they passed through the hallway. Many people told us they understood the gauntlet to be a Tailhook tradition in which women willingly walked through columns of drunken aviators and were fondled, grabbed, groped, pinched or otherwise consensually touched.

Numerous others told us the gauntlet involved uninvited, assaultive behavior against unsuspecting women entering the third floor hallway. Many of the witnesses and victims said they were alarmed and disturbed by the severity of the indecent assaults they either witnessed or had been subjected to at Tailhook 91. Finally, a substantial number of people we interviewed said that, although they had never heard the word gauntlet used in the context of the Tailhook conventions, they had observed assaultive behavior in the third floor hallway at Tailhook 91 and earlier Tailhook conventions.

Our investigation confirmed that the gauntlet did indeed exist and at one time or another involved all of the behaviors described above. Based on the reports and descriptions we received, we found that the "gauntlet" evolved over the years from somewhat innocuous nonassaultive behavior to the assaultive acts that occurred in recent years. The gauntlet existed in some form for many years and was well known within the naval aviation community.

Literally hundreds of witnesses reported they either witnessed or were aware of behavior at past Tailhook conventions consistent with the descriptions of the gauntlet at Tailhook 91. Some of those people specifically referred to the gauntlet by name, while others simply described unruly behavior in the hallway. . . .

Regardless of when the term gauntlet was first applied to behavior at Tailhook, it is clear from the many interviews that the nature of the hallway activity changed over the years. Descriptions of early Tailhook conventions included aviators drinking and singing, standing against the wall and "cheering" as women walked through the most crowded parts of the hallway. There were also accounts that as women walked through the hallway, officers would call out ratings as to the women's attractiveness. Witnesses said that type of activity later changed to "horse-play" with aviators pushing, shoving and throwing beer on one another. . . .

The nature of the gauntlet activities apparently changed some time in the mid to late 1980's when the gauntlet started to involve males touching women who walked through the hallway. Some witnesses suggested this was a progression from the cheering, catcalls and ratings of women typical of earlier Tailhook conventions, to more physical contact in which officers would pinch and grab women's breasts, buttocks and crotch areas as the women attempted to traverse the hallway. The descriptions suggested that, initially, touching was consensual and that the women involved were aware and tolerant of the consequences of walking through a hallway lined with drunken male aviators. Some accounts of prior Tailhook conventions described the women touching and grabbing the men in response to the men's actions. Descriptions of the gauntlet in the mid to late 1980's also included reports of women being passed overhead down the hallway, similar to a type of activity seen at some high school or college football games. . . .

Our investigation disclosed that gauntlet-related indecent assaults dated back to at least Tailhook 88. Ten women reported to us that they were assaulted when they attended Tailhook conventions between 1988 and 1990. The women reported they had been grabbed on the breasts, buttocks and/or crotch area. None of the women are known to have reported their assaults to authorities until after Tailhook 91. A number of male aviators also reported that they witnessed assaults on women at Tailhook conventions in the late 1980's.

During that time period, gauntlet participants were first observed acting in an organized fashion and using schemes apparently designed to lure women into the gauntlet. Witnesses told us that, as women approached the gauntlet, officers in the hallway pretended to be merely socializing in small groups. The witnesses described how the men would quiet down and create an opening in the crowd that unsuspecting women might think to use as a passageway. Witnesses went on to describe how women who entered the crowded portion of the hallway would then be suddenly surrounded by the gauntlet participants who groped them and prevented their exit.

Perhaps the best description of the gauntlet is contained in the testimony of a Navy commander:

Q. During your interview on October 3, 1992, you discussed incidents which occurred on the third floor of the Hilton Hotel late Saturday evening, September 7, after the hours of 2200 [10:00 p.m.].

Could you explain what you witnessed? You had related an incident, I believe, regarding a woman who had passed through The Gauntlet, and if you could just briefly explain the Gauntlet.

A. Okay. My definition of The Gauntlet—it is a term that I've heard used at Tailhook or around Tailhook for several years. And I believe it comes from an old Clint Eastwood movie of the same name, about a street or an avenue that starts wide and narrows into a funnel area that's hard to get through. I think that's where the term "The Gauntlet" originated in regards to Tailhook.

And The Gauntlet would be pretty much in progress on late Friday or late Saturday nights, and it would consist of again, my estimate, two to three hundred young people—young men. And that's just my estimate. I can tell you the hallway—probably as long as maybe 30 yards or so—is absolutely packed with bodies. And I would say the majority of them are between 21-to-26-year-old young men, mostly on the lower, probably the 21-to-24-year-olds and mostly, in my judgment, just by the attendance at Tailhook, mostly, young Naval officers, but also Marine officers and some Air Force guys; and I did see some people there in '91 that, by their dress and their hair, were not in the military at all. They were civilians that came from the local areas to attend the party.

The group mainly stands out there and drinks and chants and sings songs. And, on the occasion when a female would pass through the area, they would chant or, as it occurred on the late Saturday night, they would grab a girl's butt or breasts, apparently, as she went through.

That's, I guess, the best way I can describe The Gauntlet.

The third floor east wing hallway of the Las Vegas Hilton Hotel is approximately 6 feet wide, dimly lighted, and somewhat wider in the area of the guest elevators and service area. It narrows as it extends eastward into the suite corridor. By all accounts, the third floor hallway was extremely crowded on Friday and Saturday evenings. Witnesses described the hallway as nearly impassable at times because of the large number of people standing, loitering or attempting to walk through the hallway.

The hallway curves from the area of the main guest elevators to that straight section where gauntlet activity took place. Witnesses said that the curvature of the hallway, combined with the crowded conditions, made it very easy for someone to walk well into the third floor hallway before realizing that anything unusual was taking place. . . .

The gauntlet operated intermittently, but most of the activity reportedly occurred between the hours of 9:00 p.m. and midnight on Friday and Saturday nights. Just as gauntlet activity escalated over the years, so too did the intensity and frequency of hallway assaults increase over the three nights of Tailhook 91.

Our investigation revealed that many women freely and knowingly participated in gauntlet activities. A significant number of witnesses reported that women went through the gauntlet and seemed to enjoy the attention and interaction with the aviators. Those witnesses, both men and women, generally stated they could tell the women were enjoying themselves because, despite being grabbed and pushed along through the crowd, they were smiling and giggling. Some of the women were observed going repeatedly through the gauntlet. Many women who went through the gauntlet told us they did so willingly and were not offended by the men touching them. A civilian woman employed by the Navy told us of a conversation she had with another young woman whom she met while on a commercial flight into Las Vegas to attend Tailhook 91. The young woman described the gauntlet and said that, at about 3:00 a.m., things get "real rough" and wild on the third floor. According to the Navy employee, the young woman implied that she enjoyed this type of activity and that was the reason she was going to Tailhook 91.

Our investigation also revealed a much more sinister aspect to the gauntlet at Tailhook 91 which involved assaults on unsuspecting women. Of those assaults which occurred in the hallway, 5 took place on Thursday, 11 on Friday, and 53 on Saturday. Individual witness descriptions best portrayed the assaults and related activities. The following are but a few of the many eyewitness accounts reported during the investigation.

A female Navy lieutenant described the spontaneous formation of the gauntlet. She said that squadron mates told her about the gauntlet prior to attending Tailhook and warned her "don't be on the third floor after 11:00 p.m." Even though she was never told of the assaultive aspects of the gauntlet, she realized that something happened to women who walked through the gauntlet. She explained that in a matter of 30 minutes on Saturday night the hallway underwent a major transformation. At 10:00 p.m., it was a quiet place with 20 people. By 10:30 p.m., it had become an absolute mob scene. It was apparent to her that the gauntlet she had heard about was starting up, and she opined that people appeared to be exiting the suites into the hallway at a preplanned time for the gauntlet. . . .

A male Marine Corps first lieutenant said that on Friday night he saw about a dozen women walk through the gauntlet, and approximately half of those appeared to be happy and enjoying themselves. The other half appeared displeased and at least one appeared seriously distressed. A crowd of about 200 males bunched together in the hall pounding the wall and shouting "gauntlet, gauntlet." Periodically, males shouted "mill about" at which time the people in the gauntlet would begin feigning "milling about" and the general noise level would lower. When a female entered the gauntlet, the participants would surround her and touch, pat and grab her while she was funneled down the hall. He heard shouts of "shut the doors," which he deduced was intended to prevent women from escaping to the suites and to channel them through the length of the gauntlet. He said the general noise level increased substantially when an attractive female entered the gauntlet. He also heard shouts of "wave off," which he believed was a code indicating an older or "unattractive" female was entering the gauntlet. The participants did not touch women rated as "wave off." . . .

There were numerous accounts of how women were lured into the gauntlet. For example, some witnesses heard men in the gauntlet yell out that they needed more women, and men would then go down to the casino area to recruit them. . . .

Many eyewitness accounts described women who had articles of clothing ripped or removed as they went through the gauntlet. One particularly disturbing incident involved an intoxicated college freshman who was stripped from the waist down as she was passed overhead through the gauntlet and then left on the hallway floor. Although she had not attained legal drinking age in Nevada, she was served a considerable amount of alcohol by the officers in the HS-1 hospitality suite. After becoming intoxicated, she was placed by those officers in the hallway in the vicinity of the gauntlet. Once in the hallway, she was lifted above the crowd of men and passed hand-over-hand down the hallway. As she was passed over the crowd, the men removed her slacks and underpants. At the end of the gauntlet, they dumped her on the floor, and cleared out of the hallway as hotel security officers came to the victim's assistance. . . .

The Executive Director of the Tailhook Association told us that he learned of this incident shortly after it occurred. When questioned about how he viewed the matter, he responded:

I looked at it as a spontaneous incident, more along the line of a prank, not a prank in good taste, but I . . . that's my view of the situation at the time.

During the investigation, we obtained a photograph taken just after this incident occurred. It shows the victim, nude from the waist down, being escorted by security officials through the hallway as a group of aviators looks on. The hallway is littered with plastic drinking cups and the victim's pants. We chose not to publish the photograph out of consideration for the victim. However, we note that during several interviews we conducted in which the officer being interviewed expressed his belief that the events at Tailhook 91 were "no big deal," showing the officer a copy of the photograph had a dramatic effect. Several of the officers who viewed the photograph were visibly shaken.

The gauntlet was also vividly described to us by several victims. One female civilian victim, who was in Las Vegas on vacation with a female friend, told us she was walking through the third floor hallway with her friend when a group of men in the hallway began chanting and yelling. The men reached out and began to grab at her breasts, buttocks and crotch. They tried to lift her skirt and grabbed at her legs and buttocks while she desperately tried to hold down her skirt. As she looked back she saw that her friend was also being assaulted. The men also threw drinks on the victim, soaking her clothing with alcohol.

Another female civilian victim told us that, as she walked up the hallway, at least seven men suddenly attacked her. They pulled down her "tube top" and grabbed at her exposed breasts while she attempted to cover herself with her arms. She fell to the ground and the assault continued. She bit several of her attackers in an attempt to stop their assault. After a few moments, they stopped their attack and she was allowed to get up from the floor. She turned and looked back down the hallway and observed another woman screaming and fighting her way down the hallway as she too was attacked. The victim was crying profusely when she was approached by a Marine Corps aviator whom she had met earlier. He told her that it is an annual tradition at Tailhook conventions to harass women physically and verbally in the hallway and she should not worry about it. The victim later told her boyfriend, a Navy officer, about the attack but he advised her not to tell anyone about it because they would think she was a "slut."

In another incident, a 24-year-old female Navy officer told us that she entered the third floor hallway and was immediately surrounded by five or six men who groped and grabbed at her breasts and buttocks. While she struggled to escape, she saw two male Navy officers she recognized standing in the hallway close to where she was being attacked. Although she believed the men witnessed her attack and failed to help her, both men denied having seen or heard anything unusual. The victim saw one of the Navy officers several months after Tailhook 91. He told the victim that men have been treating women like that "since caveman days," and that she had no business being there (Tailhook 91) in the first place because she was not an aviator.

One victim, a 32-year-old female, reported that she attended Tailhook 91 with her spouse, a Navy officer; her mother; and two of her mother's female friends. As the group walked through the hallway the victim, who was wearing a formal cocktail dress, was suddenly grabbed around the waist and lifted above the crowd by two men. The men lifted the skirt of her dress above her waist and pushed their hands between her legs in an attempt to get their fingers inside her panties. Our investigation revealed that the victim's mother as well as one of her mother's friends were also indecently assaulted as they walked through the hallway.

LT Paula Coughlin, the Navy officer who first publicly revealed allegations of impropriety at Tailhook 91, told us that she entered the third floor hallway of the Hilton Hotel and, as she walked up the hallway and into a crowd of men, someone began to yell "Admiral's Aide!" She was grabbed on the buttocks from behind with such force that she was lifted up off the ground. As she turned to confront the man, another man behind her grabbed her buttocks and she was pushed from behind into a crowd of men who collectively began pinching her body and pulling at her clothing. One man put both his hands down the front of her tank top, inside her brassiere and grabbed her breasts. LT Coughlin told us that she crouched down and bit the man on his forearm and on his right hand. As the man released his grip on her breasts, another man reached up under her skirt and grabbed her panties. She then kicked out at her attackers. She stated "I felt as though the group was trying to rape me." LT Coughlin told us that she saw one of the men in the group turn to walk away so she "reached out and tapped him on the hip, pleading with the man to just let me get in front of him." The man turned around to face her, raised both his hands, and placed them on her breasts. . . .

Our investigation disclosed that, despite statements by many senior officers to the contrary, the fact that the gauntlet was in operation was well known. As previously mentioned, a large number of officers said they had witnessed or heard of the gauntlet at prior Tailhook conventions. Many others, particularly female officers, said they had been forewarned to avoid the third floor hallway at certain times. Even many civilians who were in attendance at Tailhook 91 said they were aware of the gauntlet. Several witnesses described seeing similar gauntlet activity at settings other than Tailhook, such as at officers' clubs. A number of officers said they felt confident the gauntlet was common knowledge among military attendees at Tailhook. Several officers stated that anyone who spent time in the area of the third floor hallway on Friday or Saturday night and said they were unaware of the gauntlet activity "must be lying." . . .

Of the many officers and civilian Tailhook attendees who admitted witnessing the gauntlet, only a few witnesses stated they were able to identify anyone else who was in the hallway at the time they witnessed the gauntlet in operation. In light of statements by most aviators that one of the primary reasons for attending Tailhook was to socialize with friends and former squadron mates, we found the inability of witnesses to identify gauntlet observers or participants to be incredible. The statements were also questionable in light of the fact that many of those same officers could identify persons in their company at other times during Tailhook 91.

When one Navy commander was queried as to the likelihood of an aviator being in the third floor hallway without seeing anybody whom that person knew, the commander responded: "You couldn't have done that, I don't think . . . well, maybe in the morning and the afternoon but, you know, in the evenings, I don't think you could have done that." When asked, hypothetically, about witnesses who stated that they were in the hallway and did not see anybody that they knew, this witness stated: "I would say that the person would be lying, and I don't see how he could do that. I was an ensign the first time that I went there, and I knew people, even inside the air wing, okay? You would almost have to know somebody there. So I'm sure there's an isolated case, but I don't think so. . . ."

B. Victims

From Thursday, September 5, 1991[,] through the early morning hours of Sunday, September 8, 1991, at least 90 people were victims of some form of indecent assault while at Tailhook 91. Of that number, 83 were women and 7 were men. Our investigation also disclosed information pertaining to 10 women who told us they were assaulted at previous Tailhook conventions. This report focuses on the Tailhook 91 assault victims. . . .

The assault victims range from 18 to 48 years of age. Eight victims were assaulted more than once. Of those, four victims were assaulted on more than one evening and four were each assaulted at two different locations on the same night.

Victims

Govt. Empl. (Female) (6)

USN (Male) (5)

USN (Female) (21)

USMC (Male) (2)

USAF (Female) (1)

Military Spouse (Female) (6)

Civilian Other (Female) (49)

Total Victims: 90

* * *

Eleven assaults, involving 10 women, took place on Thursday evening. Five took place in the hallway, five in administrative suites, and one on the pool patio.

Eighteen assaults occurred on Friday night. Eleven took place in the hallway, five in administrative suites, and two on the pool patio.

The greatest number of assaults occurred on Saturday evening, when there were a total of 68 assaults involving 63 victims. Fifty-three of those assaults took place in the third floor hallway, eight in suites, six on the pool patio and one victim was assaulted in one of the guest rooms on another floor. Of the assaults that took place in the third floor hallway on Saturday night, 36 took place between 9:00 pm. and 12:00 midnight. . . .

. . . The assaults varied from victims being grabbed on the buttocks, to victims being groped, pinched and fondled on their breasts, buttocks and genitals. Some victims were bitten by their assailants, others were knocked to the ground and some had their clothing ripped or removed. Some of the victims confronted their attackers and felt they had handled the situation to their own satisfaction.

Few victims were able to identify positively their assailants. Typically, they attributed their inability to identify their attackers to several factors, including poor lighting in the hallway, the confusion resulting from the crowded conditions and their shock at being assaulted. The victims also said most of the men in the hallway looked alike in that they were young, physically fit, Caucasian males with short military style haircuts and typically dressed in T-shirts and shorts.

. . . Of the victims, nine did not consider themselves to be a "victim" even though they had been subjected to indecent assault. . . .

SECTION X
OFFICER ATTITUDES AND LEADERSHIP ISSUES

A. Officer Attitudes

A discussion of the attitudes of the officers in attendance is central to an understanding of the misconduct at Tailhook 91. Until this point, we have focused on "what" happened with little discussion or commentary as to "why" events at the convention degenerated to a point where indecent assaults, indecent exposure and excessive alcohol consumption became commonplace.

Navy and Marine Corps aviation officers are well educated, physically fit, technically proficient and well trained. Many are Naval Academy graduates or alumni of other top colleges and universities and certainly have the education and background to recognize societal issues such as sexual harassment. Yet some of these individuals acted with disregard toward individual rights and failed by a wide margin to conduct themselves as officers and gentlemen in the Armed Forces of the United States.

Although there were approximately 4,000 naval officers at Tailhook 91, and significant evidence of serious misconduct involving 117 officers has been developed, the number of individuals involved in all types of misconduct or other inappropriate behavior was more widespread than these figures would suggest. Furthermore, several hundred other officers were aware of the misconduct and chose to ignore it. We believe that many of these officers deliberately lied or sought to mislead our investigators in an effort to protect themselves or their fellow officers. On the other hand, there were hundreds of other officers who, when questioned, gave full and truthful accounts of their actions and observations while at Tailhook 91. Similarly, there were several hundred officers who spent their time at Tailhook 91 attending symposium events, visiting tourist sites and otherwise occupying themselves in places other than the third floor. Unfortunately, the reputations of those officers, who are guilty of no wrongdoing, have been tarnished by the actions of their fellow officers.

Officers who engaged in misconduct gave a variety of reasons for their behavior at Tailhook 91. Perhaps the most common rationale was that such behavior was "expected" of junior officers and that Tailhook was comprised of "traditions" built on various lore. Another reason given by many attendees was that their behavior was somehow justified or at least excusable, because they were "returning heroes," from Desert Storm. Many attendees, especially younger officers, viewed Tailhook as a means of celebrating the United States' victory over Iraqi forces. Numerous officers expressed their belief that Tailhook was a type of "free fire zone" where they could celebrate without regard to rank or ordinary decorum. As one Navy officer opined, "It was condoned early in some of the senior officers' careers. It was probably condoned back when Tailhook started. . . . And I imagine one time when this first—the thing started, they were the elite, they thought they could [do] anything they wanted in Naval aviation and not have to answer the questions we're answering today about it."

Many officers told us they believed they could act free of normal constraints because Tailhook was an accepted part of a culture in some ways separate from the main stream of the Armed Forces. They stated that the career progression for naval aviators is such that most do not bear the leadership responsibilities of commanding a unit until they approach the 10-year point in their careers. (Aviation officers do not follow the career progression of command of increasingly larger units from the outset of their Military Service. Unlike Army ground units, where the newest second lieutenant is trained to be a unit leader, aviators for the most part are viewed as unit members for the initial portion of their careers.)

Some senior officers blamed the younger officers for rowdy behavior and cited a "Top Gun" mentality. They expressed their belief that many young officers had been influenced by the image of naval aviators portrayed in the movie "Top Gun". The officers told us that the movie fueled misconceptions on the part of junior officers as to what was expected of them and also served to increase the general awareness of naval aviation and glorify naval pilots in the eyes of many young women.

One female Navy commander opined that the 1991 Tailhook convention was different in some ways from previous years, in part because of the recent Gulf War and the congressional inquiries regarding women in combat.

The heightened emotions from the Gulf War were also enhanced with the forthcoming . . . downsizing of the military, so that you had people feeling very threatened for their job security and to more than just their jobs, their lifestyle. So you had people worried about what was coming down with the future. You had quite a bit of change. You had people that had been to the Gulf War. You had alcohol. You had a convention that had a lot of ingredients for any emotional whirlwind of controversy.

She went on to say that these potentially explosive ingredients combined at Tailhook 91, and resulted in ". . . an animosity in this Tailhook that existed that was telling the women that 'We don't have any respect for you now as humans'." The animosity, in this officer's opinion, was focused on women:

"This was the woman that was making you, you know, change your ways. This was the woman that was threatening your livelihood. This was the woman that was threatening your lifestyle. This was the woman that wanted to take your spot in that combat aircraft."

We found that all those factors were at play among the Tailhook 91 attendees. One rationale, that of the returning heroes, emphasizes that naval aviation is among the most dangerous and stressful occupations in the world. During Desert Storm, for example, the U.S. Navy suffered six fatalities, all of whom were aviation officers. We also found that the "live for today for tomorrow you may die" attitude expressed by many officers is a fact of life for many aviation officers. Over 30 officers died in the one-year period following Tailhook 91 as a result of military aviation related accidents. Others were found to have died in nonmilitary plane accidents, in vehicle crashes and, in at least one incident, by suicide. Although none of these factors justify the activities at Tailhook, they help illuminate the attitudes of many attendees.

Many officers likened Tailhook to an overseas deployment, explaining that naval officers traditionally live a spartan existence while on board ship and then party while on liberty in foreign ports. Dozens of officers cited excessive drinking, indecent exposure and visits to prostitutes as common activities while on liberty. That was acknowledged by virtually all interviewees, from junior officers through flag officers. The most frequently heard comment in that regard was "what happens overseas, stays overseas." Officers said that activities such as adultery, drunkenness and indecent exposure which occur overseas are not to be discussed or otherwise revealed once the ship returns to home port.

A similar attitude carried over to the annual Tailhook conventions. Countless officers told us it was common knowledge that "what happened at Tailhook stayed at Tailhook" and there were unwritten rules to enforce the policy. . . .

One disturbing aspect of the attitudes exhibited at Tailhook 91 was the blatant sexism displayed by some officers toward women. That attitude is best exemplified in a T-shirt worn by several male officers. The back of the shirt reads "WOMEN ARE PROPERTY," while the front reads "HE-MAN WOMEN HATER'S CLUB." The shirts, as well as demeaning posters and lapel pins, expressed an attitude held by some male attendees that women were at Tailhook to "serve" the male attendees and that women were not welcome within naval aviation. . . .

During the course of our investigation, an incident involving sexual harassment came to our attention. One of the squadron hospitality suites provided the forum for an informal job interview between a Navy captain and a civilian female. The woman had applied for a GM-I5 position within the captain's command. The captain was the hiring official for the position. Our investigation determined that the captain made numerous sexually oriented comments to the woman, questioned her sexual preferences and also directed her to stand up and turn around in front of him so as to enable him to view her buttocks. The incident was witnessed by other naval officers, as well as a civilian. Details of this matter have been referred under separate cover to Navy authorities.

B. The Failure of Leadership

One of the most difficult issues we sought to address was accountability, from a leadership standpoint for the events at Tailhook 91. The various types of misconduct that took place in the third floor corridor and in the suites, if not tacitly approved, were nevertheless allowed to continue by the leadership of the naval aviation community and the Tailhook Association.

The military is a hierarchical organization, which requires and is supposed to ensure accountability at every level. As one moves up through the chain of command, the focus on accountability narrows to fewer individuals. At the highest levels of the command structure, accountability becomes less dependent on actual knowledge of the specific actions of subordinates. At some point, "the buck stops here" applies. In the case of Tailhook 91, the buck stops with the senior leaders of naval aviation.

Tailhook 91 is the culmination of a long-term failure of leadership in naval aviation. What happened at Tailhook 91 was destined to happen sooner or later in the "can you top this" atmosphere that appeared to increase with each succeeding convention. Senior aviation leadership seemed to ignore the deteriorating standards of behavior and failed to deal with the increasing disorderly, improper and promiscuous behavior.

Throughout our investigation, officers told us that Tailhook 91 was not significantly different from earlier conventions with respect to outrageous behavior. Most of the officers we spoke to said that excesses seen at Tailhook 91 such as excessive consumption of alcohol, strippers, indecent exposure and other inappropriate behavior were accepted by senior officers simply because those things had gone on for years. Indeed, heavy drinking, the gauntlet and widespread promiscuity were part of the allure of Tailhook conventions to a significant number of the Navy and Marine Corps attendees.

In seeking to identify the measure of responsibility properly borne by senior officers, it would be unfair to focus solely on the senior officers who attended Tailhook 91. Some measure of responsibility is also borne by other senior officers, some still on active duty and others now retired who attended previous Tailhook conventions and permitted the excesses of the annual conventions to continue unchecked.

As we reported in Tailhook 91, Part 1, the nature of the misconduct at the annual conventions was well-known to senior aviation leaders. However, although aware of the activities and atmosphere, they were incapable of dealing with the increasingly indulgent behavior. The efforts taken to control their subordinates at Tailhook, through the years, were sometimes effective but only for limited periods. In our view, by September 1991, both individually and collectively, the senior leaders of naval aviation were unwilling to take the kinds of measures necessary to effectively end the types of misconduct that they had every reason to expect would occur at Tailhook 91. . . .

. . . Some senior officers themselves had participated in third floor improprieties in previous years when they were junior officers to the extent that certain offensive activities had become a matter of tradition. For example, we found that officers, including some field grade officers, engaged in improper conduct such as indecent exposure and physical contact with strippers.

In that regard, one Navy lieutenant told us, ". . . I don't think that anybody saw anything that they felt hadn't happened in the past. And so . . . if it had been allowed to happen in the past, they'd just let it go. They felt there was no reason to stop anything that they hadn't [sic] seen before." . . .

Another junior officer, who admitted to participating in the gauntlet, told us "If I thought that going around and goosing a few girls on the breasts was going to create a national incident, do you think I would have done that? We only did it because the party atmosphere seemed to promote that . . . Admiral Dunleavy and the rest of his cronies who go to Hook every year, man, they must be wearing some blinders, because it has been happening every single year that I know of."

Senior officers, on the other hand, referred to their perception that the third floor was somehow the domain of the younger officers. Senior officers, including an admiral, told us there was a lack of respect exhibited toward older officers by some junior officers and noted their belief that they would have been powerless to act successfully in attempting to stop third floor improprieties. . . .

Many factors contributed to a feeling of resentment by junior officers toward higher ranking officers. One aspect related to a perception that, despite their success in Desert Storm, junior officers would be adversely affected by the anticipated drawdown of troops. Yet another factor related to us was the squadron officers' use of their personal funds to pay for the suites, alcohol and entertainment. Flag officers and many of the Navy captains and Marine Corps colonels in attendance did not help fund the third floor activities. That fact, together with the lack of uniforms and absence of any official Navy participation with regard to squadron hospitality suites contributed to a perception held by many attendees that the party was a private one hosted by junior officers.

Numerous officers attributed the perception that they could act with impunity to the uniqueness of the naval aviation community. They explained that aviators are used to working in a rank-neutral environment frequently addressing more senior officers by their pilot "call signs" rather than by their rank. The witnesses also noted that aviation officers are less rank conscious and, therefore, less intimidated by the presence of more senior officers.

The demarcation between junior and senior officers was further blurred by the abundance of alcohol and nearly everyone's dressing in T-shirts and shorts as opposed to Navy or Marine Corps uniforms. As told to us by one officer, ". . . the more you drink, the less noticeable any ranks would be, from looking upward and looking downward, you know." . . .

SECTION XI
CONCLUSIONS

There was a serious breakdown of leadership at Tailhook 91. Misconduct went far beyond the "treatment of women" issues for which the Navy had enacted new policies in the years preceding Tailhook 91. Tailhook "traditions" such as the gauntlet, ballwalking, leg shaving, mooning, streaking and lewd sexual conduct significantly deviated from the standards of behavior that the Nation expects of its military officers. The disparity between the espoused Navy policies regarding officer conduct and the actual conduct of significant numbers of officers at Tailhook 91 could not have been greater. Officers who assaulted women, as well as those who engaged in improper sexual behavior, knew that their actions would not be condoned under any objective standard. These officers needed no "policeman at the elbow" to warn them of the wrongful nature of their actions and they, therefore, must bear a major portion of the blame.

Leaders in naval aviation, ranging from the squadron commanders to flag officers who tolerated a culture that engendered the misconduct also bear a portion of the blame. The damage suffered by the Navy as a result of Tailhook cannot be fully repaired until the integrity of the Navy is restored, which, in turn, depends on the integrity of each of its members. The senior officers must lead the way in that endeavor. For the credibility of the Navy and Marine Corps as institutions, each senior officer who attended Tailhook 91, or previous Tailhook symposia, should consider the extent to which he bears some personal responsibility for what occurred there and how he can best serve the Navy and the Marine Corps in the future.

Navy Department leadership, military and civilian, will face many difficult decisions as it comes to grips with the issues raised in this report and the individual misconduct referrals that accompany the report. Personal friendship, knowledge of past service and sacrifice by the officers involved, and a general reluctance to end or adversely impact otherwise promising military careers will further complicate the matter.

The Acting Secretary of the Navy has appointed two convening authorities, a Marine Corps lieutenant general and a Navy vice admiral, who we expect will deal with the disciplinary and military judicial aspects of this matter with dispatch, equality and compassion. The next Secretary of the Navy, the Chief of Naval Operations and the Commandant of the Marine Corps are left with the more difficult problem of determining how to resolve and correct the long-term failure of leadership that characterized Tailhook 91.

We have every expectation that the Navy will address the causes and conduct that combined to produce the disgrace of Tailhook 91, and therefore, we offer no recommendations.

Source: Office of Inspector General, Department of Defense, *Tailhook 91*, Part 2: "Events at the 35th Annual Tailhook Symposium," February 1993 (footnotes omitted).

> Several of the women assaulted at the Tailhook convention brought civil lawsuits for money damages. For example, Lieutenant Coughlin sued the Tailhook Association and Hilton Hotels. The Tailhook Association settled the lawsuit by paying her $400,000; after trial, Hilton Hotels and the Las Vegas Hilton were ordered to pay her more than $5 million. Courts held, however, that the Navy did not have to pay damages to the women who were assaulted, because the service members who committed the assaults were not acting within the scope of their employment.
>
> In the end, the Tailhook scandal shortened the careers of several prominent naval officers, including Secretary Garrett. He resigned under pressure in 1992 after it was discovered that a statement by a witness placing him near the scene of some of the misbehavior had been deleted from an original investigative report prepared by the Navy.

DOCUMENT 57: Statement by Press Secretary Fitzwater on the Resignation of H. Lawrence Garrett III as Secretary of the Navy (1992)

President Bush accepts the resignation of Secretary of the Navy, H. Lawrence Garrett III. Secretary Garrett today submitted his letter of resignation to the President, accepting full responsibility for the Tailhook incident involving naval aviators.

President Bush today received a briefing by Secretary Cheney on the status of the Department of Defense investigations into the Tailhook incident. The Inspector General of the Navy has investigated the matter.

A second investigation by the Inspector General of the Department of Defense was ordered last week.

The President seeks a full, thorough, and expedited investigation that will result in actions to ensure the highest standards of equality and conduct among all members of the Navy. Sexual harassment will not be tolerated.

Source: 28 *Weekly Compilation of Presidential Documents* 1150 (June 26, 1992).

MILITARY REGULATION OF SEXUAL HARASSMENT

The Department of Defense (DoD) establishes policy for all branches of the military. It first issued a policy prohibiting sexual harassment within the military in 1981. It revised this policy in 1989, when it promulgated regulations entitled "The Department of Defense Military Equal Opportunity Program" (Document 58). Like the EEOC, the DoD prohibits both quid pro quo and hostile environment harassment. Indeed, the DoD borrowed language from the EEOC guidelines in defining these offenses. The military's definition is broader than the EEOC's in one respect because it is also unlawful for supervising officers to "condone" sexual harassment.

DOCUMENT 58: "The Department of Defense Military Equal Opportunity Program" (1989)

§ 51.3 *Definitions.*

* * *

Sexual Harassment. A form of sex discrimination that involves unwelcomed sexual advances, requests for sexual favors, and other verbal or physical conduct of a sexual nature when:

(a) Submission to or rejection of such conduct is made either explicitly or implicitly a term or condition of a person's job, pay, or career, or

(b) Submission to or rejection of such conduct by a person is used as a basis for career or employment decisions affecting that person, or

(c) Such conduct interferes with an individual's performance or creates an intimidating, hostile, or offensive environment.

Any person in a supervisory or command position who uses or condones implicit or explicit sexual behavior to control, influence, or affect the career, pay, or job of a military member or civilian employee is engaging in sexual harassment. Similarly, any military member or civilian employee who makes deliberate or repeated unwelcomed verbal comments, gestures, or physical contact of a sexual nature is also engaging in sexual harassment. . . .

§ 51.4 *Policy.*
It is DoD policy to:

* * *

(e) Provide for an environment that is free from sexual harassment by eliminating this form of discrimination in the Department of Defense. . . .

§ 51.5 *Responsibilities.*

* * *

(b) The Heads of DoD Components shall be responsible for equal opportunity within their respective jurisdictions (to include their Reserve components) and shall: . . .

(6) Establish policies and procedures to prevent sexual harassment and to ensure that appropriate action is taken against individuals who commit sexual harassment offenses, in accordance with the Secretary of Defense Memorandums.

(7) Ensure that all military personnel, including command-selectees and flag and general officers, receive training in equal opportunity, human relations, and prevention of sexual harassment on a recurring basis. . . .

Source: 32 *Code of Federal Regulations* §§ 51.3–51.5.

The DoD's policy leaves it up to each branch of the service to "[e]stablish policies and procedures to prevent sexual harassment." The U.S. Navy's policy (Document 59) was substantially revised in 1993 in response to the Tailhook scandal. This policy makes it a criminal offense to engage in sexual harassment. Under the Uniform Code of Military Justice (UCMJ), service members who engage in sexual harassment can be imprisoned and dishonorably discharged from the service. Lesser sanctions, such as counseling or negative comments in fitness reports, can be imposed in appropriate cases.

DOCUMENT 59: *Department of the Navy (DON) Policy on Sexual Harassment* (1993)

---

6. Background
a. The Navy-Marine Corps Team must be comprised of an optimally

integrated group of men and women who must be able to work together to accomplish the mission. Each member of the team is entitled to be treated fairly, with dignity and respect, and must be allowed to work in an environment free of unlawful discrimination.

b. The economic costs of sexual harassment are significant. Even more harmful, however, are the negative effects of sexual harassment on productivity and readiness, including increased absenteeism, greater personnel turnover, lower morale, decreased effectiveness, and a loss of personal, organizational, and public trust. While not easily quantified, these costs are real and seriously affect DON's ability to accomplish its mission.

c. We must ensure that all DON military and civilian personnel are treated fairly with dignity and mutual respect, and that sexual harassment does not adversely affect the DON's ability to accomplish its mission. While the EEOC regulations . . . establish a standard for determining employer liability for sexual harassment under Title VII of the Civil Rights Act, the DOD definition . . . establishes a standard that exceeds the EEOC definition. This more comprehensive standard expands on the definition to include identifying supervisors and those in command positions who use or condone implicit or explicit sexual behavior to affect another's career, pay, or job as engaging in sexual harassment.

7. **Policy**. The DON is committed to maintaining a work environment free from unlawful discriminatory practices and inappropriate behavior. Leadership is the key to eliminating all forms of unlawful discrimination. Sound leadership must be the cornerstone of the effort to eliminate sexual harassment. In support of this commitment, it is DON policy that:

a. Sexual harassment is prohibited. All DON personnel, military and civilian, will be provided a work environment free from sexual harassment.

b. All DON personnel, military and civilian, will be educated and trained, upon accession (within 90 days to the extent possible) and annually thereafter, in the areas of identification, prevention, resolution, and elimination of sexual harassment. . . .

c. Individuals who believe they have been sexually harassed will be afforded multiple avenues to seek resolution and redress. Commanders and those in supervisory positions will ensure that notification of sexual harassment can be made in a command climate that does not tolerate acts of reprisal, intimidation, or further acts of harassment. All personnel will be made aware of the avenues of resolution and redress that are available.

d. All reported incidents of sexual harassment will be investigated and resolved at the lowest appropriate level. The nature of the investigation will depend upon the particular facts and circumstances and may consist of all informal inquiry where the action is sufficient to resolve factual issues. All incidents will be resolved promptly and with sensitivity. Confidentiality will be maintained to the extent possible. Feedback will be provided to all affected individuals consistent with the requirements of the Privacy Act and other pertinent laws, regulations, and negotiated agreements.

e. Counseling support or referral services will be made available for all involved in incidents of sexual harassment.

8. Accountability

a. Sexual harassment is prohibited.

b. No individual in the DON shall:

(1) Commit sexual harassment, as defined in [the DoD regulations];

(2) Take reprisal action against a person who provides information on an incident of alleged sexual harassment;

(3) Knowingly make a false accusation of sexual harassment.

(4) While in a supervisory or command position, condone or ignore sexual harassment which he or she has knowledge or has reason to have knowledge.

c. The rules in subparagraphs 8b are regulatory orders and apply to all DON personnel individually without further implementation. A violation of these provisions by military personnel is punishable in accordance with the UCMJ, and is the basis for disciplinary action with respect to civilian employees. The prohibitions in subparagraph 8b apply to all conduct which occurs in or impacts a DOD working environment. . . . The reasonable person standard . . . shall be used to determine whether a violation of these provisions has occurred.

d. The appropriate action to resolve an incident of sexual harassment will depend on the circumstances surrounding the incident. Incidents of sexual harassment cover a wide range of behaviors, from verbal comments to rape. Likewise, the full range of administrative and disciplinary actions is available to address sexual harassment. In the case of military personnel, these include informal counseling, comments in fitness reports and evaluations, administrative separation, and punitive measures under the UCMJ. In the case of civilians, options include informal counseling, comments in performance evaluations, and disciplinary action including removal from the Federal Service.

e. Administrative Separation. Military personnel of the Navy and Marine Corps shall be processed for administrative separation on the first substantiated incident of sexual harassment involving any of the following circumstances (for the purposes of this subparagraph, an incident is substantiated if there has been a court-martial conviction of if the commanding officer determines that sexual harassment has occurred):

(1) Actions, threats, or attempts to influence another's career or job in exchange for sexual favors; or

(2) Physical contact of a sexual nature which, if charged as a violation of the UCMJ, could result in punitive discharge.

f. Commanders are not precluded from initiating administrative separation proceedings for reasons set forth in the appropriate service regulations for individuals whose conduct warrants separation not covered in subparagraph 83.

9. Responsibility

a. **Commanders and supervisors** are responsible for leading the men and women under their control. It is not the intent of this instruction to impair their ability to take appropriate actions to carry out leadership responsibilities. They must set the example in treating all people with mutual respect and dignity, fostering a climate free from all forms of discrimination and eliminating sexual harassment. Such a climate is essential to maintain high morale, discipline, and readiness. Commanders and supervisors are responsible for and must be committed to preventing sexual harassment in their commands and work environments. They must not ignore or condone sexual harassment in their commands and work environments. They must not ignore or condone sexual harassment in any form, and they must take whatever action is required to ensure that a recipient of sexual harassment is not subsequently also the victim of reprisal or retaliation. These responsibilities regarding sexual harassment are part of the broader responsibility of commanders and supervisors to foster a positive climate and take appropriate corrective action when conduct is disruptive, provoking, discriminatory, or otherwise unprofessional.

b. **Individuals who believe they have been sexually harassed** are encouraged to address their concerns or objections regarding the incident directly with the person demonstrating the harassing behavior. Persons who are subjected to or observe objectionable behavior should promptly notify the chain of command if:

(1) The objectionable behavior does not stop; or

(2) The situation is not resolved; or

(3) Addressing the objectionable behavior directly with the person concerned is not reasonable under the circumstances; or

(4) The behavior is clearly criminal in nature.

If the person demonstrating the objectionable behavior is a direct superior in the chain of command or the chain of command condones the conduct or ignores a report, individuals who have been subjected to or who observe objectionable behavior are encouraged to promptly communicate the incident through other available means.

c. **All personnel** are responsible for treating others with mutual respect and dignity. This means fully and faithfully complying with this instruction. All DON personnel are accountable for their actions.

Source: SECNAV Instruction 5300.26B, pp. 2–4 (January 6, 1993).

An enclosure accompanying the Navy's policy explains the policy in simpler terms geared toward laypeople. This document divides behaviors into three zones—green, yellow, and red—using the colors of a traffic light. Behaviors in the green zone, such as polite compliments, are not sexual harassment. Behaviors in the yellow zone—such as "suggestive comments" and "off-color jokes"—can be sexual harassment, particularly if repeated over a period of time. Behaviors in the red zone—such as making threats if sexual favors are not provided or making obscene comments—are always considered to be sexual harassment.

DOCUMENT 60: *Department of the Navy (DON) Policy on Sexual Harassment,* **Enclosure (3) (1993)**

RANGE OF BEHAVIORS WHICH CONSTITUTE SEXUAL HARASSMENT

1. Introduction. This enclosure explains and illustrates behaviors which may constitute sexual harassment by describing in layperson's terms what sexual harassment is and how it occurs in the work environment. This enclosure is intended to be used as a guide for developing training programs and to assist military members and civilian employees in distinguishing between acceptable and unacceptable behavior in the work environment. . . .

2. Background

a. The world has changed dramatically in recent years, and America's national security policy has also changed. . . . The new vision represents a fundamental shift away from open-ocean warfare on the sea toward joint operations *from* the sea, as part of the nation's "sea-air-land" team. The need to maximize efficiency and teamwork remains firm. The Navy-Marine Corps Team must be comprised of an optimally integrated group of men and women, who must be able to work together to get the job done. Each member of the team is entitled to be treated fairly, with dignity and respect, and must be allowed to work in an environment free of discrimination.

b. Sex discrimination in the workplace is not a new problem; however, prior to 1964 there were inadequate legal protection [*sic*] against it. In

1964, the U.S. Congress passed Title VII of the Civil Rights Act, which prohibits various forms of discrimination in employment. In 1972, the Civil Rights Act was made applicable to federal employees . . . but it was not until the late 1970's that sexual harassment began to be recognized as a form of sex discrimination. In 1980, the EEOC, established to enforce Title VII, issued . . . regulations . . . [which] include a definition of sexual harassment and conditions under which an employer may be held liable for its occurrence. They have been used as a basis for legal actions brought against employers for violating the Civil Rights Act. The EEOC definition of sexual harassment has been upheld by the Supreme Court and has also been used as a basis for DOD policies on sexual harassment. . . .

c. In the 1990's sexual harassment is receiving increased attention. The costs to resolve incidents of sexual harassment are significant. Even more harmful and costly, however, are the negative effects sexual harassment has on productivity and readiness. These include costs associated with increased absenteeism, greater personnel turnover, lower morale, decreased effectiveness, and a loss of personal, organizational, and public trust. While not easily quantified these costs are just as real and seriously affect the DON's ability to meet the needs of our Nation.

3. Sexual Harassment. Basically, sexual harassment means bothering someone in a sexual way. In the context of this instruction, it is behavior that is unwelcome, is sexual in nature, and is connected in some way with a person's job or work environment. A wide range of behaviors can meet these criteria, and therefore, constitute sexual harassment. Even with this rather simplistic way of explaining it, trying to determine exactly what kinds of behavior constitute sexual harassment often is not easy. The policy established by this instruction is not intended to prevent the types of behavior which are appropriate in normal work settings and which contribute to camaraderie.

4. Discussion. For a person's behavior to be considered sexual harassment, it must meet three criteria: it must be unwelcome, be sexual in nature, and occur in or impact on the work environment.

a. **Unwelcome** behavior is behavior that a person does not ask for and which that person considers undesirable or offensive. Not everyone has the same perception of "undesirable or offensive." What is acceptable for some people is not acceptable for others. So whose perception should be used? Since the person being subjected to the behavior—the recipient—is the one being affected, it is the recipient's perception that courts use. As long as the recipient is a reasonable person and not overly sensitive, behavior which the recipient finds unwelcome should be stopped. Using this "reasonable person standard," from the perspective of the recipient, is really no more than using common sense.

b. Behavior which is **sexual in nature** is fairly easy to determine. Telling sexually explicit jokes, displaying sexually suggestive pictures, and talking about sex are obviously "sexual in nature." Some people would consider other behaviors, such as touching, to be sexual in some cases but not in others. Not all touching is sexual in nature, but if the touching is to certain parts of the body or is done suggestively, it definitely is. Again, using common sense will normally be enough to determine whether or not a certain behavior is sexual in nature.

c. For sexual harassment to occur, unwelcome sexual behavior must **occur in or impact on the work environment**:

(1) When recipients are offered or denied something that is work-connected in return for submitting to or rejecting unwelcome sexual behavior, they have been subjected to a type of sexual harassment known as "quid pro quo" ("this for that"). Examples include: getting or losing a job, a promotion or demotion, a good or bad performance evaluation, etc. Basically if any work-connected decisions are made based on the submission to or rejection of the unwelcome sexual behavior, sexual harassment has occurred. Normally, this is from a senior to a junior, because the senior person has something to offer.

(2) When the unwelcome sexual behavior of one or more persons in a workplace interferes with another person's work performance, sexual harassment has occurred. If the behavior produces a work atmosphere which is offensive, intimidating, or abusive to another person, whether or not work performance is affected, a type of sexual harassment has occurred called "hostile environment." The following are a few examples of behavior that could create a hostile environment:

(a) Using sexually explicit or sexually offensive language.

(b) Displaying sexually-oriented posters or calendars of nude or partially clad individuals.

(c) Touching someone in a suggestive manner (e.g., intentionally brushing against them or pinching).

(d) Giving someone unwelcome letters, cards, or gifts of a personal nature, when these items have sexual overtones.

(e) Unwanted or uninvited pressure for dates.

(3) Certain types of unwelcome sexual behavior do not have to create a "hostile environment" to be considered sexual harassment. If the behavior occurs in the work environment and is unreasonable, such as fondling or groping, it would be considered sexual harassment, even if it were displayed only once. Other less obvious behaviors can become sexual harassment if they are repeated.

5. Range of Behaviors. There is a wide range of behaviors, from leering to rape, which can be unwelcome, sexual, and work-connected and can, therefore, constitute sexual harassment. Some behavior may be unwelcome and work-connected, but not sexual (for example, performance counseling). This behavior is not sexual harassment. To make it easier to understand, it is helpful to think of the entire range of possible behavior in terms of a traffic light. The traffic light has three colors, and behavior may be divided into three zones. **Green** on the traffic light means "go"; **Red** on the traffic light means "stop"; the red behavior zone means "don't do it." It is sexual harassment. The third color on the traffic light, **yellow**, means "use caution." The yellow behavior zone may be sexual harassment. Just as with a traffic light, if the yellow zone is long enough, the light will turn red. If yellow zone behavior is repeated enough, especially after having been told it is unwelcome, it becomes red zone behavior—sexual harassment. The following examples illustrate these three types of behavior, but they are certainly not all-inclusive.

a. **Green zone**. These behaviors are not sexual harassment: performance counseling, touching which could not reasonably be perceived in a sexual way (such as touching someone on the elbow), counseling on military appearance, social interaction, showing concern, encouragement, a polite compliment, or friendly conversation.

b. **Yellow zone**. Many people would find these behaviors unacceptable, and they could be sexual harassment: violating personal "space", whistling, questions about personal life, lewd or sexually suggestive comments, suggestive posters or calendars, off-color jokes, leering, staring, repeated requests for dates, foul language, unwanted letters or poems, sexually suggestive touching, or sitting or gesturing sexually.

c. **Red zone**. These behaviors are always considered sexual harassment: sexual favors in return for employment rewards, threats if sexual favors are not provided, sexually explicit pictures (including calendars or posters) or remarks, using status to request dates, or obscene letters or comments. The most severe forms of sexual harassment constitute criminal conduct, e.g. sexual assault (ranging from forcefully grabbing to fondling, forced kissing, or rape).

Note: Keep in mind that the above examples are used as guidance only, that individuals believe they are being sexually harassed based on their perceptions, that each incident is judged on the totality of facts in that particular case, and that individuals' judgment may vary on the same facts. Therefore, caution in this area is advised. **Any time sexual behavior is introduced into the work environment or among co-workers, the individuals involved are on notice that the behavior may constitute sexual harassment**.

Source: SECNAV Instruction 5300.26B, enclosure (3) (January 6, 1993).

One commentator, Lieutenant Commander J. Richard Chema, a lawyer with the military, has criticized the Navy's new policy criminalizing sexual harassment. He points out that many forms of sexual harassment were already prohibited by the UCMJ before the Navy instituted its new policy, since the UCMJ explicitly prohibits such offenses as rape, assault, fraternization, and conduct unbecoming an officer. Thus, he argues that the new guidelines will not help victims of sexual harassment.

Furthermore, he is concerned that the new guidelines create vaguely defined criminal offenses that can provide a trap for the unwary and interfere with free speech. Instead of changing the rules, he argues, what is needed is dedication by the leadership to enforce the rules that already existed.

DOCUMENT 61: "Arresting 'Tailhook': The Prosecution of Sexual Harassment in the Military" (Lieutenant Commander J. Richard Chema, 1993)

VII. Conclusion

The main effect of directly criminalizing sexual harassment [through the Navy's new Instruction on sexual harassment] is to outlaw the amorphous area of hostile environment conduct. Doing this, however, creates numerous legal and practical difficulties. Problems arise initially because the criminalization is based on the transfer of a civil standard into the military criminal law. Although Title VII terminology and concepts have been used, they have failed to provide an unambiguous, constitutionally viable standard for criminality. The artificial assimilation of civil employment discrimination law concepts into a regulation defining a criminal act fails to provide proper notice of what is prohibited conduct because civil law sexual harassment is aligned inherently with the subjective feelings of individuals who perceive the alleged criminal conduct or words. Therefore, the very same conduct might be acceptable or criminal, depending upon the perceptions of two different observers. Such vagaries are neither workable nor likely to pass constitutional muster.

An additional major constitutional problem with the criminalization of sexual harassment is that it attempts to regulate offensive speech. By precluding a wide array of speech, and only one type of offensive speech, the sexual harassment prohibition is subject to First Amendment challenges under various theories.

The other potential problems with criminalizing a civil concept are not as yet readily apparent. Criminalization, however, is certainly unnecessary because the UCMJ has an expansive set of criminal prohibitions that cover almost all imaginable criminal conduct that fits within the rubric

of sexual harassment. These criminal statutes already have passed constitutional muster, provide adequate notice to satisfy the requirements
of due process, and have a long history available for bench and bar to
draw upon during prosecution of real sexual harassment crimes. Resort
to special regulations or statutes was not needed to combat racial discrimination, and they are unnecessary to combat sexual harassment.

The heart of the problem in redressing sexual harassment in the armed
forces has not been Congress's failure to expand the traditional coverage
of the UCMJ so that it directly criminalizes specific forms of hostile environment conduct such as sexist remarks, tasteless jokes, and other offensive gestures. Instead, the problem has been the military leadership's
failure to recognize that in many cases, like those arising in Tailhook,
sexual mistreatment actually constitutes a serious assaultive crime that
must be prosecuted accordingly.

Ironically, direct criminalization likely will cause two opposite, but yet
related, damaging reactions to resolving the problem of sexual harassment in the military. First, because the regulation sweeps far too broadly
in criminalizing conduct, the focus of attention changes from the truly
criminal conduct that must be eliminated, to debates about the type of
conduct that constitute "sexual harassment" and the overreaction of the
regulation.

Second, because of the highly charged nature of the sexual harassment
issue, the political agenda of interested parties, the inherently ambiguous
and subjective nature of hostile environment sexual harassment, and the
dynamics of fear of being criminally tolerant of subordinates' sexual harassment, an overaggressive enforcement of the regulation inevitably will
occur. Individual rights will be victimized, and this misuse of the legal
system will strengthen the resolve of those who are not serious about
focusing on the main issue of real sexually-motivated crimes in the military. Accordingly, by focusing on "yellow zone" type conduct, the real
problem will be obscured because all the energy of the participants in
the controversy will be centered on the periphery.

None of the problems that the military, especially the Navy, has encountered in the area of sexual harassment stem from the inadequacy of
its laws or its policies. The anti-sexual harassment policies have been in
effect throughout the entire period when the most egregious and publicized abuses have occurred. These policies are more than adequate vehicles to prosecute the assaults, indecent exposures, and drunken
conduct unbecoming officers for all past and future Tailhook-type incidents. Education, training, and administrative measures to resolve the
sociological and institutional aspects of discrimination based on sex are
being implemented widely. Victims must be encouraged to report misconduct immediately, and commands must investigate and adequately
dispose of charges in a timely fashion. The present law, however, is more

than adequate to support the policies against sexual harassment. Extensive substantive changes are not needed. What has been missing, and what is essential, is the leadership, dedication, and political will necessary to expose and timely resolve the problems. Without this type of dedication, no existing or future laws can do the job. With it, the existing legal tools for eradicating sexual mistreatment are in place and fully operational.

The Navy should revoke the punitive aspect of its regulation, and the other services should resist any movement toward direct criminalization of sexual harassment. . . .

Tinkering with the substantive law is simply not the answer to resolving the sociological problem of sexual harassment. Instead, the law as presently constituted will work effectively when officials display the resolve to do justice and enforce current policies and standards for equal treatment of men and women in the military.

Source: LCDR J. Richard Chema, "Arresting 'Tailhook': The Prosecution of Sexual Harassment in the Military," *Military Law Review* 140 (Spring 1993): 62–64.

In 1994, in response to the Tailhook scandal and to allegations of sexual abuse of female military personnel by their fellow soldiers during the Gulf War, Senator Dennis DeConcini of Arizona introduced an amendment to the bill setting the military budget for Fiscal Year 1995. This amendment would have created an independent civilian office of investigations, which would have been charged with investigating allegations of sexual misconduct in the military and with compiling data on the topic. In addition, the amendment would have made it a criminal offense for commanding officers to fail to report allegations of sexual misconduct to this new office. In his remarks, accompanying the introduction of the amendment, Senator DeConcini detailed the two facets of the problem of sexual harassment in the military—that such sexual misconduct seems to occur frequently and that military authorities have often failed to respond appropriately when being informed of such misconduct. The Senate, however, did not enact this proposed legislation.

DOCUMENT 62: National Defense Authorization Act for Fiscal Year 1995, Proposed Amendment No. 2146, Remarks of Senator DeConcini (1994)

Mr. DECONCINI.

* * *

Women in the U.S. Armed Forces are being subjected daily to sexual harassment ranging from verbal abuse to forcible rape. Who does the harassing. Men whom these women trust as fellow comrades-in-arms or—even worse—superiors who use their authority to sexually coerce lower echelon military women and then intimidate them into silence.

When victims of such abuse attempt to report it to higher military officials, they find their experience discounted as of minor importance, or as part of being in the military. The Tailhook scandal is only one example of the military's efforts to cover up and discount the magnitude of the sexual abuse problems of military women. Hundreds of individual, if not thousands of incidents occur every year. Both the incidents themselves and the subsequent cavalier treatment of the victims are unconscionable and can not be tolerated.

Mr. President, I sat in horror 2 years ago as I heard Reservist Jackie Ortiz testify before the Committee on Veterans Affairs. Ms. Ortiz was sodomized by her company's first sergeant while on duty 18 miles northwest of the Iraqi border during Operation Desert Storm. Ms. Ortiz immediately reported the incident. Instead of providing the immediate medical attention she required, her commanders placed her on unneeded guard duty for 6 straight hours and, then for 12 hours at a time. When the CID investigator finally arrived, Jackie was subjected to 6 hours of interrogation during which she was required to describe the incident in graphic detail time after time after time. For the next 2 ½ months, Jackie remained under the command of her attacker, requiring face to face confrontation almost daily, and continued denial of medical attention. Despite the first sergeant's later confession, he received a promotion and was allowed to retire. Jackie received counseling from the Chaplain, the tentmate of the company physician.

This is a real honest to goodness story, what happened to one of our military personnel in the Persian Gulf war.

The committee that held those hearings under the distinguished chairman, Senator Cranston, also heard appalling testimony indicating that one study conducted by Dr. Jessica Wolfe showing that nearly 29 percent of 113 Vietnam Era women had fallen victim to attempted or actual sexual assault, and that the rate is probably higher for war zone service. This is more than double the experience of American women as a whole. Not one of these women was raped by the enemy.

Mr. President, it is true that the survey sample was small, but I am afraid Dr. Wolfe's study accurately reflects what is going on in the military and we must put a stop to it. The fact that no reliable data exists highlights the shocking indifference to this problem. Even if the 29 percent incident rate of that survey is ignored, the 1988 Department of Defense [sic] own study of women who were on active duty indicated that 5 percent of the respondents reported actual rape or attempted rape or sexual assault. Even if one applies that very conservative estimate to all women in the military, as many as 11,000 military women would have been victims in 1 year alone. . . .

Mr. President, as most Members in this body know, at least 83 women and 7 men were sexually harassed and physically abused during Tailhook's 35th annual convention. About half the 140 cases were dismissed for lack of evidence, 40–45 received letters of reprimand, but no courts martial were taken. Thirty-two Navy admirals and one Marine general were cited for failure to stop the abuses; all but two received nonpunitive letters of reprimand. Seven admirals lost their commands, were disciplined, or took early retirements in Tailhook's wake. And just 3 weeks ago today, the Marine Corps announced the dismissal of the last pending military case arising from the Tailhook scandal of sexual misconduct.

Mr. President, when I heard that not one person accused of sexual misconduct went to trial, much less [was] convicted, it sent a cold chill up my spine, and I will not forget it. . . .

The amendment I am offering today to the Defense authorization bill creates an Office of Special Investigations at the Department of Defense level. This new office will have oversight and audit jurisdiction over all reports of sexual harassment, abuse, and assault, and other related offenses by active-duty military personnel against other active-duty personnel and civilians. The Secretary of Defense is also empowered to direct the new office to investigate or assist in the investigation of cases being conducted by any military investigative service.

Military victims of sexual assault will also be able to address their complaints directly to this office, rather than through the military chain of command, which we know does not work. In turn, this office would make the appropriate referral back to the chain of command and defense criminal investigative organizations. Most victims I have talked to simply do not believe that their allegations will be taken seriously and/or pursued vigorously by their supervisors in a male-dominated profession. We need to assure them that will be done.

The Office of Criminal Investigations will have a separate investigative staff with, to the fullest extent possible, professional expertise in sexual assault investigations. It will be independent and will have absolute authority to collect evidence and compel testimony and, when requested, secure appropriate, immediate medical treatment and psychological counseling for victims of sexual abuse.

A principal element of the office will be the collection of data so we can get a better handle on the extent of the problem, including the number of cases that go to prosecution. The cost of operating this new office and staff is modest and expected to be no more than $1 million to possibly $4 million per year. This includes an office, a staff of approximately 15 to 20 support personnel and investigators, computer capability for a data base, equipment, travel, and medical and psychiatric support availability.

This amendment would also establish a new Federal crime for failure by any commanding officer to promptly notify this new Office of Investigations of any report of sexual misconduct. Failure by a commanding officer to report sexual misconduct would be a felony punishable by imprisonment for up to 10 years.

Mr. President, no other aspect of this bill is more important than the criminalization of the coverup of sexual misconduct. Without this provision, any data collected on reports will continue to be inaccurate and perpetuate an institutional culture of coverups of sexual violence against military women that has been going on probably since women have been in the military. Are we going to stand by when there are over 200,000 fighting women who are defending our liberties and not do anything? We have an opportunity to do something. This is a tough measure, but I think it is long overdue. . . .

Mr. President, a great number of women choose to serve their country through careers in the military. American service women should not be subjected to this type of humiliation. They should not experience a sense of vulnerability engendered by the current permissive military environment. They should not be subjected to the terror and long-term incapacitation resulting from sexual assault. And they should not be subject to indifference from supervisors who are responsible for their safety.

We need to send a message to our military that such an environment and such a behavior will not be tolerated. We can fix the problem by establishing an independent unit with jurisdiction over these offenses.

I urge my colleagues to support this amendment.

Source: Congressional Record, July 1, 1994, 140, 103rd Cong., 2d sess., S8159–01, S8161–S8167.

MORE RECENT MILITARY SEXUAL HARASSMENT SCANDALS

Despite the promulgation of new rules prohibiting sexual harassment in the wake of the Tailhook scandal, the military has continued to be plagued by sexual harassment scandals.

Incidents at the Aberdeen Proving Ground

In September 1996, a group of women who received basic training at the Aberdeen Proving Ground in Aberdeen, Maryland, complained to superiors about sexual abuse by drill sergeants who were responsible for training them. In November 1996, these allegations became public when two drill sergeants were charged with rape. This, however, was just the tip of the iceberg.

Eventually the Army's investigation led to complaints by approximately fifty women of sexual abuse at Aberdeen. Twelve drill sergeants were charged with misconduct, ranging from sexual harassment, to illegal consensual sex between drill sergeants and privates, to rape. Furthermore, the Army uncovered evidence of similar abuses at other Army training centers.

The drill sergeant charged with the most serious offenses, Staff Sergeant Delmar Simpson, pled guilty to eleven counts of having consensual sex with subordinates and five counts of sexual harassment. He was later convicted of eighteen counts of rape. He was sentenced to twenty-five years in a military prison.

When the scandal came to light, the Army responded by setting up a toll free number for military personnel to use to report claims of sexual harassment and receive counseling. The Army discontinued this system, however, several months later because anonymous callers allegedly had been using the hot line to get back at soldiers against whom they had grudges. Testimony by the Secretary of the Army, Togo D. West, Jr., before the Senate Armed Services Committee (Document 63), explains in more detail the ways in which the Army has been dealing with the Aberdeen scandal.

DOCUMENT 63: Testimony Before the Senate Armed Services Committee, *Hearings on Sexual Harassment in Armed Services* (Togo D. West, Jr., 1997)

STATEMENT BY THE HONORABLE TOGO D. WEST, JR.
SECRETARY OF THE ARMY ON THE ISSUE OF SEXUAL
HARASSMENT AND MISCONDUCT IN THE UNITED STATES
ARMY

Mr. Chairman and members of the committee, I welcome the opportunity to appear before you today to report on the recent incidents of sexual misconduct at Aberdeen Proving Ground and the progress the Army is making to eliminate sexual harassment and misconduct from our ranks. This Committee and the Department of Defense have shared concerns about sexual harassment in the Armed Forces for many years. ... We will continue to work with you to ensure that our soldiers are treated with dignity and respect. We have made progress—but there is a long road ahead.

On November 7, 1996, the Chief of Staff of the Army and the Commanding General of U.S. Army Training and Doctrine Command reported to you in separate statements and to the American people that we had received allegations of sexual harassment and misconduct at Aberdeen Proving Ground, allegations that struck at the very heart of the Army's traditional commitment to soldiers and threatened the bond of trust that we hold so dear. We took immediate action to ensure that the victims were properly cared for, that the rights of the accused were protected, and that the specific incidents were addressed swiftly and appropriately.

Let me be clear: from the number and nature of the allegations, we in the Army have a problem of significant proportions. It is not clear yet what the entire list of corrective actions will turn out to be. We will come to that conclusion in time. What we know is that we have been entrusted with the lives and welfare of American sons and daughters. We know we must not—and we will not—fail that trust.

Let me state, in my own words and in the clearest terms, the Army's policy on sexual harassment: sexual harassment is unacceptable conduct. As Secretary of Defense William Cohen recently stated, "[T]here is zero tolerance for sexual harassment. It is not tolerable." That has always been our position, and that will always be our position. Sexual harassment runs counter to the values we teach our soldiers and demand in our leaders. Sexual harassment is not compatible with the Army's traditional beliefs in individual professionalism and respect for others. It has no place in our Army. . . .

What is alleged to have occurred at Aberdeen was particularly troublesome to us because it involved abuses of authority and it appeared that the incidents either had gone unreported or were not addressed. We initiated a series of actions to determine how that happened and how our system is working throughout the Army.

First, the Criminal Investigation Command (CID) immediately investigated each and every criminal allegation. On November 7, 1996, we established a toll-free hotline number for our soldiers to use to report instances of sexual harassment and misconduct. As [of] January 30, 1997, 6,979 calls had been placed to the hotline. Since the inception of the hotline, 1,025 calls have been referred to CID. CID has committed to contacting the complainants within five days of receiving the referral.

In addition, CID was directed to personally interview every female soldier currently stationed at Aberdeen Proving Ground as well as every female soldier who had trained at that post in the previous two years. Of the 990 female soldiers in the category, approximately 800 have been contacted and interviewed. This comprehensive investigation allows us to uncover the circumstances surrounding these events, and we will follow those leads wherever they take us.

Second, I directed the Department of the Army Inspector General to review and assess the sexual harassment policies and procedures at Basic and Advanced Individual Training sites throughout the Army Training Base. Concurrently, the Inspector General is conducting an inspection of the equal opportunity and sexual harassment training we provide all soldiers during their initial entry training. This special inspector is focusing on the training new soldiers receive on sexual harassment and equal opportunity, the avenues for complaints that are open to those soldiers, and the reporting systems that are in place to make sure that commanders hear the voices of soldiers who have complaints. This system must work, and it is important for all leaders to ensure that all our soldiers have complete knowledge of and confidence in this system.

Third, we convened a Senior Review Panel on Sexual Harassment, which we are pleased to note that you, Mr. Chairman, endorsed and have strongly supported. The panel is undertaking a comprehensive review of the present human relations environment in the Army and the policies and procedures that contribute to that environment. . . .

Let me address the issue of accountability. All of us—including the Secretary of the Army—are accountable for the Army's actions with respect to its soldiers. That accountability matters to you, the American people, and the Army. As you are aware, the Secretary of the Army has a role in the military justice system and must take care not to prejudice, or even be perceived to prejudice, the investigation or disposition of any individual case. I want to make it clear, here and now, that while we will not tolerate sexual abuse in America's Army, neither will we abridge the rights of soldiers accused in these matters or otherwise prejudge the results of our investigation and inquiry. We have acted quickly to stop the harm and help the victims. Conversely, we will act deliberately in sifting the facts before we assign punishment or assess blame. Each case must be judged on its own merits. That is what you expect of us, and it is the entitlement of each individual. . . .

The Army, however, is not simply awaiting the results of these investigations. We are moving forward to address the issue of sexual harassment in other ways. The Chief of Staff has ordered all major commanders to complete a chain teaching program on sexual harassment and has place [sic] renewed emphasis on the process that selects and educates those soldiers who will lead and instruct our trainees. His concern, and his emphasis on the need to prevent sexual harassment, is absolutely vital if we are to solve this problem.

We will continue our candid reporting and honest assessment of what we are doing and how we are doing it. These events—the allegations and the misconduct they imply—cut to the very heart of an Army that prides itself on taking care of its own, living life honorably, and performing its duty with integrity and courage. The Army values that every soldier must embrace—courage, candor, competence, and commitment—

cannot be destroyed by the actions of a few. We will correct these failures, and we will go on to be an even better Army in the coming century than we have been in the more than two centuries of service to our Nation.

Source: U.S. Senate Armed Services Committee, *Hearings on Sexual Harassment in Armed Services*, 105th Cong., 1st sess., February 4, 1997, 1997 Westlaw 8218692 (CONGTMY Library).

The Army's handling of the Aberdeen matter attracted the criticism of the National Association for the Advancement of Colored People (NAACP) and the Congressional Black Caucus. These groups were concerned about the racial implications of the matter; all of the accused drill sergeants were African American, and most of the accusers were white. Some members of the NAACP, along with lawyers for some of the accused, alleged that the sergeants were specifically targeted for prosecution because of their race. In March 1997, the NAACP sponsored a press conference at which five women alleged that Army investigators had attempted to coerce them into accusing their supervisors of rape.

The Congressional Black Caucus asked the Secretary of the Army to authorize an independent probe of the Army's handling of the incidents at Aberdeen. Secretary West, however, refused out of concern that such an investigation could jeopardize the criminal prosecutions. An article published in the *Washington Post* (Document 64) discusses the racial implications of the Aberdeen scandal.

DOCUMENT 64: "Issue of Race Emerges in Aberdeen Courtroom; Defense Says Army Targets Black Instructors" (Dana Priest and Jackie Spinner, 1997)

For the first time, a defense attorney for a drill sergeant accused of raping an Army trainee at Aberdeen Proving Ground argued yesterday inside the courtroom what others have argued from the sidelines: that ongoing trials and criminal investigations have unfairly targeted black men.

"We have seen a pattern of who's being charged in all these cases— African American males," said Capt. Arthur J. Coulter, an attorney for Staff Sgt. Vernell Robinson Jr., whose court-martial proceedings began yesterday at the northern Maryland military post. "Our contention is that he was only charged because he is African American and a male."

The Army's prosecutor called the defense accusation "absurd," and the presiding military judge said he would rule later on Coulter's motions to dismiss the case on grounds that the Army selectively targeted blacks.

His ruling is unlikely to resolve the question for many black members of Congress and others. They point to an all-black defendant list and to what they say are overzealous investigators as proof that the Army is out to get the black instructors.

Race was not made an issue in the trial of Staff Sgt. Delmar G. Simpson, who last week became the first of the Aberdeen drill sergeants to be convicted in the widespread scandal that has emerged at the base. He was convicted of raping six trainees: four whites, one black and one Hispanic. He also was found guilty of indecent assault and other lesser charges involving six other trainees: three blacks, one white, one Hispanic and one Pacific Islander.

Although about 60 percent of the 42 drill sergeants at the Ordnance Center and School are black, all 12 men charged with various sexual crimes are black. About 60 percent of the 2,300 trainees are white, and most of the alleged victims are white.

The NAACP and the Congressional Black Caucus, which has called for an independent investigation of the Army's handling of the cases after the trials, point to the unusual public statements of five white female soldiers to bolster their contention that the Army is overzealous in pursuing the cases.

In March, the women attended a news conference near the base called by the Harford County chapter of the NAACP and accused Army investigators of trying unsuccessfully to get them to say the instructors coerced them into having sex.

At least three of those women are to testify against Robinson, 32, who is accused of one count of rape, as well as sodomy, extortion, adultery and other crimes involving seven women and one man. Their statements will be scrutinized and questioned in court by defense attorneys looking for lies or inconsistencies. The jury will be free to judge the veracity of each statement and of the investigative process as a whole in determining whether to convict or absolve Robinson, a 12-year member of the Army from Mississippi.

But that may not be enough for some people who believe the military justice system itself is not fair.

"A great deal of pressure was brought to bear on the females to make the case the military wanted to make," said Rep. Earl F. Hilliard (D-Ala.), first vice chairman of the Congressional Black Caucus. "These women were forced to lie in many instances.

"This is just the beginning of the judicial process. But when you have a case, like this situation, where you single out people because of their race, we can't continue to sit back and let it happen."

The Aberdeen cases set off alarms immediately with black members of Congress and others because of the explosive nature of the cases: black men accused of raping white women.

"It's the history of black men and white females" that attracted attention, argued John S. Butler, professor of sociology and management at the University of Texas at Austin and co-author of a recent book on race relations in the Army. "I think the entire [racial segregation of the United States] was done to protect white females from black men. And any time a white female had sex with a black man and someone found out about it, she had to say it was rape or else the family would be ostracized."

Juanita Firestone, a military sociologist at the University of Texas at San Antonio, said survey data she has analyzed show that female soldiers are not more likely to accuse male soldiers of a different race of sexual harassment in what might be construed as inappropriate remarks or actions.

Still, she said, race "is part of the mix" at Aberdeen. "It makes trying to figure out what happened more complicated, because people are worried about the idea that women would be more likely to accuse or see harassment by a male of a different race."

She said it is wrong to focus on race and gender at Aberdeen, because it detracts from the central question of the clear-cut responsibilities of a drill sergeant in the unique training environment. "If he can't control himself, he has no right to the job," she said.

Yesterday, Robinson's attorney said another indication that the Army is selectively prosecuting black instructors is the fact that none of the accusers has been charged with violating the same Army rule that bans sexual relationships between instructors and trainees.

Army officials have said the women will not be prosecuted, in part because they believe it would have made it harder to get them to testify against the instructors. The Army also points out that most of the women had been in the Army fewer than four months and would not have understood how serious an infraction it is to have sex with their drill instructor.

"The accused is a drill sergeant with over 12 years in the Army," said the Army prosecutor, Capt. Scott Lawson. "The privates had about four months in the Army. . . . He has pages and pages of charges and has violated the regulation on numerous occasions with numerous individuals."

Source: Dana Priest and Jackie Spinner, "Issue of Race Emerges in Aberdeen Courtroom; Defense Says Army Targets Black Instructors," *The Washington Post*, May 6, 1997, p. A–1. © 1997, The Washington Post. Reprinted with Permission.

Investigation of the Sergeant Major of the Army

The most recent sexual harassment scandal in the military involved accusations against Gene McKinney, who was the sergeant major of the Army, the Army's highest ranking enlisted man. As an article published in the *New York Times* (Document 65) explains, in February 1997, Sergeant Major Brenda Hoster, who had served as Sergeant Major McKinney's public affairs specialist, accused him of sexual harassment. Specifically, she alleged that he asked her to have sex with him and forcibly kissed her. Although Sergeant Major Hoster reported the incident to her superiors, no action was taken against Sergeant Major McKinney. Sergeant Major Hoster, who subsequently retired from the Army, finally filed a formal complaint after hearing that Sergeant Major McKinney had been appointed to a panel charged with reviewing the Army's policies on sexual harassment, which was formed in response to the Aberdeen scandal.

In the following months, five other women leveled similar charges of sexual harassment and abuse against Sergeant Major McKinney. The allegations included claims that the sergeant major had directed inappropriate sexual comments to subordinates, had propositioned them for sex, and, in one instance, had sex with a subordinate against her wishes. Sergeant Major McKinney denied all of the allegations. In some cases, the women bringing the charges were threatened and harassed by other soldiers in retaliation for coming forward.

In March 1997, the Army reversed its initial position of allowing Sergeant Major McKinney to remain on the job during its investigation of the allegations, and he was suspended from his duties.

Sergeant Major McKinney was court-martialed in the spring of 1998. He was acquitted of all counts relating to sexual misconduct. He was convicted on one count of obstructing justice, based on a conversation in which he tried to coach one of his accusers about what she should tell military investigators. At his sentencing, he received a one-step demotion but was not sentenced to jail.

McKinney recently filed a lawsuit against Sergeant Major Hoster alleging that she libeled him by accusing him of sexual harassment. He is seeking $500,000 in actual damages and $1 million in punitive damages. Hoster had retired from the military before making her accusations.

McKinney is not permitted to sue his other accusers because the law prohibits active duty military personnel from getting damages from either a superior or a subordinate. This same legal principle also precludes any of the accusers, including Hoster, from suing McKinney.

As in the Aberdeen scandal, the situation involving Sergeant Major

McKinney had racial overtones. Sergeant Major McKinney is an African American; all of his accusers were white. He charged that the Army's investigation of him was tainted by racism.

DOCUMENT 65: "Top Enlisted Man in the Army Stands Accused of Sex Assault" (Eric Schmitt, 1997)

A 22-year Army veteran has accused her former boss, who is the Army's top-ranking enlisted soldier and a member of the commission charged with reviewing the Army's sexual harassment policies, of sexually assaulting her in her hotel room during an official trip to Hawaii in April. She says at least one senior Army officer then tried to cover up the incident.

As a result of the allegations, made formally in a complaint mailed to the Army on Friday, Gene C. McKinney, the Sergeant Major of the Army, today asked to be excused from his duties on the review panel until the matter is resolved. In a statement tonight, Sergeant Major McKinney denied "that he had ever engaged in any form of sexual misconduct."

Army officials said today that they had granted his request to be excused and that they would investigate the charges when the formal complaint arrived.

The woman, Sgt. Maj. Brenda L. Hoster, said that after she overcame her initial fears about reporting the incident, she told her superiors at the Pentagon about it seven weeks later. But, she said, they took no action against Sergeant Major McKinney and had suppressed her complaint. They also ignored her pleas for a job transfer and left her with no other choice but to retire early, she said.

That could have ended the matter. Sergeant Major Hoster, a 39-year-old Army journalist and public affairs specialist, said she reluctantly agreed to leave quietly in August, partly "for the good of the Army" and partly because she feared that no one would believe her if she pressed her case.

But when Army Secretary Togo D. West Jr. appointed Sergeant Major McKinney, 46, to the senior panel in November, Sergeant Major Hoster said, she could no longer stay silent. Not when the man she says kissed her, grabbed her and asked her for sex—even as his own wife was in another room just a few doors away—was to help set the Army's future policies against sexual misconduct.

"It wasn't right," Sergeant Major Hoster said in an emotional three-hour interview at her lawyer's office in Denver last Friday. "He doesn't have any business being on that panel."

The Sergeant Major of the Army—the senior person of that rank, chosen from among the service's sergeants major—is the top adviser to the Army Chief of Staff, a four-star general, on all matters, from housing to health care, relating to the Army's 410,000 enlisted soldiers. Enlisted soldiers make up 85 percent of the Army's ranks. Sergeant Major Hoster was Sergeant Major McKinney's public affairs specialist, responsible for helping him write his speeches and arranging interviews with reporters. She acknowledged that her boss had often expressed unhappiness with her performance during the 13 months they worked together. . . .

The most serious incident in Sergeant Major Hoster's complaint, she said, happened last April on an official trip to Hawaii. She said Sergeant Major McKinney had shown up at her hotel room door, casually dressed and wanting to continue a discussion that he had angrily broken off a half-hour earlier. Once inside the room, he made several sexual overtures, she said. " 'I could take you right here, right now,' " Sergeant Major McKinney said, according to her statement, a copy of which was provided by her lawyer to The New York Times.

" 'Ah, what a nice body you have,' " she said he had told her moments later, after he grabbed her by the waist and lifted her a foot off the ground.

The complaint also suggests that at least one high-ranking Army public-affairs officer covered up Sergeant Major Hoster's allegations and hid the damaging information from the Army's senior leaders.

In a three-paragraph response today to questions from a reporter, the Army said that Col. Robert Gaylord, the deputy chief of Army public affairs who heard Sergeant Major Hoster's complaint in June, had no comment, pending an investigation. . . .

Sergeant Major Hoster's complaint may undermine the credibility of the senior review panel at a time when only 47 percent of the Army women surveyed in 1995 said they believed that their leaders were serious about stopping sexual harassment. In its statement, the Army said Mr. West had not been aware of the complaint until a reporter brought it to his attention today.

Sergeants Major McKinney and Hoster were alone in the room at the Hale Koa military hotel in Honolulu when, she said, he assaulted her. Six people interviewed for this article, including civilian friends and Army co-workers, said Sergeant Major Hoster had told them about such an incident shortly after that time. Later, she told many of the same people about the Army's response.

Sergeant Major Hoster, who now earns $10 an hour as an office manager for a dentist in Santa Teresa, N. M., said she felt betrayed by an Army she had trusted. "Here's a bunch of people I would have stood in any foxhole with," she said in the interview, weeping softly, "and defended their lives with mine. They sold me out."

Source: Eric Schmitt, "Top Enlisted Man in the Army Stands Accused of Sex Assault," *New York Times*, February 4, 1997, p. A–1, col. 2.

Some critics, like former soldier Richard Cohen, in the following op-ed piece, contend that the military has gone too far in policing sexual harassment. Cohen argues that, in the interests of being politically correct, the military has too quickly rushed to punish those, like Sergeant Major McKinney, who have been accused of sexual harassment.

DOCUMENT 66: "Presumed Innocent; But Not for Long" (Richard Cohen, 1997)

At Fort Dix, N.J., where I did my basic training, we budding soldiers were told that the infantryman was the "Ultimate Weapon." No longer, though, can any grunt believe such nonsense. The ultimate weapon in today's Army is a charge of sexual harassment.

The latest to fall victim to this modern-day dumdum bullet is the very sergeant major of the Army, Gene C. McKinney. The highest-ranking enlisted man of them all, a 29-year veteran and a Legion of Merit holder, he was accused of sexual harassment by yet another sergeant major, the recently retired Brenda Hoster, and—after a principled pause—suspended from his job. In effect, he has been fired.

As is often the case in such matters, this is a he-says, she-says situation in which what Hoster says appears to have great credibility. Those who saw her interviewed on "60 Minutes"—I did not—came away impressed. She alleges that when she was serving as McKinney's public affairs specialist he demanded sex from her while on an official trip. She also says McKinney grabbed her and kissed her.

As for McKinney, he said nothing like this happened. You may or may not believe him—frankly, I have my doubts—but that is not the point. He remains, in the tradition for which he has solemnly pledged to give his life, innocent until found guilty. This, touchingly, was the Army's initial position.

"We are in a country where allegations are not proven fact, where charges are not convictions, where accuseds, no matter the seriousness of the charge, are not assumed guilty until proven guilty," said Togo D. West Jr., the secretary of the Army. A day later, he folded. It turns out we are in a country where you are assumed guilty until proven innocent. It is but a minor variation on the old theme.

As is often the case, the Army sounded retreat when it looked into the eyes of Congress. There, various members wondered why drill sergeants charged with sexual harassment were immediately suspended, while the sergeant major was not. Drill sergeants, though, are the authorized petty despots of the troops they command. Their powers are so vast that if mine suddenly materialized I think I would still bolt out of my chair and bellow out, "Good Afternoon, Sir!" Sergeant majors never had that effect on me.

I entertain no jolly boys-will-be-boys casualness about sexual harassment. It is serious stuff. But the fight against it cannot take precedence over our traditional notions of fair play. In McKinney's case, however, not only was he virtually fired from his job but we have now learned—on the front page of the New York Times, no less—that maybe two other women also have complained about him. "We're not talking physical stuff," an anonymous source told the Times. "We may be talking about approaches to women."

Approaches to women? Is this front-page news? Is this a firing offense? Is this even true? We cannot, of course, know. But we do know that the flimsiest and yet the most poisonous of charges have been aired about a man whose career, I take it, has been exemplary. He is the sergeant major of the Army, after all—no small honor where I used to be employed. Now he suffers a great public mortification on the front page of a great newspaper.

By now, there is ample evidence to suggest that the military is stumbling around in a state of shock from its various sexual scandals and outrages. A PC mentality grips the services. It seems officers may beach their ships or lose their planes, but they better not commit adultery or have been anywhere near the 1991 Tailhook convention. One Navy officer had a promotion denied for watching a stripper strip—not, mind you, for participating in any of the activities that made Tailhook synonymous with barbaric behavior.

When it comes to integrating women into what was a men-only occupation, that of warrior, the military has its work cut out for it. In some respects—joint training of men and women, for instance—it may have attempted the impractical. The rest of society watches transfixed: Why else is a single alleged episode involving two obscure noncoms given front-page treatment? Only ideological zealots know the absolute role of women in the military. The rest of us confess occasional confusion.

In McKinney's case, it may turn out that he dehumanized Hoster, turning her into an object. But that does not excuse or permit his own dehumanization. Until guilty, he is innocent. He may no longer be the ultimate weapon, but the presumption of innocence still remains our ultimate value.

Source: Richard Cohen, "Presumed Innocent; But Not for Long," *The Washington Post*, February 13, 1997, p. A–25. © 1997, The Washington Post. Reprinted with Permission.

PART III: FOR FURTHER READING

Francke, Linda Bird. *Ground Zero: The Gender Wars in the Military*. New York: Simon and Schuster, 1997.

McMichael, William H. *The Mother of All Hooks: The Story of the U.S. Navy's Tailhook Scandal*. New York: Transaction, 1997.

Office of the Inspector General. *The Tailhook Report*. New York: St. Martin's Press, 1993.

Zimmerman, Jean. *Tailspin: Women at War in the Wake of Tailhook*. New York: Doubleday, 1995.

Part IV

Sexual Harassment in Education

Another context in which sexual harassment claims arise is in the schools. Claims of sexual harassment have been brought at every level of education, from elementary schools through universities.

LAWS PROHIBITING SEXUAL HARASSMENT IN EDUCATION

Title IX of the Education Amendments of 1972 is a federal statute that prohibits educational programs or activities that receive federal funds from discriminating on the basis of sex. The vast majority of educational institutions in the United States, including primary and secondary schools and colleges and universities, receive federal funds. Some schools receive the funds through direct grants; others receive the funds indirectly, through the federal student loan program. Consequently, the vast majority of educational institutions in the United States are prohibited from engaging in sex discrimination under Title IX.

Although it does not specifically mention sexual harassment, Title IX has been interpreted to prohibit sexual harassment within educational institutions. It has been construed consistently to protect students from harassment by teachers and administrators. There is some dispute, however, among courts as to whether it makes the schools responsible for any sexual harassment by a student's peers, considered later in Documents 78–80.

DOCUMENT 67: Title IX of the Education Amendments of 1972

§ 1681. Sex

(a) Prohibition against discrimination; exceptions

No person in the United States shall, on the basis of sex, be excluded from participation in, be denied the benefits of, or be subjected to discrimination under any education program or activity receiving Federal financial assistance. . . .

(c) "Educational institution" defined

For purposes of this chapter an educational institution means any public or private preschool, elementary, or secondary school, or any institution of vocational, professional, or higher education, except that in the case of an educational institution composed of more than one school, college, or department which are administratively separate units, such term means each such school, college, or department.

Source: 20 *United States Code* § 1681 (1992).

The United States Department of Education, a federal agency, is charged with interpreting and implementing Title IX. The Office of Civil Rights of the United States Department of Education (OCR) recently promulgated a document entitled "Sexual Harassment Guidance: Harassment of Students by School Employees, Other Students, or Third Parties," in which it explains its interpretation of Title IX. The OCR takes the position that Title IX's prohibition of sexual harassment in schools should be interpreted similarly to Title VII's prohibition of sexual harassment in employment. In this regard, the OCR concludes that Title IX prohibits both quid pro quo and hostile environment sexual harassment.

DOCUMENT 68: "Sexual Harassment Guidance: Harassment of Students by School Employees, Other Students, or Third Parties" (Office for Civil Rights, United States Department of Education, 1997)

Introduction

Under Title IX of the Education Amendments of 1972 (Title IX) and its implementing regulations, no individual may be discriminated against on the basis of sex in any education program or activity receiving Federal financial assistance. Sexual harassment of students is a form of prohibited sex discrimination under the circumstances described in the Guidance. The following types of conduct constitute sexual harassment:

Quid Pro Quo Harassment

A school employee explicitly or implicitly conditions a student's participation in an education program or activity or bases an educational decision on the student's submission to unwelcome sexual advances, requests for sexual favors, or other verbal, nonverbal, or physical conduct of a sexual nature. Quid pro quo harassment is equally unlawful whether the student resists and suffers the threatened harm or submits and thus avoids the threatened harm.

Hostile Environment Sexual Harassment

Sexually harassing conduct (which can include unwelcome sexual advances, requests for sexual favors, and other verbal, nonverbal, or physical conduct of a sexual nature) by an employee, by another student, or by a third party that is sufficiently severe, persistent, or pervasive to limit a student's ability to participate in or benefit from an education program or activity, or to create a hostile or abusive educational environment.

Schools are required by the Title IX regulations to have grievance procedures through which students can complain of alleged sex discrimination, including sexual harassment. As outlined in this guidance, grievance procedures also provide schools with an excellent mechanism to be used in their efforts to prevent sexual harassment before it occurs. . . .

Applicability of Title IX

Title IX applies to all public and private educational institutions that receive Federal funds, including elementary and secondary schools, school districts, proprietary schools, colleges, and universities. The Guidance uses the term "schools" to refer to all those institutions. The "education program or activity" of a school includes all of the school's operations. This means that Title IX protects students in connection with all of the academic, educational, extra-curricular, athletic, and other programs of the school, whether they take place in the facilities of the school, on a school bus, at a class or training program sponsored by the school at another location, or elsewhere.

It is important to recognize that Title IX's prohibition of sexual harassment does not extend to legitimate nonsexual touching or other nonsexual conduct. For example, a high school athletic coach hugging a student who made a goal or a kindergarten teacher's consoling hug for a child with a skinned knee will not be considered sexual harassment. Similarly, one student's demonstration of a sports maneuver or technique requiring contact with another student will not be considered sexual harassment. However, in some circumstances, nonsexual conduct may take on sexual connotations and may rise to the level of sexual harassment. For example, a teacher's repeatedly hugging and putting his or her arms around students under inappropriate circumstances could create a hostile environment. . . .

It is also important to recognize that gender-based harassment, which may include acts of verbal, nonverbal, or physical aggression, intimidation, or hostility based on sex, but not involving conduct of a sexual nature, may be a form of sex discrimination that violates Title IX if it is sufficiently severe, persistent, or pervasive and directed at individuals because of their sex. For example, the repeated sabotaging of female graduate students' laboratory experiments by male students in the class could be the basis of a violation of Title IX. Although a comprehensive discussion of gender-based harassment is beyond the scope of this Guidance, in assessing all related circumstances to determine whether a hostile environment exists, incidents of gender-based harassment combined with incidents of sexual harassment could create a hostile environment, even if neither the gender-based harassment alone nor the sexual harassment alone would be sufficient to do so. . . .

Effect of Grievance Procedures on Liability

Schools are required by the Title IX regulations to adopt and publish grievance procedures providing for prompt and equitable resolution of sex discrimination complaints, including complaints of sexual harassment, and to disseminate a policy against sex discrimination. . . . These procedures provide a school with a mechanism for discovering sexual harassment as early as possible and for effectively correcting problems, as required by Title IX. By having a strong policy against sex discrimination and accessible, effective, and fairly applied grievance procedures, a school is telling its students that it does not tolerate sexual harassment and that students can report it without fear of adverse consequences.

Accordingly, in the absence of effective policies and grievance procedures, if the alleged harassment was sufficiently severe, persistent, or pervasive to create a hostile environment, a school will be in violation of Title IX because of the existence of a hostile environment, even if the school was not aware of the harassment and thus failed to remedy it. This is because, without a policy and procedure, a student does not know either of the school's interest in preventing this form of discrimination or how to report harassment so that it can be remedied. . . .

Welcomeness

In order to be actionable as harassment, sexual conduct must be unwelcome. Conduct is unwelcome if the student did not request or invite it and "regarded the conduct as undesirable or offensive." Acquiescence in the conduct or the failure to complain does not always mean that the conduct was welcome. For example, a student may decide not to resist sexual advances of another student or may not file a complaint out of fear. In addition, a student may not object to a pattern of sexually demeaning comments directed at him or her by a group of students out of a concern that objections might cause the harassers to make more comments. The fact that a student may have accepted the conduct does not mean that he or she welcomed it. Also, the fact that a student willingly participated in conduct on one occasion does not prevent him or her from indicating that the same conduct has become unwelcome on a subsequent occasion. On the other hand, if a student actively participates in sexual banter and discussions and gives no indication that he or she objects, then the evidence generally will not support a conclusion that the conduct was unwelcome.

If younger children are involved, it may be necessary to determine the degree to which they are able to recognize that certain sexual conduct is conduct to which they can or should reasonably object and the degree to which they can articulate an objection. Accordingly, OCR will consider the age of the student, the nature of the conduct involved, and other relevant factors in determining whether a student had the capacity to welcome sexual conduct.

Schools should be particularly concerned about the issue of welcomeness if the harasser is in a position of authority. For instance, because students may be encouraged to believe that a teacher has absolute authority over the operation of his or her classroom, a student may not object to a teacher's sexually harassing comments during class; however, this does not necessarily mean that the conduct was welcome. Instead, the student may believe that any objections would be ineffective in stopping the harassment or may fear that by making objections he or she will be singled out for harassing comments or other retaliation.

In addition, OCR must consider particular issues of welcomeness if the alleged harassment relates to alleged "consensual" sexual relationships between a school's adult employees and its students. If elementary students are involved, welcomeness will not be an issue: OCR will never view sexual conduct between an adult school employee and an elementary school student as consensual. In cases involving secondary students, there will be a strong presumption that sexual conduct between an adult school employee and a student is not consensual. In cases involving older secondary students, subject to the presumption, OCR will consider a number of factors in determining whether a school employee's sexual advances or other sexual conduct could be considered welcome. In addition, OCR will consider these factors in all cases involving postsecondary students in making those determinations. The factors include:

—The nature of the conduct and the relationship of the school employee to the student, including the degree of influence (which could, at least in part, be affected by the student's age), authority, or control the employee has over the student.

—Whether the student was legally or practically unable to consent to the sexual conduct in question. For example, a student's age could affect his or her ability to do so. Similarly, certain types of disabilities could affect a student's ability to do so.

If there is a dispute about whether harassment occurred or whether it was welcome—in a case in which it is appropriate to consider whether the conduct could be welcome—determinations should be made based on the totality of the circumstances. The following types of information may be helpful in resolving the dispute:

—Statements by any witnesses to the alleged incident.

—Evidence about the relative credibility of the allegedly harassed student and the alleged harasser. For example, the level of detail and consistency of each person's account should be compared in an attempt to determine who is telling the truth. Another way to assess credibility is to see if corroborative evidence is lacking where it should logically exist. However, the absence of witnesses may indicate only the unwillingness of others to step forward, perhaps due to fear of the harasser or a desire not to get involved.

—Evidence that the alleged harasser has been found to have harassed others may support the credibility of the student claiming the harassment; conversely, the student's claim will be weakened if he or she has been found to have made false allegations against other individuals.

—Evidence of the allegedly harassed student's reaction or behavior after the alleged harassment. For example, were there witnesses who saw the student immediately after the alleged incident who say that the student appeared to be upset? However, it is important to note that some students may respond to harassment in ways that do not manifest themselves right away, but may surface several days or weeks after the harassment. For example, a student may initially show no signs of having been harassed, but several weeks after the harassment, there may be significant changes in the student's behavior, including difficulty concentrating on academic work, symptoms of depression, and a desire to avoid certain individuals and places at school.

—Evidence about whether the student claiming harassment filed a complaint or took other action to protest the conduct soon after the alleged incident occurred. However, failure to immediately complain may merely reflect a fear of retaliation or a fear that the complainant may not be believed rather than that the alleged harassment did not occur.

—Other contemporaneous evidence. For example, did the student claiming harassment write about the conduct, and his or her reaction to it, soon after it occurred (e.g., in a diary or letter)? Did the student tell others (friends, parents) about the conduct (and his or her reaction to it) soon after it occurred?

Severe, Persistent, or Pervasive

Hostile environment sexual harassment of a student or students by other students, employees, or third parties is created if conduct of a sexual nature is sufficiently severe, persistent, or pervasive to limit a student's ability to participate in or benefit from the education program or to create a hostile or abusive educational environment. Thus, conduct that is sufficiently severe, but not persistent or pervasive, can result in hostile environment sexual harassment.

In deciding whether conduct is sufficiently severe, persistent, or pervasive, the conduct should be considered from both a subjective and objective perspective. In making this determination, all relevant circumstances should be considered:

—The degree to which the conduct affected one or more students' education. For a hostile environment to exist, the conduct must have limited the ability of a student to participate in or benefit from his or her education or altered the conditions of the student's educational environment.

——Many hostile environment cases involve tangible or obvious injuries. For example, a student's grades may go down or the student may be forced to withdraw from school because of the harassing behavior. A student may also suffer physical injuries and mental or emotional distress.

——However, a hostile environment may exist even if there is no tangible injury to the student. For example, a student may have been able to keep up his or her grades and continue to attend school even though it was more difficult for him or her to do so because of the harassing behavior. A student may be able to remain on a sports team, despite feeling humiliated or angered by harassment that creates a hostile environment. Harassing conduct in these examples alters the student's educational environment on the basis of sex.

——A hostile environment can occur even if the harassment is not targeted specifically at the individual complainant. For example, if a student or group of students regularly directs sexual comments toward a particular student, a hostile environment may be created not only for the targeted student, but also for others who witness the conduct. Similarly, if a middle school teacher directs sexual comments toward a particular student, a hostile environment may be created for the targeted student and for the students who witness the conduct.

—The type, frequency, and duration of the conduct. In most cases, a hostile environment will exist if there is a pattern or practice of harassment or if the harassment is sustained and nontrivial. For instance, if a young woman is taunted by one or more young men about her breasts or genital area or both, OCR may find that a hostile environment has been created, particularly if the conduct has gone on for some time, takes place throughout the school, or if the taunts are made by a number of students. The more severe the conduct, the less the need to show a repetitive series of incidents; this is particularly true if the harassment is physical. For instance, if the conduct is more severe, e.g., attempts to grab a female student's breasts, genital area, or buttocks, it need not be as persistent or pervasive in order to create a hostile environment. Indeed, a single or isolated incident of sexual harassment may, if sufficiently severe, create a hostile environment. On the other hand, conduct that is not severe, persistent, or pervasive will not create a hostile environment; e.g., a comment by one student to another student that she has a nice figure. Indeed, depending on the circumstances, this may not even be conduct of a sexual nature. Similarly, because students date one another, a request for a date or a gift of flowers, even if unwelcome, would not create a hostile environment. However, there may be circumstances in which repeated, unwelcome requests for dates or similar conduct could create a hostile environment. For example, a person may request dates in an intimidating or threatening manner.

—The identity of and relationship between the alleged harasser and the subject or subjects of the harassment. A factor to be considered, especially in cases involving allegations of sexual harassment of a student by a school employee, is the identity of and relationship between the alleged harasser and the subject or subjects of the harassment. For example, due to the power that a professor or teacher has over a student, sexually based conduct by that person toward a student is more likely to create a hostile environment than similar conduct by another student.

—The number of individuals involved. Sexual harassment may be committed by an individual or a group. In some cases, verbal comments or other conduct from one person might not be sufficient to create a hostile environment, but could be if done by a group. Similarly, while harassment can be directed toward an individual or a group, the effect of the conduct toward a group may vary, depending on the type of conduct and the context. For certain types of conduct, there may be "safety in numbers." For example, following an individual student and making sexual taunts to him or her may be very intimidating to that student but, in certain circumstances, less so to a group of students. On the other hand, persistent unwelcome sexual conduct still may create a hostile environment if directed toward a group.

—The age and sex of the alleged harasser and the subject or subjects of the harassment. For example, in the case of younger students, sexually harassing conduct is more likely to be intimidating if coming from an older student.

—The size of the school, location of the incidents, and context in which they occurred. Depending on the circumstances of a particular case, fewer incidents may have a greater effect at a small college than at a large university campus. Harassing conduct occurring on a school bus may be more intimidating than similar conduct on a school playground because the restricted area makes it impossible for the students to avoid their harassers. Harassing conduct in a personal or secluded area such as a dormitory room or residence hall can also have a greater effect (e.g., be seen as more threatening) than would similar conduct in a more public area. On the other hand, harassing conduct in a public place may be more humiliating. Each incident must be judged individually.

—Other incidents at the school. A series of instances at the school, not involving the same students, could—taken together—create a hostile environment, even if each by itself would not be sufficient.

—Incidents of gender-based, but non-sexual, harassment. Acts of verbal, nonverbal, or physical aggression, intimidation, or hostility based on sex, but not involving sexual activity or language, can be combined with incidents of sexual harassment to determine if the incidents of sexual harassment are sufficiently severe, persistent, or pervasive to create a sexually hostile environment.

Source: Office for Civil Rights, U.S. Department of Education, "Sexual Harassment Guidance: Harassment of Students by School Employees, Other Students, or Third Parties," 62 *Federal Register* 12034–01, 12038–39, 12040–42 (March 13, 1997) (footnotes omitted).

Title IX is different from Title VII in one important respect. Title VII specifically provides that victims of sex discrimination may sue in court and receive damages. Title IX, in contrast, does not say whether individual victims have a right to bring a lawsuit and receive individual remedies. Instead, the statute simply directs the federal government to terminate the federal funding of institutions that engage in sex discrimination. Nonetheless, in a case called *Franklin v. Gwinnett County Public Schools* (Document 69), the U.S. Supreme Court held that students who are subjected to sexual harassment in their schools may sue the schools and receive money damages.

DOCUMENT 69: *Franklin v. Gwinnett County Public Schools,* U.S. Supreme Court (1992)

I

Petitioner Christine Franklin was a student at North Gwinnett High School in Gwinnett County, Georgia, between September 1985 and August 1989. Respondent Gwinnett County School District operates the high school and receives federal funds. According to the complaint filed on December 29, 1988, in the United States District Court for the Northern District of Georgia, Franklin was subjected to continual sexual harassment beginning in the autumn of her tenth grade year (1986) from Andrew Hill, a sports coach and teacher employed by the district. Among other allegations, Franklin avers that Hill engaged her in sexually oriented conversations in which he asked about her sexual experiences with her boyfriend and whether she would consider having sexual intercourse with an older man, . . . that Hill forcibly kissed her on the mouth in the school parking lot, . . . that he telephoned her at her home and asked if she would meet him socially, . . . and that, on three occasions in her junior year, Hill interrupted a class, requested that the teacher excuse Franklin, and took her to a private office where he subjected her to coercive intercourse. . . . The complaint further alleges that though they became aware of and investigated Hill's sexual harassment of Franklin and other female students, teachers and administrators took no action to halt it and discouraged Franklin from pressing charges against Hill. . . . On April 14, 1988, Hill resigned on the condition that all matters pending against him be dropped. . . . The school thereupon closed its investigation. . . .

In this action, the District Court dismissed the complaint on the ground that Title IX does not authorize an award of damages. The Court of Appeals affirmed. . . .

. . . We reverse.

II

* * *

A

"[W]here legal rights have been invaded, and a federal statute provides for a general right to sue for such invasion, federal courts may use any available remedy to make good the wrong done." . . .

. . . From the earliest years of the Republic, the Court has recognized the power of the Judiciary to award appropriate remedies to redress injuries actionable in federal court, although it did not always distinguish clearly between a right to bring suit and a remedy available under such a right. . . . In *Marbury v. Madison* . . . (1803), for example, Chief Justice Marshall observed that our Government "has been emphatically termed a government of laws, and not of men. It will certainly cease to deserve this high appellation, if the laws furnish no remedy for the violation of a vested legal right." . . .

V

In sum, we conclude that a damages remedy is available for an action brought to enforce Title IX. The judgment of the Court of Appeals, therefore, is reversed, and the case is remanded for further proceedings consistent with this opinion.

Source: 503 *United States Reports* 60, 62–65, 66, 76 (1992) (footnotes omitted).

A number of states have laws that specifically prohibit sexual harassment in educational institutions. California has one of the most comprehensive laws. It provides that sexual harassment can be grounds for suspending or expelling a student from school, starting in the fourth grade.

DOCUMENT 70: California General Education Code §§ 212.5, 48900.2 (1995)

---

§ 212.5. *"Sexual harassment"*

For purposes of this chapter, "sexual harassment" means unwelcome sexual advances, requests for sexual favors, and other verbal, visual, or physical conduct of a sexual nature, made by someone from or in the work or educational setting, under any of the following conditions:

(a) Submission to the conduct is explicitly or implicitly made a term or a condition of an individual's employment, academic status, or progress.

(b) Submission to, or rejection of, the conduct by the individual is used as the basis of employment or academic decisions affecting the individual.

(c) The conduct has the purpose or effect of having a negative impact upon the individual's work or academic performance, or of creating an intimidating, hostile, or offensive work or educational environment.

(d) Submission to, or rejection of, the conduct by the individual is used as the basis for any decision affecting the individual regarding benefits and services, honors, programs, or activities available at or through the educational institution.

§ 48900.2. *Sexual harassment as ground for suspension or recommendation for expulsion*

In addition to the reasons specified in Section 48900, a pupil may be suspended from school or recommended for expulsion if the superintendent or the principal of the school in which the pupil is enrolled determines that the pupil has committed sexual harassment as defined in Section 212.5.

For the purposes of this chapter, the conduct described in Section 212.5 must be considered by a reasonable person of the same gender as the victim to be sufficiently severe or pervasive to have a negative impact upon the individual's academic performance or to create an intimidating, hostile, or offensive educational environment. This section shall not apply to pupils enrolled in kindergarten and grades 1 to 3, inclusive.

Source: California General Education Code §§ 212.5, 48900.2 (1995).

DEVELOPMENT OF THE LAW AGAINST
SEXUAL HARASSMENT IN EDUCATION

The first case in which students alleged sexual harassment by the educational institution that they attended involved a lawsuit brought by five women against Yale University in the late 1970s. The women sued under Title IX and asked that, as a remedy, the court declare that Yale had violated Title IX by failing to institute effective procedures to combat sexual harassment and that it order Yale to adopt such procedures.

The women, however, lost their suit. The claims of four of the women were dismissed on technical grounds. The fifth woman's claim went to trial, but the judge did not believe her claims as a factual matter. The appellate court affirmed the judgment for Yale. It reasoned that, because, by the time the court heard the dispute, all of the women had graduated, there was no longer any reason for a court to consider the case. Even if the court had awarded the remedies that the women sought, these women, since they were no longer at Yale, would receive no benefit.

The case, *Alexander v. Yale University* (Document 71), nonetheless remains an important one in the history of sexual harassment litigation. Although the plaintiffs lost, the case helped establish the proposition that there might be some situations in which educational institutions would be deemed to have violated the law by failing to remedy complaints of sexual harassment. The litigation also served as a spur to Yale and to other universities to begin adopting policies prohibiting sexual harassment and procedures under which students affected by harassment could have their complaints heard.

DOCUMENT 71: *Alexander v. Yale University*, U.S. Court of Appeals for the Second Circuit (1980)

Five women who were students at Yale University appeal from a judgment entered by Judge Burns on July 3, 1979, in the United States District Court for the District of Connecticut. The appellants alleged in their complaint that Yale was violating Title IX of the Education Amendments of 1972 . . . by refusing to consider seriously women students' complaints of sexual harassment by male faculty members and administrators. . . . We affirm the judgment of the district court for Yale as to all of the plaintiffs.

I.

Section 1681 of Title IX (hereinafter "Title IX") states: No person in the United States shall, on the basis of sex, be excluded from participation in, be denied the benefits of, or be subjected to discrimination under any education program or activity receiving Federal financial assistance. . . .

In an amended complaint filed on November 15, 1977, three female students, two female graduates, and one male professor at Yale alleged that Yale's "failure to combat sexual harassment of female students and its refusal to institute mechanisms and procedures to address complaints and make investigations of such harassment interferes with the educational process and denies equal opportunity in education" in violation of Title IX. . . . [P]laintiffs sought as relief (1) a declaratory judgment that Yale's policies and practices regarding sexual harassment violate Title IX and (2) an order enjoining Yale, among other duties, "to institute and continue a mechanism for receiving, investigating, and adjudicating complaints of sexual harassment, to be designed and implemented under the supervision" of the district court. . . .

Ronni Alexander, a 1977 graduate of Yale College, alleged that she "found it impossible to continue playing the flute and abandoned her study of the instrument, thus aborting her desired professional career," because of the repeated sexual advances, "including coerced sexual intercourse," by her flute instructor, Keith Brion. Alexander further alleged that she attempted to complain to Yale officials about her harassment, but "was discouraged and intimidated by unresponsive administrators and complex and ad hoc methods."

Margery Reifler, a member of the Class of 1980, alleged that Richard Kentwell, coach of the field hockey team, "sexually harassed" her while she was working as that team's manager, and that she "suffered distress and humiliation . . . and was denied recognition due her as team manager, all to her educational detriment." Reifler further alleged that she "wanted to complain to responsible authorities of defendant about said sexual harassment but was intimidated by the lack of legitimate procedures and was unable to determine if any channels for complaint about sexual harassment were available to her."

Pamela Price, a member of the Class of 1979, alleged that one of her course instructors, Raymond Duvall, "offered to give her a grade of 'A' in the course in exchange for her compliance with his sexual demands," that she refused, and that she received a grade of "C" which "was not the result of a fair evaluation of her academic work, but the result of her failure to accede to Professor Duvall's sexual demands." She further alleges that she complained to officials of Yale who failed to investigate her complaint and told her that "nothing could be done to remedy her situation."

Lisa Stone, a member of the Class of 1978, alleged that her discussions with a woman student who had been sexually harassed and the absence of an "established, legitimate procedure" for complaints of such harassment caused her "emotional distress," deprived her of "the tranquil atmosphere necessary to her pursuit of a liberal education," and put her "in fear of her own associations with men in positions of authority at Yale."

Ann Olivarius, a 1977 graduate, alleged that the absence of a procedure for complaining about sexual harassment "forced (her) to expend time, effort and money in investigating complaints herself, preparing them to be presented to responsible officials of defendant, and attempting to negotiate the complexities of ad hoc 'channels.' " Olivarius further alleged that she was "subjected to threats and intimidation from individuals involved in her investigations and was given no protection or encouragement by responsible officials of defendant."

Then District Judge Newman . . . dismissed all the plaintiffs but Price in an order entered on December 21, 1977. . . .

After the trial of Price's claim, Judge Burns found that "the alleged incident of sexual proposition did not occur and the grade of 'C' which Miss Price received on the paper submitted to Professor Duvall and the grade of 'C' which she received in his course did not reflect consideration of any factor other than academic achievement." Accordingly, although the district court agreed that Yale's procedures for handling complaints of sexual harassment were inadequate, it refused to enjoin Yale to establish a different procedure, concluding, "(I)t does not follow that, if Yale University failed to articulate appropriate procedures to deal with such a claim, a plaintiff who can show neither an improper advance nor the injury she claimed has a grievance to be redressed by this court." The district court therefore entered judgment for Yale, and the five female plaintiffs (hereinafter "appellants") brought their appeal.

II.

* * *

Olivarius's claim on appeal from her dismissal presents the weakest case. . . . Olivarius spent her time and money upon her own volition. The allegation that Yale failed to protect and encourage her in her investigations does not allege an injury, for it does not allege that Olivarius was hurt—in any way—by Yale's failure. Accordingly, we affirm the dismissal of her complaint.

As for the other plaintiffs, including Price, whose claim we discuss below, their graduations appear to prevent the courts both from addressing the predominant injury relied upon—deprivation of an educational environment free from condoned harassment—and from awarding the relief requested—an order directing Yale to institute effective procedures for receiving and adjudicating complaints of sexual harassment. None of these plaintiffs at present suffers from the alleged injury. Nor would the grant of the requested relief aid these plaintiffs in the slightest. Thus their claims appear moot.

It is perhaps more important to note that, as Yale's counsel has assured us in brief and oral argument, Yale in fact has adopted a set of procedures for hearing such complaints. The procedures were proposed by a committee consisting of faculty, administrators and students, in a report published March 1979, following a year of careful study specifically limited to the problems involved in structuring procedures appropriate for consideration of student complaints of sexual harassment. . . . We have no reason to doubt that the procedures now in effect will tend to alleviate the "atmosphere of inequality" alleged by plaintiffs in this suit. Thus, it appears that the major relief sought in this suit has already been granted. . . .

Both Alexander and Reifler, however, allege additional personal injuries. Nevertheless, what remains of their claims does not seem sufficient to justify judicial action. Their alleged injuries are too speculative. Alexander asserts that sexual harassment by her flute instructor in a University-sponsored music program deterred her from a successful career as a flutist. Needless to say, this is a highly conjectural claim. Reifler claims that sexual harassment by her field hockey coach caused her to leave the team and fail to receive a varsity letter. What harm she has suffered as a result is not specified. . . .

Moreover, it is difficult to imagine what relief a court could possibly award Reifler and Alexander. No money damages have been requested, and as already noted, graduation has mooted their claims for grievance procedures. As the district court remarked, there is nothing left that a court could do to redress Alexander's injury "absent sheer conjecture that (she) may in the future wish to resume study in a field allegedly abandoned at Yale because of 'sexual demands' by her tutor." . . . In appellants' brief on appeal a suggestion has been made that a court might award Reifler a varsity letter, yet we do not believe that such a possibility warrants judicial scrutiny, particularly when the alleged injury is so uncertain. Because we do not believe that the courts should indulge in speculation of the sort required here, we also affirm the dismissal of the complaints of Alexander and Reifler.

We thus agree with the district court that only plaintiff Price presented a justiciable claim for relief under Title IX. That claim, however, was tried and dismissed.

Source: 631 *Federal Reporter 2d* 178, 180–85, 186.

THE PREVALENCE OF SEXUAL HARASSMENT IN EDUCATIONAL INSTITUTIONS

Primary and Secondary Schools

In 1993 the National Organization for Women's Legal Defense and Education Fund, together with the Wellesley College Center for Research on Women, published a study documenting sexual harassment in elementary and secondary schools. The study was based on a survey published in *Seventeen* magazine. Readers of that magazine were encouraged to answer a range of questions about whether they had experienced sexual harassment and, if so, what actions they took in response. Over 4,200 girls responded to the survey. The study concludes that sexual harassment is rampant in elementary and secondary schools.

DOCUMENT 72: *Secrets in Public: Sexual Harassment in Our Schools* (Nan Stein, Nancy L. Marshall, and Linda R. Tropp, 1993)

Sexual harassment is rampant in elementary and secondary schools. It is a "well-known secret" that takes place in public every day in schools across the nation. While sometimes identified and curtailed, more often than not sexual harassment is tolerated. It is labeled as "flirting" or dismissed as part of an acceptable developmental stage in adolescence. "No harm done" and "no big deal" are the often cited excuses.

Regardless of the ways school authorities rationalize its appearance, sexual harassment is a form of sex discrimination, and therefore illegal. It is a violation of Title IX of the Educational Amendments of 1972, Title VII of the Civil Rights Act of 1964 as amended in 1972, the equal protection clause of the U.S. Constitution, and numerous state criminal and civil statutes. Sexual Harassment is defined by the person who is the target of the harassment. It is any form of unwanted sexual attention.

The dilemma facing victims of sexual harassment is how to handle upsetting and degrading incidents—especially since they have become so acceptable, ordinary and public. Sexual harassment in schools operates in full and plain view of others. Boys harass girls with impunity while others stand by.

Too many of our schools have become unsafe, uncaring and unjust. Students have a right to expect that if something frightening, unpleasant or illegal is happening in school—especially if it is occurring in public—someone in authority will intervene to stop it. They also deserve to be believed when they report an incident. Yet sexual harassment seems, for the most part, to proceed without adult interventions. The lessons of silence and neglect resulting from official inaction not only affect the subjects of sexual harassment, they also spread to the bystanders and witnesses. Boys as well as girls become mistrustful of adults who fail to intervene, to provide equal protection and to safeguard the educational environment.

To learn more about sexual harassment in schools, the Wellesley College Center for Research on Women and the NOW Legal Defense and Education Fund collaborated on a survey that was published in *Seventeen*

Magazine (September 1992). Over 4,200 girls completed and returned surveys.

Survey results show that:

- The most common forms of sexual harassment are: receiving sexual comments, gestures or looks (reported by 89 percent of the girls and young women); being touched, pinched or grabbed (reported by 83 percent).
- When sexual harassment occurs, it is not a one-time-only event: 39 percent of the girls and young women reported being harassed at school on a daily basis during the last year.
- Almost two-thirds of the girls told their harassers to stop. Over a third resisted with physical force.
- Most harassed girls and young women tell someone when they have been harassed. Three-quarters (76%) of all the girls and young women in the sample told at least one person about being harassed in school.
- Harassment is a public event; other people are present at over two-thirds of the incidents reported.
- Sexual harassment happens in all kinds of schools, to all kinds of girls—there are few differences by type of school attended or by racial or ethnic background.
- Girls are most often harassed by fellow students, but 4 percent of the girls reported being harassed by teachers, administrators or other school staff.
- Most harassers are male.
- Girls are more likely to do nothing or to walk away without telling the harasser to stop if the harasser is a teacher, administrator or other staff member than if the harasser is a fellow student.
- Schools are less likely to do something about a harassment incident when the harasser is a teacher.
- Even when girls told a teacher or administrator about the harassment, nothing happened to the harasser in 45 percent of the incidents reported.
- Only 8 percent of the girls reported that their schools had, and enforced, a policy on sexual harassment.

Source: Nan Stein, Nancy L. Marshall, and Linda R. Tropp, *Secrets in Public: Sexual Harassment in Our Schools* (Center for Research on Women, Wellesley College, 1993), pp. 1–2 (footnotes omitted).

Also in 1993, the American Association of University Women (AAUW) commissioned a similar study to assess the prevalence of sexual harassment in public schools. Professionally trained facilitators administered anonymous surveys to girls and boys in grades eight through eleven in randomly selected classes at randomly selected public schools; 1,632 surveys were completed.

The AAUW study also concluded that sexual harassment was rampant in public schools. Interestingly, the study found that very large majorities of both boys and girls had experienced some form of sexual harassment. Girls, however, report suffering more as a result of the harassment, disproportionately saying that the harassment caused them to want to avoid school and undermined their self-esteem. The AAUW study also focused on ethnic variations in the prevalence and reactions to sexual harassment. For example, African American boys were much more likely than white or Hispanic boys to report that they had experienced sexual harassment, while white girls were slightly more likely to report experiences of sexual harassment than African American and Hispanic girls.

DOCUMENT 73: *Hostile Hallways: The AAUW Survey on Sexual Harassment in America's Schools* **(American Association of University Women, 1993)**

Key Findings

Sexual harassment in school is widespread.

- Four in 5 students (81%) say they have experienced some form of sexual harassment during their school lives; 85% of girls and 76% of boys. . . .
- More than half the students surveyed (58%) report that they have been targeted "often" or "occasionally."

There are notable gender and racial/ethnic gaps.

- Nearly 1 in 3 girls (31%) who have been harassed have experienced unwanted advances "often," compared with fewer than 1 in 5 boys (18%). . . .
- For girls, 87% of whites report having experienced sexual harassment, compared with 84% of African Americans and 82% of Hispanics.
- Among boys, African Americans (81%) have experienced sexual harassment, compared with whites (75%) and Hispanics (69%).

In grades 7, 8, and 9, many more girls than boys first experience sexual harassment in school.

* * *

- For 6% of students who have been harassed, the first experience of sexual harassment took place before grade 3. . . .

Sexual comments, jokes, looks, and gestures—as well as touching, grabbing, and/or pinching in a sexual way—are commonplace in school.

- Two in 3 of all students surveyed (66%) have been targets of the above forms of verbal/gestural abuse. . . .

The third most common form of sexual harassment in school involves intentionally brushing up against someone in a sexual way—something girls experience far more often than boys.

* * *

Students say they would be very upset if they were called gay or lesbian. Being called gay would be more upsetting to boys than actual physical abuse.

* * *

- For boys, this is the most disturbing form of unwanted behavior: 88% of Hispanic boys and 85% of both African American and white boys would be troubled by being called gay. . . .

Experiences of student-to-student harassment outnumber all others, with notable gender and ethnic/racial gaps.

- Nearly 4 in 5 students (79%) who have been harassed have been targeted by peers: current or former students.
- Two in 3 (66%) of all boys and more than half (52%) of all girls say they have sexually harassed someone in the school setting. . . .

Adult-to-student harassment is nonetheless considerable, with notable gender and ethnic/racial gaps.

- 18% of students who have been harassed cite adults as the perpetrators.
- One in 4 girls (25%) and 1 in 10 boys (10%) who have been harassed say they have been harassed by a school employee (such as a teacher, coach, bus driver, teacher's aide, security guard, principal, or counselor).
- Among girls, adult-student harassment is more commonly experienced by African Americans (33%) than whites (25%) and Hispanics (17%).

Harassing others is a routine part of school culture—more so for boys than for girls.

* * *

Public areas are the most common harassment sites—especially as reported by girls.

- Two in 3 students who have been harassed (66%) say they have been harassed in the hallway.
- More than half (55%) of those who have been harassed cite the classroom. . . .

Students usually do not report incidents to adults. Boys are more likely than girls to tell no one.

- Fewer than 1 in 10 students who have been harassed (7%) say they have told a teacher, although girls are twice as likely to have done so as boys.
- Fewer than 1 in 4 students who have been harassed (23%) say they told a parent or other family member—roughly 1 in 3 girls (34%) and 1 in 10 boys (11%).
- 63% of harassed students say they told a friend—77% of girls and 49% of boys.
- 23% of harassed students say they told no one—27% of boys and 19% of girls.

Notably higher numbers of girls than boys say they have suffered as a result of sexual harassment in school; African American girls have suffered the most.

- Nearly 1 in 4 students (23%) who have been sexually harassed say that as a result they did not want to attend school: 33% of girls, compared with 12% of boys. The numbers are very similar for those who say they do not want to talk as much in class after having experienced harassment.
- Among harassed girls: 39% of African Americans did not want to attend school, in contrast with 33% of whites and 29% of Hispanics. Among harassed boys, the numbers are: 14% of whites, 9% of African Americans, and 8% of Hispanics. . . .
- Nearly half the students (48%) who were harassed say they were "very upset" or "somewhat upset" after having been harassed—an alarming 70% of girls respond this way. Twice as many boys (25%) as girls (13%) say they were not sure how they felt.
- One in 4 students (24%) of those harassed say the experience left them feeling afraid or scared—39% of girls and 8% of boys. . . .

Boys routinely experience harassment. Among African Americans, the incidence of harassment involving direct physical contact is alarming.

- 57% of boys who have been harassed have been targeted by a girl, 35% by a group of girls.
- 25% of boys who have been harassed have been targeted by another boy, 14% by a group of boys.
- 10% of harassed boys have been targeted by a teacher or other school employee. . . .

• One in 5 African American boys surveyed (22%) have been forced to kiss someone; 19% have been forced to do something sexual other than kissing.

Source: American Association of University Women, *Hostile Hallways: The AAUW
Survey on Sexual Harassment in America's Schools* (Washington, DC: The American
Association of University Women, 1993) pp. 22–25.

Institutions of Higher Education

Title IX also prohibits sexual harassment at colleges, universities, and
other institutions of higher education. Fewer recent surveys have been
done of the prevalence of sexual harassment in higher education; however, a survey conducted at Harvard University in 1983 suggests that
both female faculty members and female students are frequent victims
of harassment.

DOCUMENT 74: "Female Faculty Members and Students at Harvard Report Sexual Harassment" (Nina McCain, 1983)

Sexual harassment affects the life and work of a substantial number
of female faculty members and students at Harvard University, according to the results of a survey presented to the Faculty Council last week.

The survey, which was commissioned by the Faculty of Arts and Sciences and carried out last spring by two students under the supervision
of a dean, found that 32 per cent of the tenured female professors, 49
per cent of those without tenure, 41 per cent of female graduate students,
and 34 per cent of the undergraduate women had encountered some
form of harassment from someone in authority at least once during their
time at Harvard.

While looks, gestures, or verbal harassment accounted for one-third to
two-thirds of those figures, from 3 to 16 per cent of the women in the
various categories reported more serious incidents. For instance, 12 per
cent of the tenured women professors, 10 per cent of the non-tenured
faculty members, 6 per cent of the graduate students, and 3 per cent of
the undergraduates reported on the written questionnaires that they had
been subjected to pressure for sexual favors.

The women said the incidents had caused them personal distress and
affected the quality of their work. Of those reporting harassment, 15 per
cent of the graduate students and 12 per cent of the undergraduates
changed their academic programs because of the incidents.

The overwhelming majority did not report the incidents to the university authorities. Half of those said they had not made reports because
they feared reprisals.

Source: Nina McCain, "Female Faculty Members and Students at Harvard Report Sexual Harassment," *Chronicle of Higher Education* 27, no. 10 (November 2, 1983): 1, 14.

HARASSMENT BY SCHOOL EMPLOYEES

Since 1980 courts have recognized that schools can be held legally responsible for sexual harassment of students by employees of the school, such as teachers and administrators. Schools can be responsible for both quid pro quo harassment (for example, when a teacher conditions a grade on submission to sexual favors) and hostile environment harassment (for example, when a teacher makes continuing unwelcome sexual advances to a student).

There was some debate, however, over the issue of when a school can be held responsible for the behavior of an individual employee. The Office for Civil Rights of the United States Department of Education (OCR) took the position that schools are absolutely responsible for acts of quid pro quo harassment committed by their employees. In contrast, according to the OCR, schools should be liable for instances of hostile environment harassment only if the employee "(1) acted with apparent authority (i.e., because of the school's conduct, the employee reasonably appears to be acting on behalf of the school, whether or not the employee acted with authority); or (2) was aided in carrying out the sexual harassment of students by his or her position of authority with the institution," or if the school fails to take appropriate steps to end harassment that it knew about or should have known about.

DOCUMENT 75: "Sexual Harassment Guidance: Harassment of Students by School Employees, Other Students, or Third Parties" (Office for Civil Rights, United States Department of Education, 1997)

Liability of a School for Sexual Harassment by Its Employees

A school's liability for sexual harassment by its employees is determined by application of agency principles, i.e., by principles governing the delegation of authority to or authorization of another person to act on one's behalf.

Accordingly, a school will always be liable for even one instance of quid pro quo harassment by a school employee in a position of authority, such as a teacher or administrator, whether or not it knew, should have known, or approved of the harassment at issue. Under agency principles, if a teacher or other employee uses the authority he or she is given (e.g., to assign grades) to force a student to submit to sexual demands, the employee "stands in the shoes" of the school and the school will be responsible for the use of its authority by the employee or agent.

A school will also be liable for hostile environment sexual harassment by its employees, i.e., for harassment that is sufficiently severe, persistent, or pervasive to limit a student's ability to participate in or benefit from the education program or to create a hostile or abusive educational environment if the employee—(1) acted with apparent authority (i.e., because of the school's conduct, the employee reasonably appears to be acting on behalf of the school, whether or not the employee acted with authority); or (2) was aided in carrying out the sexual harassment of students by his or her position of authority with the institution. For example, a school will be liable if a teacher abuses his or her delegated authority over a student to create a hostile environment, such as if the teacher implicitly threatens to fail a student unless the student responds to his or her sexual advances, even though the teacher fails to carry out the threat.

As this example illustrates, in many cases the line between quid pro quo and hostile environment discrimination will be blurred, and the employee's conduct may constitute both types of harassment. However, what is important is that the school is liable for that conduct under application of agency principles, regardless of whether it is labeled as quid pro quo or hostile environment harassment.

Whether other employees, such as a janitor or cafeteria worker, are in positions of authority in relation to students—or whether it would be reasonable for the student to believe the employees are, even if the employees are not (i.e., apparent authority)—will depend on factors such as the authority actually given to the employee (e.g., in some elementary schools, a cafeteria worker may have authority to impose discipline) and the age of the student. For example, in some cases the younger a student is, the more likely it is that he or she will consider any adult employee to be in a position of authority.

Even in situations not involving (i) quid pro quo harassment, (ii) creation of a hostile environment through an employee's apparent authority, or (iii) creation of a hostile environment in which the employee is aided in carrying out the sexual harassment by his or her position of authority, a school will be liable for sexual harassment of its students by its employees under the same standards applicable to peer and third party hostile environment sexual harassment, as discussed in the next section. That is, if the school fails to take immediate and appropriate steps to remedy known harassment, then the school will be liable under Title IX. It is important to emphasize that under this standard of liability the school can avoid violating Title IX if it takes immediate and appropriate action upon notice of the harassment.

Source: Office for Civil Rights, U.S. Department of Education, "Sexual Harassment Guidance: Harassment of Students by School Employees, Other Students, or Third Parties," 62 *Federal Register* 12034–01, 12039 (March 13, 1997) (footnotes omitted).

Lower courts agreed with the OCR's position of absolute liability with regard to quid pro quo harassment. Prior to 1998, however, when the Supreme Court resolved the issue, they split about when to make schools pay for hostile environment harassment perpetrated by school employees. Some courts, like the court in *Pallett v. Palma*, agreed with the Department of Education that schools should be liable for hostile environment harassment by employees if they knew or should have known of the harassment and failed to take appropriate corrective action.

DOCUMENT 76: *Pallett v. Palma*, U.S. District Court (1996)

Plaintiff Darleen E. Pallett filed her lawsuit on January 17, 1995. She was, at relevant times, an undergraduate student at Iona College. . . .

Defendant Michael Palma, referred to as Professor Palma, is a tenured full time faculty member in the English Department of the School of Arts and Sciences of Iona College. . . .

The complaint of Ms. Pallett alleges that on or about May 19, 1994, she was falsely imprisoned and sexually harassed in the office of Professor Palma at an on-campus facility known as English House.

Ms. Pallett alleges in lurid detail . . . a conversation with Professor Palma beginning at 1:00 P.M. and lasting between two and two and one half hours. According to her version of the discussion, she had attended at the office of Professor Palma to protest a failing grade on a paper and seek to have her grade raised. During that lengthy time period, she alleges that defendant, in lewd and vulgar language, discussed in detail his own prior sexual experiences, ordered her to read pornographic poetry which contained extensive sexually explicit references and recitals regarding sexual intercourse, inquired as to her own sexual experiences, and made vivid expressions of his own imagination of her reactions to sexual intercourse with him and of having sexual relations with her, recited the content of sexually oriented dreams he had regarding another student named Laurie, and said that he could imagine her naked. . . . The complaint also alleges that he sat close to her and that his desk was between her and the only door to exit the office; that he kept raising the volume of the radio to prevent anyone outside the office from over-hearing the conversation, and that she was thereby falsely imprisoned as well as being sexually harassed.

. . . At the end of the conversation, defendant Palma explicitly warned plaintiff not to go home and tell her family about the discussion.

The complaint also alleges that Palma told other students of his sexual interest in plaintiff Pallett, and in other ways behaved like a cad. The Court accepts as valid for purposes of this motion the contention of plaintiff that the entire conversation constituted sexual harassment, and that the sexual harassment continued thereafter. However, in assessing the response of the College, we note that there was no touching during this lengthy conversation, no explicit request for specified sexual favors, either as a quid pro quo or otherwise, and no explicit threats or promises were made. . . .

The key issue in this case . . . is whether defendant has proved by un-controvertible evidence that after the point in time when it knew or should have known of the harassment, it took . . . all reasonable steps necessary to remedy the hostile environment. . . . The reasonableness of the response by the College to this sexual harassment must be tested consistently with all of the factual background known to its officials. . . . Iona maintains a Sexual Harassment Policy and detailed procedures for addressing and resolving complaints of sexual harassment. The College's Sexual Harassment Policy is set forth in the Student Handbook, the Fac-ulty Handbook, the Sexual Harassment Task Force Statement and Pro-cedures, and the College Campus Safety Manual. . . .

It was not until late September or early October during the ensuing Fall semester, that Ms. Pallett, who was then a student in another elective course taught by Palma, reported the May 1994 incident to Dean Michael McGrath. He referred her to Dr. Ingrid Grieger, Director of Iona's Coun-seling Center. After some discussion Ms. Pallett authorized Dr. Grieger to notify Dean Warren Rosenberg and Brother John Gallagher, the Vice President of Academic Affairs.

Thereafter on November 17, 1994, Palma approached Dean McGrath at a football game and acknowledged his regret and willingness to rectify the situation. From this McGrath concluded for the first time that Palma was admitting to having harassed Ms. Pallett.

Thereafter, in late November Dean McGrath met with Ms. Pallett and her parents regarding the incident. At that time he informed them that the College could not then take action to dismiss Palma absent a formal complaint because of the level of proof required where a tenured pro-fessor is involved, and furthermore that a formal complaint would be required before a hearing directed to academic tenure could be sched-uled. This advice was truthful and consistent with the faculty agreement.

On December 1, 1994, for the first time, Ms. Pallett made a formal complaint to the College. The College responded immediately by suspending Palma from teaching or advising students and thereafter he was notified that proceedings would be commenced against him pursuant to the collective bargaining agreement looking towards terminating his tenure. . . .

In early January 1995 . . . Dean Rosenberg interviewed members of the faculty and students and obtained written statements. As was to be expected, on January 11, 1995, the AAUP, the collective bargaining representative for the faculty, through Dr. Pendelton advised the college that the AAUP would object to any disciplinary action taken against Palma, presumably for lack of competent proof. Palma remains suspended, but his tenure has not been revoked.

The record submitted in connection with the motions is clear that immediately upon being informed of these complaints the College made continued reasonable efforts to resolve the problems of the plaintiffs and to gain their participation in investigation of their allegations and their cooperation in connection with due process proceedings to terminate Professor Palma. They refused or failed to do so, apparently being more interested in pursuing their litigation. . . .

. . . [T]his Court concludes that on the undisputed facts no reasonable trial juror could find liability on the part of the College, because the College upon learning of plaintiff's sexual harassment allegations took appropriate remedial action and to the extent that it was unable to or failed to take appropriate remedial action the College was prevented from doing so by the failure and active refusal of the plaintiff[] to cooperate with the College administration in pressing formal charges and testifying at the necessary faculty hearing to terminate Palma's tenure upon the required finding of gross misconduct.

Our Court of Appeals has concluded that "in a Title IX case for gender discrimination based upon the sexual harassment of a student, an educational institution may be held liable under standards similar to those applied in cases under Title VII." . . . While formulating this rule, the . . . court did not have occasion to determine what standard of constructive notice should be applied in Title IX cases. In a commercial context under Title VII, an employee's conduct will be imputed to the employer where (1) the employee is in a supervisory role and uses actual or apparent authority to further the harassment or if the supervisor was otherwise aided in accomplishing the harassment by the existence of an agency relationship; (2) the employer provided no reasonable avenue of complaint; or (3) that the employer knew of the complaint but did nothing about it. . . .

Under agency principles, Professor Palma obviously did not have actual authority of the college to act as he allegedly did. Nor would it have been reasonable for the plaintiff to have believed that Professor Palma was acting with apparent authority. Accepting the allegations as true, it is clear that Professor Palma was acting adversely to the institution itself, unlawfully, and in contravention of its express, detailed published policies previously noted. Under these circumstances, this Court concludes that any alleged harassment in the present case was not furthered by Professor Palma's actual or apparent authority nor was he otherwise aided by the existence of an agency relationship and thus no liability should attach to the college on that basis. . . .

That a faculty member on occasion will violate the published policies of an institution and do so clandestinely, as here, is not a basis for students or employees who have eschewed the established procedures for rectifying the wrong done to them, to run instead to the courts, to mulct the charitable funds of a non-profit teaching institution. Those funds could be used better for the instruction of other students.

While our Court of Appeals on occasion has applied Title VII precedent to Title IX claims, the question of whether the "employer", here the teaching institution, either failed to provide a reasonable remedy or knew of the harassment but did nothing about it, remains an issue in such cases, which must be proved by plaintiff. . . . The institution of higher learning satisfies its legal obligation under facts similar to these cases unless it provided no reasonable avenue for complaint or knew of the harassment but did nothing about it. . . .

Iona College complied in full with its obligations under the law by providing a policy against sexual harassment and a complaint procedure, copies of which were properly provided to all students and faculty. The College responded adequately to the complaints, which as to Pallett were somewhat late in arriving. That rumors may have circulated prior thereto, as plaintiffs claim but have not proved, does not substitute for actual or constructive notice of the existence of the problem, nor do rumors trigger a duty to respond. Immediately upon receiving notice, the College responded to these cases promptly, effectively and sympathetically. . . .

The conflict between the obligations of a teaching institution under Title IX and its obligations to its faculty members under the First and Fourteenth Amendment and the principles of academic freedom which necessitate faculty tenure, were known to Congress in enacting Title IX and are a part of the historical and factual background against which the adequacy of the response of the College is to be judged. As noted earlier, the College did all it could, and was, and indeed remains, powerless to do anything more about terminating Professor Palma, absent further voluntary participation of the victims. This has not been forthcoming because litigation for money damages in this Court appears to be more attractive to them.

Source: 914 *Federal Supplement* 1018, 1019–25 (S.D.N.Y. 1996).

In contrast, the U.S. Court of Appeals for the Fifth Circuit made it much more difficult for students attending schools in that jurisdiction who have suffered hostile environment sexual harassment to recover damages from the school that employed the harasser. In *Rosa H. v. San Elizario Independent School District,* the court held that school districts are not responsible for sexual harassment perpetrated by employees against students unless the school actually knew in advance that students faced a substantial threat of sexual harassment. Simply showing that the school should have known about the harassment would not be enough. Nor would it be enough for the victim to show that the school found out about the harassment after the fact and did nothing, unless the victim was subjected to more harassment after the school discovered the problem. Furthermore, according to that court, a school will be deemed to have knowledge of the harassment only if someone who had the power to supervise the offending employee knew about it.

DOCUMENT 77: *Rosa H. v. San Elizario Independent School District*, U.S. Court of Appeals for the Fifth Circuit (1997)

This case requires us to decide whether Title IX . . . creates liability on the part of a public school district that negligently fails to prevent an instructor from sexually abusing a student. We hold that it does not. In order to hold a school district liable under Title IX for teacher-student sexual harassment based on a hostile educational environment, a plaintiff must show that an employee who has been invested by the school board with supervisory power over the offending employee actually knew of the abuse, had the power to end the abuse, and failed to do so. . . .

II.

* * *

. . . [W]e hold that when a teacher sexually abuses a student, the student cannot recover from the school district under Title IX unless the school district actually knew that there was a substantial risk that sexual abuse would occur. . . .

A.

. . . When the school board accepted federal funds, it agreed not to discriminate on the basis of sex. We think it unlikely that it further agreed to suffer liability whenever its employees discriminate on the basis of sex. . . .

It is important to note that agency principles would create liability for school districts in virtually every case in which a teacher harasses, se-duces, or sexually abuses a student. . . . The teacher's status as a teacher often enables the teacher to abuse the student. . . . We conclude that Title IX does not contemplate a theory of recovery based purely on agency law.

B.

In addition to the argument based on the law of agency, the plaintiff urges us to look to Title VII law in applying Title IX. Under Title VII, a plaintiff "can demonstrate constructive notice by 'showing the perva-siveness of the harassment, which gives rise to the inference of knowl-edge or constructive knowledge.' " . . . Applying this principle here would mean that if the school district should have known about [the teacher's] abuse, it could be liable on the basis of its constructive notice of sex discrimination. . . .

Under Title VII law, an employer has constructive notice of sexual harassment if it "knew or should have known" that the harassment was taking place. . . . In other words, if an employer fails to exercise reason-able care in learning of sexual harassment by employees, Title VII treats the employer as if it had actual notice of the harassment. As other courts have remarked, the constructive-notice standard is essentially grounded in negligence. . . .

Although the school district may be somewhat less vulnerable under the constructive-notice standard than under the pure agency standard, we think that importing this aspect of Title VII law stretches Title IX beyond its language and purpose. Congress did not enact Title IX in order to burden federally funded educational institutions with open-ended negligence liability.

In prohibiting employment discrimination, Title VII establishes limits on liability to ensure that private actions against employers do not be-come excessive. . . . Title VII regulations state forthrightly that "an em-ployer . . . is responsible for its acts and those of its agents and supervisory employees with respect to sexual harassment." . . . Title IX, by contrast, does not create any administrative body to regulate private claimants' rights, and the regulations promulgated under Title IX make no mention of sexual harassment. . . . [T]his does not mean that private parties may not recover damages under Title IX for sexual harassment. Rather, it means that we should be reluctant to treat Title IX's anti-discrimination provisions in the same way that we treat Title VII's pro-visions. . . .

III.

Having rejected the pure agency and constructive-notice theories, we are left with the rule that a school district is not liable under Title IX for a teacher's sexual harassment unless it has actual notice of the harassment. . . .

Title IX liability depends on a school district's act of discriminating on the basis of sex. . . . [A] school district has not sexually harassed a student unless it knows of a danger of harassment and chooses not to alleviate that danger. . . .

. . . Students need not show that the district knew that a particular teacher would abuse a particular student; the plaintiff could prevail in this case, for example, by establishing that the school district failed to act even though it knew that Contreras [the teacher who harassed her] posed a substantial risk of harassing students in general. But Title IX liability for sexual harassment will not lie if a student fails to demonstrate that the school district actually knew that the students faced a substantial threat of sexual harassment. . . .

IV.

One major question remains before we can resolve this appeal. To this point, we have referred simply to the school district's knowledge and the school district's actions. But the district knows and acts only through individuals, whether they be members of the school board, administrators at particular schools, or classroom teachers. We have yet to decide which individuals within the school district must have known of [the] abuse . . . in order for us to conclude that the school district knew of the abuse.

At one end of the spectrum, liability might lie only when a member of the school board actually knows of the abuse and fails to take prompt remedial action. Under this rule, a school district would virtually never face penalties for sexual abuse of students unless school board members themselves intended the harm. By the same token, victims of abuse would virtually never be able to recover, especially in large school districts, in which school board members have little contact with the day-to-day interactions between teachers and students. . . . At the other end of the spectrum, liability might lie whenever any school employee other than the perpetrator has actual knowledge of the abuse and fails to take prompt remedial action. Although more protective of victims of abuse, this scheme would vitiate the premise that has guided our analysis of Title IX sexual-abuse cases: that Title IX creates liability for school districts only when the school district intentionally breaks the strings attached to those funds.

Formulating . . . meaningful tort liability . . . while recognizing that Title IX generates liability only for intentional wrongs requires us to chart a middle way between these extremes.... [S]chool districts contain a number of layers of responsibility below the school board: superintendents, principals, vice-principals, and teachers and coaches, not to mention specialized counselors such as Title IX coordinators. Different school districts may assign different duties to these positions or even reject this traditional hierarchical structure all together. We do not wish to restrict the applicability of our analysis by keying liability to certain job titles within the school system. Whether the school official is a superintendent or a substitute teacher, the relevant question is whether the official's actual knowledge of sexual abuse is functionally equivalent to the school district's actual knowledge.

We hold that a school district can be liable for teacher-student sexual harassment under Title IX only if a school official who had actual knowledge of the abuse was invested by the school board with the duty to supervise the employee and the power to take action that would end such abuse and failed to do so. This inquiry circumscribes those school employees in the chain of command whom the school board has appointed to monitor the conduct of other employees and, as distinguished from reporting to others, remedy the wrongdoing themselves. At the same time, it locates the acts of subordinates to the board at a point where the board's liability and practical control are sufficiently close to reflect its intentional discrimination. It does so by omitting the bulk of employees, such as fellow teachers, coaches, and janitors, unless the district has assigned them both the duty to supervise the employee who has sexually abused a student and also the power to halt the abuse....

As in Title VII cases, "[w]hat is appropriate remedial action will necessarily depend on the particular facts of the case—the severity and persistence of the harassment, and the effectiveness of any initial remedial steps."... Of course, prompt termination or suspension of the offender would ordinarily be sufficient. In some situations, transferring the teacher to another school might be adequate. But merely reporting the abuse to superiors or to law enforcement is insufficient. Anyone can make reports. Indeed, Texas law imposes a duty to report child abuse. ... In order to qualify as a supervisory employee whose knowledge of abusive conduct counts as the district's knowledge, a school official must at least serve in a position with the authority to "repudiate that conduct and eliminate the hostile environment" on behalf of the school district.

Source: 106 *Federal Reporter* 3d 648, 650–61 (5th Cir. 1997).

In 1998, the U.S. Supreme Court resolved this issue. In *Gebser v. Lago Vista Independent School District*, reprinted in Part VI (Document 96), a majority of the Supreme Court agreed with the Fifth Circuit's limited approach to school district liability. Consequently, the current universal rule in the United States is that educational institutions are not legally responsible under federal law for sexual harassment of students by school employees unless a person in the school hierarchy with actual power to redress the harassment knew of it but failed to take action to end it.

HARASSMENT BY PEERS

The most common perpetrators of sexual harassment against students are their peers. While some schools try to combat such harassment, other schools are content to look the other way.

Courts disagree about whether schools are legally responsible if they do not protect students from peer sexual harassment. Some courts hold that the schools are responsible if they knew about the harassment and failed to redress it. They reason that similar principles of law should apply to educational institutions as apply in the employment context; since employers are responsible for failing to remedy hostile environment harassment by coworkers, schools should also be responsible for failing to remedy hostile environment harassment by peers. One case in which a court took this position is *Bruneau v. South Kortright Central School District.* The court cautioned, however, that the school district will be responsible only if it actually knew about the harassment and failed to take appropriate corrective action or if it had no complaint procedure that was reasonably available to victims. It would not be enough if the school had only what lawyers call "constructive notice," which means that the school should have known about the harassment.

The effect of the court's decision in the *Bruneau* case was that the plaintiff was entitled to bring her claim of peer sexual harassment to a jury. The jury, however, ultimately rejected her claim that the behavior that she was subjected to amounted to sexual harassment. According to the jury foreman, who was interviewed after the case, although the jurors agreed that Ms. Bruneau had been harassed, they were not convinced that the behavior was severe or pervasive enough to violate the law. Furthermore, they were convinced that the school district had taken sufficient action to end the abuse.

DOCUMENT 78: *Bruneau v. South Kortright Central School District*, U.S. District Court (1996)

I. BACKGROUND AND FACTS

The Plaintiff, Eve Bruneau, was a student in the sixth grade at South Kortright Central School District. . . . The Defendants are: South Kortright Central School (hereinafter "SKCS"), a public school which receives Federal financial assistance; Lynda Race, an assistant superintendent of the school; William Parker, the Plaintiff's former sixth grade teacher; and the South Kortright Central School Board. . . .

ii. The Plaintiff's Case

The Plaintiff alleges that she and other girls in her class were subjected to verbal and physical sexual harassment beginning in September, 1993, until she was forced to transfer from SKCS on March 1, 1994. The Plaintiff claims that such sexual harassment made her feel unsafe and depressed. . . . Additionally, the harassment created an intimidating, abusive and hostile learning environment which interfered with her education. . . . The Plaintiff and other girls were often referred to as "lesbian", "prostitute", "retard", "scum", "bitch", "whore" and "ugly dog faced bitch." . . . The physical harassment included the boys' snapping the girls' bras, running their fingers down the girls' backs, stuffing paper down the girls' blouses, cutting the girls' hair, grabbing the girls' breasts, spitting, shoving, hitting and kicking. . . .

The Plaintiff alleges that Mr. Parker and Ms. Race were aware of the sexually harassing conduct and failed to take any action to stop it. . . . At a meeting on or about November 16, 1993, the Plaintiff alleges that all the girls in the class, including herself, informed Mr. Parker of the sexual harassment. . . . Additionally, the Plaintiff contends that in meetings on November 3, 1993, November 19, 1993, and March 25, 1994, the Plaintiff and her parents brought the sexually harassing conduct to the attention Mr. Parker, Mrs. Race, and other school officials. . . . Allegedly Mr. Parker responded by telling her that he believed that the boys' conduct was normal flirting and teasing and that "Eve was so beautiful that the guys would be all over her in a couple of years." . . .

II. DISCUSSION

* * *

2. Peer-on-Peer Sexual Harassment

As pointed out by the Plaintiff, Title VII principles impose liability on employers for knowingly failing to act to remedy a hostile working environment created by sexual harassment between co-workers. . . . The Plaintiff argues that because Title VII jurisprudence has been held to apply to analyses of Title IX claims generally, educational institutions should also be liable, just as employers under Title VII, for knowingly failing to act to remedy a hostile learning environment created by peer-on-peer sexual harassment. . . . The Plaintiff further argues that institutional liability for peer-on-peer sexual harassment is based on agency principles and agency principles support a finding that constructive notice of peer-on-peer sexual harassment is sufficient to establish institutional liability. . . .

The Defendants argue that the peer-on-peer situation in a classroom is very different from the employee/employee or employer/employee situation in the workplace. . . . Title VII proscribes actions by adults, rather than children, and arises in an agency relationship. . . . Both of the aforementioned characteristics of a Title VII claim, according to the Defendants, are absent in the school setting. This is particularly true in the context of a hostile learning environment created by peer-on-peer sexual harassment. Accordingly, the Defendants urge the Court, at a minimum, to apply some modified version of Title VII.

Title VII requires employers to take steps to assure their employees a work environment free from sexual harassment, regardless of whether the harassment or hostile environment is caused by a supervisor or other co-workers. . . . When an employer fails to act to remedy a hostile environment created by co-workers the employer discriminates against an individual in violation of Title VII. . . . Similarly, the Court finds that in the Title IX context, when an educational institution fails to take steps to remedy peer-on-peer sexual harassment, it should be held liable to the harassed student for that discriminatory conduct.

Just as a working woman should not be required to "run a gauntlet of sexual abuse in return for the privilege of being allowed to work and make a living," *Meritor*, . . . a female student should not be required to run a gauntlet of sexual abuse in return for the privilege of being allowed to obtain an education. . . .

"A student should have the same protection in school that an employee has in the workplace." . . . Moreover, "as economically difficult as it may be for adults to leave a hostile workplace, it is virtually impossible for children to leave their assigned school." . . . "A sexually abusive environment inhibits, if not prevents, the harassed student from developing her full intellectual potential and receiving the most from the academic program." . . .

Yet, "importing a theory of discrimination from the adult employment context into a situation involving children is highly problematic." . . . "At a theoretical level, the problem with sexual harassment is 'the unwanted imposition of sexual requirements in the context of unequal power.' " . . . In the context of unwanted peer-on-peer sexual harassment such a power relationship does not exist. "Unwanted sexual advances of fellow students do not carry the same coercive effect or abuse of power as those made by a teacher, employer or co-worker." . . .

Therefore, the issue remains under what parameters a Court may find an educational institution to be liable for failing to act to remedy a hostile learning environment created by peer-on-peer sexual harassment. In other words, to what extent must the institution (and the school board in this case) be on notice of the alleged ongoing harassing conduct, i.e., must notice be actual, or may notice be constructive, for Title IX liability to attach.

3. Notice

Title VII jurisprudence applies an actual and constructive notice standard for determining if an employer knowingly failed to act to remedy a hostile working environment created by peer-on-peer harassment. . . .

Constructive notice is a substitute for actual notice and will be found to exist "where a defective condition has existed for such a length of time that knowledge thereof should have been acquired in the exercise of reasonable care." . . . This is, in essence, a negligence standard. . . . For the reasons stated below, this Court finds that to establish a Title IX claim for a hostile learning environment created by peer-on-peer sexual harassment the Plaintiff must show that the school and/or school board received actual notice of the sexual harassing conduct and failed to take action to remedy it. Liability will not lie if the Plaintiff can show only constructive notice. . . .

Although an employee is an agent of an employer, a student, of an educational institution is not, per se, an agent of that institution. . . . In order for agency principles to attach between a student and their school there must be some manifestation of consent by the student to the school that the student shall act on the school's behalf and subject to the school's control, as well as, consent from the school to the student's actions. The Plaintiff has not alleged, nor provided any evidence, that the harassing students were acting on behalf of or with authority from SKCS. Therefore, although constructive notice principles properly attach between employer and employee in the Title VII context, they do not attach between the alleged harassing student and the Defendants' in this Title IX case. . . .

v. Institutional Liability

. . . In the context of Title IX, this Court, for the reasons set forth above, has held that such notice must be actual notice of the sexually harassing conduct. . . .

. . . [A]n educational institution will not be held liable for alleged peer-on-peer sexual harassment unless the school provided no reasonable avenue of complaint or knew of the harassment but did nothing about it.

It is not disputed that SKCS did provide a reasonable avenue for complaint. The school district has an established Title IX policy in effect during the time period relevant to this case. Moreover, given that certain complaints relating to peer conduct against the Plaintiff were expressed to Mr. Parker and Mrs. Race, it is clear that avenues to express and redress behavior problems among students were available. It is because of these complaints that the Plaintiff alleges that SKCS faculty and administrators, Mr. Parker and Mrs. Race in particular, had knowledge of the alleged peer-on-peer sexual harassment yet failed to act to remedy it.

As to the issue of actual notice, the Plaintiff alleges that the Defendants were aware of the hostile environment yet failed to act to remedy it. Such awareness, or actual notice, allegedly came from meetings with the Plaintiff and/or her mother where they repeatedly notified Mr. Parker and Mrs. Race of the sexual harassment that was occurring in their classroom and school. . . .

It is undisputed by the parties that the Plaintiff and/or [her mother] made verbal complaints to Mr. Parker and/or Mrs. Race concerning alleged peer sexual harassment on or about November 3, 1993, and November 10, 1993. . . . Yet, the Defendants state that they were not notified of pervasive and regular sexual harassment sufficient to constitute a hostile learning environment. It is the Defendants' position that each complaint related to a single incident where a fellow student referred to the Plaintiff as a "dog faced bitch." . . . Additionally, Mr. Parker, the Plaintiff's classroom teacher, contends that, other than the Plaintiff's complaint brought at the outset of this suit, he has "never heard Eve Bruneau, Pat Schofield, or any other student or parent allege that there was sexual harassment occurring in my classroom." . . . He did not observe any sexual activity between any children and does not believe that any sexual harassment occurred in his classroom. . . .

Based on the foregoing, and particularly in light of the Court's recognition that it must not decide issues but merely identify those issues that are in dispute, the Court can not find, as a matter of law, that the school and/or the school board were not on actual notice of ongoing peer-on-peer sexual harassment. [Thus, the issue should go to the jury.]

Source: 935 *Federal Supplement* 162, 166–77 (N.D.N.Y. 1996).

The United States Department of Education's Office of Civil Rights (OCR) agrees that peer sexual harassment can violate the law. Indeed, the OCR's position is even more favorable to students alleging sexual harassment than the *Bruneau* court's decision. The OCR argues that a school district should be responsible either if it knew or if it should have known of the harassment.

The OCR's expansive position on this issue, however, may be rejected by courts based on the U.S. Supreme Court's decision in 1998 in *Gebser v. Lago Vista Independent School District* (Document 96). In *Gebser*, a majority of the Supreme Court held that school districts cannot be liable for harassment of students by school employees unless an official in the district with power to redress the harassment actually knows that it is occurring. It is extremely unlikely that the Supreme Court would adopt a more liberal standard for school district liability in cases of peer harassment. Thus, the OCR's proposed standard, making the districts responsible in some cases even if they did not actually know of the harassment, is likely to have little legal force in the future.

DOCUMENT 79: "Sexual Harassment Guidance: Harassment of Students by School Employees, Other Students, or Third Parties" (Office for Civil Rights, United States Department of Education, 1997)

Liability of a School for Peer or Third Party Harassment

In contrast to the variety of situations in which a school may be liable for sexual harassment by its employees, a school will be liable under Title IX if its students sexually harass other students if (i) a hostile environment exists in the school's programs or activities, (ii) the school knows or should have known of the harassment, and (iii) the school fails to take immediate and appropriate corrective action.... Under these circumstances, a school's failure to respond to the existence of a hostile environment within its own programs or activities permits an atmosphere of sexual discrimination to permeate the educational program and results in discrimination prohibited by Title IX. Conversely, if, upon notice of hostile environment harassment, a school takes immediate and appropriate steps to remedy the hostile environment, the school has avoided violating Title IX. Thus, Title IX does not make a school responsible for the actions of harassing students, but rather for its own discrimination in failing to remedy it once the school has notice....

Notice

A school will be in violation of Title IX if the school "has notice" of a sexually hostile environment and fails to take immediate and appropriate corrective action. A school has notice if it actually "knew, or in the exercise of reasonable care, should have known" about the harassment. In addition, as long as an agent or responsible employee of the school received notice, the school has notice.

A school can receive notice in many different ways. A student may have filed a grievance or complained to a teacher about fellow students sexually harassing him or her. A student, parent, or other individual may have contacted other appropriate personnel, such as a principal, campus security, bus driver, teacher, an affirmative action officer, or staff in the office of student affairs. An agent or responsible employee of the school may have witnessed the harassment. The school may receive notice in an indirect manner, from sources such as a member of the school staff, a member of the educational or local community, or the media. The school also may have received notice from flyers about the incident or incidents posted around the school.

Constructive notice exists if the school "should have" known about the harassment—if the school would have found out about the harassment through a "reasonably diligent inquiry." For example, if a school knows of some incidents of harassment, there may be situations in which it will be charged with notice of others—if the known incidents should have triggered an investigation that would have led to a discovery of the additional incidents. In other cases, the pervasiveness of the harassment may be enough to conclude that the school should have known of the hostile environment—if the harassment is widespread, openly practiced, or well-known to students and staff (such as sexual harassment occurring in hallways, graffiti in public areas, or harassment occurring during recess under a teacher's supervision).

In addition, if a school otherwise has actual or constructive notice of a hostile environment and fails to take immediate and appropriate corrective action, a school has violated Title IX even if the student fails to use the school's existing grievance procedures.

Recipient's Response

Once a school has notice of possible sexual harassment of students—whether carried out by employees, other students, or third parties—it should take immediate and appropriate steps to investigate or otherwise determine what occurred and take steps reasonably calculated to end any harassment, eliminate a hostile environment if one has been created, and prevent harassment from occurring again. These steps are the school's responsibility whether or not the student who was harassed makes a complaint or otherwise asks the school to take action. . . . What constitutes a reasonable response to information about possible sexual harassment will differ depending upon the circumstances.

Response to Student or Parent Reports of Harassment; Response to Direct Observation by a Responsible Employee or Agent of Harassment

If a student or the parent of an elementary or secondary student provides information or complains about sexual harassment of the student, the school should initially discuss what actions the student or parent is seeking in response to the harassment. The school should explain the avenues for informal and formal action, including a description of the grievance procedure that is available for sexual harassment complaints and an explanation of how the procedure works. If a responsible school employee or agent has directly observed sexual harassment of a student, the school should contact the student who was harassed (or the parent, depending upon the age of the student), explain that the school is responsible for taking steps to correct the harassment, and provide the same information described in the previous sentence.

Regardless of whether the student who was harassed, or his or her parent, decides to file a formal complaint or otherwise request action on the student's behalf (including in cases involving direct observation by a responsible school employee or agent), the school must promptly investigate to determine what occurred and then take appropriate steps to resolve the situation. . . .

It may be appropriate for a school to take interim measures during the investigation of a complaint. For instance, if a student alleges that he or she has been sexually assaulted by another student, the school may decide to immediately place the students in separate classes or in different housing arrangements on a campus, pending the results of the school's investigation. Similarly, if the alleged harasser is a teacher, allowing the student to transfer to a different class may be appropriate. . . . In all cases, schools should make every effort to prevent public disclosure of the names of all parties involved, except to the extent necessary to carry out an investigation.

If a school determines that sexual harassment has occurred, it should take reasonable, timely, age-appropriate, and effective corrective action, including steps tailored to the specific situation. Appropriate steps should be taken to end the harassment. For example, school personnel may need to counsel, warn, or take disciplinary action against the harasser, based on the severity of the harassment or any record of prior incidents or both. A series of escalating consequences may be necessary if the initial steps are ineffective in stopping the harassment. In some cases, it may be appropriate to further separate the harassed student and the harasser, e.g., by changing housing arrangements or directing the harasser to have no further contact with the harassed student. Responsive measures of this type should be designed to minimize, as much as possible, the burden on the student who was harassed. . . .

Steps also should be taken to eliminate any hostile environment that has been created. For example, if a female student has been subjected to harassment by a group of other students in a class, the school may need to deliver special training or other interventions for that class to repair the educational environment. If the school offers the student the option of withdrawing from a class in which a hostile environment occurred, the school should assist the student in making program or schedule changes and ensure that none of the changes adversely affect the student's academic record. Other measures may include, if appropriate, directing a harasser to apologize to the harassed student. . . .

. . . [I]f a school delays responding or responds inappropriately to information about harassment, such as a case in which the school ignores complaints by a student that he or she is being sexually harassed by a classmate, the school will be required to remedy the effects of the harassment that could have been prevented had the school responded promptly and appropriately.

Finally, a school should take steps to prevent any further harassment and to prevent any retaliation against the student who made the complaint (or was the subject of the harassment), against a person who filed a complaint on behalf of a student, or against those who provided information as witnesses. At a minimum, this includes making sure that the harassed students and their parents know how to report any subsequent problems and making follow-up inquiries to see if there have been any new incidents or any retaliation.

Source: Office for Civil Rights, U.S. Department of Education, "Sexual Harassment Guidance: Harassment of Students by School Employees, Other Students, or Third Parties," 62 *Federal Register* 12034–01, 12039–40, 12042–43 (March 13, 1997) (footnotes omitted).

In contrast, some courts, like the U.S. Court of Appeals for the Fifth Circuit, in a case called *Rowinsky v. Bryan Independent School District*, have decided that schools are not legally obligated to protect students from harassment by their peers. That court reasoned that Title IX only prohibits discrimination by the entities that receive grants of federal money themselves and by their agents; although teachers and administrators are agents of the school that receives the grant, students are not. Thus, the only thing that schools are prohibited from doing with regard to peer harassment, according to this court, is remedying sexual harassment complaints brought by students of one gender while ignoring those brought by students of the other gender. So long as the school ignores complaints from all students, according to this court, it is not violating the law.

In September 1998, the Supreme Court agreed to resolve the issue as to whether schools are responsible for peer sexual harassment. That case, *Davis v. Monroe County Board of Education*, should be decided by the court by July 1999.

DOCUMENT 80: *Rowinsky v. Bryan Independent School District*, U.S. Court of Appeals for the Fifth Circuit (1996)

This appeal presents the question of whether title IX of the Education Amendments of 1972 . . . imposes liability on a school district for peer hostile environment sexual harassment. We conclude that title IX does not impose such liability, absent allegations that the school district itself directly discriminated based on sex. . . .

I.

During the 1992–93 school year, students proceeding in this litigation under the pseudonyms of Jane and Janet Doe were eighth graders at Sam Rayburn Middle School in the Bryan Independent School District ("BISD") who rode a BISD school bus to and from school. Boys and girls were required to sit on different sides of the bus, and the bus driver, Bob Owens, enforced the restriction, even, on occasion, telling Jane and Janet not to sit on the boys' side of the bus.

Beginning in September 1992, a male student, whom we identify only by his initials, "G. S.," physically and verbally abused Janet on the bus. . . .

Janet complained to Owens no fewer than eight times that G. S. had swatted her and Jane on their bottoms and used foul language. Owens took down names on a pad of paper. Janet eventually stopped reporting the incidents.

On September 24, G. S. grabbed Jane in her genital area, and, a few minutes later, grabbed her breasts. Jane, Janet, and their parents visited Assistant Principal Randy Caperton the next day to complain about the incident. Caperton told the Rowinsky family that he had already heard about the sexual assault from another student and that he believed the nature of the assault merited expelling G. S. Caperton suspended G. S. from riding the bus for three days and required him to sit in the second row behind the driver.

On September 29, Mrs. Rowinsky visited Caperton again to discuss the incident, complaining that other girls were being harassed on the bus. Caperton showed her a bus report that documented the incident with Jane. The report, however, contained numerous inaccuracies, including the fact that it did not name G. S. and listed the wrong date and length of punishment. Caperton corrected the assailant's name in a new report.

The three-day suspension did not deter G. S. He violated the seating requirement, and, as a result, Owens restricted Jane and Janet to the front of the bus. Mrs. Rowinsky called Jay Anding, assistant director of the transportation office, and demanded that he restrict G. S. to the second row seat because of the continuing remarks and misbehavior. Anding told Mrs. Rowinsky that he would speak with Owens. In late November 1992, G. S., with Owens nearby, called the girls offensive names and slapped Janet's buttocks. Owens did nothing, and the girls did not file any complaints.

One morning in December 1992, another male student, whose initials are "L. H.," reached up Janet's skirt, made a crude remark about what he almost touched, and then grabbed her genital area. Janet complained to Owens at the next stoplight, but he "just stared into space." On the afternoon of December 16, L. H. reached up Jane's skirt, touching her near her panty line. Jane did not tell Owens about the incident.

On December 18, Mrs. Rowinsky contacted Anding regarding L. H.'s behavior and told Anding that other girls were being sexually assaulted and gave him their names. Anding said he would investigate the alleged problems on the bus and take action.

On January 12, 1993, Mrs. Rowinsky contacted Caperton to find out the results of the investigation. Caperton told her that Anding had not conducted the investigation but that L. H. had been suspended for three days.

On January 13, Mrs. Rowinsky contacted Dr. Tom Purifoy, BISD director of secondary education, and described the assaults to him. Purifoy did not conduct an independent investigation but referred her to C. W. Henry, Anding's assistant.

On January 14, after reviewing videotapes from the bus, Henry assigned a new driver to replace Owens. There are no further allegations of harassment by G. S. thereafter.

On January 19, the driver assigned Jane the seat next to G. S. Although G. S. made no new assaults, Mrs. Rowinsky removed her daughters from the bus and, on January 22, requested that Purifoy remove G. S. from the bus. Purifoy refused to take any further action against G. S. without proof of the assaults from juvenile records.

On March 30, during class, a third male student, with the initials "F. F.," reached under Janet's shirt and unfastened her bra. The teacher in the classroom sent both students to Vice-Principal Sandra Petty, who sent Janet back to class and suspended F. F. for the rest of the day and the next day. F. F. is not alleged to have harassed or abused the girls further. The next day, Mrs. Rowinsky visited Petty and complained about F. F.'s behavior; Petty responded that she did not consider F. F.'s conduct to be sexual.

On March 30, Mrs. Rowinsky and her attorney met with Dr. Sarah Ashburn, BISD superintendent, to complain about G. S.'s behavior. Ashburn said the three-day bus suspension was sufficient punishment. She did not inform them about the existence of title IX or any title IX grievance procedures.

On May 4, Mrs. Rowinsky met with Ashburn and complained about her failure to take action against G. S. and L. H. Ashburn considered her actions against G. S. sufficient and informed Mrs. Rowinsky that she did not deem what had happened to Jane and Janet to be assaults. She refused to take further action, in part because L. H. was no longer a student in BISD. Mrs. Rowinsky told Ashburn that she intended to file a grievance with the United States Department of Education Office of Civil Rights ("OCR") . . .

III.

Title IX provides that "[n]o person in the United States shall, on the basis of sex, be excluded from participation in, be denied the benefits of, or be subjected to discrimination under any educational program or activities receiving Federal financial assistance." . . . At issue here is whether a school district may be liable under title IX when one student sexually harasses another. At a broader level of generality, we are asked to decide whether the recipient of federal education funds can be found liable for sex discrimination when the perpetrator is a party other than the grant recipient or its agents.

The linchpin of Rowinsky's theory is the assumption that a grant recipient need not engage in prohibited conduct to violate title IX. The specific statutory phrase at issue is the prohibition that "[n]o person be subjected to discrimination under any educational program or activities." Rowinsky focuses solely upon that phrase and argues that "under" means "in" and not "by." By making this substitution, she reasons that the statute cannot be limited to acts of discrimination by grant recipients.

A.

As with any statute, our starting point in determining the scope of title IX is the statutory language. . . .

We begin by noting that the text of title IX does not provide an unambiguous answer to the question. The title contains three general prohibitions: No person shall be excluded from participation in a program, denied the benefits of a program, or subjected to discrimination under a program. As is the case with the prohibition on discrimination, each of the other prohibitions, taken in isolation, is not explicitly limited to the acts of grant recipients. . . .

Despite the ambiguity in the text, three factors weigh in favor of interpreting title IX to impose liability only for the acts of grant recipients. The first is the scope and structure of the title itself; the second is the legislative history; the third is agency interpretations of the statute.

B.

The fact that title IX was enacted pursuant to Congress's spending power is evidence that it prohibits discriminatory acts only by grant recipients. As an exercise of Congress's spending power, title IX makes funds available to a recipient in return for the recipient's adherence to the conditions of the grant. While it is plausible that the condition imposed could encompass ending discriminatory behavior by third parties, the more probable inference is that the condition prohibits certain behavior by the grant recipients themselves.

This is so because the value of a spending condition is that it will induce the grant recipient to comply with the requirement in order to get the needed funds. In order for the coercion to be effective, the likelihood of violating the prohibition cannot be too great. . . .

Imposing liability for the acts of third parties would be incompatible with the purpose of a spending condition, because grant recipients have little control over the multitude of third parties who could conceivably violate the prohibitions of title IX. Thus, the possibility of a violation would be so great that recipients would be induced to turn down the grants. We find it unlikely that Congress would impose conditions on federal funds that would render the funds so unattractive to potential recipients, because to do so would render the conditions almost useless. . . .

C.

The legislative history of title IX also supports limiting the statute to the practices of grant recipients. The Supreme Court has repeatedly stated that the purpose of title IX is to prevent discrimination by grant recipients. . . .

Throughout the legislative history, both supporters and opponents of the amendment focused exclusively on acts by the grant recipients. . . .

IV.

* * *

The mere existence of sexual harassment does not necessarily constitute sexual discrimination. . . . Both men and women can be the victims or perpetrators of sexual harassment. . . . [S]exual overtures directed at both sexes, or behavior equally offensive to both males and females, is not sex discrimination. . . .

In the case of peer sexual harassment, a plaintiff must demonstrate that the school district responded to sexual harassment claims differently based on sex. Thus, a school district might violate title IX if it treated sexual harassment of boys more seriously than sexual harassment of girls, or even if it turned a blind eye toward sexual harassment of girls while addressing assaults that harmed boys. As the district court correctly pointed out, however, Rowinsky failed to allege facts to support such a claim.

Source: 80 *Federal Reporter 3d* 1006, 1008–16 (5th Cir. 1996) (footnotes omitted).

SAME-SEX HARASSMENT

In the employment context, lower courts split about whether it is illegal for someone to sexually harass a person of the same sex (see Documents 36 and 37). The Supreme Court decided this issue in the employment context in the spring of 1998, holding that same-sex harassment can be illegal (see Document 95).

Not surprisingly, the same issue has arisen in the context of education. The Office for Civil Rights of the United States Department of Education takes the position that same-sex harassment is illegal if the victim is targeted because of his or her gender, if the conduct disproportionately affects a student because of his or her gender, or if the nature of the harassment was determined by the victim's gender (see Document 81). The few courts that have considered the issue have agreed that same-sex harassment can be illegal in an educational institution.

DOCUMENT 81: "Sexual Harassment Guidance: Harassment of Students by School Employees, Other Students, or Third Parties" (Office for Civil Rights, United States Department of Education, 1997)

Title IX protects any "person" from sex discrimination; accordingly both male and female students are protected from sexual harassment engaged in by a school's employees, other students, or third parties. Moreover, Title IX prohibits sexual harassment regardless of the sex of the harasser, i.e., even if the harasser and the person being harassed are members of the same sex.[12] An example would be a campaign of sexually explicit graffiti directed at a particular girl by other girls.

Although Title IX does not prohibit discrimination on the basis of sexual orientation, sexual harassment directed at gay or lesbian students may constitute sexual harassment prohibited by Title IX. For example, if students heckle another student with comments based on the student's sexual orientation (e.g., "gay students are not welcome at this table in the cafeteria"), but their actions or language do not involve sexual conduct, their actions would not be sexual harassment covered by Title IX. On the other hand, harassing conduct of a sexual nature directed toward gay or lesbian students (e.g., if a male student or a group of male students target a lesbian student for physical sexual advances) may create a sexually hostile environment and, therefore, may be prohibited by Title IX. It should be noted that some State and local laws may prohibit discrimination on the basis of sexual orientation. Also, under certain circumstances, courts may permit redress for harassment on the basis of sexual orientation under other Federal legal authority.

[12] Title IX and the regulations implementing it prohibit discrimination "on the basis of sex;" they do not restrict sexual harassment to those circumstances in which the harasser only harasses members of the opposite sex in incidents involving either quid pro quo or hostile environment sexual harassment. . . . In order for hostile environment harassment to be actionable under Title IX, it must create a hostile or abusive environment. This can occur when a student or employee harasses a member of the same sex. . . . It can also occur in certain situations if the harassment is directed at students of both sexes. . . .

In many circumstances, harassing conduct will be on the basis of sex because the student would not have been subjected to it at all had he or she been a member of the opposite sex; e.g., if a female student is repeatedly propositioned by a male student or employee (or, for that matter, if a male student is repeatedly propositioned by a male student or employee). In other circumstances, harassing conduct will be on the basis of sex if the student would not have been affected by it in the same way or to the same extent had he or she been a member of the opposite sex; e.g., pornography and sexually explicit jokes in a mostly male shop class are likely to affect the few girls in the class more than it will most of the boys.

In yet other circumstances, the conduct will be on the basis of sex in that the student's sex was a factor in or affected the nature of the harasser's conduct or both. Thus, in [one reported case], a supervisor made demeaning remarks to both partners of a married couple working for him, e.g., as to sexual acts he wanted to engage in with the wife and how he would be a better lover than the husband. In both cases, according to the court, the remarks were gender-driven in that they were made with an intent to demean each member of the couple because of his or her respective sex. . . .

Source: Office for Civil Rights, U.S. Department of Education, "Sexual Harassment Guidance: Harassment of Students by School Employees, Other Students, or Third Parties," 62 *Federal Register* 12034–01, 12039 (March 13, 1997) (some footnotes omitted).

WHEN THE VERY YOUNG ARE ACCUSED OF HARASSMENT

Sexual harassment was in the news in the fall of 1996, when, in two separate instances, boys aged six and seven were disciplined for "sexual harassment" after subjecting female classmates to unwanted kisses. The public outcry over these incidents led some schools to revise their sexual harassment policies to take account of the fact that young children should not be held to the same standards as older children or adults. The following newspaper articles explain the controversy.

DOCUMENT 82: "6-Year-Old's Sex Crime: Innocent Peck on Cheek" (Adam Nossiter, 1996)

It might have been the most innocent thing in the world, one 6-year-old's kiss on another child's cheek. Or, as the boy's father put it, "Every child's going to steal a little peck on the jaw, once in a while."

So when Johnathan Prevette came home from school one day last week and told his mother he was in big trouble, and told her why, she scoffed. But the little boy had suddenly become wise beyond his years—wiser than his parents Calvin and Jackie, and wiser than the unthinking kiss he gave a little classmate might suggest.

Political correctness had gained an unlikely martyr, one with Coke-bottle glasses, a crooked smile, and a fondness for noisily chasing a soccer ball around his front yard. For a whole day last week, the boy's school suspended him because, as his "discipline referral" form put it, not mincing words, "Johnathan kissed a little girl on the cheek."

The formal charge was sexual harassment, and that got people talking, not just in this industrial town of 16,000, but all across the country.

For almost a week now, the telephone in the Prevettes' cluttered little house has been ringing off the hook. Radio and television stations from as far away as Australia, New Zealand and Canada have called. The little boy has become a star of the daytime television and talk-radio scene: Oliver North has called, as has NBC's "Today Show." Rush Limbaugh has taken up Johnathan's cause, and Kathie Lee Gifford discussed it on her show. That he missed an ice-cream party because of his suspension seemed to add pathos to the tale. The talk radio station in this Piedmont furniture and textile town has been flooded with calls from other stations across the country. . . .

The reason for all the attention is not hard to fathom. The television helicopter and the satellite trucks (more than a half-dozen on Wednesday), the movie deal ("they offered us $100,000, movie rights," Mr. Prevette, a disabled construction worker, said with wonder) and the calls from the radio stations, suggest that others realize what has hit the Prevettes forcefully: a doctrine meant to protect against sexual harassment might have reached a damaging level of absurdity.

But local school officials continued to defend their punishment of Johnathan. They would not return phone calls today, but released a statement on Wednesday saying that the boy had been punished not for violating the sexual harassment code, but instead for breaking a rule prohibiting "unwarranted and unwelcome touching of one student by another."

That enrages the Prevettes, who accuse the officials of trying to cover up their mistake. When Mrs. Prevette called Lisa Horne, the principal of Southwest School, last week to ask why her son was in trouble, the response was unequivocal, as she remembers it: "Because he violated the sexual harassment policy."

And describing what happened when she visited the school on Monday to talk to Ms. Horne, Mrs. Prevette said: "She gave me the sexual harassment policy, and proceeded to tell Johnathan what he did was wrong. If he was caught again kissing, hugging or hand-holding, he would be suspended." Ms. Horne did not return a telephone call.

Mrs. Prevette has a copy of the school's policy on "student-to-student sexual harassment," which she says was given to her by the principal. It is an explicit enumeration of what constitutes sexual harassment, including pressure for sex, flirting, propositions, and "patting, pinching or constant brushing against another's body." The exact origin of the policy is unclear, since Lexington school officials would not return calls today.

But it appears to closely follow Federal definitions of sexual harassment. Under Federal education law, schools at all levels are required to have policies for dealing with sexual harassment.

Still, at least one expert suggested today that applying such policies to 6-year-olds seems odd. Dr. T. Berry Brazelton, the pediatrician and nationally syndicated columnist, said, "I think it's crazy going so far," and added, "I would want to look at the adults in that situation, because I think they need help."

The furious Mr. Prevette has other, somewhat more forceful suggestions for dealing with the officials who disciplined his son. And he is dumbfounded by the notion that the bureaucratic language of Lexington City Schools' sexual harassment policy might apply to the tow-headed little blond boy running around the house. "We might read him that sexual harassment thing all night, and he might be bright enough to remember it. But would he understand it?" Mr. Prevette asked. . . .

Even the Mayor, Richard Thomas, did not defend Johnathan's treatment. "It's somewhat of an embarrassment to the people of Lexington," he said. "It would seem to be a policy gone awry. The only thing to do is to step forward, admit the policy is flawed, correct it and move on."

The Prevettes also say they want the policy changed. "That's my baby they're talking about," Mr. Prevette said. "He's not an adult. They're 6-year-old kids, two babies kissing each other."

Johnathan had never been in trouble before, Mr. Prevette said. His only fault this time could be traced to a basic character element, his burly, genial father said. "He's just an affectionate person."

Source: Adam Nossiter, "6-Year-Old's Sex Crime: Innocent Peck on Cheek," *New York Times*, September 27, 1996, p. A-14, col. 5.

DOCUMENT 83: "Kiss Leads to a Policy Revision" (*New York Times*, 1996)

The school board that punished a 6-year-old boy for kissing a girl on the cheek voted on Monday to revise its sexual harassment policy, giving school officials more leeway in punishing violators.

The boy's mother, Jackie Prevette, appeared before the nine-member board to argue that the board should define sexual harassment clearly. She said the change did not satisfy her and said her next move would be "legal action."

Johnathan, a first-grader, was separated from his class at Southwest Elementary School for a day and banned from an ice cream party after kissing a classmate last month.

"You need to change this policy so that it is age-appropriate and so that the punishment fits the crime," Mrs. Prevette told the board. "I do not think to this day that a kiss on the cheek, whether the girl wanted it or not, had anything to do with sex. I think it was a friendly kiss."

The board approved a new subsection, titled "Appropriate Behavior in the Elementary Grades," in the student handbook. It states:

"Student-to-student sexual harassment policy shall not be applied in the case of young students unless it clearly appears that there is an intent on the part of the students to engage in harassment of a sexual nature.

"In the absence of such intent, rules which forbid other forms of personal contact or interference should be considered and applied if appropriate."

The policy on "student-to-student sexual harassment" was amended to consider "the age and maturity of the student involved, the circumstances surrounding the incident, and the past behavior of the student."

Source: "Kiss Leads to a Policy Revision," New York Times, October 9, 1996, p. B-9, col. 1.

DOCUMENT 84: "Harassment in 2d Grade? Queens Kisser Is Pardoned" (Norimitsu Onishi, 1996)

A 7-year-old Queens boy who kissed a classmate and tore a button from her skirt was suspended from school for sexual harassment, then reinstated, as chagrined school officials weathered a wave of criticism yesterday and said they would review the school system's harassment policies.

The second-grade boy, De'Andre Dearinge, missed three days of classes at Public School 104 in Far Rockaway but was permitted to return after his parents met yesterday with the school's principal, Gerri Perriott. Ms. Perriott sent the boy home last Friday with a letter handing down a five-day suspension.

The incident came on the heels of a similar case that drew worldwide attention to a small town in North Carolina and became fodder for talk-show hosts and columnists suggesting that "political correctness" was beginning to claim under-age victims.

Few voices were raised yesterday to defend the initial decision to suspend De'Andre, with everyone from Mayor Rudolph W. Giuliani to experts on sexual harassment suggesting that school officials had overreacted. But the incident, and the storm that followed, gave a hint of how sensitive the issue of sexual harassment has become, with business executives, educators and others fearful of liability if employees or students contend they have been harassed.

Still, with many companies finding it necessary to conduct seminars to explain what constitutes sexual harassment, parents, city officials and experts contended that a 7-year-old was unlikely to understand the concept.

"Clearly, Title IX doesn't reach a little boy kissing a girl," said Verna Williams, a lawyer at the National Women's Law Center, referring to the Federal law prohibiting sex discrimination in schools. "That's not pervasive harassment, it's not a pattern, it's not severe, and sometimes a kiss is just a kiss."

The Board of Education said yesterday that it would reconsider its sexual-harassment guidelines, which list examples of sexual harassment and possible penalties but do not describe how the policy should be applied to students of varying ages, from kindergarten to high school.

"Clearly, the policy needs review," said Chiara Coletti, a spokeswoman for the board. "We have to look at whether it should be specific about age, and what that age should be. One can conclude that sexual harassment is a concept that a 7-year-old can't take."

School officials would not discuss details of the incident between De'Andre and his classmate, nor would they release the girl's name.

Despite the reversal of the suspension, Kenneth Grover, deputy superintendent of District 27, said that the initial decision was not made lightly, and that the boy's behavior had been serious enough to warrant some action.

"The principal made a decision based on the facts that she had at the moment," Mr. Grover said. "And possibly the use with a 7-year-old of the term 'sexual harassment' was inappropriate. But certainly the behavior dictated a stronger look at what the child did."

But the boy's mother, Erica White, and stepfather, Michael Bryan, said the principal had misinterpreted a child's innocent peck on the cheek, and instead of reprimanding him for his action, had overreacted by charging him with sexual harassment.

"Sexual harassment is too harsh a charge for an elementary school child," said Ms. White, 23. "My main concern is how this is going to affect his next 10 years in school."

Inside her uncle's house on Mott Avenue, a few blocks from the school, the mother said she had fought the charge because she did not want her son, who sings in the choir at St. John's Baptist Church and wants to be a writer, to have a tainted record. "It's going to be off his record now," she said of the charge. "That's all I wanted."

The parents said they learned of the suspension when De'Andre returned from school Friday afternoon, carrying a letter from the principal. "He thought it was a good letter, since he felt he'd had a good day at school," the mother said.

Instead, the letter, dated Sept. 27 and signed by the principal, said to keep De'Andre out of school Monday to Friday. In the middle of the one-page letter, two short paragraphs, the second one in bold capital letters, said: "Reason for suspension: SEXUAL HARASSMENT."

The letter omitted details of the incident. But after speaking to her son and school officials, Ms. White said that as De'Andre was sitting next to a girl during Friday's lunch break, he kissed her.

"She was sad," De'Andre later told his mother, describing his class-mate's reaction. "She didn't want to be kissed."

Outside P.S. 104 after the meeting yesterday, De'Andre, surrounded by a throng of reporters, explained that he had torn the button from the girl's skirt because the character in his favorite book, a bear, found him-self in a similar predicament.

Asked to name the book, the boy said softly: "Corduroy."

Asked what the bear was missing, the boy answered, "A button," then ran away from the media crush. . . .

The board's guidelines include "inappropriate physical contact of a sexual nature such as touching, patting, pinching" as sexual harassment.

Ms. Coletti, the board spokeswoman, said principals at all schools held frequent meetings to discuss sexual harassment and received training on how to handle the problem.

She added that the district superintendent had called the parents on Tuesday and asked them to a meeting yesterday. De'Andre had no pre-vious record of trouble or suspensions and no history of trying to kiss other girls, she said. . . .

"I think there are serious questions about the appropriateness of sus-pending a 6-year-old or 7-year-old for displaying the innocence of child-hood," said Carol A. Gresser, the Queens representative to the board. "I have a problem with holding little ones to the same standard you would hold adults to in the workplace."

But some other students—although older and perhaps more sophis-ticated than the second grader at the center of attention—were less for-giving of De'Andre's actions.

"In my opinion, he had no right to do it," said Melvin Martelly, 10, a fifth grader who was discussing the case with some classmates after school yesterday. "It's against the privacy of a female."

Diane Blair, also 10, added: "His parents should have told him not to do it in the first place. Common sense should have told you that, as well."

Source: Norimitsu Onishi, "Harassment in 2d Grade? Queens Kisser Is Par-doned," *New York Times*, October 3, 1996, p. A-1, col. 3.

SEXUAL HARASSMENT AND ACADEMIC FREEDOM

Some critics of the law against sexual harassment, like Michael S. Greve, the director of the Center for Individual Rights in Washington, D.C., argue that the law infringes on professors' rights to academic freedom (see Document 85). They argue that the law stifles what should be permissible forms of academic discourse—such as the use of sexual metaphors in the classroom. These commentators are concerned that the integrity of academic institutions is being undermined by those trying to police professors' speech in the name of political correctness.

Others, however, like law professor Linda Hirshman, defend the law against sexual harassment (see Document 86). They argue that it is proper to discourage professors from speaking in ways that intimidate female students, especially since these students often constitute a captive audience. This debate mirrors the debate about whether the regulation of sexual harassment in the workplace stifles free speech in violation of the First Amendment of the United States Constitution (see Documents 42 and 43).

DOCUMENT 85: "First Amendment: Do 'Hostile Environment' Charges Chill Academic Freedom? Yes: Call It What It Is—Censorship" (Michael S. Greve, 1994)

J. Donald Silva is a pastor at the New Castle Congregational Church in New Castle, N.H. Until April 1993, he was also a creative writing teacher at the University of New Hampshire. His 30-year tenure was terminated for having created a "hostile environment." The evidence consisted of two offbeat remarks Silva had made in class—one comparing "focus" in the writing process to sexual activity, the other elucidating the meaning of simile with a famed belly dancer's description of her craft.

Silva v. University of New Hampshire may be unique in its particulars. But it shows that the current, untempered enthusiasm for stamping out "hostile environment" harassment may produce huge social costs, including the suppression of free speech.

To date, First Amendment concerns have played only a marginal role in sexual harassment litigation. . . . But this is changing rapidly. Complaints over a hostile work or learning environment are proliferating on college campuses, which are disproportionately populated by individuals with exquisite sensibilities or, less charitably but perhaps more to the point, with a politically and sexually correct agenda.

Conflicts between harassment claims and free speech will be much sharper on campus than in the ordinary employment context, and the effort to produce a harmonious environment by means of civil rights litigation will entail far higher social costs in the form of "lost" speech.

Widget Inc. and its employees will function with or without pin-up posters and other forms of employee "speech" that have occasionally attracted harassment complaints. In higher education, in contrast, free speech is central both to the purpose of the institution and to the employee's profession and performance.

Academia cannot function under a legal regime that punishes speech in the name of combating a "hostile environment." This, alas, is the legal regime we have. One may argue that Professor Silva is a rare exception. But the question is not what Professor Silva said; it is what professors and students on campuses across the country will refrain from saying.

Vague Rules Stifle Speech

The current legal rules, which define a "hostile environment" on the basis of a case-by-case, multifactor analysis and with reference to the perception of a "reasonable person," are exceedingly vague. By that very virtue, they deter not only genuine harassment but also harmless and desirable speech; faced with legal uncertainty, individuals will avoid any speech that might be interpreted as creating a hostile environment.

Nor is it enough that the innocent victims of the anti-harassment campaign eventually can obtain judicial relief; mere complaints of misconduct, and their adjudication by university committees that operate with less than mathematical precision and are fearful of EEOC sanctions and investigations by the Office of Civil Rights, are in and of themselves a powerful deterrent.

A more reasonable set of rules would afford comprehensive First Amendment protection for all academic speech: Subject to liability only speech that is targeted at particular individuals and amounts to an intentional infliction of severe emotional distress; and authorize disciplinary measures and compensatory damages against individuals who knowingly bring false and frivolous charges of harassment (much like some "hate crime" statutes impose liability for such charges).

This arrangement would have the great advantage of curbing genuine harassment without intrusions into free speech and academic freedom. Naturally, it would fail to satisfy the apostles of sexual correctness, who view the First Amendment as merely one more policy consideration and the delicate sensibilities of freshwomen as an absolute limit to academic discourse.

But, as any student with strong religious convictions can testify, we have never considered subjective perceptions of a "hostile environment" as a limit to robust dialogue. Professor Silva's case illustrates why we should not do so now.

Source: Michael S. Greve, "First Amendment: Do 'Hostile Environment' Charges Chill Academic Freedom? Yes: Call It What It Is—Censorship," *American Bar Association Journal* 80 (February 1994): 40.

DOCUMENT 86: "First Amendment: Do 'Hostile Environment' Charges Chill Academic Freedom? No: This Is Teaching?" (Linda Hirshman, 1994)

I belong to the Ruth Bader Ginsburg generation of liberal feminists. I read "The Feminine Mystique" when it was published, was one of eight women in law school, and thought I could be as good a lawyer as any man. So, for a long time, I thought the focus of Catharine MacKinnon on sexual subordination and harassment was eccentric. Equal pay, reproductive rights—those were my issues.

But, in the last few years, the teachers who talk dirty to their female students have made a believer out of me. I began to ask what conceivable justification there could be for Professor J. Donald Silva to have to teach his students that writing "is like sex. You seek a target. You zero in on your target. You move from side to side. You close in on the subject. . . . You and the center become one."

In this . . . era, can you imagine your law partner describing legal writing to your associates this way? College tuition these days is a pretty high price to pay for something you can get from a 900 number for a lot less money. Worse still, if Greve has his way, and the colleges can't offer students alternatives to Silva's sex talk, the students will continue to be his captive audience.

Professors like Silva and their defenders say that the students should lighten up. Such sex talk is important, they say. Yet the more I know about the offending teachers, the more I realize that what really matters to them is the privilege of sexual abuse. The academics' attachment to acting out has made me realize the importance of this issue.

Another tactic is to compare people who oppose the harassment to Hitler. Legal commentators argue that law suddenly loses all capacity for sensible distinctions when sex is involved. Don't believe it. First, calling someone Hitler (the "reductio ad Hitlerium") is a desperate move, which people make only because their other arguments aren't very good. Historical exceptions to the First Amendment—for instance, limiting lawyers soliciting captive clients at bedside—exist to this day. Free countries like Canada and Britain regulate pornography and defamation without turning into the Third Reich.

Education Needn't Be X-rated

Constitutional law aside, the professors' defenders invoke the serious and worthy value of "academic freedom," implying that nothing less than the future of Western civilization rests on the freedom to engage in such exhibitions. This suggestion defames the very concept of "teachers."

Since women entered higher education in numbers, a whole generation of American women have been lucky enough to know teachers who managed to achieve excellence without insulting female students. . . .

My own First Amendment teacher and one of its greatest advocates, Harry A. Kalven Jr., of the University of Chicago, derived his love of free speech from its role in the 1960s enabling black Americans to march for full citizenship after centuries of subordination.

None of us who were privileged to sit in Harry's classroom could remotely imagine him offering to relieve an 18-year-old student of her virginity, as did 54-year-old William Kerrigan of the University of Massachusetts in a recent issue of Harper's.

In Europe, liberal equality put an end to *droit du seigneur*, the feudal lord's privilege of sexual access to the females on his lands. University campuses are one of the last refuges of the practice, and it's beyond time for the Middle Ages to come to an end there, too.

Source: Linda Hirshman, "First Amendment: Do 'Hostile Environment' Charges Chill Academic Freedom? No: This Is Teaching?" *American Bar Association Journal* 80 (February 1994): 41.

In 1997 the Office for Civil Rights of the United States Department of Education gave its position on the debate, arguing that the law against sexual harassment in education, when properly construed, does not raise First Amendment problems.

DOCUMENT 87: "Sexual Harassment Guidance: Harassment of Students by School Employees, Other Students, or Third Parties" (Office for Civil Rights, United States Department of Education, 1997)

First Amendment

In cases of alleged harassment, the protections of the First Amendment must be considered if issues of speech or expression are involved. Free speech rights apply in the classroom (e.g., classroom lectures and discussions) and in all other education programs and activities of public schools (e.g., public meetings and speakers on campus; campus debates, school plays and other cultural events; and student newspapers, journals and other publications). In addition, First Amendment rights apply to the speech of students and teachers.

Title IX is intended to protect students from sex discrimination, not to regulate the content of speech. OCR recognizes that the offensiveness of particular expression as perceived by some students, standing alone, is not a legally sufficient basis to establish a sexually hostile environment under Title IX. In order to establish a violation of Title IX, the harassment must be sufficiently severe, persistent, or pervasive to limit a student's ability to participate in or benefit from the education program or to create a hostile or abusive educational environment.

Moreover, in regulating the conduct of its students and its faculty to prevent or redress discrimination prohibited by Title IX (e.g., in responding to harassment that is sufficiently severe, persistent, or pervasive as to create a hostile environment), a school must formulate, interpret, and apply its rules so as to protect academic freedom and free speech rights. For instance, while the First Amendment may prohibit a school from restricting the right of students to express opinions about one sex that may be considered derogatory, the school can take steps to denounce those opinions and ensure that competing views are heard. The age of the students involved and the location or forum may affect how the school can respond consistent with the First Amendment. As an example of the application of free speech rights to allegations of sexual harassment, consider the following:

Example 1: In a college level creative writing class, a professor's required reading list includes excerpts from literary classics that contain descriptions of explicit sexual conduct, including scenes that depict women in submissive and demeaning roles. The professor also assigns students to write their own materials, which are read in class. Some of the student essays contain sexually derogatory themes about women. Several female students complain to the Dean of Students that the materials and related classroom discussion have created a sexually hostile environment for women in the class. What must the school do in response?

Answer: Academic discourse in this example is protected by the First Amendment even if it is offensive to individuals. Thus, Title IX would not require the school to discipline the professor or to censor the reading list or related class discussion.

Example 2: A group of male students repeatedly targets a female student for harassment during the bus ride home from school, including making explicit sexual comments about her body, passing around drawings that depict her engaging in sexual conduct, and, on several occasions, attempting to follow her home off the bus. The female student and her parents complain to the principal that the male students' conduct has created a hostile environment for girls on the bus and that they fear for their daughter's safety. What must the school do in response?

Answer: Threatening and intimidating actions targeted at a particular student or group of students, even though they contain elements of speech, are not protected by the First Amendment. The school must take reasonable and appropriate actions against the students, including disciplinary action if necessary, to remedy the hostile environment and prevent future harassment.

Source: Office for Civil Rights, U.S. Department of Education, "Sexual Harassment Guidance: Harassment of Students by School Employees, Others Students, or Third Parties," 62 *Federal Register* 12034–41, 12045–46 (March 13, 1997).

PART IV: FOR FURTHER READING

Benson, Katherine A. "Comment on Crocker's 'An Analysis of University Definitions of Sexual Harassment.' " *Signs: Journal of Women in Culture and Society* 9:3 (Spring 1984), 516–19.

Dziech, Billie Wright, and Linda Weiner. *The Lecherous Professor: Sexual Harassment on Campus*. 2d ed. Urbana: University of Illinois Press, 1990.

Hoffman, Frances L. "Sexual Harassment in Academia: Feminist Theory and Institutional Practice." *Harvard Educational Review* 56:2 (May 1986), 105–21.

Layman, Nancy S. *Sexual Harassment in American Secondary Schools*. Dallas: Contemporary Research Press, 1994.

Paludi, Michele A., ed. *Sexual Harassment on College Campuses: Abusing the Ivory Power*. Albany: State University of New York Press, 1996.

Schneider, Beth E. "Graduate Women, Sexual Harassment, and University Policy." *Journal of Higher Education* 58:1 (January/February 1987), 46–65.

Shoop, Robert J., and Jack W. Hayhow, Jr. *Sexual Harassment in Our Schools: What Parents and Teachers Need to Know to Spot It and Stop It*. Boston: Allyn and Bacon, 1994.

Stein, Nan D., and Lisa Sjostrom. *Flirting or Hurting: A Teacher's Guide to Student-on-Student Sexual Harassment in Schools (Grades 6 Through 12)*. Washington, DC: National Educational Association, 1994.

Part V

New Frontiers in Sexual Harassment Law

SEXUAL HARASSMENT IN HOUSING

Another context in which sexual harassment can occur is in housing, although there has been less litigation in this area than in employment and education. A federal statute called the Fair Housing Act (FHA) (Document 88) prohibits sex discrimination in the provision of housing.

Victims of housing discrimination who want to sue under the FHA may first present their claims either in court or before an administrator employed by the United States Department of Housing and Urban Development (HUD), the agency charged with implementing the FHA. Either way, their claims eventually can be reviewed by a federal court of appeals. Those who violate the provisions of the FHA can be forced to pay money damages to the victim and can also be subjected to orders requiring them to cease their discriminatory behavior.

Some state courts have also found that sexual harassment violates state laws against discrimination in housing or state tort laws prohibiting the intentional infliction of emotional distress.

DOCUMENT 88: Fair Housing Act (1968)

§ 3604. Discrimination in the sale or rental of housing and other prohibited practices.
[I]t shall be unlawful— ...

(b) To discriminate against any person in the terms, conditions, or privileges of sale or rental of a dwelling, or in the provision of services or facilities in connection therewith, because of race, color, religion, sex, familial status, or national origin.

Source: 42 *United States Code* § 3604 (1997).

> Landlords, property managers, and rental agents often have substantial power over tenants, particularly poorer tenants who may have little ability to move elsewhere. They can exploit this power by demanding sexual favors from tenants or by treating tenants in a sexually hostile or abusive manner. In 1987 a student author surveyed 150 agencies across the country, who work to implement fair housing laws, about the prevalence of sexual harassment. She found that sexual harassment in housing occurred frequently.

DOCUMENT 89: "Home Is No Haven: An Analysis of Sexual Harassment in Housing" (Regina Cahan, 1987)

The fair housing representatives who responded to the [author's] Survey described five different types of activity as sexual harassment:
(1) Abusive Remarks. . . .
(2) Unsolicited Sexual Behavior. . . .
(3) Solicitation of Sexual Behavior by Promise or Award. . . .
(4) Coercion of Sexual Activity by Threat or Punishment. . . .
(5) Punishment upon Rejection of Sexual Overtures. . . .

II. SURVEY RESULTS

A. Extent of Sexual Harassment in Housing and an Examination of the Factors that May Explain the Underreporting of Sexual Harassment in Housing

. . . The FHA Survey was sent to 150 public and private fair housing centers, agencies, and organizations across the country to determine the number of sexual harassment complaints received and to analyze specific characteristics of the complaints. The respondents were fair housing centers, not the victims themselves. Consequently, the survey results are based on information provided only by those women who reported their harassment to these centers. . . .

Taking into account the various reasons women are reluctant to report their harassment, it is likely the actual incidents of sexual harassment in housing number more than the 288 reported. In the absence of direct data regarding the emotional responses of victims of sexual harassment in housing, it is necessary to make analogies from the studies examining sexual harassment in the workplace and academia. The factors that deter women from reporting sexual harassment are fear of retaliation, silence as the chosen form of coping, aversion to the stigma attached to victims of sexual harassment, anticipation of ridicule, and a desire not to prolong suffering.

One reason women do not report their victimization is economic: they literally cannot afford to risk eviction or blacklisting. Of the sexual harassment reports in the survey for which specific characteristics were included, seventy-five percent of the women possessed annual incomes under $10,000, twenty-three percent between $10,000–$20,000 and the remaining two percent between $20,000–$30,000. Moreover, there is fertile ground for exploitation of tenants with low incomes because affordable housing options are limited and the effects of blacklisting are severe. Thus, the landlord's threat to evict the tenant unless granted sexual favors is especially menacing. Even if eviction does not take place, the fear of retaliation strikes when the unwelcome comment, gesture or behavior occurs. Moreover, instead of choosing eviction, the landlord or building superintendent may make the tenancy more burdensome by refusing to make repairs, enforcing rules more rigidly, or charging more rent. Recognizing that the landlord has the power to evict or to make the tenant's life more difficult, the victim has a strong disincentive to report the harassment.

Often, women remain silent for the sake of their family's physical well-being. Landlords frequently threaten the tenants' family members when subjecting women to harassment. In response, instead of risking their family's safety, women choose to be silent and endure the harassment. For instance, one woman reported that her landlord threatened to throw her child down the elevator shaft if the woman refused to have sexual intercourse with him. Confronted with such threats, silence and compliance become forms of coping, not acquiescence.

In addition to protecting their families, women also choose to remain silent because they do not want to be stigmatized as victims of sexual harassment: it is humiliating and embarrassing. A stigma persists because society often blames the victim. . . . In response to society's skepticism, the victim feels guilty and questions her behavior prior to the sexual harassment. Victims often feel that they should have prevented the occurrence by foreseeing it, handling it differently or simply not being at that place at that time.

A perception that other women were ridiculed, ignored or discredited when they reported incidents of sexual harassment is another factor that deters women from reporting. . . . Instead of support, the victim suffers further harassment. She learns that it is easier to endure alone than to report.

Furthermore, many women choose not to report because they do not wish to relive the incident. They feel that they have suffered enough. The FHA Survey indicated that agencies received many inquiries from women who did not pursue their complaints because the women did not want to continue their suffering by repeating the sordid details of the incident. Moreover, many women choose not to report because they perceive their harassment as unique. Victims do not know about each other's plight because of the paucity of public attention paid to this issue.

In addition to the forces that deter reporting, there are two other indications that the number of reported complaints in the FHA Survey represent a low estimate of the actual incidents of sexual harassment in housing. First, victims in the workplace and academia rarely file formal internal complaints. . . . Taking into account that the agencies who responded to the FHA Survey receive formal complaints, and assuming that the reporting rate in housing is as meager as the reporting rate in the workplace, the approximately 300 sexual harassment in housing cases found in the survey may represent only two to four percent of the actual occurrences. Thus, applying these statistics to the base of 300 reported incidents, 6,818 to 15,000 cases of sexual harassment in housing may have occurred.

The second factor suggesting that the FHA Survey under-reports the amount of sexual harassment in housing is the relative obscurity of the problem. Victims are only beginning to acquire and learn their legal rights. Recognition of sexual harassment in housing is recent and the law is in its infancy; hence, public education is vital at this time. As the law develops and more people become informed, the number of complaints is likely to increase. . . .

Taking into account the reasons women are reluctant to report their harassment in conjunction with the acknowledgement that sexual harassment in housing is a recently recognized fair housing issue, the 288 cases reported in the FHA Survey probably reflect only a small number of the actual incidents of sexual harassment in housing.

B. Specific Characteristics of Sexual Harassment in Housing

One goal of the FHA Survey was to determine whether sexual harassment occurred in housing and, if so, to gather data on the severity of the harassment. The forty-eight agencies that provided specific characteristics of the harassment gave specific characteristics on ninety complaints. The complaints were divided into behavioral components: request for sexual intercourse, request to pose for nude pictures, request for sexual exposure, indecent exposure, unsolicited and improper touching, abusive remarks, and other. The agencies reported 138 behavioral components within the ninety complaints. A complaint may include one or more components. For instance, if a complaint included both a request for sexual intercourse and abusive remarks, it was tallied under both

Table 1
Frequency Distribution of Behavioral Components

Code	Behavior Component	Actual Number	Percentage
A	Request for sexual intercourse	61	67.7
B	Abusive remarks	35	38.8
C	Unsolicited & Improper touching	31	34.4
D	Request for sexual exposure	3	3.0
E	Request to pose for nude pictures	1	1.0
F	Indecent exposure	1	1.0
G	Other	6	6.6
		(n=138)	(N=90)

behaviors. The survey demonstrated the [above] frequency distribution of the behavioral components[.]

Table 1 illustrates that 67.7 percent of the complaints included at least a request for sexual intercourse. As the survey requested information concerning the most severe complaints, the respondents distinguished requests for sexual intercourse, abusive remarks, and unsolicited and improper touching as the most severe sexual harassment in housing today. Additionally, taking into account the request for the most severe complaints, the data demonstrated that at least two-thirds of the women subjected to sexual harassment in their homes were asked to have sexual intercourse. . . .

The Survey also elicited details concerning the frequency of the harassment. Table 3 illustrates the frequency of sexual harassment in housing[.]

Although the majority of sexual harassment in housing incidents involved between one and four occurrences, complaints cited up to twenty-five events. As Table 3 indicates, the mode, the most cited number, was 1–2 occurrences.

Finally, the survey data also demonstrated the duration of the sexual harassment incidents. Table 4 displays the frequency distribution of the duration of the complaints received[.]

The duration of sexual harassment occurrences varied from one event in one day to many events over seven years. Although the mode is one day, more than half of the complaints lasted between one and six months.

C. Effects of Sexual Harassment

Masquerading as acceptable behavior, sexual harassment is often treated as a trivial issue and its debilitating effects are often ignored. . . . Although the research on the effects of sexual harassment in the work-

Table 3
Frequency of Sexual Harassment in Housing

Number of Occurrences	Frequency
1–2 occurrences	20
3–4 occurrences	14
5–6 occurrences	5
More than 8 occurrences	5

place and academia is relevant, the implications of being harassed in one's home may be even more traumatic. When sexual harassment occurs at work, at that moment or at the end of the workday, the woman may remove herself from the offensive environment. She will choose whether to resign from her position based on economic and personal considerations. In contrast, when the harassment occurs in a woman's home, it is a complete invasion in her life. Ideally, home is the haven from the troubles of the day. When home is not a safe place, a woman may feel distressed and, often, immobile.

Although accounts of sexual harassment differ, the similarities in women's responses are striking. Whether receiving leering looks, pinches, or demands for sexual intercourse, women report feeling nervous, irritable, frustrated and powerless. Similar to the reactions of a rape survivor, women who have experienced sexual harassment feel a loss of control over their lives. As her boss, teacher or landlord, the harasser usually possesses power over the woman. In fear of alienating this power, sexually harassed women often internalize their anger and fright, which may result in physical illness, decreased work productivity and depression.

Moreover, the victim's feeling of powerlessness is exacerbated by the fact that in small apartments, duplexes, or rented rooms, there is usually only one owner, the harasser. The FHA Survey demonstrated that thirty percent of sexual harassment of tenants occurs in small apartment complexes from two to twenty apartments, twenty-five percent in duplexes, and eight percent in rented rooms in private homes. Therefore, in sixty-three percent of the cases, the harasser was likely to be the only person in charge. Thus, the power to evict as well as the power to withhold repairs and services are in the hands of the harasser.

In larger complexes, victims are in a similarly powerless position because harassers' supervisors are inaccessible or unreceptive. The FHA Survey illustrated that seventeen percent of sexual harassment of tenants occurs in apartment complexes with more than a hundred units, fourteen percent in large complexes consisting of fifty to one hundred units, and five percent in apartment complexes with twenty to fifty units. Owners

Table 4
Duration of Sexual Harassment in Housing

Length of Time	Frequency
One day	15
One week	3
1–3 months	9
4–6 months	8
7–10 months	1
11 months–1 year	2
More than one year	5

and managers of large complexes tend to insulate themselves from the day-to-day problems of their building employees, and especially from the problems of their tenants. Even when a supervisor is accessible, an attempt at an informal resolution may prove meaningless for the following reasons: (1) the supervisor has a better relationship with the harasser than with the victim [and] tends to believe him; (2) the supervisor feels the woman can take care of the problem herself; or (3) the supervisor suggests that she is exaggerating the problem. Therefore, in order for a tenant to seek redress, she must become involved in a formal complaint process such as reporting to the local housing authority or human rights agency. Instead of preparing for this legal battle, the sexually harassed woman often chooses to endure the harassment in the hope it will cease.

Source: Regina Cahan, "Home Is No Haven: An Analysis of Sexual Harassment in Housing," *Wisconsin Law Review* (1987): 1061, 1064–74 (footnotes and Table 2 omitted).

In 1989 HUD issued regulations banning quid pro quo harassment. The agency declared that such activity constitutes unlawful sex discrimination within the meaning of the FHA. The regulations, however, are silent about hostile environment harassment.

DOCUMENT 90: "Regulations Relating to Housing and Urban Development, Discriminatory Conduct under the Fair Housing Act, Housing Practices" (1989)

(a) It shall be unlawful, because of race, color, religion, sex, handicap, familial status, or national origin, to impose different terms, conditions or privileges relating to the sale or rental of a dwelling or to deny or limit services or facilities in connection with the sale or rental of a dwelling.

(b) Prohibited actions under this section include, but are not limited to: . . .

(5) Denying or limiting services or facilities in connection with the sale or rental of a dwelling, because a person failed or refused to provide sexual favors.

Source: 24 *Code of Federal Regulations* § 100.65 (1997).

> Courts, like the court of appeals in *DiCenso v. Cisneros*, have held that hostile environment harassment of tenants is also illegal under the FHA. The courts reason that the law in this area should be substantially the same as the law that governs sexual harassment in employment, because of the similarities between the language of and purposes behind Title VII and the FHA. As the *DiCenso* case illustrates, however, just as in the employment context, there can be disagreement about how severe the harasser's behavior must be in order to create a hostile environment.

DOCUMENT 91: *DiCenso v. Cisneros*, U.S. Court of Appeals for the Seventh Circuit (1996)

This case raises the question of whether one incident of harassment was sufficiently egregious to create a hostile environment sex discrimination cause of action under the Fair Housing Act. . . .

Background

The events of this lawsuit arose in the context of Christina Brown's tenancy at 522 ½ West Allen Street in Springfield, Illinois. Brown, who at the time was 18 years old, lived in one of the four apartment units with Thomas Andrews and their infant daughter Sara. Beginning in June 1990, they leased the apartment from Albert DiCenso, who owned and managed the building, did most of the cleaning and maintenance, and collected the rents.

Brown and Andrews signed a six-month lease with an option for six more months. During the first few months a family friend stayed with them, and their rent was $300 per month. When the friend moved out in September, DiCenso reduced the rent to $275 per month. At first, Brown and her co-tenants delivered the rent checks to DiCenso's home, but eventually, DiCenso started going to the apartment to collect the payments.

Sometime in mid-October or early November, DiCenso came to

Brown's apartment to collect the rent. . . . [T]he following exchange took place: While [Brown] stood at the door, [DiCenso] asked about the rent and simultaneously began caressing her arm and back. He said to her words to the effect that if she could not pay the rent, she could take care of it in other ways. [Brown] slammed the door in his face. [DiCenso] stood outside calling her names—a "bitch" and "whore," and then left. On January 15, 1991, DiCenso again went to the apartment to collect the monthly rent. While there, he became involved in a confrontation with Andrews and the police were called. DiCenso informed the police that the disagreement was over Andrews' refusal to pay the rent. Brown and Andrews told DiCenso that they would be leaving the apartment within the next ten days. According to the police report, the two parties "both came to the decision of settling the matter in court."

Brown and Andrews did not move out, however, and in late January, DiCenso served them with a five-day notice to quit the premises. On January 31, Brown filed a housing discrimination complaint alleging that DiCenso had harassed her and her boyfriend, and had made sexual advances toward her. DiCenso denied the allegations, and asserted that he had had problems collecting the December 1990 and January 1991 rent, and that Andrews not only refused to pay the rent, but had threatened to hurt him. DiCenso felt that the discrimination complaint was a "plot" by Brown and Andrews to avoid paying the rent that was due.

The Department [of Housing and Urban Development ("HUD")] investigated Brown's complaint and determined that reasonable cause existed to believe that discrimination had occurred. On June 22, 1994 the Department issued a charge against DiCenso for violations of sections 804(b) and 818 of the Fair Housing Act. Section 804(b) prohibits discrimination "against any person in the terms, conditions, or privileges of [the] rental of a dwelling . . . because of . . . sex." . . . Section 818 makes it illegal to "coerce, intimidate, threaten, or interfere with any person in the exercise or enjoyment of . . . any right" granted or protected by the Fair Housing Act. . . .

Analysis

* * *

B. Hostile Environment Sex Discrimination

Title VII of the Civil Rights Act of 1964 . . . allows a cause of action for harassment that creates a hostile or offensive working environment. . . . Claims of hostile environment sex discrimination in the housing context have been far less frequent. . . . [C]ourts that have found harassment to create an actionable form of housing discrimination also have incorporated Title VII doctrines into their analyses. . . .

Like [other courts], we recognize a hostile housing environment cause of action, and begin our analysis with the more familiar Title VII standard. For sexual harassment to be actionable in the Title VII context, it must be sufficiently severe or pervasive to alter the conditions of the victim's employment and create an abusive working environment. . . . "Conduct that is not severe or pervasive enough to create an objectively hostile or abusive work environment—an environment that a reasonable person would find hostile or abusive—is beyond Title VII's purview." *Harris v. Forklift Systems, Inc.* . . . Applied to the housing context, a claim is actionable "when the offensive behavior unreasonably interferes with use and enjoyment of the premises." . . . Whether an environment is "hostile" or "abusive" can be determined only by looking at all the circumstances, and factors may include the frequency of the discriminatory conduct; its severity; whether it is physically threatening or humiliating, or a mere offensive utterance; and whether it unreasonably interferes with an employee's work performance. *Harris.* . . .

We repeatedly have held that isolated and innocuous incidents do not support a finding of sexual harassment. . . . "Though sporadic behavior, if sufficiently abusive, may support a [discrimination] claim, success often requires repetitive misconduct." . . .

In this context, the problem with Brown's complaint is that although DiCenso may have harassed her, he did so only once. Moreover, DiCenso's conduct, while clearly unwelcome, was much less offensive than other incidents which have not violated Title VII. DiCenso's comment vaguely invited Brown to exchange sex for rent, and while DiCenso caressed Brown's arm and back, he did not touch an intimate body part, and did not threaten Brown with any physical harm. There is no question that Brown found DiCenso's remarks to be subjectively unpleasant, but this alone did not create an objectively hostile environment.

We stress in closing that our decision today should not be read as giving landlords one free chance to harass their tenants. We do not condone DiCenso's conduct, nor do we hold that a single incident of harassment never will support an actionable claim. . . . Considering the totality of the circumstances in this case . . . DiCenso's conduct was not sufficiently egregious to create an objectively hostile housing environment. . . .

FLAUM, Circuit Judge, dissenting.

The majority correctly notes that this case raises the purely legal issue of whether a particular incident of harassment was sufficiently egregious to create a hostile housing environment claim under the Fair Housing Act (the "FHA"). The majority reviews this legal issue de novo and concludes that Albert DiCenso's conduct did not create an objectively hostile environment. Because, in my view, we must defer to HUD's reasonable interpretation of what constitutes a hostile housing environment, I respectfully dissent from the majority's decision.

It is well-established that considerable weight should be given to an agency's construction of a statutory scheme that it has been entrusted to administer. . . . The Supreme Court has held that HUD's interpretation of the FHA "ordinarily commands considerable deference" since "HUD [is] the federal agency primarily assigned to implement and administer Title VIII." . . .

In the current case, the Secretary of HUD has taken the position that DiCenso's conduct was sufficiently severe as to create a claim for hostile housing environment under the FHA. Section 804(b) of the FHA prohibits gender-based discrimination in the sale or rental of a dwelling, or in the "provision of services" in connection with such sale or rental. . . . The Secretary, consistently with the approach adopted by the majority, believes that a hostile housing environment claim is actionable "when the offensive behavior unreasonably interferes with use and enjoyment of the premises." . . . The Secretary concludes that DiCenso's offensive conduct was sufficiently severe to satisfy this test, despite the fact that the conduct only occurred once. DiCenso's unwelcome caressing of Brown, combined with his offer of "sex for rent" and his hurling of gender-oriented epithets after Brown's rejection of his offer, certainly provides the Secretary with ample support for this conclusion. Although the majority may very well be correct in stating that DiCenso's conduct would not be sufficient to give rise to a claim for sexual harassment under our Title VII precedent, the majority provides no basis for doubting the reasonableness of the Secretary's interpretation of the FHA. In conclusion it is my judgment that the Secretary's interpretation of the FHA is a reasonable one and is therefore entitled to deference.

Source: 96 *Federal Reporter 3d* 1004, 1005–06, 1008–10 (footnotes omitted).

SEXUAL HARASSMENT IN OTHER CONTEXTS

The state of California has been at the forefront of expanding the situations in which sexual harassment is illegal. In an amendment to a statute called the Unruh Civil Rights Act, adopted in 1994, California prohibited sexual harassment in the context of any "business, service, or professional relationship," including such relationships as physician/patient, attorney/client, and landlord/tenant. These are situations, like employment and education, in which one person can have power over another and can use that power in an abusive or exploitative manner.

DOCUMENT 92: Unruh Civil Rights Act (1994)

§ 51.9. Sexual harassment

(a) A person is liable in a cause of action for sexual harassment when the plaintiff proves all of the following elements:

(1) There is a business, service, or professional relationship between the plaintiff and defendant. Such a relationship includes any of the following:

(A) Physician, psychotherapist, or dentist-patient.

(B) Attorney, marriage, family or child counselor, licensed clinical social worker, master of social work, real estate agent, real estate appraiser, accountant banker, trust officer, financial planner loan officer, collection service, contractor, or escrow loan officer-client.

(C) Executor, trustee, or administrator beneficiary.

(D) Landlord or property manager-tenant.

(E) Teacher-student.

(F) A relationship that is substantially similar to any of the above.

(2) The defendant has made sexual advances, solicitations, sexual requests, or demands for sexual compliance by the plaintiff that were unwelcome and persistent or severe, continuing after a request by the plaintiff to stop.

(3) There is an inability by the plaintiff to easily terminate the relationship without tangible hardship.

(4) The plaintiff has suffered or will suffer economic loss or disadvantage or personal injury as a result of the conduct described in paragraph (2).

(b) In an action pursuant to this section, damages shall be awarded. . . .

(c) Nothing in this section shall be construed to limit application of any other remedies provided under the law.

Source: California Civil Code, § 51.9 (1995).

PART V: FOR FURTHER READING

Butler, Kathleen. "Sexual Harassment in Rental Housing." *University of Illinois Law Review* 1989:1 (Winter 1989), 175–214.

Honigsberg, Peter Jan, Marilyn Tham, and Gary Alexander. "When the Client Harasses the Attorney—Recognizing Third Party Sexual Harassment in the Legal Profession." *University of San Francisco Law Review* 28:3 (Spring 1994), 715–37.

Rosenthal, Robert. "Landlord Sexual Harassment: A Federal Remedy." *Temple Law Review* 65:2 (Summer 1992), 589–613.

Part VI

The Supreme Court's Decisions from 1998

In 1998 the Supreme Court rendered four decisions about issues relating to sexual harassment—more than it had issued in all previous years combined. Three of the decisions dealt with issues relating to sexual harassment in employment; the other decision addressed sexual harassment in the context of education.

The first of the decisions handed down by the Supreme Court resolved the issue whether same-sex harassment in employment can constitute illegal sex discrimination under Title VII. (For a discussion of this issue, see Documents 36–37, above). In *Oncale v. Sundowner Offshore Services, Inc.* (Document 93), the Court held unanimously that such harassment can be illegal. It reasoned that it is possible for members of a particular group (like men) to discriminate against other members of the same group.

In order to prevail in such a lawsuit, the plaintiff must establish that he or she is being targeted because of his or her gender. A plaintiff may do this by establishing that the harasser is homosexual and therefore is directing his or her sexual attentions only at people of the same sex. Or, if a female harasser's comments demonstrate that he or she is hostile to the presence of women in the workplace, that would be sufficient. Similarly if, for whatever reason, the harasser has been confining his or her objectionable behavior to other workers of the same gender, that would constitute sexual harassment.

DOCUMENT 93: *Oncale v. Sundowner Offshore Services, Inc.,* U.S. Supreme Court (1998)

This case presents the question whether workplace harassment can violate Title VII's prohibition against "discriminat[ion] . . . because of . . . sex," . . . when the harasser and the harassed employee are of the same sex.

I

. . . In late October 1991, Oncale was working for respondent Sundowner Offshore Services on a Chevron U.S.A., Inc., oil platform in the Gulf of Mexico. He was employed as a roustabout on an eight-man crew which included respondents John Lyons, Danny Pippen, and Brandon Johnson. Lyons, the crane operator, and Pippen, the driller, had supervisory authority. . . . On several occasions, Oncale was forcibly subjected to sex-related, humiliating actions against him by Lyons, Pippen and Johnson in the presence of the rest of the crew. Pippen and Lyons also physically assaulted Oncale in a sexual manner, and Lyons threatened him with rape.

Oncale's complaints to supervisory personnel produced no remedial action; in fact, the company's Safety Compliance Clerk, Valent Hohen, told Oncale that Lyons and Pippen "picked [on] him all the time too," and called him a name suggesting homosexuality. . . . Oncale eventually quit—asking that his pink slip reflect that he "voluntarily left due to sexual harassment and verbal abuse." . . . When asked at his deposition why he left Sundowner, Oncale stated "I felt that if I didn't leave my job, that I would be raped or forced to have sex." . . .

II

* * *

Title VII's prohibition of discrimination "because of . . . sex" protects men as well as women, . . . and in the related context of racial discrimination in the workplace we have rejected any conclusive presumption that an employer will not discriminate against members of his own race. "Because of the many facets of human motivation, it would be unwise to presume as a matter of law that human beings of one definable group will not discriminate against other members of that group." . . . If our precedents leave any doubt on the question, we hold today that nothing in Title VII necessarily bars a claim of discrimination "because of . . . sex" merely because the plaintiff and the defendant (or the person charged with acting on behalf of the defendant) are of the same sex. . . .

We see no justification in the statutory language or our precedents for a categorical rule excluding same-sex harassment claims from the coverage of Title VII. As some courts have observed, male-on-male sexual harassment in the workplace was assuredly not the principal evil Congress was concerned with when it enacted Title VII. But statutory prohibitions often go beyond the principal evil to cover reasonably comparable evils, and it is ultimately the provisions of our laws rather than the principal concerns of our legislators by which we are governed. Title VII prohibits "discriminat[ion] . . . because of . . . sex" in the "terms" or "conditions" of employment. Our holding that this includes sexual harassment must extend to sexual harassment of any kind that meets the statutory requirements.

Respondents . . . contend that recognizing liability for same-sex harassment will transform Title VII into a general civility code for the American workplace. But that risk is no greater for same-sex than for opposite-sex harassment, and is adequately met by careful attention to the requirements of the statute. Title VII does not prohibit all verbal or physical harassment in the workplace; it is directed only at "discriminat[ion] . . . because of . . . sex." We have never held that workplace harassment, even harassment between men and women, is automatically discrimination because of sex merely because the words used have sexual content or connotations. "The critical issue, Title VII's text indicates, is whether members of one sex are exposed to disadvantageous terms or conditions of employment to which members of the other sex are not exposed." . . .

Courts and juries have found the inference of discrimination easy to draw in most male-female sexual harassment situations, because the challenged conduct typically involves explicit or implicit proposals of sexual activity; it is reasonable to assume those proposals would not have been made to someone of the same sex. The same chain of inference would be available to a plaintiff alleging same-sex harassment, if there were credible evidence that the harasser was homosexual. But harassing conduct need not be motivated by sexual desire to support an inference of discrimination on the basis of sex. A trier of fact might reasonably find such discrimination, for example, if a female victim is harassed in such sex-specific and derogatory terms by another woman as to make it clear that the harasser is motivated by general hostility to the presence of women in the workplace. A same-sex harassment plaintiff may also, of course, offer direct comparative evidence about how the alleged harasser treated members of both sexes in a mixed-sex workplace. Whatever evidentiary route the plaintiff chooses to follow, he or she must always prove that the conduct at issue was not merely tinged with offensive sexual connotations, but actually constituted "discrimina[tion] . . . because of . . . sex."

And there is another requirement that prevents Title VII from expanding into a general civility code: . . . the statute does not reach genuine but innocuous differences in the ways men and women routinely interact with members of the same sex and of the opposite sex. The prohibition of harassment on the basis of sex requires neither asexuality nor androgyny in the workplace; it forbids only behavior so objectively offensive as to alter the "conditions" of the victim's employment. "Conduct that is not severe or pervasive enough to create an objectively hostile or abusive work environment—an environment that a reasonable person would find hostile or abusive—is beyond Title VII's purview." . . . We have always regarded that requirement as crucial, and as sufficient to ensure that courts and juries do not mistake ordinary socializing in the workplace—such as male-on-male horseplay or intersexual flirtation— for discriminatory "conditions of employment."

We have emphasized, moreover, that the objective severity of harassment should be judged from the perspective of a reasonable person in the plaintiff's position, considering "all the circumstances." . . . In same-sex (as in all) harassment cases, that inquiry requires careful consideration of the social context in which particular behavior occurs and is experienced by its target. A professional football player's working environment is not severely or pervasively abusive, for example, if the coach smacks him on the buttocks as he heads onto the field—even if the same behavior would reasonably be experienced as abusive by the coach's secretary (male or female) back at the office. The real social impact of workplace behavior often depends on a constellation of surrounding circumstances, expectations, and relationships which are not fully captured by a simple recitation of the words used or the physical acts performed. Common sense, and an appropriate sensitivity to social context, will enable courts and juries to distinguish between simple teasing or roughhousing among members of the same sex, and conduct which a reasonable person in the plaintiff's position would find severely hostile or abusive.

Source: 118 Supreme Court Reporter 998, 1000–03 (1998).

In June 1998, the U.S. Supreme Court rendered two more decisions relating to sexual harassment in employment: Burlington Industries, Inc. v. Ellerth (Document 94) and Faragher v. City of Boca Raton (Document 95).

The Ellerth case raised the issue whether a plaintiff could establish quid pro quo harassment if her supervisor threatened to retaliate against her if she refused to have sex with him but then failed to carry out that threat, or whether this would constitute hostile environment harassment instead. The Supreme Court held that the labels "quid pro quo" and "hostile environment" have limited utility. Instead, the important question is whether the plaintiff suffered any tangible harm— such as being denied a raise or being demoted.

In cases in which the victim suffers a tangible harm, the employer is automatically liable for the acts of its supervisor and must compensate the victim for the harm that she has suffered. In contrast, in cases in which an employee has been harassed by a supervisor but not tangibly harmed, the majority of the court held that an employer is only presumptively responsible. The employer can rebut this presumption of liability if it establishes both "that the employer exercised reasonable care to prevent and correct promptly any sexually harassing behavior, and . . . that the plaintiff employee unreasonably failed to take advantage of any preventive or corrective opportunities provided by the employer or to avoid harm otherwise."

The *Faragher* case reiterated and applied the principles set forth in *Ellerth* with regard to when employers can be held responsible for harassment by supervisors that does not cause a tangible harm.

Justices Thomas and Scalia dissented in both cases, arguing that the majority's rule created too much liability for employers. They argued that employers should be liable only if the plaintiff establishes that the employer was negligent in permitting the supervisor's conduct to occur.

The *Ellerth* and *Faragher* cases helped clear up the standards for employer liability for sexual harassment by supervisors. The cases, however, still leave important questions unanswered. Most significantly, the requirement that an employer take reasonable care to prevent and redress harassment remains murky. An employer would be well advised to have an anti-harassment policy that is communicated to its employees, although the Court cryptically states that an employer will not necessarily lose if it does not have such a formal policy. But it remains unclear what such a policy must provide and how often and in what format it must be communicated to the employees.

Furthermore, once an employer receives a claim of sexual harassment, the decisions leave it unclear exactly what is required. If the employer finds credible evidence that the harassment occurred, how severely must it punish the offending supervisor? And what must an employer do if it is faced with contradictory evidence and does not know whom to believe?

Finally, these cases only discuss liability in situations in which a supervisor harasses a subordinate. The standard for employer liability for co-worker harassment remains unsettled.

DOCUMENT 94: *Burlington Industries, Inc. v. Ellerth*, U.S. Supreme Court (1998)

We decide whether, under Title VII of the Civil Rights Act of 1964, . . . an employee who refuses the unwelcome and threatening sexual advances of a supervisor, yet suffers no adverse, tangible job consequences, can recover against the employer without showing the employer is negligent or otherwise at fault for the supervisor's actions.

I

. . . The employer is Burlington Industries, the petitioner. The employee is Kimberly Ellerth, the respondent. From March 1993 until May 1994, Ellerth worked as a salesperson in one of Burlington's divisions in Chicago, Illinois. During her employment, she alleges, she was subjected to constant sexual harassment by her supervisor, one Ted Slowik.

In the hierarchy of Burlington's management structure, Slowik was a mid-level manager. Burlington has eight divisions, employing more than 22,000 people in some 50 plants around the United States. Slowik was a vice president in one of five business units within one of the divisions. He had authority to make hiring and promotion decisions subject to the approval of his supervisor, who signed the paperwork. . . . According to Slowik's supervisor, his position was "not considered an upper-level management position," and he was "not amongst the decision-making or policy-making hierarchy." . . . Slowik was not Ellerth's immediate supervisor. Ellerth worked in a two-person office in Chicago, and she answered to her office colleague, who in turn answered to Slowik in New York.

Against a background of repeated boorish and offensive remarks and gestures which Slowik allegedly made, Ellerth places particular emphasis on three alleged incidents where Slowik's comments could be construed as threats to deny her tangible job benefits. In the summer of 1993, while on a business trip, Slowik invited Ellerth to the hotel lounge, an invitation Ellerth felt compelled to accept because Slowik was her boss. . . . When Ellerth gave no encouragement to remarks Slowik made about her breasts, he told her to "loosen up" and warned, "you know, Kim, I could make your life very hard or very easy at Burlington." . . .

In March 1994, when Ellerth was being considered for a promotion, Slowik expressed reservations during the promotion interview because she was not "loose enough." . . . The comment was followed by his reaching over and rubbing her knee. . . . Ellerth did receive the promotion; but when Slowik called to announce it, he told Ellerth, "you're gonna be out there with men who work in factories, and they certainly like women with pretty butts/legs." . . .

In May 1994, Ellerth called Slowik, asking permission to insert a customer's logo into a fabric sample. Slowik responded, "I don't have time for you right now, Kim—unless you want to tell me what you're wearing." . . . Ellerth told Slowik she had to go and ended the call. . . . A day or two later, Ellerth called Slowik to ask permission again. This time he denied her request, but added something along the lines of, "are you wearing shorter skirts yet, Kim, because it would make your job a whole heck of a lot easier." . . .

A short time later, Ellerth's immediate supervisor cautioned her about returning telephone calls to customers in a prompt fashion. . . . In response, Ellerth quit. She faxed a letter giving reasons unrelated to the alleged sexual harassment we have described. . . . About three weeks later, however, she sent a letter explaining she quit because of Slowik's behavior. . . .

During her tenure at Burlington, Ellerth did not inform anyone in authority about Slowik's conduct, despite knowing Burlington had a policy against sexual harassment. . . . In fact, she chose not to inform her immediate supervisor (not Slowik) because " 'it would be his duty as my supervisor to report any incidents of sexual harassment.' " . . . On one occasion, she told Slowik a comment he made was inappropriate. . . .

In October 1994, . . . Ellerth filed suit . . . alleging Burlington engaged in sexual harassment and forced her constructive discharge, in violation of Title VII. . . .

II

At the outset, we assume an important proposition yet to be established before a trier of fact. . . . The premise is: a trier of fact could find in Slowik's remarks numerous threats to retaliate against Ellerth if she denied some sexual liberties. The threats, however, were not carried out or fulfilled. Cases based on threats which are carried out are referred to often as *quid pro quo* cases, as distinct from bothersome attentions or sexual remarks that are sufficiently severe or pervasive to create a hostile work environment. The terms *quid pro quo* and hostile work environment are helpful, perhaps, in making a rough demarcation between cases in which threats are carried out and those where they are not or are absent altogether, but beyond this are of limited utility. . . .

"*Quid pro quo*" and "hostile work environment" do not appear in the statutory text [of Title VII]. The terms appeared first in the academic literature, *see* C. MacKinnon, Sexual Harassment of Working Women (1979); found their way into decisions of the Courts of Appeals, . . . and were mentioned in this Court's decision in *Meritor Savings Bank, FSB v. Vinson.* . . .

. . . [A]s use of the terms grew in the wake of *Meritor*, they acquired their own significance. The standard of employer responsibility turned on which type of harassment occurred. If the plaintiff established a *quid pro quo* claim, the Courts of Appeals held, the employer was subject to vicarious liability. [Under the vicarious liability standard, employers are automatically legally responsible for their employees' actions]. . . .The rule encouraged Title VII plaintiffs to state their claims as *quid pro quo* claims, which in turn put expansive pressure on the definition. The equivalence of the *quid pro quo* label and vicarious liability is illustrated by this case. The question presented . . . is whether Ellerth can state a claim of *quid pro quo* harassment, but the issue of real concern to the parties is whether Burlington has vicarious liability for Slowik's alleged misconduct, rather than liability limited to its own negligence. . . .

We do not suggest the terms *quid pro quo* and hostile work environment are irrelevant to Title VII litigation. To the extent they illustrate the distinction between cases involving a threat which is carried out and offensive conduct in general, the terms are relevant when there is a threshold question whether a plaintiff can prove discrimination in violation of Title VII. When a plaintiff proves that a tangible employment action resulted from a refusal to submit to a supervisor's sexual demands, he or she establishes that the employment decision itself constitutes a change in the terms and conditions of employment that is actionable under Title VII. For any sexual harassment preceding the employment decision to be actionable, however, the conduct must be severe or pervasive. Because Ellerth's claim involves only unfulfilled threats, it should be categorized as a hostile work environment claim which requires a showing of severe or pervasive conduct. . . . For purposes of this case, we accept the District Court's finding that the alleged conduct was severe or pervasive. . . . The case before us involves numerous alleged threats, and we express no opinion as to whether a single unfulfilled threat is sufficient to constitute discrimination in the terms or conditions of employment.

When we assume discrimination can be proved, however, the factors we discuss below, and not the categories *quid pro quo* and *hostile work environment*, will be controlling on the issue of vicarious liability. That is the question we must resolve.

III

We must decide, then, whether an employer has vicarious liability when a supervisor creates a hostile work environment by making explicit threats to alter a subordinate's terms or conditions of employment, based on sex, but does not fulfill the threat. We turn to principles of agency law, for the term "employer" is defined under Title VII to include "agents." . . . In express terms, Congress has directed federal courts to interpret Title VII based on agency principles. . . .

A

. . . [A] central principle of agency law [is that]:

"A master is subject to liability for the torts of his servants committed while acting in the scope of their employment."

An employer may be liable for both negligent and intentional torts committed by an employee within the scope of his or her employment. Sexual harassment under Title VII presupposes intentional conduct. . . . [C]onduct, including an intentional tort, [is] within the scope of employment when "actuated, at least in part, by a purpose to serve the [employer]," even if it is forbidden by the employer. . . . For example, when a salesperson lies to a customer to make a sale, the tortious conduct is within the scope of employment because it benefits the employer by increasing sales, even though it may violate the employer's policies. . . .

As Courts of Appeals have recognized, a supervisor acting out of gender-based animus or a desire to fulfill sexual urges may not be actuated by a purpose to serve the employer. . . . The harassing supervisor often acts for personal motives, motives unrelated and even antithetical to the objectives of the employer. . . .

The general rule is that sexual harassment by a supervisor is not conduct within the scope of employment.

B

Scope of employment does not define the only basis for employer liability under agency principles. In limited circumstances, agency principles impose liability on employers even where employees commit torts outside the scope of employment [as follows]. . . .

"(2) A master is not subject to liability for the torts of his servants acting outside the scope of their employment, unless:
"(a) the master intended the conduct or the consequences, or
"(b) the master was negligent or reckless, or
"(c) the conduct violated a non-delegable duty of the master, or
"(d) the servant purported to act or to speak on behalf of the principal and there was reliance upon apparent authority, or he was aided in accomplishing the tort by the existence of the agency relation." . . .

Subsection (a) addresses direct liability, where the employer acts with tortious intent, and indirect liability, where the agent's high rank in the company makes him or her the employer's alter ego. None of the parties contend Slowik's rank imputes liability under this principle. There is no contention, furthermore, that a nondelegable duty is involved. . . . So, for our purposes here, subsections (a) and (c) can be put aside.

Subsections (b) and (d) are possible grounds for imposing employer liability on account of a supervisor's acts and must be considered. Under subsection (b), an employer is liable when the tort is attributable to the employer's own negligence. . . . Thus, although a supervisor's sexual harassment is outside the scope of employment because the conduct was for personal motives, an employer can be liable, nonetheless, where its own negligence is a cause of the harassment. An employer is negligent with respect to sexual harassment if it knew or should have known about the conduct and failed to stop it. Negligence sets a minimum standard for employer liability under Title VII; but Ellerth seeks to invoke the more stringent standard of vicarious liability.

Subsection . . . (d) concerns vicarious liability for intentional torts committed by an employee when the employee uses apparent authority (the apparent authority standard), or when the employee "was aided in accomplishing the tort by the existence of the agency relation" (the aided in the agency relation standard). As other federal decisions have done in discussing vicarious liability for supervisor harassment, . . . we begin with [subsection] (d).

C

As a general rule, apparent authority is relevant where the agent purports to exercise a power which he or she does not have, as distinct from where the agent threatens to misuse actual power. . . . In the usual case, a supervisor's harassment involves misuse of actual power, not the false impression of its existence. Apparent authority analysis therefore is inappropriate in this context. . . .

D

We turn to the aided in the agency relation standard. In a sense, most workplace tortfeasors are aided in accomplishing their tortious objective by the existence of the agency relation: Proximity and regular contact may afford a captive pool of potential victims. . . . Were this to satisfy the aided in the agency relation standard, an employer would be subject to vicarious liability not only for all supervisor harassment, but also for all co-worker harassment, a result enforced by neither the EEOC nor any court of appeals to have considered the issue. . . . The aided in the agency relation standard, therefore, requires the existence of something more than the employment relation itself.

At the outset, we can identify a class of cases where, beyond question, more than the mere existence of the employment relation aids in commission of the harassment: when a supervisor takes a tangible employment action against the subordinate. Every Federal Court of Appeals to have considered the question has found vicarious liability when a discriminatory act results in a tangible employment action. . . . Although few courts have elaborated how agency principles support this rule, we think it reflects a correct application of the aided in the agency relation standard.

In the context of this case, a tangible employment action would have taken the form of a denial of a raise or a promotion. . . . A tangible employment action constitutes a significant change in employment status, such as hiring, firing, failing to promote, reassignment with significantly different responsibilities, or a decision causing a significant change in benefits. . . .

When a supervisor makes a tangible employment decision, there is assurance the injury could not have been inflicted absent the agency relation. A tangible employment action in most cases inflicts direct economic harm. As a general proposition, only a supervisor, or other person acting with the authority of the company, can cause this sort of injury. A co-worker can break a co-worker's arm as easily as a supervisor, and anyone who has regular contact with an employee can inflict psychological injuries by his or her offensive conduct. . . . But one co-worker (absent some elaborate scheme) cannot dock another's pay, nor can one co-worker demote another. Tangible employment actions fall within the special province of the supervisor. The supervisor has been empowered by the company as a distinct class of agent to make economic decisions affecting other employees under his or her control. . . .

For these reasons, a tangible employment action taken by the supervisor becomes for Title VII purposes the act of the employer. Whatever the exact contours of the aided in the agency relation standard, its requirements will always be met when a supervisor takes a tangible employment action against a subordinate. In that instance, it would be implausible to interpret agency principles to allow an employer to escape liability. . . .

Whether the agency relation aids in commission of supervisor harassment which does not culminate in a tangible employment action is less obvious. Application of the standard is made difficult by its malleable terminology, which can be read to either expand or limit liability in the context of supervisor harassment. On the one hand, a supervisor's power and authority invests his or her harassing conduct with a particular threatening character, and in this sense, a supervisor always is aided by the agency relation. . . . On the other hand, there are acts of harassment a supervisor might commit which might be the same acts a co-employee would commit, and there may be some circumstances where the supervisor's status makes little difference.

. . . [W]e are bound by our holding in *Meritor* that agency principles constrain the imposition of vicarious liability in cases of supervisory harassment. . . .

Although *Meritor* suggested the limitation on employer liability stemmed from agency principles, the Court acknowledged other considerations might be relevant as well. . . . For example, Title VII is designed to encourage the creation of antiharassment policies and effective grievance mechanisms. Were employer liability to depend in part on an employer's effort to create such procedures, it would effect Congress' intention to promote conciliation rather than litigation in the Title VII context, . . . and the EEOC's policy of encouraging the development of grievance procedures. . . . To the extent limiting employer liability could encourage employees to report harassing conduct before it becomes severe or pervasive, it would also serve Title VII's deterrent purpose. . . .

In order to accommodate the agency principles of vicarious liability for harm caused by misuse of supervisory authority, as well as Title VII's equally basic policies of encouraging forethought by employers and saving action by objecting employees, we adopt the following holding in this case and in *Faragher v. Boca Raton*, . . . also decided today. An employer is subject to vicarious liability to a victimized employee for an actionable hostile environment created by a supervisor with immediate (or successively higher) authority over the employee. When no tangible employment action is taken, a defending employer may raise an affirmative defense to liability or damages, subject to proof by a preponderance of the evidence. . . . The defense comprises two necessary elements: (a) that the employer exercised reasonable care to prevent and correct promptly any sexually harassing behavior, and (b) that the plaintiff employee unreasonably failed to take advantage of any preventive or corrective opportunities provided by the employer or to avoid harm otherwise. While proof that an employer had promulgated an anti-harassment policy with complaint procedure is not necessary in every instance as a matter of law, the need for a stated policy suitable to the employment circumstances may appropriately be addressed in any case when litigating the first element of the defense. And while proof that an employee failed to fulfill the corresponding obligation of reasonable care to avoid harm is not limited to showing any unreasonable failure to use any complaint procedure provided by the employer, a demonstration of such failure will normally suffice to satisfy the employer's burden under the second element of the defense. No affirmative defense is available, however, when the supervisor's harassment culminates in a tangible employment action, such as discharge, demotion, or undesirable reassignment.

IV

Relying on existing case law which held out the promise of vicarious liability for all *quid pro quo* claims, . . . Ellerth focused all her attention in the Court of Appeals on proving her claim fit within that category. Given our explanation that the labels *quid pro quo* and *hostile work environment* are not controlling for purposes of establishing employer liability, Ellerth should have an adequate opportunity to prove she has a claim for which Burlington is liable. . . .

Justice Thomas, with whom Justice Scalia joins, dissenting.

The Court today manufactures a rule that employers are vicariously liable if supervisors create a sexually hostile work environment, subject to an affirmative defense that the Court barely attempts to define. This rule applies even if the employer has a policy against sexual harassment, the employee knows about that policy, and the employee never informs anyone in a position of authority about the supervisor's conduct. As a result, employer liability under Title VII is judged by different standards depending upon whether a sexually or racially hostile work environment is alleged. The standard of employer liability should be the same in both instances: An employer should be liable if, and only if, the plaintiff proves that the employer was negligent in permitting the supervisor's conduct to occur.

I

Years before sexual harassment was recognized as "discrimination . . . because of . . . sex," . . . the Courts of Appeals considered whether, and when, a racially hostile work environment could violate Title VII. In the landmark case *Rogers v. EEOC*, . . . the Court of Appeals for the Fifth Circuit held that the practice of racially segregating patients in a doctor's office could amount to discrimination in " 'the terms, conditions, or privileges' " of employment, thereby violating Title VII. . . . The principal opinion in the case concluded that employment discrimination was not limited to the "isolated and distinguishable events" of "hiring, firing, and promoting." . . . Rather, Title VII could also be violated by a work environment "heavily polluted with discrimination," because of the deleterious effects of such an atmosphere on an employee's well-being. . . .

In race discrimination cases, employer liability has turned on whether the plaintiff has alleged an adverse employment consequence, such as firing or demotion, or a hostile work environment. If a supervisor takes an adverse employment action because of race, causing the employee a tangible job detriment, the employer is vicariously liable for resulting damages. . . . This is because such actions are company acts that can be performed only by the exercise of specific authority granted by the employer, and thus the supervisor acts as the employer. If, on the other hand, the employee alleges a racially hostile work environment, the employer is liable only for negligence: that is, only if the employer knew, or in the exercise of reasonable care should have known, about the harassment and failed to take remedial action. . . . Liability has thus been imposed only if the employer is blameworthy in some way. . . .

This distinction applies with equal force in cases of sexual harassment. When a supervisor inflicts an adverse employment consequence upon an employee who has rebuffed his advances, the supervisor exercises the specific authority granted to him by his company. His acts, therefore, are the company's acts and are properly chargeable to it. . . .

If a supervisor creates a hostile work environment, however, he does not act for the employer. As the Court concedes, a supervisor's creation of a hostile work environment is neither within the scope of his employment, nor part of his apparent authority. . . . Indeed, a hostile work environment is antithetical to the interest of the employer. In such circumstances, an employer should be liable only if it has been negligent. That is, liability should attach only if the employer either knew, or in the exercise of reasonable care should have known, about the hostile work environment and failed to take remedial action.

Sexual harassment is simply not something that employers can wholly prevent without taking extraordinary measures—constant video and audio surveillance, for example—that would revolutionize the workplace in a manner incompatible with a free society. . . . Indeed, such measures could not even detect incidents of harassment such as the comments Slowick allegedly made to respondent in a hotel bar. The most that employers can be charged with, therefore, is a duty to act reasonably under the circumstances. . . .

Under a negligence standard, Burlington cannot be held liable for Slowick's conduct. Although respondent alleged a hostile work environment, she never contended that Burlington had been negligent in permitting the harassment to occur, and there is no question that Burlington acted reasonably under the circumstances. The company had a policy against sexual harassment, and respondent admitted that she was aware of the policy but nonetheless failed to tell anyone with authority over Slowick about his behavior. . . . Burlington therefore cannot be charged with knowledge of Slowick's alleged harassment or with a failure to exercise reasonable care in not knowing about it.

II

* * *

The Court's holding does guarantee one result: There will be more and more litigation to clarify applicable legal rules in an area in which both practitioners and the courts have long been begging for guidance. It thus truly boggles the mind that the Court can claim that its holding will effect "Congress' intention to promote conciliation rather than litigation in the Title VII context."

Source: 118 Supreme Court Reporter pp. 2257, 2262–75 (1998); available on the internet at http://www.supct.law.cornell.edu/supct/supct.June.1998.html.

DOCUMENT 95: *Faragher v. City of Boca Raton*, U.S. Supreme Court (1998)

This case calls for identification of the circumstances under which an employer may be held liable under Title VII of the Civil Rights Act of 1964, . . . for the acts of a supervisory employee whose sexual harassment of subordinates has created a hostile work environment amounting to employment discrimination. We hold that an employer is vicariously liable for actionable discrimination caused by a supervisor, but subject to an affirmative defense looking to the reasonableness of the employer's conduct as well as that of a plaintiff victim.

I

Between 1985 and 1990, while attending college, petitioner Beth Ann Faragher worked part time and during the summers as an ocean lifeguard for the Marine Safety Section of the Parks and Recreation Department of respondent, the City of Boca Raton, Florida (City). During this period, Faragher's immediate supervisors were Bill Terry, David Silverman, and Robert Gordon. In June 1990, Faragher resigned.

In 1992, Faragher brought an action against Terry, Silverman, and the City . . . [alleging] that Terry and Silverman created a "sexually hostile atmosphere" at the beach by repeatedly subjecting Faragher and other female lifeguards to "uninvited and offensive touching," by making lewd remarks, and by speaking of women in offensive terms. The complaint contained specific allegations that Terry once said that he would never promote a woman to the rank of lieutenant, and that Silverman had said to Faragher, "Date me or clean the toilets for a year." Asserting that Terry and Silverman were agents of the City, and that their conduct amounted to discrimination in the "terms, conditions, and privileges" of her employment, . . . Faragher sought a judgment against the City for nominal damages, costs, and attorney's fees.

. . . [T]hroughout Faragher's employment with the City, Terry served as Chief of the Marine Safety Division, with authority to hire new lifeguards (subject to the approval of higher management), to supervise all aspects of the lifeguards' work assignments, to engage in counseling, to deliver oral reprimands, and to make a record of any such discipline. . . . Silverman and Gordon were responsible for making the lifeguards' daily assignments, and for supervising their work and fitness training. . . .

The lifeguards and supervisors were stationed at the city beach and worked out of the Marine Safety Headquarters, a small one-story building containing an office, a meeting room, and a single, unisex locker room with a shower.... Their work routine was structured in a "paramilitary configuration,"... with a clear chain of command. Lifeguards reported to lieutenants and captains, who reported to Terry. He was supervised by the Recreation Superintendent, who in turn reported to a Director of Parks and Recreation, answerable to the City Manager.... The lifeguards had no significant contact with higher city officials like the Recreation Superintendent....

In February 1986, the City adopted a sexual harassment policy, which it stated in a memorandum from the City Manager addressed to all employees.... In May 1990, the City revised the policy and reissued a statement of it.... Although the City may actually have circulated the memos and statements to some employees, it completely failed to disseminate its policy among employees of the Marine Safety Section, with the result that Terry, Silverman, Gordon, and many lifeguards were unaware of it....

From time to time over the course of Faragher's tenure at the Marine Safety Section, between 4 and 6 of the 40 to 50 lifeguards were women. ... During that 5-year period, Terry repeatedly touched the bodies of female employees without invitation, ... would put his arm around Faragher, with his hand on her buttocks, ... and once made contact with another female lifeguard in a motion of sexual simulation.... He made crudely demeaning references to women generally, ... and once commented disparagingly on Faragher's shape.... During a job interview with a woman he hired as a lifeguard, Terry said that the female lifeguards had sex with their male counterparts and asked whether she would do the same....

Silverman behaved in similar ways. He once tackled Faragher and remarked that, but for a physical characteristic he found unattractive, he would readily have had sexual relations with her.... Another time, he pantomimed an act of oral sex.... Within earshot of the female lifeguards, Silverman made frequent, vulgar references to women and sexual matters, commented on the bodies of female lifeguards and beachgoers, and at least twice told female lifeguards that he would like to engage in sex with them....

Faragher did not complain to higher management about Terry or Silverman. Although she spoke of their behavior to Gordon, she did not regard these discussions as formal complaints to a supervisor but as conversations with a person she held in high esteem.... Other female lifeguards had similarly informal talks with Gordon, but because Gordon did not feel that it was his place to do so, he did not report these complaints to Terry, his own supervisor, or to any other city official.... Gordon responded to the complaints of one lifeguard by saying that "the City just [doesn't] care." . . .

In April 1990, however, two months before Faragher's resignation, Nancy Ewanchew, a former lifeguard, wrote to Richard Bender, the City's Personnel Director, complaining that Terry and Silverman had harassed her and other female lifeguards. . . . Following investigation of this complaint, the City found that Terry and Silverman had behaved improperly, reprimanded them, and required them to choose between a suspension without pay or the forfeiture of annual leave. . . .

II

A

* * *

While indicating the substantive contours of the hostile environments forbidden by Title VII, our cases have established few definite rules for determining when an employer will be liable for a discriminatory environment that is otherwise actionably abusive. . . .

. . . [I]n *Meritor [Savings Bank, FSB v. Vinson],* . . . [w]e observed that the very definition of employer in Title VII, as including an "agent," . . . expressed Congress's intent that courts look to traditional principles of the law of agency in devising standards of employer liability in those instances where liability for the actions of a supervisory employee was not otherwise obvious. . . .

B

* * *

2

[Agency law provides] that an employer "is not subject to liability for the torts of his servants acting outside the scope of their employment unless . . . the servant purported to act or speak on behalf of the principal and there was reliance on apparent authority, or he was aided in accomplishing the tort by the existence of the agency relation." Faragher points to several ways in which the agency relationship aided Terry and Silverman in carrying out their harassment. She argues that in general offending supervisors can abuse their authority to keep subordinates in their presence while they make offensive statements, and that they implicitly threaten to misuse their supervisory powers to deter any resistance or complaint. Thus, she maintains that power conferred on Terry

and Silverman by the City enabled them to act for so long without provoking defiance or complaint. . . .

We . . . agree with Faragher that in implementing Title VII it makes
sense to hold an employer vicariously liable for some tortious conduct
of a supervisor made possible by abuse of his supervisory authority, and
that the aided-by-agency-relation principle . . . provides an appropriate
starting point for determining liability for the kind of harassment presented here. Several courts, indeed, have noted what Faragher has argued, that there is a sense in which a harassing supervisor is always
assisted in his misconduct by the supervisory relationship. . . . The
agency relationship affords contact with an employee subjected to a supervisor's sexual harassment, and the victim may well be reluctant to
accept the risks of blowing the whistle on a superior. When a person
with supervisory authority discriminates in the terms and conditions of
subordinates' employment, his actions necessarily draw upon his superior position over the people who report to him, or those under them,
whereas an employee generally cannot check a supervisor's abusive conduct the same way that she might deal with abuse from a co-worker.
When a fellow employee harasses, the victim can walk away or tell the
offender where to go, but it may be difficult to offer such responses to
a supervisor, whose "power to supervise—[which may be] to hire and
fire, and to set work schedules and pay rates—does not disappear . . .
when he chooses to harass through insults and offensive gestures rather
than directly with threats of firing or promises of promotion." . . . Recognition of employer liability when discriminatory misuse of supervisory
authority alters the terms and conditions of a victim's employment is
underscored by the fact that the employer has a greater opportunity to
guard against misconduct by supervisors than by common workers; employers have greater opportunity and incentive to screen them, train
them, and monitor their performance.

In sum, there are good reasons for vicarious liability for misuse of
supervisory authority. That rationale must, however, satisfy one more
condition. We are not entitled to recognize this theory under Title VII
unless we can square it with *Meritor*'s holding that an employer is not
"automatically" liable for harassment by a supervisor who creates the
requisite degree of discrimination, and there is obviously some tension
between that holding and the position that a supervisor's misconduct
aided by supervisory authority subjects the employer to liability vicariously; if the "aid" may be the unspoken suggestion of retaliation by
misuse of supervisory authority, the risk of automatic liability is high.
To counter it, [one option is] to recognize an affirmative defense to liability in some circumstances, even when a supervisor has created the
actionable environment. . . .

. . . [This] alternative to automatic liability would . . . allow an employer to show as an affirmative defense to liability that the employer had exercised reasonable care to avoid harassment and to eliminate it when it might occur, and that the complaining employee had failed to act with like reasonable care to take advantage of the employer's safeguards and otherwise to prevent harm that could have been avoided. This composite defense would, we think, implement the statute sensibly, for reasons that are not hard to fathom.

Although Title VII seeks "to make persons whole for injuries suffered on account of unlawful employment discrimination," . . . its "primary objective," like that of any statute meant to influence primary conduct, is not to provide redress but to avoid harm. . . . As long ago as 1980, the Equal Employment Opportunity Commission (EEOC), charged with the enforcement of Title VII, . . . adopted regulations advising employers to "take all steps necessary to prevent sexual harassment from occurring, such as . . . informing employees of their right to raise and how to raise the issue of harassment." . . . [A]nd in 1990 the Commission issued a policy statement enjoining employers to establish a complaint procedure "designed to encourage victims of harassment to come forward [without requiring] a victim to complain first to the offending supervisor." . . . It would therefore implement clear statutory policy and complement the Government's Title VII enforcement efforts to recognize the employer's affirmative obligation to prevent violations and give credit here to employers who make reasonable efforts to discharge their duty. Indeed, a theory of vicarious liability for misuse of supervisory power would be at odds with the statutory policy if it failed to provide employers with some such incentive.

The requirement to show that the employee has failed in a coordinate duty to avoid or mitigate harm reflects an equally obvious policy imported from the general theory of damages, that a victim has a duty "to use such means as are reasonable under the circumstances to avoid or minimize the damages" that result from violations of the statute. . . . An employer may, for example, have provided a proven, effective mechanism for reporting and resolving complaints of sexual harassment, available to the employee without undue risk or expense. If the plaintiff unreasonably failed to avail herself of the employer's preventive or remedial apparatus, she should not recover damages that could have been avoided if she had done so. If the victim could have avoided harm, no liability should be found against the employer who had taken reasonable care, and if damages could reasonably have been mitigated no award against a liable employer should reward a plaintiff for what her own efforts could have avoided.

In order to accommodate the principle of vicarious liability for harm caused by misuse of supervisory authority, as well as Title VII's equally basic policies of encouraging forethought by employers and saving action by objecting employees, we adopt the following holding in this case and in *Burlington Industries, Inc. v. Ellerth,* . . . also decided today. An employer is subject to vicarious liability to a victimized employee for an actionable hostile environment created by a supervisor with immediate (or successively higher) authority over the employee. When no tangible employment action is taken, a defending employer may raise an affirmative defense to liability or damages, subject to proof by a preponderance of the evidence. . . . The defense comprises two necessary elements: (a) that the employer exercised reasonable care to prevent and correct promptly any sexually harassing behavior, and (b) that the plaintiff employee unreasonably failed to take advantage of any preventive or corrective opportunities provided by the employer or to avoid harm otherwise. While proof that an employer had promulgated an antiharassment policy with complaint procedure is not necessary in every instance as a matter of law, the need for a stated policy suitable to the employment circumstances may appropriately be addressed in any case when litigating the first element of the defense. And while proof that an employee failed to fulfill the corresponding obligation of reasonable care to avoid harm is not limited to showing an unreasonable failure to use any complaint procedure provided by the employer, a demonstration of such failure will normally suffice to satisfy the employer's burden under the second element of the defense. No affirmative defense is available, however, when the supervisor's harassment culminates in a tangible employment action, such as discharge, demotion, or undesirable reassignment. *See Burlington.* . . .

Applying these rules here, we [find for the plaintiff]. The District Court found that the degree of hostility in the work environment rose to the actionable level and was attributable to Silverman and Terry. It is undisputed that these supervisors "were granted virtually unchecked authority" over their subordinates, "directly controlling and supervising all aspects of [Faragher's] day-to-day activities." . . . It is also clear that Faragher and her colleagues were "completely isolated from the City's higher management." . . .

While the City would have an opportunity to raise an affirmative defense if there were any serious prospect of its presenting one, it appears from the record that any such avenue is closed. The District Court found that the City had entirely failed to disseminate its policy against sexual harassment among the beach employees and that its officials made no attempt to keep track of the conduct of supervisors like Terry and Silverman. The record also makes clear that the City's policy did not include any assurance that the harassing supervisors could be bypassed in registering complaints. . . . Under such circumstances, we hold as a matter of law that the City could not be found to have exercised reasonable care to prevent the supervisors' harassing conduct. Unlike the employer of a small workforce, who might expect that sufficient care to prevent tortious behavior could be exercised informally, those responsible for city operations could not reasonably have thought that precautions against hostile environments in any one of many departments in far-flung locations could be effective without communicating some formal policy against harassment, with a sensible complaint procedure. . . .

Justice Thomas, with whom Justice Scalia joins, dissenting.

For the reasons given in my dissenting opinion in *Burlington Industries v. Ellerth*, absent an adverse employment consequence, an employer cannot be held vicariously liable if a supervisor creates a hostile work environment. Petitioner suffered no adverse employment consequence; thus the Court of Appeals was correct to hold that the City is not vicariously liable for the conduct of Chief Terry and Lieutenant Silverman. Because the Court reverses this judgment, I dissent.

As for petitioner's negligence claim, the District Court made no finding as to the City's negligence, and the Court of Appeals did not directly consider the issue. I would therefore remand the case to the District Court for further proceedings on this question alone. I disagree with the Court's conclusion that merely because the City did not disseminate its sexual harassment policy, it should be liable as a matter of law. . . . The City should be allowed to show either that: (1) there was a reasonably available avenue through which petitioner could have complained to a City official who supervised both Chief Terry and Lieutenant Silverman, . . . or (2) it would not have learned of the harassment even if the policy had been distributed. Petitioner, as the plaintiff, would of course bear the burden of proving the City's negligence.

Source: 118 *Supreme Court Reporter* pp. 2275, 2280–86, 2290–94 (1998); available on the internet at http://www.supct.law.cornell.edu/supct/supct.June.1998.html.

The fourth Supreme Court decision in 1998 relating to sexual harassment dealt with the question of when an educational institution must pay if a student has been sexually harassed by a school employee. (This issue is also discussed in Documents 75–77, above.) In the case of *Gebser v. Lago Vista Independent School District* (Document 96), a five Justice majority of the Supreme Court made it very difficult for plaintiffs to win in such cases. The Court adopted the very restrictive standard originally announced by the U.S. Court of Appeals for the Fifth Circuit in *Rosa H. v. San Elizario Independent School District* (Document 77). Under this standard, the plaintiff cannot recover money from the educational institution "unless an official who at a minimum has authority to address the alleged discrimination and to

institute corrective measures on the recipient's behalf has actual knowledge of discrimination in the recipient's programs and fails adequately
to respond."

Indeed, the Supreme Court majority went even further than this in
restricting liability. The Fifth Circuit in the *Rosa H.* case did not resolve
the question of whether an educational institution would be legally
responsible if it negligently failed to respond to known harassment. The
Supreme Court answered this question by saying that mere negligence
on the part of the institution is not enough. The victim needs to establish
that the institution was "deliberately indifferent" to her plight, a much
tougher standard.

It is thus much more difficult to hold an educational institution legally responsible for harassment of students than it is to hold an employer responsible for harassment of workers. Employers can be liable
even if they had no knowledge of the harassment, and if they did not
take reasonable steps to make sure that harassment did not happen in
their institution. Educational institutions cannot be liable, in contrast,
without actual knowledge of the harassment by a person with authority
to take action coupled with deliberately indifferent inaction by that
person.

The majority of the Supreme Court justifies this result by pointing to
differences between Title VII, the employment statute, and Title IX, the
education statute. Title VII specifically provides that victims of discrimination can receive money damages and has compensation of victims
as one of its central purposes. Furthermore, it specifically provides that
employers are responsible for actions of their agents.

In contrast, Title IX is silent on the issue of whether money damages
can be recovered. Although the Supreme Court has held that despite
this silence plaintiffs can sometimes get such damages (as discussed in
Document 69, above), the Court sees the silence as an indication that
the right to money damages should be fairly narrow.

The four other Supreme Court Justices dissented bitterly. In an opinion authored by Justice Stevens, they argued both that the majority had
misinterpreted Congress's intent in enacting Title IX and, further, that
the decision was harmful as a policy matter. They complained that
rather than encouraging educational institutions to adopt policies
against sexual harassment and to make strong efforts to uncover and
redress sexual harassment, the majority's decision had the opposite
effect. It creates a perverse incentive for the school to turn a blind eye
to sexual harassment, since the school can only be forced to pay money
damages if it knows that harassment is occurring.

And in a separate dissent, joined by two other Justices, Justice Ginsburg set forth what she thought the correct standard for assessing school
liability should be. The standard that these Justices advocated (but that

the majority of the Court rejects) is very similar to the standard that applies in employment cases. Under this proposed test, educational institutions would not be liable for sexual harassment if they could establish that they had "an effective policy for reporting and redressing such misconduct."

DOCUMENT 96: *Gebser v. Lago Vista Independent School District*, U.S. Supreme Court (1998)

The question in this case is when a school district may be held liable in damages . . . under Title IX of the Education Amendments of 1972 . . . for the sexual harassment of a student by one of the district's teachers. We conclude that damages may not be recovered in those circumstances unless an official of the school district who at a minimum has authority to institute corrective measures on the district's behalf has actual notice of, and is deliberately indifferent to, the teacher's misconduct.

I

In the spring of 1991, when petitioner Alida Star Gebser was an eighth-grade student at a middle school in respondent Lago Vista Independent School District (Lago Vista), she joined a high school book discussion group led by Frank Waldrop, a teacher at Lago Vista's high school. Lago Vista received federal funds at all pertinent times. During the book discussion sessions, Waldrop often made sexually suggestive comments to the students. Gebser entered high school in the fall and was assigned to classes taught by Waldrop in both semesters. Waldrop continued to make inappropriate remarks to the students, and he began to direct more of his suggestive comments toward Gebser, including during the substantial amount of time that the two were alone in his classroom. He initiated sexual contact with Gebser in the spring, when, while visiting her home ostensibly to give her a book, he kissed and fondled her. The two had sexual intercourse on a number of occasions during the remainder of the school year. Their relationship continued through the summer and into the following school year, and they often had intercourse during class time, although never on school property.

Gebser did not report the relationship to school officials, testifying that while she realized Waldrop's conduct was improper, she was uncertain how to react and she wanted to continue having him as a teacher. In October 1992, the parents of two other students complained to the high school principal about Waldrop's comments in class. The principal arranged a meeting, at which, according to the principal, Waldrop indicated that he did not believe he had made offensive remarks but apologized to the parents and said it would not happen again. The principal also advised Waldrop to be careful about his classroom comments and told the school guidance counselor about the meeting, but he did not report the parents' complaint to Lago Vista's superintendent, who was the district's Title IX coordinator. A couple of months later, in January 1993, a police officer discovered Waldrop and Gebser engaging in sexual intercourse and arrested Waldrop. Lago Vista terminated his employment, and subsequently, the Texas Education Agency revoked his teaching license. During this time, the district had not promulgated or distributed an official grievance procedure for lodging sexual harassment complaints; nor had it issued a formal anti-harassment policy.

Gebser and her mother filed suit against Lago Vista and Waldrop . . . in November 1993. . . . They sought compensatory and punitive damages from both defendants. . . .

II

* * *

[Petitioners] advance two possible standards under which Lago Vista would be liable for Waldrop's conduct. First, relying on a 1997 "Policy Guidance" issued by the Department of Education, they would hold a school district liable in damages under Title IX where a teacher is " 'aided in carrying out the sexual harassment of students by his or her position of authority with the institution,' " irrespective of whether school district officials had any knowledge of the harassment and irrespective of their response upon becoming aware. . . . That rule is an expression of respondeat superior liability, i.e., vicarious or imputed liability, . . . under which recovery in damages against a school district would generally follow whenever a teacher's authority over a student facilitates the harassment. Second, petitioners and the United States submit that a school district should at a minimum be liable for damages based on a theory of constructive notice, i.e., where the district knew or "should have known" about harassment but failed to uncover and eliminate it. . . . Both standards would allow a damages recovery in a broader range of situations than the rule [that the defendant proposes] which hinges on actual knowledge by a school official with authority to end the harassment. . . .

[The standard for liability under Title IX should not be the same as under Title VII. The Court's rationale in *Meritor Savings Bank, FSB v. Vinson*] for concluding that agency principles guide the liability inquiry under Title VII rests on an aspect of that statute not found in Title IX: Title VII, in which the prohibition against employment discrimination runs against "an employer," . . . explicitly defines "employer" to include "any agent," . . . Title IX contains no comparable reference to an educational institution's "agents," and so does not expressly call for application of agency principles.

. . . [Furthermore,] [u]nlike Title IX, Title VII contains an express cause of action, . . . and specifically provides for relief in the form of monetary damages. . . . Congress therefore has directly addressed the subject of damages relief under Title VII and has set out the particular situations in which damages are available as well as the maximum amounts recoverable. . . . With respect to Title IX, however, the private right of action is judicially implied, . . . and there is thus no legislative expression of the scope of available remedies, including when it is appropriate to award monetary damages. . . .

III

Because the private right of action under Title IX is judicially implied, we have a measure of latitude to shape a sensible remedial scheme that best comports with the statute. . . . That endeavor inherently entails a degree of speculation, since it addresses an issue on which Congress has not specifically spoken. . . . To guide the analysis, we generally examine the relevant statute to ensure that we do not fashion the parameters of an implied right in a manner at odds with the statutory structure and purpose. . . .

Applying those principles here, we conclude that it would "frustrate the purposes" of Title IX to permit a damages recovery against a school district for a teacher's sexual harassment of a student . . . without actual notice to a school district official. Because Congress did not expressly create a private right of action under Title IX, the statutory text does not shed light on Congress' intent with respect to the scope of available remedies. . . . Instead, "we attempt to infer how the [1972] Congress would have addressed the issue had the . . . action been included as an express provision in the" statute. . . .

As a general matter, it does not appear that Congress contemplated unlimited recovery in damages against a funding recipient where the recipient is unaware of discrimination in its programs. When Title IX was enacted in 1972, the principal civil rights statutes containing an express right of action did not provide for recovery of monetary damages at all, instead allowing only injunctive and equitable relief. . . . It was not until 1991 that Congress made damages available under Title VII, and even then, Congress carefully limited the amount recoverable in any individual case, calibrating the maximum recovery to the size of the employer. . . . Adopting petitioners' position would amount, then, to allowing unlimited recovery of damages under Title IX where Congress has not spoken on the subject of either the right or the remedy, and in the face of evidence that when Congress expressly considered both in Title VII it restricted the amount of damages available.

Congress enacted Title IX in 1972 with two principal objectives in mind: "to avoid the use of federal resources to support discriminatory practices" and "to provide individual citizens effective protection against those practices." . . . The statute was modeled after Title VI of the Civil Rights Act of 1964, . . . which is parallel to Title IX except that it prohibits race discrimination, not sex discrimination, and applies in all programs receiving federal funds, not only in education programs. . . . The two statutes operate in the same manner, conditioning an offer of federal funding on a promise by the recipient not to discriminate, in what amounts essentially to a contract between the Government and the recipient of funds. . . .

That contractual framework distinguishes Title IX from Title VII, which is framed in terms not of a condition but of an outright prohibition. Title VII applies to all employers without regard to federal funding and aims broadly to "eradicate discrimination throughout the economy." . . . Thus, whereas Title VII aims centrally to compensate victims of discrimination, Title IX focuses more on "protecting" individuals from discriminatory practices carried out by recipients of federal funds. . . .

Title IX's contractual nature has implications for our construction of the scope of available remedies. When Congress attaches conditions to the award of federal funds under its spending power, . . . as it has in Title IX and Title VI, we examine closely the propriety of private actions holding the recipient liable in monetary damages for noncompliance with the condition. . . . Our central concern in that regard is with ensuring "that the receiving entity of federal funds [has] notice that it will be liable for a monetary award." . . . If a school district's liability for a teacher's sexual harassment rests on principles of constructive notice or respondeat superior, it will . . . be the case that the recipient of funds was unaware of the discrimination. It is sensible to assume that Congress did not envision a recipient's liability in damages in that situation. . . .

Most significantly, Title IX contains important clues that Congress did not intend to allow recovery in damages where liability rests solely on principles of vicarious liability or constructive notice. Title IX's express means of enforcement—by administrative agencies—operates on an assumption of actual notice to officials of the funding recipient. The statute entitles agencies who disburse education funding to enforce their rules implementing the non-discrimination mandate through proceedings to suspend or terminate funding or through "other means authorized by law." . . . Significantly, however, an agency may not initiate enforcement proceedings until it "has advised the appropriate person or persons of the failure to comply with the requirement and has determined that compliance cannot be secured by voluntary means." . . .

Presumably, a central purpose of requiring notice of the violation "to the appropriate person" and an opportunity for voluntary compliance before administrative enforcement proceedings can commence is to avoid diverting education funding from beneficial uses where a recipient was unaware of discrimination in its programs and is willing to institute prompt corrective measures. The scope of private damages relief proposed by petitioners is at odds with that basic objective. When a teacher's sexual harassment is imputed to a school district or when a school district is deemed to have "constructively" known of the teacher's harassment, by assumption the district had no actual knowledge of the teacher's conduct. Nor, of course, did the district have an opportunity to take action to end the harassment or to limit further harassment. . . .

IV

Because the express remedial scheme under Title IX is predicated upon notice to an "appropriate person" and an opportunity to rectify any violation, . . . we conclude, in the absence of further direction from Congress, that the implied damages remedy should be fashioned along the same lines. An "appropriate person" . . . is, at a minimum, an official of the recipient entity with authority to take corrective action to end the discrimination. Consequently, in cases like this one that do not involve official policy of the recipient entity, we hold that a damages remedy will not lie under Title IX unless an official who at a minimum has authority to address the alleged discrimination and to institute corrective measures on the recipient's behalf has actual knowledge of discrimination in the recipient's programs and fails adequately to respond.

We think, moreover, that the response must amount to deliberate indifference to discrimination. The administrative enforcement scheme presupposes that an official who is advised of a Title IX violation refuses to take action to bring the recipient into compliance. The premise, in other words, is an official decision by the recipient not to remedy the violation. That framework finds a rough parallel in the standard of deliberate indifference. Under a lower standard, there would be a risk that the recipient would be liable in damages not for its own official decision but instead for its employees' independent actions. . . .

Applying the framework to this case is fairly straightforward, as petitioners do not contend they can prevail under an actual notice standard. The only official alleged to have had information about Waldrop's misconduct is the high school principal. That information, however, consisted of a complaint from parents of other students charging only that Waldrop had made inappropriate comments during class, which was plainly insufficient to alert the principal to the possibility that Waldrop was involved in a sexual relationship with a student. Lago Vista, moreover, terminated Waldrop's employment upon learning of his relationship with Gebser. . . .

Petitioners focus primarily on Lago Vista's asserted failure to promulgate and publicize an effective policy and grievance procedure for sexual harassment claims. They point to Department of Education regulations requiring each funding recipient to "adopt and publish grievance procedures providing for prompt and equitable resolution" of discrimination complaints, . . . and to notify students and others "that it does not discriminate on the basis of sex in the educational programs or activities which it operates," . . . Lago Vista's alleged failure to comply with the regulations, however, does not establish the requisite actual notice and deliberate indifference. And in any event, the failure to promulgate a grievance procedure does not itself constitute "discrimination" under Title IX. Of course, the Department of Education could enforce the requirement administratively: Agencies generally have authority to promulgate and enforce requirements that effectuate the statute's nondiscrimination mandate, . . . even if those requirements do not purport to represent a definition of discrimination under the statute. . . . We have never held, however, that the implied private right of action under Title IX allows recovery in damages for violation of those sorts of administrative requirements.

V

The number of reported cases involving sexual harassment of students in schools confirms that harassment unfortunately is an all too common aspect of the educational experience. No one questions that a student suffers extraordinary harm when subjected to sexual harassment and abuse by a teacher, and that the teacher's conduct is reprehensible and undermines the basic purposes of the educational system. The issue in this case, however, is whether the independent misconduct of a teacher is attributable to the school district that employs him under a specific federal statute designed primarily to prevent recipients of federal financial assistance from using the funds in a discriminatory manner. Our decision does not affect any right of recovery that an individual may have against a school district as a matter of state law or against the teacher in his individual capacity . . . : Until Congress speaks directly on the subject, however, we will not hold a school district liable in damages under Title IX for a teacher's sexual harassment of a student absent actual notice and deliberate indifference. . . .

Justice Stevens, with whom Justice Souter, Justice Ginsburg, and Justice Breyer join, dissenting.

* * *

The Court ... holds that the law does not provide a damages remedy for the Title IX violation alleged in this case because no official of the school district with "authority to institute corrective measures on the district's behalf" had actual notice of Waldrop's misconduct.... That holding is at odds with settled principles of agency law, under which the district is responsible for Waldrop's misconduct because "he was aided in accomplishing the tort by the existence of the agency relation." ... This case presents a paradigmatic example of a tort that was made possible, that was effected, and that was repeated over a prolonged period because of the powerful influence that Waldrop had over Gebser by reason of the authority that his employer, the school district, had delegated to him. As a secondary school teacher, Waldrop exercised even greater authority and control over his students than employers and supervisors exercise over their employees. His gross misuse of that authority allowed him to abuse his young student's trust.

Reliance on th[is] principle ... comports with the relevant agency's interpretation of Title IX. The United States Department of Education, through its Office for Civil Rights, recently issued a policy "Guidance" stating that a school district is liable under Title IX if one of its teachers "was aided in carrying out the sexual harassment of students by his or her position of authority with the institution." ... As the agency charged with administering and enforcing Title IX, ... the Department of Education has a special interest in ensuring that federal funds are not used in contravention of Title IX's mandate. It is therefore significant that the Department's interpretation of the statute wholly supports the conclusion that respondent is liable in damages for Waldrop's sexual abuse of his student, which was made possible only by Waldrop's affirmative misuse of his authority as her teacher.

The reason why the common law imposes liability on the principal in such circumstances is the same as the reason why Congress included the prohibition against discrimination on the basis of sex in Title IX: to induce school boards to adopt and enforce practices that will minimize the danger that vulnerable students will be exposed to such odious behavior. The rule that the Court has crafted creates the opposite incentive. As long as school boards can insulate themselves from knowledge about this sort of conduct, they can claim immunity from damages liability. Indeed, the rule that the Court adopts would preclude a damages remedy even if every teacher at the school knew about the harassment but did not have "authority to institute corrective measures on the district's behalf." ... It is not my function to determine whether this newly fashioned rule is wiser than the established common-law rule. It is proper, however, to suggest that the Court bears the burden of justifying its rather dramatic departure from settled law, and to explain why its opinion fails to shoulder that burden. ...

Justice Ginsburg, with whom Justice Souter and Justice Breyer join, dissenting.

...I join [Justice Stevens'] opinion, which reserves the question whether a district should be relieved from damages liability if it has in place, and effectively publicizes and enforces, a policy to curtail and redress injuries caused by sexual harassment. . . . I think it appropriate to answer that question. . . .

In line with the tort law doctrine of avoidable consequences, . . . I would recognize as an affirmative defense to a Title IX charge of sexual harassment, an effective policy for reporting and redressing such misconduct. School districts subject to Title IX's governance have been instructed by the Secretary of Education to install procedures for "prompt and equitable resolution" of complaints, . . . and the Department of Education's Office of Civil Rights has detailed elements of an effective grievance process, with specific reference to sexual harassment. . . .

The burden would be the school district's to show that its internal remedies were adequately publicized and likely would have provided redress without exposing the complainant to undue risk, effort, or expense. Under such a regime, to the extent that a plaintiff unreasonably failed to avail herself of the school district's preventive and remedial measures, and consequently suffered avoidable harm, she would not qualify for Title IX relief.

Source: 118 Supreme Court Reporter pp. 1989, 1993–2000, 2003–4, 2007; (1998) available on the internet at http://www.supct.law.cornell.edu/supct/supct. June.1998.html.

Index

About the Author

LAURA W. STEIN is a graduate of Yale University and Harvard Law School and has published articles about labor and employment law and feminist theory. She was formerly an Associate Professor of Law at New York Law School.

Recent Titles in the Series
Primary Documents in American History and Contemporary Issues

The Abortion Controversy: A Documentary History
Eva R. Rubin, editor

Women's Rights in the United States: A Documentary History
Winston E. Langley and Vivian C. Fox, editors

Founding the Republic: A Documentary History
John J. Patrick, editor

Major Crises in Contemporary American Foreign Policy: A Documentary
History
Russell D. Buhite, editor

Capital Punishment in the United States: A Documentary History
Bryan Vila and Cynthia Morris, editors

The Gun Control Debate: A Documentary History
Marjolijn Bijlefeld, editor

The AIDS Crisis: A Documentary History
Douglas A. Feldman and Julia Wang Miller, editors